D1496530

STUDIES IN MODERN BRITISH RELIGIOUS HISTORY

Volume 1

Friends of Religious Equality:
Nonconformist Politics in Mid-Victorian England

During the middle decades of the nineteenth century the English Nonconformist community developed a coherent political philosophy of its own, of which a central tenet was the principle of religious equality (in contrast to the stereotype of Evangelical Dissenters). The Dissenting community fought for the civil rights of Roman Catholics, non-Christians and even atheists, on an issue of principle which had its flowering in the enthusiastic and undivided support which Nonconformity gave to the campaign for Jewish emancipation.

This study examines the political efforts and ideas of English Nonconformists during the period, covering the whole range of national issues raised, from state education to the Crimean War. It offers a case study of a theologically conservative group defending religious pluralism in the civic sphere, showing that the concept of religious equality was a grand vision at the centre of the political philosophy of the Dissenters.

Dr TIMOTHY LARSEN is the Principal of Covenant College, Coventry, where he was formerly Lecturer in Church History.

STUDIES IN MODERN BRITISH RELIGIOUS HISTORY

ISSN: 1464–6625

General editors
Stephen Taylor
Arthur Burns
Kenneth Fincham

This series aims to differentiate 'religious history' from the narrow confines of church history, investigating not only the social and cultural history of religion, but also theological, political and institutional themes, while remaining sensitive to the wider historical context; it thus advances an understanding of the importance of religion for the history of modern Britain, covering all periods of British history since the Reformation.

Friends of Religious Equality

Nonconformist Politics in
Mid-Victorian England

TIMOTHY LARSEN

THE BOYDELL PRESS

First published 1999
The Boydell Press, Woodbridge

ISBN 0 85115 726 2

ISSN 1464–6625

The Boydell Press is an imprint of Boydell & Brewer Ltd
PO Box 9, Woodbridge, Suffolk IP12 3DF, UK
and of Boydell & Brewer Inc.
PO Box 41026, Rochester, NY 14604–4126, USA
website http://www.boydell.co.uk

A catalogue record for this book is available
from the British Library

Library of Congress Cataloging-in-Publication Data
Larsen, Timothy, 1967–
    Friends of religious equality: nonconformist politics in mid-
Victorian England/Timothy Larsen,
        p.   cm. – (Studies in modern British religious history; v. 1)
    Includes bibliographical references and index.
    ISBN 0–85115–726–2 (alk. paper)
    1. Freedom of religion – England – History – 19th century.
2. Dissenters, Religious – England – Political activity – History – 19th
century.   I. title.   II. Series.
BR759.L27   1999
323.44′2′0882044–dc21   98–43277

This publication is printed on acid-free paper

Printed in Great Britain by
St Edmundsbury Press Ltd, Bury St Edmunds, Suffolk

For my father, KENNETH W. LARSEN, who sang to me the songs cherished by generations long past, took me to the unmarked battlefields of wars long ceased, and taught me to believe that, for those who have ears to hear, the dead continue to speak.

CONTENTS

Acknowledgements   ix

Introduction   1

Part I: Nonconformity and English Society

1. The Nonconformists   15

2. Nonconformist Grievances   39

Part II: The Gospel of Religious Equality

3. Disestablishment   79

4. Religious Equality   110

5. State Education   137

Part III: Another Gospel?

6. Moral Reform   171

7. National Identity   207

Conclusion   251

Bibliography   271

Index   290

ACKNOWLEDGEMENTS

I am grateful to the librarians and staff members of numerous archives and libraries. I would like to acknowledge, in particular, the helpfulness and the kindness of Mrs. Susan J. Mills, the Librarian and Archivist at Regent's Park College, Oxford; the Librarian, Mr John Creasey, and the staff at Dr Williams's Library, London, including Mrs. Janet Barnes, who is now retired; Miss M. Smith, Social Sciences Information Services, Birmingham Central Library; and Mrs. J. G. Baldry, Assistant Archivist, Manchester Central Library. I am grateful to the archivists or librarians of the following institutions for permission to quote from unpublished manuscripts in their care: the British Library, Dr Williams's Library, the Congregational Library, London Metropolitan Archives, Manchester Central Library, the West Yorkshire Archives Service in Leeds and the Guildhall Library, London. The Protestant Dissenting Deputies of the Three Denominations graciously gave me permission to quote from their records, as did the Free Churches' Council for the Liberation Society papers and Sir William Gladstone for the Gladstone papers. My brother, the historian and librarian David Larsen, and my friend and local book dealer in Loughborough, Malcolm Hornsby, helped me track down some elusive sources, and Mrs. Sophy Walker, our college administrator, helped with the compilation of the index. I wish to thank Covenant Ministries International and its founder, Bryn Jones, for generously supporting this research project. My wife, Jane, has been a valuable encourager. Finally, I owe one of my greatest debts to my former supervisor, David Bebbington, who has been my indispensable guide into the historiography of Dissent. He is an extraordinarily kind, helpful and generous person.

INTRODUCTION

This is a study of the national political efforts, ambitions and ideas of English Dissenters during the middle decades of the nineteenth century. In addition to providing a detailed account of the political stances and activities of Nonconformists during this period, two primary strands of inquiry and argument emerge. Firstly, in contrast to the popular stereotype of Evangelical Nonconformists as 'Puritans' who wished to promote their own religion and impose its values on others by means of legislation, this study explores the degree to which the goal of religious equality before the law was sincerely and uniquely embraced by this community. The declared commitment to religious equality by Dissenters was more than just rhetoric: they really did champion, to a surprising extent, the right to political equality of Jews, Roman Catholics and others whose religious convictions subjected them to legalised forms of discrimination. Secondly, whilst research in this area in recent decades has usually focused upon the social, economic, environmental and philosophical factors which shaped the ideas and motivations of Non-conformist politics, this study seeks to add to these emphases an exploration of the theological underpinnings of the Dissenting political worldview. Theology played a crucial part in forming and informing the political philosophy of Nonconformists and, unless its influence is adequately taken into account, our understanding of their behaviour in the public sphere will always be incomplete.

Although the origins of struggles, ideas and patterns of behaviour will often be traced back into the years prior to 1847 and the development of political campaigns will be tracked into the years beyond 1867, those two dates serve as the chronological boundaries for the main focus of this study. The terminal date hardly needs explanation: the Reform Act of 1867 is commonly recognised as a moment when a new chapter in English politics began. Moreover, a study ending in 1867, falling as this date does between the death of Palmerston in 1865 and the defeat of Disraeli in the general election of 1868, may reasonably be seen as one which finishes all that comes before the Gladstonian era – a less precisely datable event which also marks a new political climate for the English people, and not least for the Nonconformists amongst them.

1847 cannot boast a sweeping change in the wider political world to rival these. It is, however, not devoid of national significance. 1847 was an election year and this was the first election when the adherents of

Conservatism were divided between Protectionists and Peelites. A related factor which was an even more important national political event for Nonconformists was that this was the first election since the triumph of the Anti-Corn Law League. This victory ushered in a new era of respect for the power of pressure group politics – a climate which was peculiarly compatible with the Dissenting mindset. D. A. Hamer suggests that the 'heyday' of favourable conditions for effective pressure group politics was 'the period between the first and second Reform Acts'.[1] 1847 was the first general election since Dissenters had discovered this truth for themselves by defeating Sir James Graham's Factory Bill in 1843 because of its offensive educational clauses. This fight had politicised Dissent in a new way. One result had been the founding of the Anti-State Church Association in 1844, and the 1847 election was the first one subjected to the influence of its electoral activities, falling conveniently in the year of its first triennial conference. State education had become suspect and many Dissenters also wanted to express their disapproval of the Minutes of Education which Lord John Russell had instituted. Moreover, orthodox Dissenters (those who affirmed traditional Christian doctrines such as the Trinity and the deity of Christ) now fought on the general front of wanting to see members of their own community represent them in Parliament. In 1847, the Congregational textile manufacturer, Samuel Morley, chaired a Dissenters' Parliamentary Committee, formed specifically to organise electoral action for the pending election. He listed the names of over fifty Nonconformists whom he thought should be encouraged to become candidates in Parliamentary elections sometime in the future.[2] A special publication, the *Nonconformist Elector*, even emerged for the duration of the campaign in order to help mobilise the Dissenting vote.[3]

Nonconformists did not fill the Commons' benches in the new Parliament. Many of their most full-blooded candidates were soundly defeated, notably Edward Miall at Halifax and Joseph Sturge at Leeds. Dissenters had some success in ousting Whigs who would not bend toward their agenda – English Dissenters took vicarious pleasure in Macaulay's defeat at Edinburgh. Norman Gash sees the Dissenting electoral strategy in this election as a senseless lashing out at one's allies (Anglican Whigs) 'to no practical purpose', viewing the new

---

[1] D. A. Hamer, *The Politics of Electoral Pressure*, Hassocks, Sussex: Harvester, 1977, p. 10.
[2] Edwin Hodder, *The Life of Samuel Morley*, 3rd ed., London: Hodder and Stoughton, 1887, pp. 100–3.
[3] Josef L. Altholz, *The Religious Press in Britain, 1760–1900*, New York: Greenwood, 1989, p. 61.

emphasis on disestablishment as 'an academic gesture, not a real issue'.[4] There are, however, factors which need to be weighed against such an assessment. Evangelical Nonconformists and Unitarians had split in 1836 over increasing tensions which were, at root, primarily theological.[5] The Presbyterian denomination that had largely turned Unitarian had always provided the bulk of the political leadership for the Dissenting community as a whole and therefore the rest of Old Dissent now needed to start to build its own political base. Moreover, by their efforts in education and their lack of efforts on religious grievances, the Whigs had proved that they could not be trusted to act on behalf of the Nonconformists. Gash seems to see the energy Dissenters expended helping Baron Rothschild, 'an ineligible Jew', secure a seat, as part of their wasted effort, but it could be argued that focusing public attention on the importance of the principle of religious equality was just as valuable an achievement as placing a friend in the Commons.[6] In short, a deeper exploration needs to be made of the distinctive agenda Dissenters were seeking to establish. In a different light, the 1847 election is the first deliberate effort by Evangelical Nonconformists to carve out a distinctive political agenda of their own, to demand that it should be taken seriously in national politics, to articulate long-term goals, to begin to pursue them and to attempt to find men from their own ranks who would represent them in Parliament.[7] Therefore, the dates of this study may be said to cover the period from the time when English Evangelical Nonconformists began to mobilise as a self-conscious, distinctive force within national politics – replacing a trust in the leadership of the Whigs with a desire to place their own people in Parliament – until many of those very people, by then securely in the Commons, as well as their Nonconformist supporters, began to place their trust in the leadership of Gladstone.

There is therefore at least the potential that this unique period between their estrangement from the Whigs and their marriage to Gladstone will provide a particularly clear picture of what the Nonconformists themselves actually believed and wanted politically. Nevertheless, a detailed study of Dissenting politics in this era has not yet been attempted. Raymond Cowherd's *The Politics of English Dissent* (by now over forty

---

[4] Norman Gash, *Reaction and Reconstruction in English Politics, 1832–1852*, Oxford: Clarendon, 1965, p. 105.
[5] K. R. M. Short, 'London's General Body of Protestant Ministers: its Disruption in 1836', *Journal of Ecclesiastical History*, XXIV, 4 (October 1973), pp. 377–93.
[6] Gash, *Reaction and Reconstruction*, p. 105.
[7] Machin also notes that the significance of this election has been underestimated. G. I. T. Machin, *Politics and the Churches in Great Britain, 1832 to 1868*, Oxford: Clarendon, 1977, p. 191.

years old) ends in 1848.[8] *The Nonconformist Conscience* by David Bebbington begins in 1870.[9] There is no equivalent study to bridge the gap between these two important works. Moreover, various inaccurate statements in more sweeping studies or ones with an overlapping specialist focus clearly indicate that a reliable guide to Dissenting politics in this era is needed, although this study is able to build upon the valuable work already done in this area by scholars such as G. I. T. Machin and Clyde Binfield.[10]

There has long been a popular stereotype that Victorians were moralising hypocrites who sought to enforce Protestant Christian mores on the populace by the power of the law, that Victorians behaved in this way because of the influence of Evangelicalism and that the most rabid of the Evangelicals were the Nonconformist ones.[11] If one has imbibed these assumptions, even in a diluted form, then one would expect Nonconformist politics in the mid-Victorian era to consist of narrow and oppressive goals such as enshrining the Christian Sabbath in law and barring atheists and Roman Catholics from playing a full part in civil society. In fact, as soon as serious historians begin to study the actual political behaviour of these Dissenters, they find them refusing to co-operate with this caricature. Nevertheless, if an alternative Nonconformist political worldview is not grasped and put in its place – and it is a premise of this book that this task has not yet been satisfactorily done – then historians are left with merely a vague sense of frustration that their subjects are not acting in the way one assumes they ought to. This tendency can sometimes even be seen in the best of the available research. For example, Michael Watts, in his recent, impressive work, *The Dissenters: Volume II*, paints the refusal to participate in anti-Catholic politics by an influential figure in Nonconformist politics, Edward Miall, as a tactical move in order not to

[8] Raymond G. Cowherd, *The Politics of English Dissent*, London: Epworth, 1959 [originally 1956].
[9] D. W. Bebbington, *The Nonconformist Conscience*, London: George Allen & Unwin, 1982. The final decades of the century and beyond are also explored in Stephen Koss, *Nonconformity in Modern British Politics*, London: B. T. Batsford, 1975, and James Munson, *The Nonconformists*, London: SPCK, 1991. On the other side of the timeline, James E. Bradley, *Religion, Revolution and English Radicalism*, Cambridge: Cambridge University Press, 1990, offers on account of Nonconformist politics in the eighteenth century.
[10] Machin, *Politics and the Churches in Great Britain*; Clyde Binfield, *So Down to Prayers: Studies in English Nonconformity, 1780–1920*, London: J. M. Dent & Sons, 1977.
[11] Indeed, the Victorians themselves were the authors of some enduring stereotypical notions of the Dissenters of their day. Valentine Cunningham, *Everywhere Spoken Against: Dissent in the Victorian Novel*, Oxford: Clarendon Press, 1975.

alienate Irish Catholics whose support he needed in order to secure Irish disestablishment.[12] To whatever extent this might have been a motivation of his, what is lacking in Watts' analysis which this study hopes to add is a consideration of the possibility that rejecting the politics of anti-Catholicism might actually have been a part of the Dissenting political worldview at a fundamental level.

A by-product of this lingering caricature is an assumption that those who hold conservative religious convictions almost inevitably also hold conservative political ones. Once again, Watts is not alone in seeking to show that there was a 'connection between religious heterodoxy and political radicalism', but he can only show a one-way connection – that some of the heterodox supported radicalism – for his own evidence (as he concedes) shows that so did some of the orthodox.[13] Moreover, it is not hard to imagine that someone who was willing to defy the main-stream of religious opinion might also be willing to defy the mainstream of political thinking. A fresh look does need to be made, however, at the remarkable extent to which theological conservatism was combined with political radicalism in this period and an explanation offered for this phenomenon.

There are at least three contributing factors to a confused under-standing of Nonconformist politics in this era. Firstly, as the stereotype outlined above indicates, there is an assumption that Nonconformists may best be viewed through the lens of Evangelicalism, with a resulting failure adequately to distinguish the politics of Dissenters from those of Evangelical Churchmen. For example, William Gibson claims that Evangelicals 'like Palmerston and his mentor Shaftesbury sought to relieve the dissenters from their disabilities'.[14] Shaftesbury, however, was decidedly in favour of protecting the privileges of the Established Church against the encroachments of Nonconformists, and Palmerston was no deliverer of oppressed Dissenters either. The political views of Dissenters during this period will never be adequately understood until they are no longer viewed as merely a manifestation of the preoccupa-tions of Evangelicals.

Secondly, there is a tendency to impose ideas derived from notions of the 'Nonconformist conscience' in the closing decades of the century on to mid-Victorian politics. For example, Owen Chadwick writes:

> The triumph at the Crystal Palace stimulated demand for
> Sabbath laws. The leaders in the movement were evangelicals

---

[12] Michael R. Watts, *The Dissenters: Volume II*, Oxford: Clarendon, 1995, p. 569.
[13] *Ibid.*, p. 514.
[14] William Gibson, *Church, State and Society, 1760–1850*, Basingstoke, Hampshire: Macmillan, 1994, p. 171.

of the Church of England. But their power rested upon a
constituency wider than the Church of England. Wesleyans,
Baptists and Independents were decisively behind Lord Shaftesbury and Archbishop Sumner. The campaign for a godly Sunday
was another wave in English politics of what later in the century
was called the Nonconformist conscience. When the petitions for
Sunday laws were analysed they were found to include a large
number of petitions from Wesleyan congregations; still more
from the united inhabitants of villages; fewer from Independents
and Baptists . . .[15]

This passage illustrates much of what has already been argued in this
introduction: an assumption is apparently held about where Nonconformists stand which seems to have clouded the fact that the evidence
given does not reinforce it ('fewer' petitions from the Nonconformist
denominations), the impression that Evangelical Churchmen and Dissenters have a great deal in common politically (Dissenters 'decisively
behind' the Anglican Evangelicals), and finally – the point in hand – the
indication that this is quintessentially Dissenting behaviour by trans-
planting the label 'Nonconformist conscience' from the late Victorian era
to an earlier period – and this banner is flown despite the fact that this
movement was led exclusively by Churchmen. This study, by focusing in
detail on the mid-Victorian behaviour of Nonconformists, hopes to
enable future studies of the politics of Dissenters to be better able to
understand their preoccupations at mid-century on their own terms
rather than by importing views of their concerns in subsequent (or
indeed prior) generations. Whilst crude labels and generalisations can
be easily criticised, a rough guide to the periodisation offered here might
be as follows: if (rightly or wrongly) the 'Nonconformist conscience' of
the closing decades of the nineteenth century is seen as an attempt at
'domination' of the national culture through legislation, and the political
agenda of Dissenters in the first decades of the century is seen as
'toleration', the period in-between is marked by a commitment to the
goal of 'equalisation'.

The third factor, however, is the one which most makes this study
necessary: a failure adequately to grasp and explore the political philosophy of Dissenters during this period. In recent years, Eugenio Biagini
has provided us with a valuable and long-needed analysis of the political
worldview of plebeian Liberals.[16] This work sets a new standard for
taking seriously the thinking of a group which has been too often

[15] Owen Chadwick, *The Victorian Church*, Part I, London: Adam & Charles Black,
1966, p. 464.
[16] Eugenio F. Biagini, *Liberty, Retrenchment and Reform: Popular Liberalism in the
Age of Gladstone, 1860–1880*, Cambridge: Cambridge University Press, 1992.

patronised in the past. Biagini, however, downplays the role of theological ideas in the politics of Dissenters, pronouncing their attacks on
the Church Establishment in Ireland as 'about church power, not
religious principles' and arguing that 'as far as theology was concerned,
the differences between Church and Dissent . . . were politically
uninspiring'.[17] Just as Biagini has convincingly defended the integrity
of plebeian political thinking, this study seeks to demonstrate that
Nonconformists developed a coherent political worldview and that
theological ideas were more influential than has previously been
assumed.

A concentrated look at the political thinking of mid-Victorian Dissenters is needed. Owen Chadwick spends several pages recounting the
disputes over a sum of money which the government granted to be
distributed to poor Dissenting ministers. As he presents it, this is a
struggle between insensitive propagandists looking for the Victorian
equivalent of a publicity stunt and the poor, voiceless families who
desperately needed this money. Whilst Chadwick is right to have
reminded us of 'the rags of children and the tea without sugar', the
dilemmas of conscience which caused a community to refuse money
which the government was freely offering it are left largely unexplored.[18]
Chadwick writes, 'No one knows whether their principles would have
been so strong if the grant had been larger.'[19] There is, however, an
obvious parallel case which helps to answer this question (and in the
opposite direction from the one signalled by its suspicious tone):
Dissenters were, during these same years, refusing much larger sums of
money which the government was offering for their much-loved network
of schools. Chadwick's account does not shed much light on the
intellectual framework which made these sacrifices seem the necessary
path of duty; yet an explanation of this mindset would significantly aid
our understanding of the political behaviour of Dissenters.

It would be inaccurate, however, to give the impression that no one
has previously attempted the task of exploring the ideological roots of
Nonconformist politics. Notably, Richard Helmstadter has sought to
explain Dissenting political thought. He has contributed to a better
understanding of Nonconformist politics by noting that the political
agenda of Dissenters in the middle decades of the century was different in
significant ways from that of the Gladstonian period and by making the
effort to explore the intellectual foundations of Nonconformist politics.
His analysis, however, raises as many problems as it solves. By attempt-

---

[17] *Ibid.*, p. 16.
[18] Chadwick, *Victorian Church*, I, pp. 409–12.
[19] *Ibid.*, p. 410.

ing to root Dissenting political notions in the ideology of Evangelicalism, he has provided a variation of the pan-Evangelicalism view which has been advocated more recently by E. D. Steele. This approach, however, fails to explain the deep political cleavage between Evangelical Churchmen and Evangelical Nonconformists which becomes apparent when one actually compares the legislative agendas of these two groups.[20]

Many historians have resorted to dualistic models in order to explain the relationship between Dissent and politics. Norman Gash sees the development and articulation of a distinctive political theory by Dissenters as inversely related to their actual political maturity and engagement: 'Retreat into voluntaryism in fact was a retreat from politics.'[21] In other words, whilst Gash may be aware that a political worldview was emerging within Nonconformity, he views it as at the opposite pole from serious political efforts. He seems to imply that Dissenters should have focused on special-interest group politics without having the ambition to attempt to undergird their actions with political theory. A related version of this kind of dualism is offered by Watts. For example, he writes:

> But the great crime of the slave owners, in the eyes of Evangelical Dissenters, was not that they tortured the negroes' bodies by overworking them, but that they imperilled their souls by denying missionaries access to them. . . . But heterodox Dissenters such as Joseph Rayner Stephens, Joseph Livesey, James Taylor, and John Fielden were more concerned with their fellow countrymen's bellies than with their souls. . . . By contrast the great strength of Evangelical Nonconformity was that it offered consolation, companionship, and ultimately eternal salvation, to a working class threatened by disease, natural disaster, and early death. Yet for this very reason the great weakness of orthodox Dissent was its inability to offer convincing solutions when working people began to see the cause of their problems not in natural disasters or immutable laws, but in the policies of government, the demands of factory owners, and the tight-fistedness of poor law guardians.[22]

Here we have, instead of the escapist political ideology presented by Gash, an escapist religious ideology. Watts paints a picture of a dualism between souls and bodies – between spiritual revival and social reform – and argues that even when Evangelical Nonconformists appear to be

---

[20] Richard J. Helmstadter, 'The Nonconformist Conscience', in Gerald Parsons (ed.), *Religion in Victorian Britain*, vol. 4, Manchester: Manchester University Press, 1988, pp. 61–95.
[21] Norman Gash, *Reaction and Reconstruction in English Politics, 1832–52*, Oxford: Clarendon, 1965, p. 76.
[22] Watts, *Dissenters*, II, pp. 510–11.

interested in the latter it is only a round about way of getting at the former. From this perspective, the sole concern of Evangelical Non-conformists seems to be with people's religious life. Such a view does not adequately appreciate the genuine political philosophy and agenda which these Dissenters did possess.

John Vincent captured what was happening in the Dissenting political camp well when he wrote:

> . . . denominational differences were not important within the [Liberation] Society. Caught up in the web of their own logic, Liberationists took pride in supporting Roman Catholics and appearing on platforms with the godless John Morley, and common allegiance to the principle of a free church diluted or replaced specifically denominational belief.[23]

Vincent adds to a better understanding of at least one section of Nonconformist politics by noting that these Dissenters had an inter-connected political worldview and that this might even have caused them freely and without grumbling to reject the politics of anti-Catholicism. It was not Vincent's task, however, to explore the indigenous roots within Dissent of this way of thinking and, by confusing a willingness to orchestrate activities irrespective of the personal convictions of the participants with the specific theological sources for the intellectual rationale of Dissenting political goals ('denominational belief'), he does not help to point the way to where such an exploration ought to begin.

The dualism between theology and political philosophy, between interest in things spiritual and things temporal, taught by Watts, is stood on its head by J. P. Ellens in another recent book. Ellens, far from seeing Dissenters as unable to progress politically because of their orientation towards progressing spiritually, actually theorises a dualism working in the opposite direction: according to him, Nonconformist politics was hampering Dissenting spirituality. He writes:

> The liberalism inherent in voluntaryism offered a type of salvation. The passions of mid-nineteenth-century Dissent were redirected to yearn for the establishment of an earthly kingdom of peace and justice to be inaugurated with the lifting of government restrictions from commerce and religion.[24]

Ellens and Watts cannot both be right. Dissenters could have substituted

---

[23] John Vincent, *The Formation of the British Liberal Party, 1857–68*, Harmonds-worth, Middlesex: Penguin, 1966, p. 106.
[24] J. P. Ellens, *Religious Routes to Gladstonian Liberalism: The Church Rate Conflict in England and Wales, 1832–68*, University Park, Pennsylvania: Pennsylvania State University Press, 1994, pp. 85–6.

religious goals for political ones or temporal ends for spiritual ones, but it is implausible to imagine both happening to the same people simultaneously. As a way of moving the discussion beyond these conflicting interpretations, perhaps the very dualistic mode of thinking which provides the context for many of these studies needs to be re-examined. Perhaps it is possible for theology and politics to have a symbiotic relationship rather than a competitive one.

One of the fullest and best attempts at explaining the political world-view and agenda of Dissenters during this era is an unpublished doctoral thesis by K. G. Brownell: 'Voluntary Saints: English Congregationalism and the Voluntary Principle, 1825–62'. Brownell insightfully shows how Congregationalists moved from a general pan-Evangelicalism in the early years of the century to nurturing their own, distinctive theological roots and how this doctrinal line of thinking – labelled at the time as 'Voluntaryism' – was applied to political and social issues, a process which he calls 'externalizing the voluntary community'.[25] Brownell's insights need to be refined and developed and explored beyond the context of a single denomination.[26]

Studies of education in the mid-Victorian era have often noted the influence of the commitment of many Dissenters to educational Voluntaryism (a stance which was anti-state education), but have largely failed to explore the theological foundations of this position. This omission significantly hinders one's understanding of this stance because educational Voluntaryism was seen by the Nonconformists themselves as an extension of religious Voluntaryism – a theological line of thinking well developed amongst Dissenters. Indeed, the anti-state education organisation, the Voluntary School Association, was undoubtedly echoing in its name the Voluntary Church Associations of the 1830s. Our comprehension of the nature of much of Nonconformist politics in this period will be aided by exploring the tradition of religious thought which was one of its main sources. Owen Chadwick sought to brace his readers for the onslaught of historical realities revealed in his work by conceding in his introduction that: 'Free competition in religion is so repellent to religious instinct that we shrink from an evident truth of history . . .'[27] Yet mid-Victorian Nonconformists, far from finding free trade in religion repulsive, were

[25] K. G. Brownell 'Voluntary Saints: English Congregationalism and the Voluntary Principle, 1825–62', Ph.D. thesis, St Andrews University, 1982, p. 97.
[26] Briefer comments which also demonstrate a measure of awareness and sensitivity to this set of ideas can be found in another work on this denomination: R. Tudur Jones, *Congregationalism in England, 1662–1962*, London: Independent Press, 1962, for example, p. 194.
[27] Chadwick, *Victorian Church*, I, p. 4.

often imbued by their Voluntaryism with something akin to the faith
Elijah had when he called for a free and fair contest between himself
and the prophets of Baal.

Adherents of politicised Voluntaryism are generally referred to as the
'militant' or 'radical' portion of Nonconformist politics in this era. An
assessment needs to be made of the extent to which this group dominated
Dissenting politics as a whole. Steele has argued that militant Dissent
was losing influence in this period as Palmerston successfully wooed
many Dissenters back on to the moderate ground.[28] Steele's study is a
fuller attempt to bolster Chadwick's earlier claim that Palmerston
'attracted many dissenters'.[29] Likewise, Watts argues that the militants
were not the dominant force, claiming that the advocates of disestablishment and educational Voluntaryism spoke for 'fewer than half of the
politically aware Nonconformists'.[30] Nevertheless, the evidence offered
for these assessments deserves a critical re-appraisal. W. R. Ward notes
that in 'the later 'thirties the dissenters divided for the first time on this
insoluble problem of tactics', which is arguably a backhanded way of
acknowledging the hegemony of the political *principles* championed by
the militants – and the philosophy which undergirded them.[31] In short,
the whole rhetoric of 'moderates' and 'militants' might prove overplayed
– or even largely illusory – when applied to ideological convictions.
Arguably, 'moderates' were merely Dissenters who were uneasy with the
way that 'militants' were pursuing goals which they all desired to see
achieved, derived from principles which they all shared. The useful terms
'moderate' and 'militant' are not to be abandoned, but it will be argued
that their meaning for mid-Victorian English Dissenting politics relates
to tactics rather than principles.

The very title of this study contains the words 'religious equality' and,
as already has been indicated, part of its task is to investigate the extent
to which Dissenters defended the civil rights of people from other
religious (and non-religious) traditions. There is enough evidence already
available in existing secondary sources to make it clear that they sometimes did support measures for securing greater equality for members of
other groups such as Jews and Roman Catholics. The questions this
raises are: How sincere was this effort? Was it merely a reluctant decision
not to act on the desire to cut these groups out of civil society which was
allegedly in Dissenting hearts or primarily a matter of tactics or were
there genuinely held convictions which prompted this attitude? Also, if it

[28] Steele, *Palmerston*, for example, pp. 173–83.
[29] Chadwick, *Victorian Church*, I, p. 471.
[30] Watts, *Dissenters*, II, p. 551.
[31] W. R. Ward, *Religion and Society in England, 1790–1850*, London: B. T. Batsford,
1972, p. 193.

11

is conceded that religious equality was part of the political philosophy of Nonconformists, was this merely because they had imbibed their civic worldview from other sources, or could it have evolved from their own theological framework? Did being a 'friend of religious equality' mean friendship with 'the world' or could it be seen as a logical implication of friendship with Christ?

Part I

NONCONFORMITY AND
ENGLISH SOCIETY

Chapter One

THE NONCONFORMISTS

One could argue that as long as there have been state churches there has been religious nonconformity. For there to be an on-going, identifiable nonconformist community, however, there must be some measure of religious toleration – whether by design, or merely through apathy or incompetence. In an English context, the term 'Nonconformity' usually refers only to Protestant Dissenters during times when the Established Church was itself Protestant. Such communities can be identified in the sixteenth century, but a continuous, stable Nonconformist tradition is better traced from the second half of the seventeenth century. During that period, several major branches of Dissent found a secure rooting. The Great Ejectment of 1662 pushed a significant number of Puritan ministers into the arms of Dissent and thereby helped to produce a permanent Nonconformist community of some weight and note.[1] The two largest branches of Dissent objected to the Episcopal polity of the Established Church. The Presbyterians followed a Reformed tradition in ecclesiology which taught that any rulings which were meant to be binding upon local churches should be made by a synod of local elders. An offshoot from this stem in the nineteenth century were the Unitarians. They were members of congregations which were historically Presbyterian whose commitment to rationalistic thinking led them to reject the doctrine of the Trinity.[2] The other main branch was the Congregationalists (or Independents). They taught that every local church had complete autonomy and was not answerable to any human authority outside itself.[3] Their offshoot, already well-established in the

---

[1] The pre-nineteenth-century history of Nonconformity can be found in Michael R. Watts, *The Dissenters*, vol. 1, Oxford: Clarendon, 1978.

[2] Wigmore-Beddoes has explored the religious sentiments of Victorian Unitarians. Dennis G. Wigmore-Beddoes, *Yesterday's Radicals: A Study of the Affinity between Unitarianism and Broad Church Anglicanism in the Nineteenth Century*, Cambridge: James Clarke & Co., 1971.

[3] The history of this denomination from the Great Ejection to the mid-twentieth century has been written by R. Tudur Jones, *Congregationalism in England, 1662–1962*, London: Independent Press, 1962.

15

seventeenth century, were the Baptists. Baptists concurred with Congregational thinking on matters of church government, but also maintained the distinctive conviction that a person was not eligible for baptism until he or she was old enough to become personally convinced of the truth of the gospel.[4] A final group, the Society of Friends, was more idiosyncratic than the others and, like Unitarianism, was sometimes shunned or persecuted as heretical. The Quakers (as members of the Society of Friends were commonly called) respected experiences of personal illumination of truth and set themselves apart from the rest of society by such traits as their pacifism and their austere and quaint habits in dress, decoration, entertainment and language.[5] Presbyterians, Congregationalists, Baptists and Quakers were the main varieties of Dissent in the decades after the Restoration.

For purposes of studying the mid-nineteenth century, Congregationalists, Baptists and Presbyterians are identified as 'Old Dissent', as they were in contemporary usage. By this time, although it was the predominant expression of Christianity in Scotland, Presbyterianism in England had shrunk dramatically in relation to the two other groups, and what remained of English Presbyterianism which was not receiving its life blood from Scots residing in England had become overwhelmingly Unitarian.[6] Evangelicalism had become a strong influence in the bulk of Nonconformity, causing Unitarians to remain suspect in the eyes of many other Dissenters.[7] Some Quakers, on the other hand, had imbibed many Evangelical convictions and traits and were therefore on far friendlier terms with the other groups than had been the case in the days when John Bunyan, the Congregational-Baptist minister remembered as the author of *Pilgrim's Progress*, denounced them so

---

[4] Several histories of the Baptists in England were written in the first half of this century. The best of these is A. C. Underwood, *A History of the English Baptists*, London: Baptist Union, 1947. In recent decades, the Baptist History Society has been publishing a series of volumes on the history of English Baptists from the seventeenth century. The volume relevant to the dates of this study is J. H. Y. Briggs, *The English Baptists in the Nineteenth Century*, Didcot, Oxfordshire: Baptist Historical Society, 1994.

[5] The nineteenth-century history of this denomination may be found in Elizabeth Isichei, *Victorian Quakers*, Oxford: Oxford University Press, 1970.

[6] For a history of orthodox English Presbyterianism during the years of this study, see A. H. Drysdale, *History of the Presbyterians in England: Their Rise, Decline and Revival*, London: Presbyterian Church of England, 1889.

[7] The transformation of the bulk of English Presbyterians into Unitarians and the transformation of the bulk of orthodox Dissenters into Evangelicals who found it increasingly difficult to keep their disapproval of heterodox views from straining their relations with Unitarians is clearly presented in Bernard Lord Manning, *The Protestant Dissenting Deputies*, Cambridge: Cambridge University Press, 1952, chapter 5.

unequivocally.[8] The Congregationalists were the largest group of Old Dissenters during the period under consideration; and the Baptists, who were very similar to them in both theology and politics, were the second, well ahead of the remaining historic groupings.[9] Therefore, this study will chiefly concentrate on these two denominations which together represent the vast majority of mid-Victorians in the direct spiritual lineage of historic Dissent.

The 'New Dissent' which made the distinction of 'the old' necessary consisted of those groups which had arisen through the Methodist movement. Of these, Wesleyan Methodism, the body which continued the work which John Wesley had left upon his death, was by far the largest.[10] Indeed, it was the largest of all the religious groupings outside the Established Church and it looked upon its separation from that greater body as more an unfortunate (but perhaps necessary) circumstance rather than a point of principle to be trumpeted. For example, an article in the *Wesleyan Methodist Magazine* in 1854 noted:

> . . . the Wesleyan is not committed to any opposition, and is never included under either the terms Churchman and Dissenter, (as these terms are understood by those to whom they primarily belong,) he stands in such a relation to both these parties as neither of them does to the other.[11]

Wesleyan Methodism, therefore, was in the anomalous position of being numerically the most significant, yet nevertheless being unrepresentative of Dissenting thought. In this study, as in contemporary usage, references to 'Dissenters' and 'Nonconformists' are not intended to include Wesleyans.[12] Wesleyan opinions on various matters discussed will be dealt with explicitly and separately.

---

[8] John Bunyan, *Grace Abounding to the Chief of Sinners*, (ed. W. R. Owens), London: Penguin, 1987, p. 33. For Evangelical Quakers see Isichei, *Victorian Quakers*, pp. 3–16.
[9] Statistical evidence for this can be found in *Census of Great Britain, 1851. Religious Worship. England and Wales*, London: George E. Eyre and William Spottiswoode, 1853 (reprinted in *British Parliamentary Papers: 1851 Census*, Population 10, Shannon, Ireland: Irish University Press, 1970). (The worth and reliability of this data is discussed below.) Baptists divided into several groupings, but the largest, the Particular Baptist denomination, was, by itself, significantly larger than all the other historic Dissenting denominations apart from the Congregationalists.
[10] The origins of Methodism and especially Wesleyan Methodism can be found in Rupert Davies and Gordon Rupp (eds), *A History of the Methodist Church in Great Britain*, vol. 1, London: Epworth Press, 1965.
[11] *Wesleyan Methodist Magazine*, June 1854, p. 536. Similar comments were still being made in the closing years of this study. *Wesleyan Methodist Magazine*, January 1865, p. 29.
[12] The *Eclectic Review*, for example, when it wished to be inclusive spoke of 'every dissenting and methodist minister': n.s., vol. XXI (Jan.–June 1847), p. 362.

17

Most of the other Methodist bodies were groupings which had split away from this parent body due to some disagreement with the workings or decisions of the Wesleyan governmental machinery and leadership. The Primitive Methodists and the Bible Christians offered a more populist form of Methodist religion. The New Connexion, the Wesleyan Methodist Association and the other groups which joined with the latter to create the United Methodist Free Churches in 1857 were formed in protest against what they perceived to be the heavy-handed, authoritarian way in which the parent body was governed. These splinter groups, unlike Wesleyan Methodism, tended to identify themselves unequivocally and unashamedly as part of Dissent.[13] Some of them, however, like the Primitive Methodists and Bible Christians, for reasons unrelated to deference for the Establishment such as a shortage of the kind of prominent laymen and ministers who could spend a portion of their time sitting on committees and a lack of organs of expression such as a newspaper controlled by one of their own, were often content to plough their own furrows without being represented in the various co-operative efforts undertaken in the name of Nonconformity.[14]

In terms of social composition, mid-Victorian Nonconformity was overwhelmingly from the middle classes or lower. Nonconformity had no champion in the House of Lords and loyal Dissenters amongst the aristocracy were virtually non-existent. Those of high social standing were normally committed – however indifferently – to the Church of England, and even the Church of Rome was far better represented amongst the titled and landed classes than the Protestant Dissenters. One Nonconformist minister, seeking to sum up the plight of Dissent in this matter, grumbled that a peeress had once been interested in joining his congregation, but this exciting possibility had come to nothing because 'I had not a single member who was adequate to converse with her in the usual mode.'[15] Many of the poor, on the other hand, tended to withhold their full support and participation from all organised religion.[16] Moreover, they typically viewed their religion, when

---

[13] For example, the editor of the *Methodist New Connexion Magazine* felt free to remark on behalf of the body he served 'we are professedly a dissenting community'. vol. 51 (1848), p. 444.

[14] For example, whilst the Congregationalists had the layman, Edward Baines, to lead the campaign against the Education Minutes of 1846, the *Primitive Methodist Magazine*, which – unlike the voices of Wesleyanism – agreed with this Dissenting campaign, had to be content with reprinting an article Baines had written for his own newspaper. *Primitive Methodist Magazine*, vol. XXVIII (1847), pp. 232–40.

[15] John Waddington, *Congregational History, 1850–1888* (vol. 5 of series), London: Longmans, Green, and Co., 1880, p. 137.

[16] Hugh McLeod, *Religion and the Working Class in Nineteenth-Century Britain*, Basingstoke, Hampshire: Macmillan, 1984, pp. 57–66. cf. Mark Smith, *Religion in*

forced to consider it, as Church of England by default, and usually looked to the Established Church to perform any rites of passage which were deemed necessary. The very poor did not flock anywhere, but if forced to state an opinion, they would usually deny atheism and not affirm any Dissenting denomination. Positively, Dissent was particularly attractive to the aspiring middle classes who found in it – in addition to spiritual benefits – community, identity, respectability (in comparison to the non-religious) and habits of living conducive to upward social mobility.

This situation led some Victorian Congregationalists to view their denomination as primarily appealing to the middle classes. The *Eclectic Review* claimed in 1867: 'Our churches [i.e. the Establishment] are for the rich, our chapels [i.e. Dissent] for the lower half of the middle class, and the working man seldoms [sic] finds his way to either.'[17] Some made a virtue of this (apparent) fact. The Congregational minister and scholar, Robert Vaughan, wrote at the end of the 1830s:

> Another point observable – but observable as one of perpetuity, and not of contrast – is the fact that Congregationalism still finds *the body of its adherents among the middle class*. We do not scruple to say, that we look with some pleasure on this manifest aptitude of our system to commend itself to that part of the community which all wise men regard as the most sound – as having in it much the larger portion of real social health.[18]

In 1848, the Congregational minister, Thomas Binney, one of the most prominent Nonconformist preachers of the age, said of his denomination in an address to the Congregational Union:

> Our special mission is neither to the very rich nor to the very poor. We have a work to do upon the thinking active, influential classes – classes which fill neither courts nor cottages; but which, gathered into cities, and consisting of several gradations there, are the modern movers and moulders of the world.[19]

Likewise Joshua Wilson, an influential Congregational layman, said in 1862, 'It is an unquestionable fact, that our strength as a denomination lies in the large cities and towns, as our special vocation is to the middle classes of people, who form the chief portion of their inhabitants.'[20]

Industrial Society: Oldham and Saddleworth, 1740–1865, Oxford: Clarendon Press, 1994.

[17] *Eclectic Review*, n.s., vol. XIII (July–Dec. 1867), p. 427.

[18] Robert Vaughan, *Religious Parties in England*, London: Thomas Ward, 1839 [originally 1838], pp. 97–8.

[19] *Congregational Year Book* for 1848, p. 9.

[20] Autumnal Assembly of the Congregational Union, 9 October 1861: *Congregational Year Book* for 1862, London: 1862, p. 63

These assessments should not be applied to Dissent collectively. Congregationalists were more middle class than some other denominations such as the Primitive Methodists. Moreover, Michael Watts has recently offered statistical evidence showing that the appeal of Dissent as a whole, with Congregationalists included, 'continued to be primarily to the working class' during the decades covered in this study.[21] He suggests that comments on the predominance of the middle classes by people like Binney reflected the composition of the kind of metropolitan congregations they served rather than the situation in the whole of Congregationalism throughout the country.[22] Therefore, although these Victorian Dissenters were right to note that most working-class people and particularly the very poor abstained from regular attendance at any house of worship, nevertheless it seems clear that the members and adherents which they did draw included, not only members of the middle classes, but a significant number of people from the labouring classes.

One of the benefits which comes with studying the mid-nineteenth century is the location within this period of a unique source of information concerning English religious life: the Religious Census of 1851. On Sunday, 30 March 1851, an official attempt was made to count all the various places of worship throughout England and Wales, the seating capacity of these venues and the number of people who attended the meetings held in them throughout that day. Ever since the census was first proposed, attacks have been made on its accuracy and usefulness. Scholars cannot help but be irritated by the fact that the structure of the census (counting the attendance at the morning, afternoon and evening meetings of a single congregation) makes it impossible to say with confidence how many individuals were actually involved. The census has other inherent weaknesses as well, in addition to the separate question of the accuracy of the information. Nevertheless, for all its faults, the 1851 Religious Census is a valuable source of information. Recent historians, whilst not failing to expound its inherent drawbacks, have defended its essential accuracy and usefulness.[23]

The results of the census were said to have revealed two important

---

[21] Michael R. Watts, *The Dissenters: Volume II*, Oxford: Clarendon, 1995, p. 597. The evidence on which this statement is based is presented in tables in the appendix, pp. 718–76.

[22] *Ibid.*, pp. 317, 322, 598.

[23] K. S. Inglis, 'Patterns of Religious Worship in 1851', *Journal of Ecclesiastical History*, 11, 1 (1960), pp. 74–86. W. S. F. Pickering, 'The 1851 religious census – a useless experiment?', *The British Journal of Sociology*, 18 (1967), pp. 382–407. David M. Thompson, 'The 1851 religious census: problems and possibilities', *Victorian Studies*, 11, 1 (September 1967), pp. 87–97. David M. Thompson, 'The Religious Census of 1851', in *The Census and Social Structure*, Richard Lawton (ed.), London: Frank Cass, 1978, pp. 241–86.

facts. The first one, which we shall not dwell on here, was that, when the statistics were examined in the light of those compiled at the same time regarding the size of the English (and Welsh) population as a whole, however one looked at it, it was an unavoidable conclusion that there was a large section of the population which must have willingly refrained from attending worship services altogether. The second major finding derived from the census was that close to half of the worshipping community was attending the meetings of some body other than the Established Church. The question which this raised in people's minds was: to what extent can a church which does not have the loyalty of the majority of the worshipping population be legitimately considered the national one? If the percentage of the worshipping population which the Church of England could secure was on a downward trend, then at some point its position would surely become untenable. Perhaps it was already perilously close to that point. Dissenters, particularly those pre-occupied with the goal of disestablishment, leapt to this interpretation of the census. When the results were ready for publication at the start of 1854, but had not yet been made available to the general public, the militant newspaper, the *Nonconformist*, boasted that it was 'the first journal in this country to give an account of this publication' and it knew immediately what lesson it thought should be drawn from it:

> A religious Establishment co-extensive with a people we can well understand – but a religious Establishment which does not half the spiritual work of the nation, and that the lesser half, is an anomaly which no sophistry can defend when once the facts of the case are thoroughly known.[24]

Because the census was not repeated in this form – due to the fears of those loyal to the Church of England of what new returns might indicate – Dissenters referred to these figures as evidence of their strength for decades to come. Herbert Skeats' book, *A History of the Free Churches of England*, which he published in 1868, begins its tale with the Glorious Revolution and ends on the results of the Religious Census of 1851.[25] Even those who were not obsessed with disestablishment used the figures to bolster Dissenting claims.[26] The government, egged on by some Churchmen, devised a plan in 1860 to include a statement of religious

---

[24] *Nonconformist*, 4 January 1854, p. 2.
[25] H. S. Skeats, *History of the Free Churches of England, 1688–1851*, London: Arthur Miall, 1868.
[26] The moderate *British Quarterly Review*, for example, claimed in 1862 that the census demonstrated that establishing a particular denomination was not effective in terms of its own stated goals, because it did not result in it growing and other ones declining. XXXV, LXIX (January 1862), pp. 206–7.

profession in the forthcoming census. This alteration of the nature of the census suddenly caused the Nonconformists themselves to be the ones who were worried about the results. Dissenters feared that the large number of people who comprised the irreligious world would call themselves 'Church of England' just because they were being forced to say something and that this would therefore give a false impression of the true strength of the Church in relation to Dissent. Nonconformity was able to exercise its political muscle in order to have the offending question removed, ironically proving, despite its fear of the proposed data, that there was truth in the interpretation of the 1851 Census which said that Dissent was a considerable force to be reckoned with in the land.[27]

As Thomas Binney and Joshua Wilson's coupling of Congregationalism's middle-class constituency with its location in cities suggests, Nonconformity in this era was particularly strong – relative to the Established Church – in the cities and large towns. Certainly, the metropolis and the old cathedral cities were still dominated by the Church, but the urban areas which had come into vitality through industrialisation and the development of manufacturing were much more the domain of Dissent.[28] Places like Manchester, Birmingham, Leicester, Rochdale, Leeds and Bradford might be justly seen as centres of Dissent. Although it is unquestionably true that a good portion of their teeming masses was not actively committed to any religious body, the civic affairs of these places were usually in the hands of Dissenters and Nonconformity was often thriving, and organised on the ground, in a way which the Church clearly was not.[29] Nevertheless, it is easy to overplay the significance of the large industrial towns of the north due to the wealthy laymen from them which were so vital and visible when Nonconformists set out to act collectively on national issues. David Thompson has shown that the most important Dissenting political organisation of this period, the Liberation Society, was numerically stronger in midland and southern provincial market towns rather than in the industrial towns of the north.[30] The influence of Dissenters in the

---

[27] H. S. Skeats and C. S. Miall, *History of the Free Churches of England, 1688–1891*, London: Alexander & Shepheard, 1891, pp. 561–3.
[28] A useful guide to the geographical strength of the Established Church during this period is: B. I. Coleman, *The Church of England in the Mid-Nineteenth Century: A Social Geography*, London: The Historical Association, 1980.
[29] See, for example, A. Temple Patterson, *Radical Leicester*, Leicester: University College, 1954; Jack Reynolds, *The Great Paternalist: Titus Salt and the Growth of Nineteenth-Century Bradford*, London: Maurice Temple Smith, 1983.
[30] David M. Thompson, 'The Liberation Society, 1844–1868', in Patricia Hollis (ed.), *Pressure from Without*, London: Edward Arnold, 1974, p. 229 (see his appendix, pp. 237–8, for the evidence on which this statement is based).

industrial towns of both the north and the midlands were vital to the interests of Nonconformity as a whole in this era, but we must look beyond them to understand the full geographical range of the sources of its strength.

On a county basis, Cornwall shows itself to be the least willing to express its spirituality through the ministrations of the Established religion. This independently-minded county had been completely over-run by New Dissent. Wesleyan Methodists were particularly strong in a block of counties stretching down to the east midlands from the north east: Durham, Yorkshire, Lincolnshire, Nottinghamshire and Derbyshire. Old Dissent maintained as its strongest areas those which it had inherited from the preceding centuries. Baptists still held their greatest concentration in John Bunyan's Bedfordshire and a block of interconnected counties spread around it: Huntingdonshire, Buckinghamshire and Cambridgeshire, and further beyond this core into Hertfordshire, Suffolk and right through to Leicestershire. Congregationalism did well in Dorset and the parts surrounding it, particularly in the eastward and northward directions, and in Suffolk and Essex, coming westward, passing more lightly through Bedfordshire (presumably in deference to the Baptists), but regaining impressive strength in Northamptonshire. Congregationalism also thrived in the metropolis and its suburbs.[31] It has been traditional for historians to impose meaning on this data with the generalisation that Old Dissent did well in areas where the Church of England was strong (because it was able to play the rival) and New Dissent did well where the Church of England (together with Old Dissent) was weak (because it was able to fill the void). Nevertheless, K. D. M. Snell warns that a statistically-significant correlation proves elusive when this thesis is actually put to the test.[32]

The situation in rural England and on a level lower (and arguably more telling one) has been explored by Alan Everitt. His study of Dissent in four regions (Lindsey, Leicestershire, Northamptonshire and Kent) shows that Nonconformity grew best where land was not owned and controlled by a small group of people, but rather in freeholders' parishes, and where land was subdivided. Other places identified as more typically

---

[31] This information on county distribution is primarily derived from John D. Gay, *The Geography of Religion in England*, London: Duckworth, 1971, and the geographical comments made by Horace Mann, the official compiler of the 1851 Religious Census, in his article 'On the Statistical Position of Religious Bodies in England and Wales', *Quarterly Journal of the Statistical Society*, XVIII, Part II (June 1855), pp. 155–6.

[32] K. D. M. Snell, *Church and Chapel in North Midlands: Religious Observance in the Nineteenth Century*, Leicester: Leicester University Press, 1991. Also, Alan D. Gilbert, *Religion and Society in Industrial England*, London: Longman, 1976, pp. 115–21.

receptive to the development of Dissent were: boundary settlements, decayed market towns and industrial villages.[33] Nonconformist strength in the cities and large towns, in contrast to the Church of England's relative weakness in these areas, should not be mistakenly construed as implying that Dissent was not strong in rural areas, for there was a healthy rural Dissenting tradition. No striking contrast can be drawn here, however, with the Established Church, which had even deeper roots in the land.[34]

A map of the political life of Dissent, however, is more specifically to the point of this study. In the early 1840s, Dissenters were coming out of a period in which they had largely refrained from engaging in rigorous, radical political agitation on their own behalf. This, however, was only a temporary hiatus between the Dissenting radicalism of the second half of the eighteenth century which has recently been highlighted by James E. Bradley and the militancy discussed in this study.[35] One of the main causes of this hiatus was the effect of the American and French revolutions. The unease which these events had caused in English society had provoked accusations that Dissenters were politically dangerous which, in turn, tempted the Nonconformist community to minimise the impression that it was a political force. The Congregational minister, John Blackburn, tried to thwart the new politicisation of Dissenters in the 1840s by reviewing the origins of this quietism and the benefits he felt it had produced:

> Dissenters have always displayed a generous love of liberty. This led them on the first outbreak of the French Revolution to rejoice in the dawn of freedom upon the vine-covered hills of France; and taking their position in favour of that great movement, many of them continued its advocates till the sanguinary and atheistical conduct of its leaders, and the proud aggressions of the First Consul, outraged and alarmed all true Englishmen. Thus the storm of political agitation was hushed; and even Mr. Robert Hall, the eloquent and enthusiastic apologist of the Revolution, united his voice with that of conservative orators to repel the intended aggressions of Napoleon. At that period party passions were hushed, the common dangers of the country

[33] Alan Everitt, *The Pattern of Rural Dissent: the Nineteenth Century*, Leicester: Leicester University Press, 1972.
[34] David M. Thompson, 'The churches and society in Nineteenth Century England: a rural perspective', in *Popular Belief and Practice* (Studies in Church History 8), G. J. Cuming and Derek Baker (eds), Cambridge: Cambridge University Press, 1972, pp. 267–6.
[35] James E. Bradley, *Religion, Revolution and English Radicalism: Non-conformity in Eighteenth-Century Politics and Society*, Cambridge: Cambridge University Press, 1990.

led to much special prayer, the value of the Christian religion as the divinely appointed remedy for the evils of humanity was felt, missionary, tract and Bible Societies arose; and it was during that quarter of a century, that evangelical religion and evangelical nonconformity too, made greater progress in this country than was perhaps ever witnessed.[36]

Moreover, Nonconformists in the 1830s were largely deprived of prominent leaders who were willing to articulate the political agenda of Dissenting radicalism. Edward Baines, senior, for example, used his rare position as an orthodox Nonconformist voice in the Commons to condemn his fellow Dissenter, John Thorogood, for his civil disobedience over the issue of church rates and to try to dissuade a radical, Anglican MP from bring in a bill to alleviate this grievance on the grounds that 'enough had been done that Session', even though he would not hold his ground on opinions like these when communicating exclusively to Dissenting audiences.[37] In this context, the prudence of leading a quiet life was a major signal sent by many of the prominent voices in the Dissenting world and the alternative – to agitate politically for their own community – was considered fraught with dangers. Those who engaged in the latter activity were given the pejorative label 'political Dissenters'. This taunt implied that its recipients had become side-tracked from the cause of the gospel and that their Dissent was not the holy, admirable kind which the 'the religious Dissenters' (the term of approbation given to those who refrained from political agitation) exhibited. For example, when the climate began to change in the 1840s, a noted Congregational minister in Manchester, Robert Halley, felt a need to write to John Blackburn – a prominent member in London of this old (and rapidly fading) school of thinking which discouraged political activism – and frantically attempt to downplay his role in the campaign against the corn laws 'when I heard that you imagined I had become an agitator'.[38]

What one had to do to merit the accusation of being 'a political Dissenter' moved on a sliding scale as the political situation changed. Some people gave the Birmingham Congregational minister, J. A. James, this label because of a pamphlet he published in 1830, *Dissent and the Church of England*. In the following decade, however, he was being criticised by the then 'political Dissenters' for being too timid, and once he had passed away his memory was evoked in order to conjure up the honourable way Dissenters used to behave before 'political Dissent' had

---

[36] John Blackburn, *The Three Conferences held by the Opponents of the Maynooth College Endowment Bill*, London: Jackson & Walford, 1845, pp. 91–2.
[37] London, Dr Williams's Library, New College Library MSS, Blackburn Papers, L52/6/4, John Thorogood to Edward Baines, 11 December 1840.
[38] *Ibid.*, L52/2/71, Robert Halley to John Blackburn, 3 August 1841.

come on the scene.[39] Nevertheless, throughout this period, though the taunt had diminishing effect, it was always there and could cause pangs of conscience for those unsure of how far political activity was compatible with the religious life. The great Baptist preacher, C. H. Spurgeon, whom no one could justly accuse of neglecting his spiritual work, refuted the charge at a meeting in 1866 of the Liberation Society:

> All sorts of bad names had been given to those connected with the Society, and they were called by the terrible name of "Political Dissenters;" but he had been looking round the meeting, and saw that it was composed of some of their most earnest members, deacons and ministers, and he was persuaded that they were as spiritually-minded a body of men, and as active in the spread of the Gospel, as any that could be brought together. (Hear, hear). He intended spending a few moments in expostulating with those of his brethren who thought that it was wicked thus to agitate and especially to teach anything political. Such people were inconsistent . . . He held it to be a dishonest thing to join a community and enjoy its privileges without discharging its duties. (Cheers.) Some other people said that they should have less spiritual-mindedness if they took any part in this business; but if so, the sooner they got a healthier kind of spiritual life the better.[40]

Every decade which passed in the Victorian era diminished yet further the power this charge had to cause active Dissenters to search their souls uneasily; the Nonconformity community became increasingly convinced that political and religious goals could be complementary.[41]

Some groups were particularly sensitive to the accusation of becoming political. The Wesleyans, as we have already noted, would not even officially admit that they were Dissenters, much less political ones. John Wesley had left the body a 'no politics' rule which the dominant figure in early Victorian Wesleyanism, Jabez Bunting, successfully invoked in order to suppress any calls for disestablishment or even many lesser goals such as the abolition of church rates. In 1834, Bunting succeeded in having the Wesleyan minister, Joseph Rayner Stephens, put under discipline because his work for disestablishment was said to have violated the 'no politics' rule.[42] This policy was maintained throughout

---

[39] R. W. Dale, *Life and Letters of John Angell James*, London: James Nisbet, 1861, pp. 585–9.
[40] Supplement to the *Liberator*, 5 May 1866, p. 85.
[41] Even the moderate Congregationalist, Robert Vaughan, insisted on 'the absurdity of the distinction attempted to be drawn between the "religious" and the "political" Dissenter'. *Liberator*, November 1861, p. 177.
[42] Benjamin Gregory, *Side Lights on the Conflicts of Methodism*, London: Cassell, 1899, pp. 150–64.

the period under discussion, arguably at the price of several schisms and the quiet dissatisfaction of an inestimable number of those who remained. Throughout this period, the militant Dissenters tried to coax Wesleyan sympathisers out of the closet, but with little success. For example, when feelings were running particularly high over the issue of church rates in 1861, the Liberation Society wondered if this might be the opportunity to harvest some of the goodwill which it knew, through the private correspondence it received, existed within some Wesleyan hearts and minds. An agent was employed for a three-month trial period to persuade members of that body to subscribe to the society, the sensitivity of his position made apparent by the stipulation that his name was not to appear on the letter which the society would compose. After eight months, however, the committee was forced to admit that his work 'had not been followed by any immediate results'.[43] If some of the Wesleyan crop had matured into political Dissent, it was not yet ready to stand taller than the rest and risk being lopped off. David Hempton, in an authoritative study of Wesleyanism and politics, has concluded that the Toryism of the Bunting era has been exaggerated.[44] Likewise, the pollbook evidence compiled by J. R. Vincent reveals the tendency of Wesleyans to vote Liberal.[45] Nevertheless, the ethos of the denomination did prevent it from making pronouncements as a body in favour of radical (or even Liberal) political goals and even largely succeeded in restraining individual Wesleyans from lending their names publicly to these campaigns.

The Society of Friends had practically made an aloof attitude towards the political sphere into a spiritual discipline. This stance, however, was in tension with their robust humanitarianism which led them to fight injustice wherever it was found – and by the measures which seemed likely to be most effective. The 'weighty friends' who set the tone of political renunciation for this group did not wield control as effectively as Jabez Bunting. Nevertheless, concerns over politicisation were more pronounced in the Society than in any other group of Old Dissent. In 1843, the annual epistle of the Yearly Meeting included a phrase which was meant to check the growing temptation to become political Dissenters: 'we desire ever to be found of those who are quiet in the land'. Quakers who were active in the political sphere such as John Bright and

---

[43] London, London Metropolitan Archives, Liberation Society, Minutes of the Executive Committee, A/LIB/383, 15 November 1861, minute 1228; 1 August 1862, minute 103.
[44] David Hempton, *Methodism and Politics in British Society, 1750–1850*, London: Hutchinson, 1987 [originally 1984], p. 235.
[45] J. R. Vincent, *Pollbooks: How Victorians Voted*, Cambridge: Cambridge University Press, 1968, especially pp. 69–70.

Joseph Sturge refused to accept that their activities were incompatible with their religious convictions.[46] The anti-slavery movement had already helped to erode the old Quaker political quietism and various other causes such as free trade, franchise reform and prohibition augmented this trend. By the end of the period under consideration, the Liberation Society could approach Quakers with a letter of recommendation signed by close to thirty prominent Friends, including Joseph Pease of Darlington, Samuel Bowly of Gloucester and John S. Rowntree of York (the elder brother of the entrepreneur, Joseph Rowntree).[47] Ironically, the philanthropic zeal of wealthy and prominent members of the Society sometimes caused Quaker personalities to play crucial roles in political pressure group campaigns, despite the small size of the Society's membership and its ambivalent attitude toward the broader political arena.

A final group which was particularly vulnerable to the charge of politicisation was the body of ordained ministers.[48] They, above all people, were not supposed to become deflected from the cause of advancing the gospel. They, above all people, were not supposed to allow baser concerns to impoverish the purity of their spiritual life. There is a paradox here as well though, for they, above all people, were the natural leaders of the Dissenting community, its natural spokesmen in the wider world. They had the respectability, learning, talents, communication skills and social experience to represent Dissenting concerns. If Dissenting politics simply meant defending the interests of Dissenters against the disadvantages which society might wish to impose upon them and raising a voice for righteousness and justice against public evils, then perhaps ministers were ideal for such a task. A good number of ministers did take very active parts in political pressure group campaigns, addressed the issues of the day in print and in speeches and even actively supported political candidates. Some were provoked only by a particularly heated issue, but others seemed to entangle themselves in almost every campaign going. William McKerrow, an orthodox Presbyterian minister in Manchester, for example, threw himself into the campaigns for the removal of Nonconformist grievances, disestablishment, free trade, peace and arbitration, national education and prohibition. It was not until 1857, however, by which time he already had a track record in all these issues, that he was willing publicly to endorse political

---

[46] Alex Tyrrell, *Joseph Sturge*, London: Christopher Helm, 1987, pp. 192–3; G. M. Trevelyan, *Life of John Bright*, London: Constable, 1913, pp. 104–5.

[47] *Friend*, First Month [January] 1867, p. 58.

[48] This issue is discussed and statistical evidence for the political activity of ministers is offered in Kenneth D. Brown, *A Social History of the Nonconformist Ministry in England and Wales, 1800–1930*, pp. 202–3, 208–17.

candidates (Liberals such as John Bright), and openly join the world of party politics. He declared defiantly in his first speech of this kind:

> We have, however, arrived at a particular crisis in the history of our country, and I will not abandon the duty which I owe to my conscience, to my principles, and to my fellow-citizens, in consequence of any charge of being a political minister that may be advanced against me.[49]

The ministers of the Baptist denomination seemed to lead the way in political activism; the names of men like J. H. Hinton, F. A. Cox and J. P. Mursell can be found listed in association with numerous causes of interest to political Dissent. The more unpredictable C. H. Spurgeon was also not afraid to lend his weight to pressure group politics. Congregationalism also played a strong part; it offered notable figures such as R. W. Dale, J. G. Rogers and G. W. Conder. Numerous other ministers were liable to take a very strong stand at moments of their choosing, even if their sensibilities or ministerial duties kept them from a steady involvement in the struggles of the day; men such as the Baptist, William Brock, and the Congregationalist, Thomas Binney. The High Church newspaper, the *Guardian*, published an article upon the death in 1862 of the Congregational minister, John Burnet, who had been a very active member of the Liberation Society, entitled 'A Political Dissenter'. With no sentimentality about speaking ill of the dead, it noted:

> Mr. Burnet does not appear to have considered that the salvation of souls was his proper and peculiar calling, but to have been from an early date absorbed in a great outward political object – viz., the destruction of the Established Church as an Establishment.

The paper then went on to say of any minister who believed that this was his task that 'his conception of the Christian minister's calling is singularly blind, carnal, unspiritual, and unevangelical'.[50] Despite all this activity by numerous 'political' ministers like Burnet, the old taboo did seem generally to restrain ministers from actually running for political office themselves. As late as 1880, the prominent Congregational minister, Joseph Parker, withdrew from a Parliamentary election he had joined, after having been informed by 'some Nonconformist friends' that he was violating 'an unwritten law in the city of London'.[51] Outside the metropolis, moreover, Dissenting ministers did not seem free of this law either. Those, like Edward Miall, who became politicians did so at the

[49] J. M. McKerrow, *Memoir of William McKerrow,* London: Hodder and Stoughton, 1881, p. 226.
[50] *Guardian*, 25 June 1862, pp. 604–5.
[51] William Adamson, *Life of the Rev. Joseph Parker*, London: Cassell, 1902, p. 162.

price of ceasing to be ministers. The biographer of Henry Richard, MP, comments on his subject becoming the chairman of the Congregational Union in 1876: 'it was the first time that it had been offered to a layman; for the honourable member had long since ceased to be regarded as a minister'.[52]

Much of the political work of Dissent was done by laymen. Wealthy, philanthropic men – men who bore the name of a distinguished family, well known in their region of influence, or who were running a large business with numerous employers – provided a secular alternative with many of the same advantages ministers could offer. They too possessed respectability, social experience and an ability to communicate in the wider world. Moreover, they had the added advantage of being able to add financial backing to campaigns which gained so much merely by the prestige of being associated with their names. The Congregationalist Samuel Morley, who was a wealthy textile manufacturer, was one such figure. Morley was a kind of Nonconformist Lord Shaftesbury. He was extremely generous with both his time and his money and seemed to have an insatiable appetite for adopting causes. Another noted Congregational textile manufacturer was Sir Titus Salt of Bradford. He also added his name and purse to numerous projects, but, unlike the more influential Morley, he disliked public speaking and did not move to London. Both men served in Parliament during this period, but Morley did so for longer, and with much more enthusiasm. A similar figure amongst the Baptists was Sir Morton Peto, a wealthy railway contractor who also served in Parliament. Peto and Salt each received a baronetcy for his philanthropic efforts and service to the country and, arguably, as a gesture to the Dissenting community, which was continuing to grow in influence and power, but still lacked official honour. The Quaker corn merchant, Joseph Sturge, who lived his most influential years in Birmingham, also belongs in this camp. He was not as wealthy as these other men, nor was he ever successful when he entered Parliamentary elections, but he compensated for these restraints by his generous philanthropic heart and the energy and single-minded zeal which he was willing to put into pressure group campaigns. He was the kind of man who was prepared to travel across half the globe or risk his reputation and fortune in fighting for a cause he endorsed. Another Quaker was John Bright, the well-known radical MP. Bright was also very influential in Dissenting politics due to the high esteem in which he was held by many Nonconformists during most of his career; however, he did not think of his political life in terms of Dissenting politics and therefore he fits somewhat awkwardly into this category: he is simply too big either to put in or

---

[52] C. S. Miall, *Henry Richard, MP*, London: Cassell, 1889, p. 281.

leave out. The Congregational lawyer, George Hadfield, was more willing to be seen as a spokesman for the Dissenting interest.[53] He was based in Manchester, but also spent a good many years in Parliament. He also had a name which mattered and some money with which to boost a good cause. Moreover, he also possessed a measure of dogged determination and the capacity to lead a campaign, rather than just support it. Laymen like these were crucial supporters and often central figures in Dissenting political battles.

In mid-Victorian society, if an idea or reform was to make any headway it needed to be championed in one or more of four arenas: pulpit, press, platform and Parliament. The Dissenting answer to such a world was Edward Miall: preacher, author-editor, agitator and politician.[54] Miall, born in 1809, trained for the Congregational ministry, and took up pastorates first in Ware, Hertfordshire, and then, in that centre of Dissent, Leicester. He became increasingly interested in politics. In 1841, he founded a newspaper, the *Nonconformist*. Its mission was to champion Dissenting politics in a more strident way than the existing organs such as the more moderate *Patriot*. He resigned his pastorate and his identity as a minister, though this change was purely vocational and did not represent a weakening of his theological convictions. Miall became a focal figure around whom radical Dissenters could rally. His ability to articulate the arguments and identify the next goals of militant Dissenters helped to shift the centre of Nonconformist politics in a more radical direction.

In 1844, Miall was instrumental in forming the British Anti-State Church Association, a pressure group organisation which had as its ultimate goal the disestablishment of the Church of England, but was willing to work for numerous smaller objectives *en route*, such as the removal of Nonconformist grievances. Several ineffectual organisations of similar ilk had been attempted in the past, but this one succeeded in harnessing the latent political power of Dissent. It took its place alongside, and in some areas eclipsed, another important organisation, the Dissenting Deputies. The Deputies, of longer standing, were more moderate and more narrowly focused on Dissenting grievances. Officially, they represented only the interests of Old Dissent, 'the three denominations', in the London area, and unofficially, they were meant to comprise distinguished men of influence. Nevertheless, the very

---

[53] Unlike most of the others mentioned in this chapter, Hadfield has not been the subject of a biography. His unpublished autobiography, however, can be found in the Local Studies Unit, Manchester Central Library: 'A Personal Narrative of Me, George Hadfield, M.P.', 1882.

[54] Miall's life, a sketch of which is given here, is recounted in Arthur Miall, *Life of Edward Miall*, London: Macmillan, 1884.

respectability of their established position within the traditions of political life of the metropolis, whilst it made them more staid and timid, also
afforded them real influence, albeit often of a more subtle nature than the
strong arm of the younger body.[55] In 1853, the Anti-State Church
Association changed its name to 'the Society for the Liberation of
Religion from State Patronage and Control' and therefore it is usually
referred to as 'the Liberation Society'. Many respected Dissenters
eventually came to support it, young Dissenters often revered it and
some Churchmen and party politicians learned to fear it.[56] Miall
continued to play a key role in its leadership and he fought for its
goals during those years when he managed to secure a seat in Parliament.
Dissenters in general were not necessarily as radical as Miall, but many
were sincerely willing to own him as one of their political leaders, and
more moderate voices were not as successful at creating an enduring
rallying point and a well-articulated position. Arguably, no one figure
was more important to Dissenting politics in this period than Edward
Miall and certainly the organisation which fought most forcefully for
Nonconformist political goals was the Liberation Society.

In a category of their own are the other newspapermen. Born in 1789,
Josiah Conder made some of his chief contributions to Dissent in the
early decades of the century. Nevertheless, he agreed to edit the *Patriot*
newspaper shortly after it was founded in 1832 and continued to do so
until the year of his death, 1855. This newspaper exhibited a more
moderate tone than that which was adopted, in conscious contrast to it,
by the *Nonconformist*. When Conder's memoir was published, the *Baptist
Magazine* criticised its late friend for 'the timidity . . . of his views of
Dissenting policy' and contrasted him unfavourably with the more
forceful Miall. It did not fail to acknowledge, however, that although
Miall might be the right man for mid-century Dissent, Conder had
played his part faithfully in the battles of the preceding generation.[57] The
Patriot held to its more moderate tone even after Conder's death. The
contrast must not be overplayed, however: the two papers usually took a
broadly similar line on the issues of the day and were generally working
toward the same goals.

Conder fits neatly in this category because he was not a minister

---

[55] The most important work on the Deputies is Manning, *Dissenting Deputies*.
[56] The history of the Liberation Society is explored in William H. Mackintosh,
Disestablishment and Liberation, London: Epworth Press, 1972. See also, Allen
Howard Welch, 'John Carvell Williams, the Nonconformist Watchdog (1821–
1907)', Ph.D. thesis, University of Kansas, 1968, Ellens, *Religious Routes* and
Thompson, 'Liberation Society'.
[57] *Baptist Magazine*, December 1857, p. 770. The memoir reviewed there is the only
biography: E. R. Conder, *Josiah Conder: A Memoir*, London: John Snow, 1857.

(though a lay preacher), he was not a philanthropist (being underpaid and overworked), and he did not run for political office. His working life consisted of bookselling, writing and editing. Other men brought together several of these identities. The Congregationalist Edward Baines the younger (1800–90), inherited the *Leeds Mercury* from his father. Both men's reputations were based on more than just editing a newspaper, however: they were influential and respectable figures in Leeds and beyond. Nevertheless, they were not extraordinarily wealthy men who deserve a place with the philanthropists. In our period, the name of Edward Baines certainly added prestige to a Dissenting cause, but this effect was not easily traceable to one source. Baines, like his father before him, was also a politician. He entered Parliament in 1859 and stayed there throughout the remainder of the period under consideration and beyond, championing many of the political causes dear to Dissenters.[58]

Another influential editor was Robert Vaughan (1795–68). He trained as a Congregational minister and continued to fulfil this calling full-time at varying points throughout his life. He was also an academic, educational administrator and an historian. He held the chair of history at University College, London, for a season before he embarked upon a fourteen-year period as principal of Lancashire Independent College, beginning in 1843. One of his greatest contributions to Dissenting life, however, was his editorship of the *British Quarterly Review*, a journal which he founded in 1845. Like Conder, he was more moderate than Miall, but nevertheless Vaughan and Miall were often taking the same stands and fighting for the same political goals. As will be shown in chapter five, he diverged most markedly from militant Dissent over its rejection of a publicly funded system of national education. He founded his journal, amongst other reasons, in order to create a forum for articulating his contrary view.

In particular, Vaughan wanted to counteract the influence of the *Eclectic Review*, a venerable Dissenting journal which, under the editorship of the Baptist, Dr Thomas Price, had become a uncompromising voice on behalf of the militant Dissenting political agenda. Vaughan made it clear when he was about to launch the *British Quarterly Review* that he had no qualms about what this might mean for the fate of the *Eclectic*, justifying his apathy on the grounds that that publication had fallen 'into the hands of an extreme section of our body'.[59] Dr Price and

[58] A biography of Baines has never been published either. Several modern scholars have explored his life, however, notably: Clyde Binfield, *So Down to Prayers*, London: J. M. Dent, 1977, ch. 4; Derek Fraser, 'Edward Baines', ch. 8 in Patricia Hollis (ed.), *Pressure from Without*, London: Edward Arnold, 1974.
[59] Blackburn Papers, L52/3/13, Robert Vaughan to John Blackburn, 1 July 1844.

his journal were firm allies of the Anti-State Church Association during its crucial first decade, when others still stood aloof. The *Eclectic* journal and the *Nonconformist* newspaper were a formidable team – championing together the political goals of militant Dissenters.

Finally, there was John Campbell. He also retained his identity, if not a full-time position, as a Congregational minister. Campbell founded more than his share of publications and instigated more than his share of controversies. In 1844 he launched the *Christian Witness* and in 1846 the *Christian's Penny Magazine*. He also founded and laid to rest a succession of Dissenting political newspapers: the *British Banner*, the *British Standard* and the *British Ensign*. Through these publications, he also tried to lay to rest a succession of Dissenting figures and institutions which he discovered, amid great alarm, to be insufficiently orthodox or to be failing to fulfil their duty in some other way. Moreover, his impression of the seriousness of his discovery tended to grow the more he thought about it and the desire of others to defend the objects of his attack often only served to bring fresh targets into his view. Thus an attack on T. T. Lynch – the 'Rivulet controversy' – caused him to escalate into an assault on the far more eminent and less vulnerable Thomas Binney.[60] Nevertheless, despite his contrary tendency, he often agreed with his fellow Dissenters on political matters and he was always most at home in a religious rather than a political fight.

It is conventional to refer to the political views of Dissenters as either 'moderate' or 'militant' – and, as has already been made apparent, this study will not break with this usage. Nevertheless, the precise meaning of these terms needs to be examined afresh. It is not accurate to imply, as some historians do, that the 'militants' were a zealous minority who held a political worldview which the majority of Dissenters rejected. Michael Watts, for example, has recently claimed that the views on disestablishment of the militant editor of the *Nonconformist*, Edward Miall, represented the views of only a minority of the Nonconformists 'for whom his newspaper by its very title claimed to speak'.[61] This statement, however, is dependent on tipping the scales in one swoop by including the Wesleyans and, as we have seen, it is clear that that body did not understand itself to be included in the Nonconformist camp for which Miall aspired to speak.

It is much more difficult for historians to locate an articulated alternative to the political philosophy of the militants within historic, orthodox Dissent during this period. The quixotic nature of this task is

---

[60] For a discussion of the 'Rivulet Controversy' and other information on Campbell, see Albert Peel, *These Hundred Years*, London: Congregational Union, 1931, pp. 216–35.
[61] Watts, *Dissenters: Volume II*, p. 551.

well illustrated by comments made in a recent study by J. P. Ellens. In a discussion of events in 1865 he notes: 'Nonconformity was becoming ever more closely identified with liberalism and the Liberal party, despite the protestations of older Evangelicals such as Dr. John Campbell and John Angell James.'[62] This is not a very impressive opposition to muster, given the fact that Dr Campbell had, by this time, retired from all his editorial endeavours and James had already been dead for five years. Moreover, these two example figures illustrate the lack of an alternative to the militant agenda in a more profound way. James, the epitome of a moderate, agreed completely with the central goal of the militants – the disestablishment of the Church of England – as did every other prominent Dissenting 'moderate' in this period whom one could name. R. W. Dale, who was James' successor and a militant, enjoyed answering those who lamented the loss of the old moderation by quoting 'from Mr. James's writings to show that he had never spoken as strongly as Mr. James about the evils of an Established Church'.[63] Moreover, James' moderation did not prevent him from voting in Parliamentary elections for two of the most militant, political Dissenters of his day: John Bright and Joseph Sturge.[64] James can be considered a moderate because he held aloof from using the tactics of pressure group politics in order to achieve disestablishment and felt uneasy about Nonconformity throwing itself behind such a campaign.

Dr Campbell hardly even qualifies by this narrow definition. Leaving aside a misguided assumption that a heresy-hunting Evangelical must inevitably be fairly conservative politically, he has principally been cast as a moderate because of his attack on the Anti-State Church Association in 1850:

> It is time that all right-minded men should know, that a SCHOOL OF ANARCHY is being formed among the British Churches; and what if it be already formed? And what if the Anti-State Church Association be gradually converted into an instrument for the promotion of its object?[65]

This attack has tempted several historians into presenting Campbell as a prominent political moderate. For example, Owen Chadwick writes of Campbell, 'About the assault on the Church of England he held moderate views, and assailed those Congregationalists who planned for

[62] J. P. Ellens, *Religious Routes to Gladstonian Liberalism*, University Park, Pennsylvania: Pennsylvania State University Press, 1994, p. 218.
[63] A. W. W. Dale, *The Life of R. W. Dale*, London: Hodder and Stoughton, 1898, pp. 384–5.
[64] R. W. Dale, *The Life and Letters of John Angell James*, London: 1861, p. 583.
[65] *British Banner*, 3 April 1850, pp. 227–8.

a political programme of disestablishment.'[66] This, however, is not an entirely accurate description, and this peculiar man is not easily pigeonholed. Campbell's attack on the Association should be viewed primarily as a tribute to his talents as a controversialist. Campbell had, unlike the genuine moderates at that time, attended the founding conference of the Association and supported it in the press. He was even on its Executive Committee until immediately before he launched his attack. Campbell had consistently supported the militant agenda up to that point: including a regular section in the *Christian Witness* on 'Church and State', hounding another supporter of the Association, Dr Pye Smith, for not being sufficiently militant over the issue of the government grant to poor Dissenting ministers and, to provide a random illustration, writing in his *British Banner*:

> The Dissenting Members [in the Commons] now possess suffi-
> cient strength . . . to encounter the whole House on the subject of
> Church Establishments, and no Session henceforth ought to
> pass, while these Establishments have a being, without a full
> discussion of their merits.[67]

Moreover, after having run this campaign against the Association for a few months, he settled back into supporting the militant Dissenting agenda – if not the Association – and, gravitating more and more toward religious rather than political controversies, never attempted to provide a competing political (or anti-political) worldview to the one articulated by Miall and his colleagues. Already by October of the same year of his attack, he was running an enthusiastic review of the new batch of tracts produced by the Anti-State Church Association (which included one entitled 'Political Dissenter!'), remarking that they 'are excellent, and cannot be too extensively circulated'.[68] This indicates not only that he did not wish to push his luck with this particular fight, but also that his attack cannot be construed as being the voice of an alternative political vision for Dissent, as his approach to the political issues of the day, both before and after this incident, confirms.

Moreover, if Campbell is to be accepted as a moderate, it is under the definition being developed here: moderates in the years of this study were Dissenters who agreed with the political goals and philosophy of the militants but were uneasy about the political tactics which they employed to pursue them. Campbell himself explained after his attack, 'Our friends and ourselves are at one in regard to the ultimate object, whatever differences of judgement may obtain betwixt us as to means.'[69] Likewise,

---

[66] Chadwick, *Victorian Church*, I, p. 404.
[67] *British Banner*, 30 August 1848, p. 598.
[68] *British Banner*, 16 October 1850, p. 697.
[69] *Ibid.*

Vaughan's *British Quarterly Review*, founded as a counterweight to militancy, could, in 1863, give Miall's *The Politics of Christianity* a favourable review, qualifying this endorsement only by saying: 'We do not see with him exactly on all points but the things in which we differ are the rare exception, not the rule, and have respect to means more than to ends.'[70] The *Patriot* (and its editor, Josiah Conder) qualify for the moderate title merely because this newspaper – in contrast to the *Nonconformist* in particular – was not as willing relentlessly to follow militant logic to uncomfortable conclusions. Nevertheless, it gave clear support to the Anti-State Church Association and so hardly qualifies as the organ of an imagined opposition party – even on the issue of tactics. In short, the more telling point about Dissenting politics in this period is the remarkable hegemony of the militant political worldview. Moderates only moderated this by placing a (decreasingly effective) drag on the mobilisation of Dissenters for pressure group political action and by leading a few rebellions against some of the more counter-intuitive stands militants made in the name of logical consistency. No significant voices challenged the principles or goals which the militants advocated or even found a consistent forum for advocating the abandonment of some of their tactics. The militant vision had no serious rivals.

It only remains to be said, by way of general context and background, that a Nonconformist who supported the Conservative Party was almost as rare as an aristocrat who supported Nonconformity. A tabulation of pollbook evidence shows clearly that throughout the period under consideration Dissenting ministers voted overwhelming for Liberal candidates.[71] Undoubtedly, this is why certain Conservatives were so interested in having as many Dissenting ministers struck off the list of voters as possible.[72] At the start of the century Dissenters had looked to the Whigs to secure for them their political goals, and in the chaotic party political world of the mid-Victorian era, various Dissenters might have viewed themselves as Whigs or Liberals or Radicals or Independents, but there was scarcely a single Dissenter shaping the politics of the Nonconformist community in general who was a Tory. Every one of the newspapers and journals previously mentioned supported the Whig-Liberal-Radical wing of the House of Commons. For example, the most moderate of them, the *British Quarterly Review*, noted unequivocally in 1862 the political implications of denominational loyalties:

---

[70] *British Quarterly Review*, XXXVII, LXXV (July 1863), pp. 264–5.
[71] Vincent, *Pollbooks*, pp. 67–70.
[72] For an example of this behaviour in Cambridge, see *Baptist Magazine*, December 1865, pp. 787–8.

Place the bulk of the Church and the bulk of the old Wesleyan Methodists on one side, and you have that which, on all questions, of the day, constitutes the Tory party: place, on the other, a readily understood proportion of the Church and the Dissenting bodies generally, and you have that portion of the constituencies which fills the Liberal benches. . . . it may almost be said that there would be no Liberal party at all without Dissent. There are important districts in which it seems as if there is nothing else for its electors to come from . . .[73]

No Dissenting MP mentioned in this chapter ever ran as a Conservative, Peelite or Protectionist. The only apparent exception to this rule is the Congregationalist Edward Ball who represented Cambridgeshire as a Protectionist. David Bebbington has provided biographical information on all the MPs who can be identified as being Baptists during the whole of the nineteenth century. Not one of them was a Conservative.[74] 'Liberal', therefore, would probably be as good a one-word description of where the vast majority of Nonconformists stood on party politics as any. The purpose of the rest of this study is to discover the more specific political agenda and philosophy which Nonconformists brought to this broad political camp.

[73] *British Quarterly Review*, XXXV, LXIX (January 1862), pp. 220–1. Moreover, as has been noted, the Wesleyan vote was far more Liberal than the statements of some of its leaders and official organs might lead one to believe. Hempton, *Methodist and Politics*, p. 206.
[74] David Bebbington, 'Baptist M.P.s in the Nineteenth Century', *Baptist Quarterly*, XXIX, 1 (January 1981), pp. 3–24.

Chapter Two

NONCONFORMIST GRIEVANCES

The Nonconformist grievances were forms of legal discrimination against Dissenters which placed them at a disadvantage in comparison with their conforming neighbours. Often they were referred to by Nonconformists as their 'practical grievances'. Militant Dissenters, however, wished at times that this phrase could be replaced. They felt it might be construed to mean that their objection to the very existence of a church establishment could be counted as only an 'abstract' grievance and not a tangible injustice. The *Nonconformist*, which believed that the community's higher priority should be the latter rather than the former, sometimes emphasised this point by referring to Dissenting efforts to remove these grievances as their 'minor movements'.[1] Likewise, the *Eclectic Review*, spoke of: 'The redress of some grievances, small, very insignificant indeed, when compared with the one great grievance, the standing evil of the State Church.'[2] Nevertheless, radical Nonconformists were unable to dispense with the term 'practical grievances', even in their own writings, although they occasionally placed it in quotations marks in order to indicate their sense that this usage was problematic.[3] The fully paid-up militant Nonconformist, Herbert S. Skeats, however, felt free when writing in the last year of this study to use the term without any qualification.[4] The struggle to find the right language, and its eventual abandonment, reveals some useful clues regarding the core political convictions and ideological trends within Dissent. As this chapter will show, during this period, the redress of Nonconformist grievances survived as a separate goal. This very survival, however, was partially achieved because the radical Dissenters made their peace with these causes. Nevertheless, despite the theoretical views of the militants, these grievances held a pivotal place in Dissenting politics precisely because they were felt by

[1] See, for example, *Nonconformist*, 29 July 1863, p. 597.
[2] *Eclectic Review*, n.s., XXVII (Jan.–June 1850), p. 8.
[3] *Nonconformist*, 29 July 1863, p. 597.
[4] Herbert S. Skeats, *A History of the Free Churches, 1688–1851*, London: Arthur Miall, 1868, p. 589. (He has dated the preface 'December, 1867.')

numerous Nonconformists across the land to have some 'practical' import on their lives.

These two points, slightly re-packaged as questions, need to be stated at the outset so that they can illuminate the wider political struggle behind the various specific campaigns. The first question is: what was the relationship between the fight for the removal of grievances and the militant Dissenting agenda? This question produced a considerable amount of soul-searching across the political spectrum. More conservative figures outside the Establishment were often reticent to endorse campaigns fully even when they sympathised with their objective for fear of adding fuel to the militant fire. It was important to them to distinguish these two, separate agendas carefully – as one Wesleyan remarked in regard to a grievance over rates, 'We cannot appear in alliance with the Dissenters . . . but can nothing be done in our defence?'[5] Moreover, those with their hearts in the same place did not always adhere to the same logic. No less a lover of the Established Church than W. E. Gladstone, for example, came to argue that one should support the removal of grievances precisely because this action would take the steam out of the radicals and make the Church of England more secure.[6] Within the Dissenting camp, there were those who felt at times that the fights over grievances were a distraction from the real issue of the separation of church and state (as the above quotation from the *Eclectic Review* shows), or conversely, that the disestablishment campaign had overshadowed the necessary struggle to remove their grievances. The balance between these two sets of goals was a cause for recurring *angst*. Edward Miall launched the *Nonconformist* in the early 1840s asserting that a preoccupation with their grievances meant that Dissenters had 'wasted their efforts in a series of petty skirmishes' and ignored their 'ultimate object', but within a decade the more moderate *Patriot* was announcing that the pendulum had already swung too far the other way, confessing:

> Some of us too easily suffered ourselves to be persuaded, that it was bad tactics to take our stand upon the redress of practical grievances, and better policy to devote all our strength to the separation of Church and State.[7]

[5] Letter from John Farrar to Jabez Bunting, 10 March 1849. W. R. Ward (ed.), *Early Victorian Methodism: The Correspondence of Jabez Bunting, 1830–1858*, Oxford: Oxford University Press, 1976, p. 370.
[6] G. I. T. Machin, 'Gladstone and Nonconformity in the 1860s: the Formation of an Alliance', *Historical Journal*, XVII, 2 (1974), pp. 347–64.
[7] From the first issue of the *Nonconformist* (14 April 1841), as quoted in Arthur Miall, *Life of Edward Miall*, London: Macmillan and Co., 1884, pp. 50–1. *Patriot*, 27 June 1850, p. 404.

It proved impossible for Dissenters (or their fellow citizens) to view campaigns against practical grievances in isolation from the wider political agenda of militant Nonconformists – as will become increasingly clear when they are examined in detail.

The second question is: were the practical grievances really a notable hardship for Dissenters or were they only petty, symbolic or confined in their effects to a small number of people? In short, how grievous were the grievances? With this question as well, arguments were varying, contradictory and sometimes made use of by people in opposing camps. When in his Tamworth Manifesto in 1834 Sir Robert Peel had spoken of an agenda which included 'the correction of *proved* abuses and the redress of *real* grievances' (emphasis added) he was reflecting the widespread notion amongst Churchmen that not all Dissenting complaints warranted sympathy.[8] Nonconformists were called upon to make their case. Once something had been widely accepted as a grievance, however, the campaigners would often begin to alter their tone, cautioning fellow Dissenters not to over-rate what would be only a small victory and promising Parliament that the concession could be made safely because it was only a minor one. The campaign against church rates, for example, demanded an acute balancing act with some arguments geared toward arousing the consciences of Churchmen regarding the real injustice which was being perpetrated and others re-assuring them that the amounts of money involved were so insignificant that their Church could easily manage without them.

Assessing the severity of a grievance is particularly difficult when the primary offence was the creation of a social stigma. It is easy to see such an offence as hardly being a 'practical' grievance at all, but in an age when 'respectability' was a highly valuable commodity to be marked publicly as inferior could be grievous indeed for some.[9] The *British Quarterly Review*, which had increasing the respectability of Dissent as a kind of unwritten goal, quoted a description by Thomas Binney of this social stigma at length, before pronouncing the fate of every Dissenter with social aspirations: 'If a layman, and still more if a minister, he will have to bear about with him, all his life long, this sense of social and conventional inferiority.'[10] Or as Edward Miall described it:

> we go about the world with a label on our backs, on which nothing more is written than the word 'Fool.' Nobody hinders

---

[8] W. G. Addison, *Religious Equality in Modern England, 1714–1914*, London: SPCK, 1944, p. 61.
[9] A discussion of the notion of respectability is offered in Geoffrey Best, *Mid-Victorian Britain, 1851–75*, London: Fontana Press, 1979 [originally 1971], pp. 279–86.
[10] *British Quarterly Review*, VI, XI (August 1847), p. 124.

us, we may walk where we please; but the brand is upon us, and we cannot forget it.[11]

This picture might evoke in our minds the image of Jews being forced to wear a yellow star of David – a social stigma which if followed by no more 'practical' discrimination would still rightly outrage our sensibilities – and might serve to remind today's historians, now that we are distant in many ways from the life of a Victorian Dissenter, that even social grievances have their import. Michael Watts, for example, argues that Dissenters were 'poor, ill-educated, unsophisticated, and superstitious' and comments upon these observations as if they could be explained by the nature of Dissenting religion *per se*, without ever introducing into this specific discussion the reality of legal and social discrimination against Nonconformists.[12] Contemporary opinions also varied as to the extent of the burden which Dissenters had to endure, but social inferiority cannot be glibly dismissed.

Until their repeal in 1828, the major grievance of Dissenters had been the existence of the Test and Corporation Acts. These acts were a consequence of the attempt to re-structure national religious life following the restoration of the monarchy in the latter part of the seventeenth century. Essentially, they barred those not in communion with the Established Church from holding various official offices. The Dissenting Deputies – a body consisting of lay representatives of the Presbyterian, Independent and Baptist communities in the London area – was formed in 1732 with the specific goal of obtaining the repeal of these odious acts.[13] In time, the Deputies came to be viewed as a major vehicle for expressing Nonconformist concerns regarding discrimination in its manifold forms, but it is important for grasping the dynamics of the wider debate in the mid-Victorian era to bear in mind that by that time the founding concern of the Dissenting Deputies had already been alleviated.

Moreover, it could be argued that the Test and Corporation Acts were themselves not 'practical' grievances. Since the second quarter of the eighteenth century an Indemnity Act had passed through Parliament every year.[14] These acts had the effect of removing any penalties from a person who neglected to take the oath required by the Test and

---

[11] Miall, *Life of Miall*, p. 70 (apparently Miall wrote this in 1841).
[12] Michael R. Watts, *The Dissenters: Volume II*, Oxford: Clarendon Press, 1995, pp. 326–7.
[13] Bernard Lord Manning, *The Protestant Dissenting Deputies*, Cambridge: Cambridge University Press, 1952, p. 19.
[14] These acts are discussed in K. R. M. Short, 'The English Indemnity Acts, 1726–1867', *Church History*, 42 (1973), pp. 366–76.

Corporation Acts. The *Nonconformist* described an Indemnity Act as a measure which 'annually undid with one hand what had been done by the other'.[15] Josiah Conder described their effect as:

> virtually suspending the penal operation of the Corporation and Test Acts, though allowing them still to disgrace the Statute-book, on the avowed policy of binding Dissenters to good behaviour.[16]

Undoubtedly, knowing that one's career could at any time be halted by Parliament's failure to pass an Indemnity Act that year might produce some anxiety, but this also the unsympathetic could have argued was a concern which was not sufficiently tangible. In such a vein, certain statesmen such as William Pitt were already arguing in the late eighteenth century that Dissent had been given full toleration and meeting any further demands would be to co-operate in the dismantling of the Church Establishment.[17]

As the nineteenth century progressed, it became obvious that Dissenters viewed the repeal of the Test and Corporation Acts as the beginning of a campaign to remove their grievances, rather than as the conclusion of their struggle. In 1833, the Dissenting Deputies composed a list of outstanding practical grievances, namely: the necessity of using the marriage service of the Established Church; the lack of a legal registration of births and deaths outside the Church; compulsory church rates; the possibility of poor rates being charged to Dissenting places of worship; the inability of the Dissenting community to bury its dead in the churchyard with its own ministers officiating; and religious tests which excluded them from the full privileges of the ancient universities.[18] By the opening of the period under discussion, the grievance regarding registrations had been resolved satisfactorily, a significant advance had been made in relation to Dissenting marriages and concerns about poor law rates being applied to chapels had apparently proved ill-founded. Lord John Russell's government had successfully navigated the two advances – the Registration of Births, Deaths and Marriages Bill and the Solemnisation of Marriages Bill – through Parliament in 1836, thus showing that even many influential figures outside Dissent recognised that at least some of the complaints of Nonconformists were legitimate.

[15] *Nonconformist*, 8 August 1866, p. 629.
[16] Josiah Conder, *The Political Position of Protestant Dissenters in 1853*, London: *Patriot* Office, 1853, p. 22.
[17] Addison, *Religious Equality*, p. 19.
[18] Manning, *Deputies*, p. 274. Albert Peel, *These Hundred Years*, London: Congregational Union, 1931, p. 104.

Lists of grievances inevitably varied depending on who created any particular one and when it was drafted. Coming into the period of this study, the minutes of the Deputies include a freshly devised list at the end of 1847:

1. Church Rates
2. Ecclesiastical Courts
3. Tithes
4. Drawback on Materials for Building Churches
5. Colonial Bishops
6. Maynooth Grant
7. Regium Donum
8. Exclusion of Dissenters from practising as Advocates in Doctors Commons
9. Exclusion from Universities
10. Poor Law Chaplains
11. Declaration on becoming a Member of a Municipal Corporation
12. Fees for Burial in Church Yards
13. Educational Scheme[19]

This list includes the obscure (particularly the issues regarding building materials and advocates) and items which, although clearly important to the Dissenting political agenda, are not usually considered in the category of the practical grievances (particularly the Maynooth grant, the *Regium Donum* and state education). The list reveals that at that time Dissenters were apparently still generally satisfied with the laws concerning marriage. It also offers two indications of things to come by giving church rates the place of pre-eminence and by including the issue of oaths (item 11). In the mid-Victorian era, the primary grievances vocalised by Dissenters proved to be those concerning church rates, burial laws, marriage laws, access to the benefits of Oxford and Cambridge, oaths for public offices and, to a lesser extent and still unidentified by 1847, grievances concerning endowed schools.

The most sustained campaign for the removal of a grievance during this period was the one for the abolition of church rates.[20] These rates constituted a nationally sanctioned local tax levied irrespective of religious affiliation for the purpose of maintaining the parish church building and related material items. The vast majority of Nonconformists objected to being forced to aid a religion from which they

[19] London, Guildhall Library, Deputies of Protestant Dissenters: minute books, Ms. 3083, vol. 11, 3 December 1847, p. 409.
[20] This struggle has recently been explored at length: J. P. Ellens, *Religious Routes to Gladstonian Liberalism: The Church Rate Conflict in England and Wales, 1832–1868*, University Park, Pennsylvania: Pennsylvania State University Press, 1994.

derived no benefit and which they had no desire to support. Committed members of Dissenting congregations frequently resented the double burden of ensuring the upkeep of both church and chapel. To them, it was simply unfair. In 1840, the Dissenting Deputies argued succinctly, 'It is unjust to tax one man to support another man's religion.'[21] By the opening years of the period under discussion in this study, a note of weariness had already crept into the Deputies' statements: 'the exaction of Church Rates has always been regarded by your Petitioners and Protestant Dissenters as a great grievance'.[22] The *Eclectic Review* branded it 'that shabby, unjust impost' and 'a system of legalized wrong and robbery'.[23] The *Nonconformist*, in its own inimitable way, quipped that church rates were a 'method of making the unwilling pay for the worship of the indifferent'.[24]

Dissenters felt that the injustice of church rates was compounded because the Church, unlike many chapel congregations and tax payers, already possessed enormous wealth. According to the Dissenting Deputies, a Church that was wealthy and went about expanding its interests by obtaining forcibly more money could be fittingly described as 'rapacious'.[25] In this context, every revelation regarding the Establishment's wealth and extravagance became a subtle indictment against church rates. The *Christian Witness*, for example, began an article which rambled through figures regarding church finances and the voluntary achievements of Nonconformists despite having to pay church rates with the sentence: 'The estimated value of national ecclesiastical property is £100,000,000 sterling; the annual income of that amount, at £5 [sic] per cent., £5,000,000.'[26] Essentially, many Dissenters felt that church rates were a way for the Establishment to rob the common people in order to benefit further a centre of wealth. As Edward Miall sardonically observed (in a discussion of unjust sources of church revenue which did not touch on the issue of church rates), 'In one sense the clergy are quite correct in designating the Establishment "the poor man's Church," for certainly poor men do much to support it.'[27]

Dissenters had to be careful, however, not to overplay the argument based on economic loss because those who were financially unable to pay were exempt and most of those leading the abolition campaign could afford the rate easily. Nevertheless, Nonconformists did make the most

---

[21] Manning, *Deputies*, p. 183.
[22] Dissenting Deputies Minutes, Ms. 3083, vol. 11 (1844–48), 10 July 1848 (p. 474).
[23] *Eclectic Review*, n.s. XXV (Jan.–June 1849), p. 641.
[24] *Nonconformist*, 26 June 1850, p. 509.
[25] Manning, *Deputies*, p. 183. (In an address written in 1840.)
[26] *Christian Witness*, XII (1855), p. 421.
[27] Miall, *Life of Miall*, p. 70. (Miall apparently made this comment in 1841.)

of any shocking stories which emerged. The best of these was the exception which proved the rule as it entailed churchwardens illegally enforcing a rate upon someone who was poor enough to be exempt. John Bright retold the incident in this way:

> They entered the house of an inhabitant of Spotland, poor James Brearley, who was then on his death-bed; the illegal claim upon the poor weaver was fourpence; they seized a looking-glass, but this would not cover the costs, and their ruthless hands then seized his family Bible, and sold it for an illegal rate.[28]

The Dissenting press continually carried stories of confiscations, but these were due to the common practice amongst some Nonconformists of refusing to pay the rate for conscientious reasons. If a case was highlighted as particularly outrageous it was generally due, not to the poverty of the person or the exorbitant level of a rate, but rather to the sentimental nature of the items taken or the discrepancy between their value and the amount owed. Perhaps the wittiest confiscation was when the owners of a printing company refused to pay a church rate and had removed from their premises 'a portrait of Mr. Edward Miall'.[29] Nevertheless, Dissenters could not but admit that most of the sums involved were trivial. When this point arose, the argument could simply be stood on its head, with Josiah Conder, for example, not being alone in arguing that abolition was a reasonable next step precisely because church rates were too light to generate a significant amount of revenue.[30] The *Baptist Magazine* even managed to argue that the triviality of the sums involved actually helped to expose the injustice of the church rate system:

> If it were a mere question of pounds, shillings, and pence, it might have been settled long ago; but it is a question of ecclesiastical supremacy, a question of Brahmin and Soodra.[31]

Whatever possessed the enormously wealthy textile manufacturer and philanthropist Titus Salt to send away a church rate collector with the defiant exclamation, 'I tell you I will not pay', it was not lack of funds or a miserly disposition.[32] The campaign against church rates was fuelled by

---

[28] G. M. Trevelyan, *The Life of John Bright*, London: Constable and Company, 1913, p. 36.
[29] *British Banner*, 13 December 1848, p. 831.
[30] Conder, *Political Position*, pp. 57–9.
[31] *Baptist Magazine*, June 1865, pp. 381–2. See also April 1865, pp. 239–40, where similar comments are made and the writer notes that the sums involved are small and decreasing.
[32] Jack Reynolds, *The Great Paternalist: Titus Salt and the Growth of Nineteenth-Century Bradford*, London: Maurice Temple Smith, 1983, p. 108.

Dissenting indignation, led by the middle classes and centred on issues of principle, not pence.

Having one's tableware confiscated was a minor incident when compared with being sent to gaol. To accomplish this feat, one had usually to couple non-payment with contempt of court. In 1839, the Dissenter John Thorogood began a period of incarceration which lasted almost two years, making his plight a symbol of injustice far more compelling than the six-penny rate which had originally stirred him into action.[33] Upon his release, William Baines of Leicester became the new *cause célèbre*. The heady atmosphere surrounding his imprisonment inspired 7,000 local women to send a petition to Parliament and the residents of the largest ward in the town to elect him to the council.[34] Thorogood was outraged that Edward Baines, senior, (no relation to William) had said of him in Parliament that 'his punishment had been equal to his delinquency'. When the member for Leeds grumbled that Thorogood was making him into a scapegoat, the militant Dissenter at least pretended to understand the expression in its literal, biblical sense: 'I really cannot see, what sin of omission, commission, or error of my own, I attempted to lay upon or imputed to you.'[35] In general, however, Dissenters passionately and visibly supported these men. The Yorkshire Baptist Association, for example, passed clear resolutions of support, claiming that they were 'suffering for conscience sake'.[36] Others followed their example. George Hadfield's journal records a lesser known case which occurred in 1847:

> John Bidewell, Cambridge, sentenced to six months imprison-m[en]t for disobeying a Magistrate's order to pay church rate, and his wife near confinement. I, and others, represented his cause to Government & procured a "Pardon".[37]

Indeed, the excitement surrounding the celebrated cases could tempt others to seek the glory and romantic heroism of becoming a 'church rate martyr'. Some comments by the daughter of the prominent Wesleyan Methodist Associationist, John Petrie, upon the time when their dining

[33] Ellens, *Religious Routes*, p. 73.
[34] *Ibid.*, p. 82. Raymond G. Cowherd, *The Politics of English Dissent*, London: The Epworth Press, 1959, p. 155. See also Arthur Mursell, *James Phillippo Mursell*, London: James Clarke & Co., 1886, pp. 56–8.
[35] London, Dr Williams's Library, New College London MSS, Blackburn Papers, L52/6/4, John Thorogood to Edward Baines, senior, 11 December 1840.
[36] C. E. Shipley (ed.), *The Baptists of Yorkshire*, Bradford: Wm. Byles & Sons, 1912, p. 303.
[37] Manchester, Manchester Central Library, Local Studies Unit, 'The Personal Narrative of Me, George Hadfield, M.P.', p. 154.

room table was confiscated for non-payment of church rates, capture well the potentially intoxicating nature of such actions:

> For a week or two we picnic'd in the front kitchen – we youngsters glorying in the notion of persecution for truth's sake, but enjoying the whole thing immensely. There was some talk of imprisonment, and I think we were rather disappointed that our father had not to go to prison, like John Bunyan, for conscience sake.[38]

Therefore, some Nonconformists began to think that things were getting out of hand – that it was unwise to send the signal that the whole Dissenting community would back every person who deliberately brought trouble upon himself. Even the militant *Nonconformist* became fed up with people incurring huge costs and then expecting a subscription to be raised on their behalf. It recommended that no one else follow this path of defiance and particularly no one else who could not pay his own expenses.[39] In 1856, the *Baptist Magazine* went so far as to claim:

> we think such resistance unscriptural, and believe that a man's dissent may be as firm and intelligent who thinks it right to obey the powers that be, and whilst he seeks by constitutional measures the repeal of unrighteous laws, to submit to every ordinance of man for the Lord's sake.[40]

Despite the deep sympathy which was aroused by the plight of people such as Thorogood and Baines, it was (and is) hard to dismiss totally the thought that it was partially of their own making. If church rates formed a grievance which was particularly offensive it was not primarily due to any physical discomfort which they might induce.

Instead, the main arguments of Dissenting abolitionists were based on the principles of unfair treatment, religious Voluntaryism and the violation of conscience caused by being forced to support a religion against one's convictions. The *Christian Witness*, for example, ran an article in 1854 entitled 'Are Church-Rates Sanctioned By Scripture?', answering in the negative, of course, and on the grounds of Voluntaryism, using texts such as 'of every man that giveth it willingly with his heart ye shall take my offering' (Exodus xxv. 2). Moreover, the journal

---

[38] Quoted in D. A. Gowland, *Methodist Secessions: The Origins of Free Methodism in Three Lancashire Towns*, Manchester: The Chetham Society, 1979, pp. 155–6.
[39] *Nonconformist*, 6 August 1851, p. 617.
[40] *Baptist Magazine*, April 1856, p. 226. These remarks were made in a review of a fictionalised account of a church rate martyr. The *Wesleyan Methodist Association Magazine*, by contrast, praised the novel, feeling that it would usefully promote militant ideas. December 1855, p. 584.

noted that all of this biblical evidence was in addition to the argument that compulsory church rates are directly contrary 'to the first principles of justice between man and man'.[41] The *Wesleyan Methodist Association Magazine*, also used, amongst others, the argument from Voluntaryism: 'Christianity requires not, but repudiates, support which is not given with a willing mind.'[42] Edward Miall felt that, regardless of its legality, forcibly taking another person's possessions in order to bolster one's own religion was simply wicked behaviour, leading him into wild speculations about what his local vicar might do if granted the legal right to kill him.[43]

These arguments offer a partial explanation of the fact that the abolition of church rates became the predominant short-term, political goal of the Dissenting community for much of the mid-Victorian era. Another important factor in the prominence of this issue, however, was that militant Nonconformists saw abolition as a useful tool for promoting their broader agenda. In 1855, the Liberation Society appointed a subcommittee 'for promoting & facilitating *opposition to Church Rates* in the Parishes'.[44] From this point onward, the Society was increasingly associated with the abolition cause. By the early 1860s, Sir John Trelawny, a Liberal Churchman who was leading the cause in the Commons, was co-ordinating his efforts with those of the Society; and when he became weary with his annual attempt to pass an abolition bill, the minutes of the Society clearly reveal that finding a replacement for him was indisputably the Society's responsibility.[45] Therefore, when in 1859 (rather late in the game) the Lords' Select Committee on Church Rates announced that their investigation had exposed 'ulterior objects' in the abolitionist camp, all the Liberation Society could do – in the words of its secretary – was marvel that after decades of frank, public agitation it had (adopting a phrase from Lord Byron) 'awoke one morning and found itself famous'.[46] Unquestionably, the militant Dissenters felt that the campaign against church rates was helping their cause and this same line of reasoning tempted their political opponents to become entrenched on the issue. This argument too, however, under the care of skilful agitators, was capable of performing an admirable head stand. The alternative line of reasoning claimed that if liberationists received propaganda value from the existence of compulsory church rates then

---

[41] *Christian Witness*, XI (1854), pp. 121–4.
[42] *Wesleyan Methodist Association Magazine*, March 1852, p. 122.
[43] *Nonconformist*, 3 December 1851, p. 957.
[44] London, London Metropolitan Archives, Liberation Society Papers, Executive Committee Minute Books, A/LIB/2, 10 August 1855, minute 429.
[45] *Ibid.*, A/LIB/3, 14 February 1862, minute 27; 16 February 1866, minute 659.
[46] *Nonconformist*, 21 December 1859, p. 1014.

Church defenders should welcome an opportunity to thwart this gambit by abolition. The *Nonconformist* claimed:

> in relation to our ulterior object, we are not anxious to abolish Church-rates. No doubt, we shall thereby gain a victory, but we shall also lose a most effective weapon.[47]

The Congregational minister, Newman Hall, sought to plant this kind of logic in Gladstone's mind:

> Were I more a Dissenter than a Christian I should wish their continuance – Indeed I have heard this opinion from some violent Dissenters on the ground that a practical grievance does more than great principles to keep up hostility to the Church![48]

In terms of the long game, this argument was true, as Gladstone himself was coming to see. Nevertheless, in the middle decades of the century, radical Nonconformists could still kindle deeper passions in some of their co-religionists by waving the banner of the injustice of church rates.

Since 1853 there had been a bill for the abolition of church rates before Parliament every year, and every year the divisions were more sympathetic, to the point where in 1858 Trelawny successfully navigated his bill through the Commons (but it was rejected by the Lords). In the following year, the Lords' Select Committee found its justification for the intransigence of that House on this matter in the 'ulterior objects' argument. Church defenders began to mobilise in support of church rates and, division by division, abolitionists saw their majority in the Commons narrow, until in 1861 the bill was rejected by the speaker's vote.[49] The setback was so severe that in 1864 and 1865 the abolitionists chose to refrain from presenting their desire before Parliament at all. However, a loss of a majority in the Commons did not indicate a total reversal. It was equally true that more MPs supported abolition than ever before (the earlier votes having been taken when fewer members were present) and numerous Churchmen agreed that the Dissenters had a valid case for which some solution needed to be found. The 'ulterior objects' argument produced only a hiatus in the campaign's overall forward march. As the decade progressed, no less a figure than the one cabinet member who had voted against the bill in 1859, W. E. Gladstone, felt the need to take the

---

[47] *Nonconformist*, 16 March 1859, p. 201.
[48] London, British Library, Gladstone Papers, CIII, B.L. Additional Ms. 44,188, Newman Hall to Gladstone, 26 November 1864.
[49] The rise of a politicised Church defence movement at this time is discussed in M. J. D. Roberts, 'Pressure-Group Politics and the Church of England: the Church Defence Institution, 1859–1896', *Journal of Ecclesiastical History*, 35, 4 (October 1984), pp. 560–82.

messy business in hand and find a way to pacify the Nonconformists.[50] The passing of his Compulsory Church Rates Abolition Bill in 1868 succeeded in eliminating a central rallying point for militant Dissenting politics and gave Parliament rest from an issue which had doggedly vexed it for decades.[51]

The campaign against church rates was a boon for militant Nonconformists which added strength to their cause. Virtually everyone outside the Establishment disliked church rates. The Quakers, in particular, had been waging their own private war of resistance against them long before the rest of Dissent had awakened to the issue. Many of them, therefore, were willing to be included in a wider campaign during this period. The *Friend* called for:

> A united action on the part of all dissenters, Friends as well as others, a resistance in all quarters, even when success is hopeless, to compulsory church rates . . .[52]

If this meant accepting the leadership of militant Nonconformists, so be it. Quakers were asked to prepare petitions to Parliament in favour of abolition in 1855 and instructed to entrust them to the radicals John Bright, Edward Miall or George Hadfield.[53] These were undoubtedly the right people, but a number of Churchmen and any Dissenter would have responded with good will. Even Edward Ball, the one Conservative Congregationalist MP, articulated the case for total abolition in the Commons.[54] Whilst the anti-militant credentials of someone like Ball were hardly open to question, by making themselves the champions of abolition, militant Dissenters emphasised the impression that the masses of Nonconformists who felt strongly about church rates were a part of their long tail.

This situation caused some *angst* for the Wesleyan leadership, who wanted to see the issue solved, not as a way of advancing the cause of disestablishment but, in the words of the *Wesleyan Methodist Magazine*, in order to 'remove an occasion of exasperating our differences' with the Church Establishment.[55] The Wesleyan body generally chose to steer

---

[50] Olive Anderson, 'Gladstone's Abolition of Compulsory Church Rates: a Minor Political Myth and its Historiographical Career', *Journal of Ecclesiastical History*, XXV, 2 (April 1974), pp. 185–98.

[51] Ellens, *Religious Routes*, provides a detailed account of the fortunes of the abolitionist cause in Parliament.

[52] *Friend*, Tenth Month [October] 1858, p. 185.

[53] *Ibid.*, Fourth Month [April] 1855, p. 72.

[54] *British Banner*, 7 February 1856, p. 46.

[55] *Wesleyan Methodist Magazine*, July 1855, p. 643. These comments are a rare example of a direct reference to church rates in this publication. This reticence, however, was not the result of the journal having a purely theological focus, as the

clear of the abolitionist cause. This was not because Wesleyans lacked passion when it came to issues of fairness involving petty sums: a point well illustrated by its willingness to raise the alarm when a toll-bar keeper near Oakham refused to give the complimentary right of passage usually afforded to ministers to a Wesleyan itinerant preacher.[56] No, the real issue was sharing the same banner with militant Dissenters, an act which they knew would serve to strengthen radicalism. This was not the line taken by other Methodist bodies. The *United Methodist Free Churches' Magazine*, for example, argued that it was important for members of their body to sign abolitionist petitions precisely because MPs had been arguing, on the basis of the aloofness of Conference Wesleyans, that 'Methodists' supported the rate.[57]

Moreover, the campaign against church rates actually did cause the politics of many Dissenters to drift in the direction of radicalism. Some Dissenters were drawn into militant circles by first getting entangled in a local difficulty regarding church rates and then gratefully discovering that the Liberation Society would offer them free legal advice. The Society's journal, the *Liberator*, noted in 1864:

> Experience has also shown that the Church-rate agitation is a great value, as a means of furthering the ultimate aims of the Society. The past year has greatly added to the number of its correspondents who appreciate highly the aid afforded to those who are engaged in carrying on local struggles, and who, in turn, are likely to diffuse the Society's principles in many places which could not otherwise be reached by its influence.[58]

The Society's role in this regard was all the more influential because the Dissenting Deputies were unwilling or unable to share the burden. When this more moderate body received a letter regarding a local church rate conflict, it resolved: 'That it is not thought to be desirable for the Deputies to interfere in the matter.'[59] The noted Baptist, Edward Steane, violated a lifelong habit of not joining political campaigns in order to support the abolitionist rallies of 1861.[60] Although this step did not lead him into radicalism, it undoubtedly weakened the difference between himself and the so-called 'political Dissenters'. The moderate

steady stream of comments on the government's stance on issues such as Sabbatarianism and Roman Catholicism clearly demonstrate.
[56] *Wesleyan Methodist Magazine*, February 1847, p. 193.
[57] *United Methodist Free Churches' Magazine*, April 1861, p. 225.
[58] Supplement to the *Liberator*, June 1864, p. 102.
[59] Dissenting Deputies Minutes, Ms. 3083, vol. 13, 16 April 1862, p. 264.
[60] Ernest A. Payne, *The Baptist Union: A Short History*, London: The Carey Kingsgate Press, 1959, p. 80.

British Quarterly Review conceded on the issue of church rates in 1855, 'Nothing short of its *total abolition* can now be thought of', thereby giving its blessing to the rhetoric of the militants.[61] One could even argue that the radicals themselves had been radicalised by church rates: John Bright fought his first political campaign over this issue, George Hadfield gave his first political speech in a church rate struggle and Edward Miall founded the *Nonconformist* at least partially in response to the plight of the church rate martyr, William Baines, who was a member of his own congregation.[62] Even rank-and-file Wesleyans were not immune to the effects which this issue could have on one's politics. One of their number claimed in 1865 that despite the stance taken by their leadership he had tested the general opinion amongst Wesleyans and had:

> found them quite as ready to go to the poll against Church-rates as their Congregational brethren, though perhaps not, in general, sufficiently advanced to go with the "Liberation Society" for the entire separation of Church and State.[63]

Militant Nonconformists judged correctly that adopting the campaign against church rates would serve their interests.

Grievances concerning burials were uniquely irksome to Dissenters because they inevitably were made most manifest at times when emotions were already running high. Those who survived were naturally jealous for the dignity of their lost loved one. Moreover, the universality of death ensured that, if a grievance did exist, it would touch the lives of the mass of Nonconformists. As Carvell Williams, the secretary of the Liberation Society, expressed it, the Church Establishment 'affected men as soon as they came into the world, and it could not leave untouched even their cold bodies after they had left it'.[64] Historically, every person (excepting the unbaptised, the excommunicated and suicides) was buried in the parish churchyard, thus giving the Establishment a monopoly on this final rite of passage. Only clergymen of the Church of England could perform the funeral ceremony on consecrated ground and they were required to do it according to the Prayer Book. Dissenters wanted to be able to have their own ministers officiate and to have the content of the service adapted in accordance with their own theological and spiritual sensibilities. These demands were never met during the period under discussion.

---

[61] *British Quarterly Review*, XXI, XLII (April 1855), p. 560.
[62] Trevelyan, *Bright*, pp. 35–6. Hadfield, 'Personal Narrative', p. 66. Miall, *Life of Miall*, pp. 26–33; 37–51.
[63] Letter from 'A Conference Wesleyan' dated 13 November 1865: *Liberator*, 1 December 1865, p. 198.
[64] *Nonconformist*, 21 December 1859, p. 1014.

In urban areas, one alternative approach to this problem was the creation of private cemeteries. In 1821, George Hadfield was one of a group of men in Manchester who founded the first of such ventures.[65] In the 1850s, Parliament passed several Metropolitan Interment Bills which sought to provide burial places in addition to the churchyard. When the first one of these was introduced into Parliament in 1850, the Dissenting community opposed it because of the invidious distinction it made between consecrated and unconsecrated land (Nonconformists to be segregated into the latter) and the way the bill sought to protect burial fees as a source of income for clergymen. It is perhaps not surprising that the *Eclectic Review* ended its long article on the bill with the sentence: 'THE STATE-CHURCH MUST BE DESTROYED!'[66] The Liberation Society, of course, was active in opposing these parts of the bill.[67] Moreover, the less predictable *British Banner* decided to unleash its full rhetorical potential against this bill: 'Let it suffice to say that a more outrageous, insulting and iniquitous document was never presented to the people of this country.'[68] In fact, complaints were wide-ranging, if usually more tempered. The Dissenting Deputies petitioned against it.[69] Even the *Friend*, although beginning by apologetically noting that party politics was not really within its sphere, warmed into an editorial complaining about the bill.[70] Subsequent bills sought to diminish some of the concerns of Dissenters and they did successfully eliminate, where separate cemeteries existed, ugly confrontations over the interment of specific corpses, isolating the continuing occurrence of most specific burial grievance cases to rural areas. In such places, an unsympathetic vicar could behave in a way which Dissenters found grossly insensitive and unjust.

Throughout this period, the Primitive Methodists had a steady stream of burial grievance cases. Their religion was generally viewed as of dubious respectability; even the Wesleyan leader, George Osborn, let his disdain slip out in an unguarded moment, referring to this denomination publicly as 'that unfortunate sect'.[71] This attitude, in a more pronounced form, caused some clergymen to go so far as to deny the validity of some baptisms performed by members of that body. Legally,

---

[65] Hadfield, 'Personal Narrative', p. 81. A recent study has explored these companies: Julie Rugg, 'The Rise of Cemetery Companies in Britain, 1820–53', Ph.D. thesis, University of Stirling, 1992.
[66] *Eclectic Review*, n.s. vol. XXVII (Jan.–June 1850), p. 774.
[67] Liberation Society Papers, A/LIB/1, 12 June 1850, minute 179.
[68] *British Banner*, 24 April 1850, p. 281.
[69] Dissenting Deputies Minutes, vol. 12, 27 May 1850, pp. 125–6.
[70] *Friend*, Seventh Month [July] 1850, pp. 129–30.
[71] *Primitive Methodist Magazine*, XLV (1864), pp. 702–3.

clergymen were required to accept the legitimacy of all baptisms done by the orthodox formula, no matter by whom, and therefore such incidents were in spite of, rather than because of, the existing laws. The Revd W. H. Henslowe of Wormegay, Norfolk, for example, was not deterred by having been punished three years earlier for a similar dereliction of duty, from running away when a Primitive Methodist funeral procession approached, twice forcing the family to bring the body back to their house.[72] 'So numerous have been the cases', the *Primitive Methodist Magazine* wrote in 1856, that it felt the need to offer general advice about how to handle them. Its correspondent counselled those who received such resistance: 'let them assert their right, and stand upon the law'.[73] The Primitives felt the grievousness of burial grievances in specific cases more acutely than the rest of the numerically large Dissenting denominations – except the Baptists.

Beginning in 1861, Sir Morton Peto, MP, who was a Baptist, introduced legislation in Parliament which sought to gain the right to a respectable burial in the parish churchyard for the unbaptized. This issue was of particular concern to Quakers, who did not practise baptism, and Baptists, who did not perform baptisms for infants so that many of their children who died were unbaptized. Peto wanted to spare such people from 'the indignity of being classed with the excommunicate and the suicide' and demanded to know whether the House felt that the famous Quaker reformer, Elizabeth Fry, deserved such a fate.[74] He tried to stimulate some empathy in the hearts of his hearers by warning them that if they had not received communion the preceding Easter (a situation which he intimated might be applicable to more than one respectable member) they were, by strict application of the laws of the Established Church, '*ipso facto* excommunicate'.[75] Peto was not unaware of the questions which all such campaigns raised. As to the severity of the problem, he assured the House that it was 'no mere sentimental grievance' but a real one.[76] However, not everyone was convinced. Sir George Grey, who was shortly to be appointed Secretary of State for the Home Department in Palmerston's administration, begrudgingly called it 'the admitted grievance', but S. H. Walpole, a Conservative member for Cambridge University, thought it more precise to speak of it as 'a *minimum* of grievance' and Sir William Heathcote, a fellow Tory representing the other ancient university, not ready to concede even

---

[72] *Ibid.*, XXVIII (1847), pp. 301–3.
[73] *Ibid.*, XXXVII (1856), pp. 680–2.
[74] *Hansard*, CLXI, 650–1 (19 February 1861).
[75] *Ibid.*, 653.
[76] *Ibid.*

that, retreated into legal language and referred to it as the 'alleged grievance'.[77]

Certainly, it was offensive to the families discriminated against to be treated in such a way, but often clergymen (especially those of High Church conviction) were also having their sense of propriety disturbed. Peto's bill, it was argued, would only make it worse for them as they would be forced to expose consecrated ground to ceremonies by any 'Mahommedan or Hindoo or Mormonite; and equally the abnegation of all religion in an infidel oration'.[78] The *Nonconformist*, for example, reported the case of a clergyman who would not bury a man well-known for his Unitarianism. Not surprisingly, the paper's gratuitous advice to the troubled soul was that he should do his public duty or resign.[79] The *Primitive Methodist Magazine* was equally unsympathetic with the clergyman who refused 'to admit the corpse of a Dissenter into the body of his Church' and wrote in his own defence, pleading with the Dissenting community not to burden his conscience.[80] Nevertheless, even if it was admitted that some Dissenters were subjected to some unfortunate circumstances, it was not clear whether this piece of legislation would actually alleviate grievances or only transfer them to other parties.[81]

Sir Morton Peto was also aware of another concern in the minds of some of his hearers and took pains to assure the House that this grievance campaign was not meant to further the cause of militant Dissenters. He confessed that 'he had never been an enemy of the Church of England and had never taken part in any agitation against her'. Moreover, in a burst of profound solidarity with his opponents, he claimed that, 'No one deplored more than he did the existence of such societies as the Liberation Society', promising them that, 'In introducing this Bill to the House he had no object in view to effect the achievement of any Nonconformist triumph.'[82] In short, Peto sought to make an effort on behalf of moderate Dissent. When he was preparing to introduce his bill once again in 1863, the Liberation Society wrote and informed him that it disapproved of it 'as amended by the Select Committee last session', but the Baptist MP wrote back making it clear that he was not taking any notice of the Society's

---

[77] *Hansard*, CLXII, 1050, 1047, 1025 (24 April 1861).
[78] A comment made by Sir William Heathcote: *Hansard*, CLXII, 1026 (24 April 1861).
[79] *Nonconformist*, 2 November 1864, p. 877.
[80] *Primitive Methodist Magazine*, XXXI (1850), pp. 105–7.
[81] On the counter-grievance of clergymen, see Rugg, 'Cemetery Companies', pp. 167–70.
[82] *Hansard*, CLXII, 1024.

opinions.[83] Nevertheless, despite such unequivocal language in public and careful consistency in private, it was not so easy to disentangle the practical grievances from the militant agenda. Sir William Heathcote said he was pleased to hear the baronet's denunciation of the Liberation Society, but:

> Nevertheless, his Bill is of the same character as those which that society has promoted, and wears the appearance of serving to complete the systematic series, of which parts have been already discussed in this House.[84]

Naturally, Peto's words had not endeared him to the militant Nonconformists and they took it out on him by not throwing their full energy behind his bill. The *Nonconformist* actually struck a tone of gleeful vindication when the bill was rejected in 1863.[85] The Baptists themselves, of course, mobilised behind their crusading baronet, even if he was in moderate armour. C. H. Spurgeon wrote an article in which he argued the case for the bill, the Baptist Union called for petitions on its behalf and the *Baptist Magazine*, much like the *Primitive Methodist Magazine*, began to publish accounts of local clashes between Baptists and clergymen.[86] Nevertheless, despite Baptist support and his unfurling of moderate colours, Peto's bill was never successful. Whether Sir Morton Peto and other more moderate Dissenters liked it or not, the Nonconformist grievances could not be dealt with in isolation from the militant agenda.

The bill passed in 1836 had dealt with the original grievance regarding marriage ceremonies by creating ways in which Dissenters could replace the vicar, the Prayer Book and the church building by their equivalents within their own denomination. Therefore, throughout the mid-Victorian era, marriages were never the subject of a major grievance campaign comparable to those regarding issues such as church rates and burials. Still, this issue provided its own irritations. Under the 1836 act, notification of a Dissenting marriage had to be made to the Guardians of the Poor. Many Nonconformists found this arrangement degrading, dubbing them 'work-house marriages'. Those of high social standing felt the insult all the more strongly. As Lord Brougham expressed it when the matter was discussed in the Lords in 1855: 'Many most respectable persons objected to this, and many were thereby deprived of the benefit

---

[83] Liberation Society Papers, A/LIB/3, 30 January 1863, minute 176; 27 February 1863, minute 187. The Deputies agreed to petition on behalf of the bill, but 'Sir Morton was to introduce the Bill on his own responsibility and not on that of the Committee.' Dissenting Deputies Minutes, vol. 13, 12 February 1862, p. 262.

[84] *Hansard*, CLXII, 1031.

[85] *Nonconformist*, 22 April 1863, p. 301.

[86] *Baptist Magazine*, June 1861, pp. 330–7; April 1861, pp. 232–3; June 1861, pp. 370–1.

intended by the Act of 1836.'[87] The *Methodist New Connexion Magazine* noted:

> We see no reason – except a determination to maintain offensive distinctions between Churchman and Dissenter, – why the law as to the notice required should not be the same for all marriages, wherever solemnized.[88]

The *Christian Witness* opened its letter columns for discussion on the matter. One typical correspondent wrote, 'The distinction is, at least, ungracious, and, in the eyes of some, degrading.'[89] One wonders if awareness of these feelings was one of the factors considered when it was decided that M. T. Baines, brother to the prominent Dissenter, Edward Baines, junior (though personally loyal to the Church of England), should be appointed President of the Poor Law Board in 1849. A clearer gesture was the introduction of legislation in the mid-1850s. After an unsuccessful attempt in 1855, a bill was passed in 1856 which alleviated this particular offence by shifting the place of notification to the Registrar's Office. Dissenters, of course, supported this legislation, with the Congregational Union, for example, petitioning in its favour.[90]

From the point of view of the Establishment, some MPs were concerned that clergymen would be legally obliged to perform a marriage once a licence had been obtained from the registrar and this might place them in a position where their consciences might be violated at some point. Once again, the counter-grievance of High Church clergymen was another complication in the mix. Only Sir Robert Phillimore, Liberal member for Tavistock, hinted that he was afraid of how this redress would bode for the rest of the militant agenda, commenting bitterly that:

> he did not quite understand the new doctrine of religious liberty which had been propounded that night, namely, that Dissenters should have everything they asked for, and Churchmen nothing.[91]

Marriages outside the Church of England had also required higher fees, and the same piece of legislation also dealt with this grievance. It seems, however, that the social stigma was the one which inflamed more passions. Individual cases of grievances continued, but they were despite, rather than because of, the law. The Dissenting Deputies, for example,

---

[87] *Hansard*, CXXXIX, 1335.
[88] *Methodist New Connexion Magazine*, 51 (1848), p. 95.
[89] *Christian Witness*, V (1848), p. 127.
[90] *Congregational Year Book* for 1857, pp. 18–19.
[91] *Hansard*, CXL, 1930.

dealt with the case of a clergyman 'who had remarried individuals previously married in the Independent Chapel and who in the entry in the Parochial Register were stated to be a Bachelor and Spinster'.[92] The *Primitive Methodist Magazine*, for its part, reported:

> We were recently at Louth, Lincolnshire, where we were startled to hear of a sample of establishmentarian bigotry beyond what we had heard of before, namely, that the clergy of that neighbourhood actually visit the registrars of marriages once or twice a week to ascertain what marriages are likely to take place in dissenting chapels; and they then go to the parties intending to marry and tell them their marriage in a dissenting or methodist chapel will be illegal and invalid, and urge them to go to church . . .[93]

Issues around the wedding ceremony produced Dissenting protests in this period, but marriage was much less of a concern in this era than several other practical grievances.

Long established in the lists of grievances were the religious tests which prevented Dissenters from receiving degrees from Cambridge and even gaining entrance to Oxford University. Already in 1834 the Commons had passed a bill which would have made a significant step toward dealing with this issue – had it not been rejected by the Lords. In the 1850s, a decade when the ancient universities were subject to Parliamentary scrutiny, a fresh push was made to obtain these rights. The argument was based on the general grounds of fairness, bolstered by the specific claim that the universities were national institutions and therefore should be open to all. The *Eclectic Review* noted:

> the State has recognised the universities as, in a peculiar sense, national institutions. This it has done by various acts of legislative regulation or patronage, by annual pecuniary grants out of the public purse for certain professorships . . . Why, then, should not Dissenters be admissible to study, in equality and friendship with their fellow-subjects of the Establishment . . . ?[94]

Militants, however, were not the only ones interested in this issue. It is not surprising that the *British Quarterly Review*, a journal which strove for culture and respectability, should be particularly interested in this grievance. It boasted in 1854 that it had addressed the concerns regarding the ancient universities 'more at large and more thoroughly, we think,

---

[92] Dissenting Deputies Minutes, vol. 13, 7 October 1863, p. 293.
[93] *Primitive Methodist Magazine*, XLVII (1866), p. 61.
[94] *Eclectic Review*, n.s. XXV (Jan.–June 1849), pp. 645–6.

than any of our contemporaries'.[95] Unitarians were prominent in this campaign. The Unitarian newspaper, the *Inquirer*, despite arguing that Unitarians had more in common politically with liberal Churchmen than orthodox Dissenters, nevertheless listed the campaign for opening the ancient universities as an area where Evangelical Nonconformists were their brothers-in-arms.[96] Even the *Wesleyan Methodist Magazine* was willing to remark: 'As to Oxford and Cambridge, few will say that it is not a fair thing to seek access to their literary advantages.'[97] In the last year of the period under consideration, the *English Independent* (the successor to the *Patriot*) articulated the on-going grounds of the Dissenting case passionately:

> We claim the Universities for the nation; and until their doors are thrown wide open to the people, irrespective of class, caste, or creed, the end for which they were founded can never be realized, nor can the strife and contention of religious parties give place to the calm repose of justice and truth.[98]

The logic of this argument seemed impeccable to Dissenters, but nevertheless they felt some ambivalence about the campaign. High Church and non-traditional theological ideas with which they had no desire to expose their best and brightest were known to be advocated by some people at Oxford – and there was a widespread suspicion that they might send their Dissenting sons up to the ancient universities only to receive them back as loyal Churchmen. When a bill for opening Oxford to Nonconformists passed in 1854 the *Christian Witness* rejoiced, but also noted:

> Of the perils connected with the enjoyment of that right we shall not now speak. We conceive they are very considerable, and the probabilities are that Dissenters will, for a time at least, avail themselves but sparingly of the privilege. Happily, they are under no necessity so to do. That necessity, however, is one thing, and the *right* is another; and there is great reason to rejoice that the right has been at length established.[99]

Newman Hall briefed Gladstone accurately on this point: 'while all Dissenters would maintain the theoretical *right*, very many would doubt the *expediency* of sending their sons to those Universities'.[100] The

[95] *British Quarterly Review*, XIX, XXXVIII (April 1854), p. 569.
[96] *Inquirer*, 7 February 1857, p. 81.
[97] *Wesleyan Methodist Magazine*, July 1855, p. 643.
[98] *English Independent*, 18 April 1867, p. 497.
[99] *Christian Witness*, XI (1854), p. 445.
[100] Gladstone Papers, CIII, B.L. Additional Ms. 44,188, Newman Hall to Gladstone, 24 February 1865.

Nonconformist admitted that concerns about the perils of the ancient universities were not without foundation and that in consequence of this some Dissenters were apathetic about the entire campaign. In order to bolster support, it claimed that 'although it may confer no direct benefit on Protestant Dissenters which they have reason to covet', redress of this grievance 'may be of high importance to the cause of religious liberty'.[101]

James Heywood, member for North Lancashire and a Unitarian, took the opportunity of a bill for the reform of Oxford University which was before the House in 1854, to add a clause which he proclaimed would 'open the matriculation and graduation of students at that University to the whole British people'.[102] The reality was less sweeping, certainly not envisioning anything as comprehensive as the admission of women, and limiting its benefits to the sons of Dissenters to the possibility of earning bachelor's degrees – and even this was denied in the case of divinity degrees. Lord John Russell had previously affirmed that he was still in favour of this change in principle, just as he had been in the 1830s. Edward Miall, now in Parliament, argued for the rights of Nonconformists, noting that, 'Whenever that House passed measures of taxation, he, as well as those 5,000,000 of people who were not connected with the Church of England, were considered a part of the nation', and therefore when it came to discussions of the ancient universities they should be as well.[103] Naturally, Heywood's clause met with some opposition. Gladstone, member for Oxford University, of course, was unwilling to bite the hand that fed him. C. N. Newdegate, a Conservative who was a quixotic defender of the cause of the Church and of Protestantism in the House, like the apostle Paul introducing the subject of the resurrection of the dead before the Sanhedrin, assured his fellow members that the real issue was that they were about to 'remove the Protestant safeguards of the University', though without a similar effect.[104] Instead, the bill as altered by Heywood was passed into law with remarkable ease, to the surprise of even the Nonconformists themselves.[105] The *British Quarterly Review* announced jubilantly: 'The badge of civil inferiority fastened on all Englishmen who are not churchmen, has been cast away.'[106]

In 1856, a bill concerning Cambridge University was also passed. That university had been traditionally more sympathetic to Dissenters and this

---

[101] *Nonconformist*, 8 March 1854, p. 197.
[102] *Hansard*, CXXXI, 935.
[103] *Ibid.*, 913.
[104] *Ibid.*, CXXXIV, 887–9. For Newdegate, see Walter L. Arnstein, *Protestant versus Catholic in Mid-Victorian England: Mr. Newdegate and the Nuns*, Columbia, Missouri: University of Missouri Press, 1982.
[105] *Nonconformist*, 28 June 1854, p. 525.
[106] *British Quarterly Review*, XX, XL (October 1854), p. 579.

position was restored by the provisions of this bill which allowed Nonconformists to obtain a master's as well as a bachelor's degree. Nevertheless, the traditional right to participate in the government of the university was withheld. The *Baptist Magazine*, regretting the restrictions, dubbed this process of giving specific concessions rather than establishing a general principle of complete equality 'justice by instalments'.[107] Dissenting bodies had been agitating for more openness at Cambridge as well. The Liberation Society had the member of its Executive Committee with the most distinguished academic credentials, Dr C. J. Foster, Professor of Jurisprudence at London University, lead a deputation on the Cambridge University grievance which met Lord Palmerston and the Lord Chancellor.[108] Once again, those opposed to these changes seemed to be imbued with a sense of resignation. In the Lords, Samuel Wilberforce, the bishop of Oxford, grumbled that the additional concession of master's degrees would put pressure on the university in his diocese to do likewise, but the Lord Chancellor retorted that 'it was an extraordinary argument against doing good, that it would lead to good being done elsewhere'.[109] These two pieces of legislation, supported as they were by the Unitarian community and liberal Churchmen, were the clearest redresses of long-standing grievances which were afforded to Dissenters during the period under discussion. No wonder the Liberation Society looked back on them in 1866 as its most gratifying successes up to that point.[110]

The bishop of Oxford's prophetic powers were vindicated when the issue was rekindled in the following decades. J. G. Dobson, Liberal member for East Sussex, introduced a bill in 1864 for the purpose of gaining access to post-graduate degrees at Oxford for Dissenters. Claiming that these degrees were for those who had studied their 'passport into the world', he argued that:

> it is obvious that the attractions of a University career consist not only in the education, but still more in the degrees which stamp the man as having received and profited by that education.[111]

He was seconded on the motion for its second reading by Charles Neate, member for Oxford City, who argued even more passionately, saying that access to just a bachelor's degree 'amounted to hardly any admission at all' and spoke of those who 'were to be cut off in their career there, just

---

[107] *Baptist Magazine*, July 1856, p. 434.
[108] Liberation Society Papers, A/LIB/2, 14 December 1855, minute 472.
[109] *Hansard*, CXXXVIII, 1553.
[110] Supplement to the *Liberator*, 5 May 1866, p. 90.
[111] *Hansard*, CLXXIV, 104–5.

at the time when others were about to enter upon theirs'.[112] Other members, however, felt that the Nonconformists did not have a legitimate complaint. Sir C. J. Selwyn stated bluntly that 'no real grievance existed' and, taking his constituency, Cambridge University, for his example, wondered if after someone had distinguished himself to the point of becoming a Senior Wrangler:

> Would anybody care or inquire whether afterwards he went on to take the formal degree of M.A., which was the mere result of the payment of certain fees and the lapse of a few years?[113]

John Walter sought to bolster this argument still further by providing an Oxford example from his personal experience, remarking:

> The only grievance to be dealt with, then, was of so slight and imperceptible a nature that it was difficult to understand what it was. He had himself been a Master of Arts of Oxford University for twenty years, but he had not considered it a privilege of so extraordinary a nature that he should go far out of his way to obtain it.[114]

Dissenters, by the mid-1860s, seemed to have gained an increased awareness – perhaps through the previous successes – of the relevance of concerns regarding the universities for their overall rights and interests. Certainly, the militant Dissenters were now conscious that this grievance could be put to work on behalf of their wider agenda. The Liberation Society noted in 1865:

> Hitherto the subject has been forced into prominence chiefly by those who are interested in the welfare of the Universities; but it is one which may become as useful to the Society, as a means of agitation among the educated classes as the Church rate question has been among persons of another class.[115]

Moreover, Dissenting support was visibly widespread. A petition in favour of Dobson's bill by 117 'leading Nonconformists' included amongst its signatories not just Congregationalists such as Robert Vaughan and Newman Hall and Unitarians such as James Martineau and James Heywood, but even Quakers, Joseph Pease and William Rowntree; the president of the Methodist New Connexion Conference, Robert Henshaw, and perhaps farthest from the world of Oxford of all, the prominent Bible Christians, F. W. Bourne and James Thorne.[116]

---

[112] *Ibid.*, 110.
[113] *Ibid.*, 142, 139.
[114] *Ibid.*, 153.
[115] Liberation Society Papers, A/LIB/3, 15 September 1865, minute 575.
[116] *Ibid.*, 16 June 1864, minute 400 and inserted, printed statement dated 1 July 1864.

Moreover, Dissenters no longer emphasised the hazards of exposure to this world. Certainly the Baptists were reminded that it was possible for some of their own to conquer Cambridge and offensive that they could not reap the full honours appropriate to their talent and labours through the achievements of some of their own, notably a series of three sons of John Aldis who each in turn gained a place on the honours list, beginning with a Senior Wrangler in 1861.[117] The Dissenting Deputies were now saying in their petition that 'many members of the nonconformist bodies would gladly avail themselves of the great educational facilities granted by the University'.[118] In 1864, the *Nonconformist* had confessed that it no longer saw a reason why Dissenters should not attend the ancient universities and in 1866 it was speaking of the cruel social and intellectual handicap which had been inflicted upon Dissent by centuries of exclusion from them.[119] This rhetoric was undoubtedly meant to serve the recurring need to establish the severity of a grievance.

The question of what kind of a wider trend they might be supporting also featured in the debate, with members being more suspicious now that the House had already dealt with a round of university grievances in the preceding decade. Sir William Heathcote had pieced together what was happening and sought to warn members that 'the fact was that if the Bill were carried, it would only furnish an argument for another advance in the same direction'.[120] Nevertheless, the argument that this piece of legislation was wanted, not for the specific redress it would offer, but in order to advance the cause of militant Dissenters was less potent than on some other issues. First of all, the attempts which were made in the 1860s were not initiated as a part of an orchestrated agitation but were rather the spontaneous efforts of individual members. Secondly, it was not totally clear which religious party had the most to gain. Charles Buxton, member for Maidstone, was at least getting at a truth when he told the House that:

> it was a delusion to suppose that this was in the main a Dissenter's question. No doubt the Bill might relieve a certain number of Dissenters, but its main effect would be to relieve those who, while still loyal members of the Church, were yet unable to subject their minds to every part of her dogmatic teaching.[121]

---

[117] John C. Carlile, *The Story of the English Baptists*, London: James Clarke & Co., 1905, p. 264. For an example of contemporary pride around the time of Dobson's bill, see the *Baptist Magazine*, August 1865, p. 513.

[118] Dissenting Deputies Minutes, Ms. 3083, vol. 13, 15 March 1864, p. 312.

[119] *Nonconformist*, 24 February 1864, p. 141; 19 September 1866, p. 749.

[120] *Hansard*, CLXXIV, 115.

[121] *Ibid.*, 146.

More than one wing of the Established Church contained Churchmen who were not fully at peace with everything in the Prayer Book. Although the attention is usually focused on High Churchmen and those who were finding traditional doctrines no longer tenable, it is worth remembering that some Evangelicals had their own qualms. The animating spirit of the Evangelical Alliance, Sir Culling Eardley Eardley, although he had attended Oriel College, Oxford, and had left without his degree through sheer gentlemanly disregard, later 'having scruples about some of the Thirty-nine Articles . . . dissolved his connexion with the University, and took his name off the College books'.[122] Although Dobson's bill was rejected on its third reading in 1864, militant Dissenters were thrilled that it had come as close as it did.[123] The struggle (which included a parallel campaign for further advances at Cambridge) continued without another legislative success during this period.

The effort concerning the universities was played out on a lower level with the endowed schools. The secretary of the Liberation Society, Carvell Williams, asked an audience in 1859:

> if the battering-ram had been plied so successfully against the Universities, how much longer would they submit to exclusion from the ancient Grammar Schools – numerous as they were, well endowed as they were, and which were now almost exclusively in the hands of members of the Establishment, whose clergy monopolized most of the masterships?[124]

The Welsh MP, Lewis Llewellyn Dillwyn, spearheaded the campaign in Parliament. A bill had been introduced in 1860 for the purpose of gaining for Dissenting children greater access to these schools which did pass into law, but Dillwyn sought the right for Dissenters to be trustees as well. The debate centred around whether or not references to religion made in the deeds of schools should continue to be interpreted as referring to the Established one. A strict rendering of the wishes of founders would probably not have been in the interest of the Nonconformists, but there was a common sense argument for adapting to the times. Sir C. J. Selwyn, member for the University of Cambridge, tried to help Dillwyn see the case of his opponents by having him imagine an Independent rising from his grave to discover in horror that the religious school he had sacrificed to build had been taken over by Roman Catholics, but he merely wondered in return what the good Catholics who had founded

---

[122] *Primitive Methodist Magazine*, XLV (1864), p. 154. (As a memoir, the magazine run a lengthy, serialised biography of Eardley written by the Baptist, Edward Steane.) Until he changed it to Eardley in 1847, his surname was Smith.
[123] *Nonconformist*, 6 July 1866, p. 537.
[124] *Ibid.*, 21 December 1859, p. 1014.

Selwyn's Cambridge would think of what it had become.[125] Selwyn saw the militant Dissenters lurking in the background. In a clear allusion to the Liberation Society, he appealed to the 'hon. Members opposite to exercise their own judgment in this matter, and to liberate themselves from the dictation of that society whose business it was to perpetuate and embitter religious disputes'.[126] Certainly the *Eclectic Review* was willing to see this cause captured for militancy:

> One thing is clear, however; we have had enough of these puerile attempts at compromising what does not admit of compromise; and Mr. Dillwyn must be content to do what Sir W. Clay and Sir J. Trelawney [sic] have done before him [in regard to church rates], and fight his battle on the broad ground of a great principle.[127]

Likewise, the *Nonconformist* called for petitioning on the matter and for Dissenters to 'make this as much a testing point as Church-rate abolition'.[128] Moreover, the militant element in this campaign was undoubtedly made more dominant by the decision of the Wesleyan body to pronounce against Dillwyn's bill, arguing that it might undermine the exclusively Wesleyan control and character of some of its own institutions.[129] On the other hand, the *British Quarterly Review*, with its usual concern for culture and learning, supported the bill; and in 1865 the Dissenting Deputies listed as the two great questions upon which Parliamentary candidates should be examined as, firstly, church rate abolition and secondly: 'The Abolition of Ecclesiastical Tests at the Universities & Grammar Schools'.[130] This campaign, however, was not on behalf of one of the grievances long-established in the consciousness of the Dissenting community, and no legislative progress was made during the period under consideration.

The final grievance which repeatedly aroused Dissenting passions during this period involved an oath which was officially required before one could assume an appointed office on the national level or – more relevant to the prospects of prominent Dissenting laymen during these years – any municipal office. The repeal of the Test and Corporation Acts had dealt with the original grievance by eliminating the religious test. However, rather than it simply being removed, it had been replaced by a declaration that one would not use any influence

---

[125] *Hansard*, CLXI, 679, 696.
[126] *Ibid.*, 684.
[127] *Eclectic Review*, n.s. II (July–Dec. 1859), p. 318.
[128] *Nonconformist*, 15 June 1859, p. 473.
[129] *Wesleyan Methodist Magazine*, May 1861, pp. 457–8.
[130] *British Quarterly Review*, XXXV, LXIX (January 1862), pp. 223–5. Dissenting Deputies Minutes, vol. 13, 5 July 1865, p. 340.

derived from the office to 'injure or weaken' the Established Church or to 'disturb' its clergy 'in the possession of any rights or privileges' given to them by law.[131] In practice, the oath was often not taken by those in national government because they simply neglected to swear it, a point which the Congregationalist George Hadfield (who led the fight in Parliament) made much of, mischievously noting that even the Lord Chancellor had 'pleaded ignorance of the law'.[132] Hadfield's Qualification for Offices Bill fell victim to a stalemate during the first half of the 1860s in which the Commons passed it repeatedly only to have the Lords reject it. Hadfield bitterly recorded the fact that the bishops overwhelmingly voted against his bill and this undoubtedly contributed to his decision – in the period following this study – to bring in a bill for the removal of spiritual lords from that House.[133] The debate in the Commons gravitated to familiar questions which in turn polarised members into familiar camps. When G. W. Hunt, member for North Northamptonshire, arrived late for a debate in 1866 which was a prelude to the Commons passing the bill for the seventh time, one has some sympathy with his qualifying his apology with the speculation that 'he had probably only missed hearing the same arguments over again'.[134] Indeed, many of the same arguments he could have heard used in a whole range of legislation which was periodically discussed in that House.

Dissenters generally agreed that the oath was offensive. The *Leeds Mercury*, for example, called it 'an invidious and absurd law'.[135] Edward Baines' personal papers include notes listing reasons why Hadfield's bill should pass.[136] The Dissenting Deputies passed a resolution in favour of the bill and Hadfield sought and received the support and co-operation of the Liberation Society.[137] Once again, however, it was difficult to establish the nature and severity of the offence. It is possible that the oath might have thwarted someone's career. The Revd T. Green of Ashton intimated to the delegates at the Liberation Society conference in 1862 that the oath should prevent Dissenters from holding these offices if they were true to their convictions and received a 'hear, hear' for the remark. This provoked the mayor of Ipswich to defend his position by classifying the oath as insulting rather than an obstacle to his conscience.[138] It seems

[131] *Hansard*, CLXXXI, 1241–2.
[132] *Ibid.*, CLXI, 666.
[133] Hadfield, 'Personal Narrative', pp. 219, 222.
[134] *Hansard*, CLXXXI, 1253.
[135] *Leeds Mercury*, 19 February 1862, p. 2.
[136] Leeds, West Yorkshire Archive Service, Baines Papers, Ms. 57. (These notes are not dated.)
[137] Dissenting Deputies Minutes, vol. 13, 22 February 1861, p. 232. Liberation Society Papers, A/LIB/3, 2 February 1866, minute 653.
[138] Supplement to the *Liberator*, 1 June 1862, pp. 108–9.

likely that Dissenters who had any inclination toward holding a public office almost invariably agreed with the mayor rather than the minister.

Therefore, this grievance was less 'practical' than the others. Even the *Liberator* admitted that this grievance was 'comparatively slight', but pleaded that there was an important point of principle at stake.[139] Hadfield tried to counter the accusation that the concern was trivial by arguing that the real grievance was primarily felt by the Almighty, saying:

> It might by some be considered an unimportant question; but, in his opinion, and in that of many other earnest and sincere men, it was no light matter to appeal on trifling or pretended occasions to the name of the Most High.[140]

The *Nonconformist* attempted to make the perceived smallness of the grievance serve the militant cause by claiming that the bill represented 'the *minimum* of relief which the Legislature refuses us' and tried to drive the point home in a practical way by comparing this situation to when 'a man in social life declines to favour another with so much as a pinch of snuff which he is known to carry about with him'.[141] Gladstone, who voted in favour of the bill, also seemed to see things in this light, referring to it as 'the poor little measure . . . of my hon. Friend the Member for Sheffield' (George Hadfield).[142] Naturally, others saw it differently, with C. N. Newdegate, for example, predictably referring to it as the 'supposed grievance' and voting against it.[143] The Home Secretary, Sir George Lewis, perhaps spoke for the silent majority when he said he would vote for the bill but nevertheless he thought that Hadfield had 'rather exaggerated the grievance' and that he did not think that 'this declaration acted very oppressively'.[144] W. E. Baxter, member for Montrose, in turn, might have summed up the true Nonconformist assessment of the grievance by labelling the oath 'a badge of dissenting inferiority'.[145]

The Qualification for Offices Bill finally passed into law in 1866. Alongside the crumbling of university tests, it is the other significant victory for Dissenters during these years. As with other grievances such as burials and church rates, it too was seen by friend and foe alike as a tool in the hands of militant Dissenters. The *British Quarterly Review*

---

[139] *Liberator*, May 1866, p. 90.
[140] *Hansard*, CLXI, 666.
[141] *Nonconformist*, 15 February 1865, p. 121.
[142] *Hansard*, CLXXIV, 136 (16 March 1864).
[143] *Ibid.*, CLXI, 667.
[144] *Ibid.*, 670.
[145] *Ibid.*, CLXXI, 1252.

complained in 1862 that Hadfield's bill 'is rejected by the Lords solely because it is supposed to emanate from Serjeants' Inn' (the location of the offices of the Liberation Society).[146] When its passing was imminent the *Nonconformist* relished it, not as relief from a practical grievance, but as a great moment in the march of radicalism, boasting: 'It marks the close of one era in the progress of religious equality, and indicates the commencement of another.'[147] With Gladstone on the verge of gaining a solution to the church rates issue and soon to achieve Irish disestablishment, the colourful language of this polemical publication for once does not sound over-stated. Nevertheless, before this case-by-case discussion of the Nonconformist grievances ends, perhaps it would be illuminating to see these campaigns through the eyes of the loyal Churchman, C. N. Newdegate, one last time, as he fought Hadfield's bill to the bitter end:

> I fear these piecemeal innovations. Why, some of these piecemeal innovators have not the instincts of the rat, which, when on shipboard, has the sense not to gnaw the main plank which forms the outer protection of the vessel from the waves. Some of these innovators do not care what may be the result of their attempts. They have minor or personal interests to serve, and will sacrifice great public interests to the attainment of their puny objects. Others, indeed, are actuated by great purposes, and are combined to effect some great political change through this piecemeal legislation. Although individually insignificant, collectively they are formidable. They are working piecemeal, it is true, but still it is for the purpose of overthrowing the organism which they are attacking.[148]

As has already been illustrated, the Liberation Society, and therefore militant Nonconformity, successfully moved into the position of providing the leadership and expertise to the campaign against church rates. In fact, it came to be seen as the arch-strategist on the whole range of 'practical grievance' issues. Comments made in Parliament – which already have been noted – well illustrate the way that Church defenders had developed this perception. To take one more example, in a pamphlet written by 'A Lay Churchman' in 1865 entitled *Church and Party: Being Some Remarks on the Duty of Churchmen in and out of Parliament; with Particular Reference to the Coming General Election* the author warned that all grievance bills were so much grist to the militant mill: '*The Member who votes for a bill should remember well that it is demanded as a*

---

[146] *British Quarterly Review*, XXXV, LXIX (January 1862), p. 223.
[147] *Nonconformist*, 25 April 1866, p. 321.
[148] *Hansard*, CLXXXI, 1247.

part of something more.'[149] Moreover, this perception was increasingly shared by the Dissenting community generally as well. The *Congregational Year Book* for 1857, for example, concluded a detailed article on the current legal situation regarding burial laws with the suggestion: 'On all these points further advice and information should be sought from the *Liberation of Religion Society . . .*'[150] Dissenters saw the work of the Society as vital even in the one area of grievance campaigning which was led least by orthodox Nonconformists – the ancient universities. When in 1854 the first assault was made during this period the *Wesleyan Methodist Association Magazine* credited the Society with 'having sounded the key-note' and even the *British Quarterly Review*, which held this cause dear to its heart, felt obliged to praise the radical association:

> University Reform moves slowly; but the steady pressure in that direction is doing much, and will do more. On this, and on kindred topics, the Society for the Liberation of Religion from State Control is doing good service.[151]

G. I. T. Machin has suggested that Dissenters might have obtained successes in their campaigns for the redress of grievances sooner if these struggles had not been championed by their militant wing.[152] Even if, for purposes of argument, this observation is accepted as true, it is only the beginning of a discussion. The deeper question is whether the radical Dissenters gained something in return which justified risking delays in these areas. This leads the discussion back for a final time to the issue of the severity of the grievances. Simply put, they were offensive enough to anger many Dissenters and to evoke the sympathy of more than a few Churchmen, but not so painful that their redress could not be postponed for a few years in order to pursue a higher purpose. For a small number of Nonconformists the grievances inflicted a bitter wound, but most Dissenters most of the time were not looking for a place to bury an unbaptised daughter or the prestige of an Oxford M.A. As the *Nonconformist* expressed the militant battle strategy:

> We are all, we hope, prepared to postpone any legislative realisation of minor objects, if by so doing we may place our ultimate one in a better position.[153]

---

[149] Anon. ['A Lay Churchman'], *Church and Party*, London: Rivingtons, 1865, p. 17.
[150] *Congregational Year Book* for 1857, p. 293.
[151] *Wesleyan Methodist Association Magazine*, April 1854, p. 233. *British Quarterly Review*, XX, XXXIX (July 1854), p. 272.
[152] G. I. T. Machin, *Politics and the Churches in Great Britain, 1832 to 1868*, Oxford: Clarendon Press, 1977, pp. 110, 163.
[153] *Nonconformist*, 19 October 1864, p. 837.

Church rates, the grievance which provoked the most agitation, was also the purest case for this line of reasoning. In this case, legislation which would have exempted Dissenters could probably have been obtained earlier, but most militant Dissenters were more than ready to forgo a few pennies for a few more years in order to add fuel to the radical fire. Militants saw the grievances as inhabiting the exploitable position of being indefensible without being literally unbearable.

In the medium term, this strategy was successful. The Anti-State Church Association (the Liberation Society) had set as its initial goal the greater dissemination of militant ideas within Dissent.[154] The agitation for redress of grievances served this end. E. D. Steele has recently argued that Palmerston weakened the influence of militant Dissent and facilitated the rise of moderation as a dominating influence in the Nonconformist camp.[155] Actually, the truth is just the reverse. Particularly in Palmerston's final administration, militancy was leavening the whole Dissenting lump to the point where the radicals and their institutions became the accepted leaders of Dissent in political matters. It has already been noted that the moderates did not have an agenda of their own. Moreover, most of them were from the older generation: whilst Miall's days of bringing before Parliament measures for the disestablishment of the English Church had to wait for the years beyond this study, moderates such as J. A. James and Josiah Conder did not even survive to 1860. John Campbell died before the closing date of this study and Robert Vaughan was retired and only six months short of his life's end. Sir Morton Peto's firm had had to file for bankruptcy in 1866 and therefore he was no longer a public, political influence. Who then remained to articulate the moderate position? Miall had captured much of the generation which was replacing them, men such as R. W. Dale and J. G. Rogers, with his militancy:

> Miall at once became the object of the intensest hero-worship. The old idols were utterly cast out and destroyed. Old gentlemen, who had led a pompous life for half a century, suddenly found themselves of no account. Their power had passed away as a dream. Students in Dissenting Colleges went over *en masse* to this second Daniel.[156]

---

[154] Liberation Society Papers, A/LIB/ 275, *Proceedings of the First Anti-State-Church Conference*, London: ASCA, 1844, p. 14.
[155] E. D. Steele, *Palmerston and Liberalism, 1855–1865*, Cambridge: Cambridge University Press, 1991, pp. 70, 135–6, 177.
[156] James Ewing Ritchie, *The London Pulpit*, London: Simpkin, Marshall and Co., 1854, pp. 124–5.

Moreover, the rise of radicalism can be tracked over time in denominations, journals and even the lives of individual moderates. A fine case study in this evolution is Vaughan's *British Quarterly Review*, which had been founded as a foil to militancy. By 1862, in an article which discussed the numerous grievance bills currently being promoted, it was sufficiently inspired by what the militants were saying and achieving to announce its desire to give up the trademark aloofness of the moderates and lend a helping hand:

> We beg respectfully to say, then, not to the Liberal party, but to Nonconformists – and if to any portion of them in particular, to those who, like ourselves, may have refrained hitherto from any prominent participation in the political action of Dissent – that we think the present state of things throws upon US a totally new responsibility.[157]

The Anglican Evangelical press was led to complain that men are supposed to become more moderate as they get older, but Dr Vaughan was doing the opposite.[158] As an elderly militant, J. G. Rogers could still relish this change when reflecting back on the 1860s from the vantage point of the twentieth century:

> Dr. Vaughan certainly did not like the new Radicalism, and *The British Quarterly Review* was commenced by him in the interests of a more cautious and moderate policy. It was extremely interesting to some of us to observe how the march of events gradually, but surely, forced him into an entirely different line.[159]

Even the Unitarians felt the pull of militant currents. The *Inquirer* had ridiculed the name of the Liberation Society in 1857 and proceeded to declare:

> we are reminded by the Orthodox Dissenters of our common Nonconformity, and our common subservience to a dominant Church. To this we would reply that we approve the principle of a National Church, and, as English Presbyterians, have more love for the Church of England than for the Independents or the Baptists.[160]

By 1862, however, it too had decided to defer in some measure to the leadership being offered by the radicals:

---

[157] *British Quarterly Review*, XXXV, LXIX (January 1862), p. 222.
[158] *Record*, 9 April 1862, p. 4 (in an article originally printed in the *Christian Observer*.)
[159] J. G. Rogers, *J. Guinness Rogers: An Autobiography*, London: James Clarke & Co., 1903, p. 69.
[160] *Inquirer*, 7 February 1857, p. 81.

> Our readers are well aware that on the Church and State
> Question we have clung hitherto, through constant opposition,
> to the old Presbyterian idea of comprehension. . . . we feel bound
> now to give our hearty support to many of the practical
> propositions of the Liberation Society, while not committing
> ourselves to any Anti-State Church theory.[161]

Perhaps even the emotions and will of the Wesleyan leadership were
swayed by the consciousness-raising activities of the militants. 'Practical
grievances' were certainly fewer and less grievous by the time Dr Waddy,
a former president of the Wesleyan Conference, felt moved to remark in
1864:

> He should deeply regret their being driven into a position of
> active hostility and agitation, which, however justifiable it might
> be, would, in the first instance, be greatly prejudicial to the
> spirituality of their churches; and, for a time, the work of
> conversion would be hindered. But if their dead were to be
> insulted, and if people married by them were to be told that
> they were not married at all, and their children were illegitimate;
> if the conscience of their people were to be disturbed, and the
> sacred and hallowed relations of their families to be questioned,
> then it might become necessary for them, at whatever amount of
> present risk, to take their stand and keep it.[162]

Many Wesleyans were moving closer to the militant Dissenters who had
always seen the grievances as this onerous. The campaigns for redress of
grievances were an important factor in the spread of militancy.

In the medium term, the adoption by radical Nonconformists of the
campaign against the practical grievances created a situation in which
their ultimate objectives were perceived to be furthered regardless of
whether a specific grievance was eliminated or stubbornly maintained. If
a grievance was redressed, the victory was seen to be theirs, while if the
concession was denied the outrage which resulted won them more
supporters. W. E. Baxter made this reply to C. N. Newdegate during a
discussion of Hadfield's Oaths Bill:

> Perhaps the hon. Gentleman was not aware that though the great
> body of the Dissenters of this country were anxious to remove
> grievances of this sort, there was a body whom he might call the
> extreme Dissenters, who rejoiced that there were laws of this
> kind, and that there were church rates. In their opinion the
> removal of these grievances would make the Church of England

---

[161] *Inquirer*, 29 November 1862, p. 834.
[162] *Liberator*, 1 January 1865, p. 5. These remarks are reported as having been said
'lately' by Dr Waddy.

stronger, and if it was any consolation to the hon. Member to know it, he would tell him that, in the opinion of that extreme party, he was at that moment playing their game.[163]

In truth, there was no immediate consolation for men such as New-degate. The real battle had been when public opinion had been shaped. Militant Nonconformists had succeeded in convincing a large number of people both that Dissenters were being treated unfairly and that their faction was wed to this cause and once that had happened it was not within the power of a member's vote to hold back the advancing tide. The fact that some Dissenters were still in favour of gaining only the redress of grievances and not other parts of the Liberation Society's programme actually added legitimacy and strength to the grievance campaigns which then indirectly benefited the militant Nonconformists because a win in these fights was perceived as their victory. Therefore, much of the sting was taken out of the term 'practical grievances' for the militant Dissenters as they began to exploit both the distance and the nearness of these goals in relation to their own ultimate objectives. The grievance campaigns represent one of the rare areas in which the militant Nonconformists were able to have their cake and eat it too.

In terms of the long game, however, this strategy had its limitations. Hadfield had claimed that his bill was needed in order to 'remove one of the last rags of intolerance that remained on the statute-book' and perhaps one had to wonder even then how many more the militant Dissenters would be able to find and how they would draw attention to their cause if they no longer had one to wave.[164] In 1865, J. Pillans of Camberwell justified the attention which the Liberation Society was paying to the grievances by saying:

> The great bulk of the English people would never listen to general principles by themselves, but only if they were put before them in connection with practical business . . .[165]

Such a conviction must have induced some anxiety at the thought of parting with the last of the practical grievances. As the century had progressed and old priorities had been met, Dissenters had had to re-write their list of grievances on numerous occasions. Already in 1867 – several decades before the fight against grievances had completely ceased to be a rallying cry – there was a certain pathos in the *British Quarterly Review*'s attempt to provide a rebuttal to those who said that 'Nonconformists have nothing to complain of' now that Hadfield's bill had

---

[163] *Hansard*, CLXXXI, 1252.
[164] *Ibid.*, 1239.
[165] Supplement to the *Liberator*, 1 June 1865, p. 100.

passed by exposing a whole set of little known grievances such as 'the refusal of some to let farms on their estates to Dissenters'.[166] Radical Nonconformity was indeed energised by the grievance campaigns, but the fuel was running out. Gladstone could see that the English Church was not in immediate danger of disestablishment and that removing the Dissenting grievances could well make it more immune to such an eventuality.[167] The hope of radical Dissenters would need to be pinned on converting a significant portion of society to their principles before all of the occasions for dramatically illustrating them were past. Whether or not they succeeded in this aim is a question which belongs to a study of a later period. In the middle decades, if the practical grievances were not truly 'fulcrums on which to place the levers for shaking the edifice' of the Established Church, they were at least evidence which proved useful in strengthening the conviction of the Dissenting community that there was a case for demolition.[168]

[166] These quotations are from a summary of the article made in the *Nonconformist*, 10 April 1867, p. 286.
[167] *Hansard*, CLXXIV, 136–7.
[168] Supplement to the *Liberator*, 1 June 1862, p. 109.

Part II

THE GOSPEL OF RELIGIOUS EQUALITY

Chapter Three

DISESTABLISHMENT

In 1862, some militant Nonconformists argued that, in an undeveloped form, or at least in a poetical sense, the campaign for the disestablishment of the Church of England had begun two hundred years earlier. On St Bartholomew's Day 1662 two thousand Puritan ministers had been 'ejected' from the Established Church because they could not conscientiously accept the requirements placed on them by the new Act of Uniformity. Nineteenth-century opponents of disestablishment, however, together with Nonconformists sensitive to possible attacks, were quick to point out that these early Dissenters had believed in religious establishments in principle and therefore did not affirm the central tenet of Victorian militants: the rejection of all church-state alliances as inherently wrong. The Liberation Society passed a resolution at its Triennial Conference in 1862 which expressed its carefully worded understanding of the relevance of the ejected ministers' stance:

> while aware that refusal was not attributable to any abstract objection to the union of the Church with the State, it recognises in their act a virtual denial of the right claimed by the State to exercise influence over the consciences of men.[1]

Others were content to say that they were celebrating the 'courage' or the 'fidelity to conscience' shown by their Puritan forefathers. It could not be legitimately argued that the cry for disestablishment began in 1662.[2]

In fact, even at the dawn of the nineteenth century, Dissenters were not offering a consistent, public critique of 'State-Churchism'. One does not wish to doubt the claim made in 1865 by the elderly J. H. Hinton that he had worked for the objects of the Liberation Society for over half a century and so had his father before him, but the Hinton family would

---

[1] Supplement to the *Liberator*, June 1862, p. 110.
[2] Timothy Larsen, 'Victorian Nonconformity and the memory of the ejected ministers: the impact of the bicentenary commemorations of 1862', in R. N. Swanson (ed.), *The Church Retrospective* (Studies in Church History 33), Woodbridge, Suffolk: The Boydell Press for the Ecclesiastical History Society, 1998.

have found it difficult to discover a formal outlet for their convictions until the 1830s.[3] The opening of that decade marked the beginning of an intense controversy in Scotland between Voluntaries (those who believed that religion should be supported by the voluntary aid of its friends rather than the power and resources of the state) and the defenders of church establishments. Voluntary Church Associations were formed in Scottish towns and the agitation began to inspire English Dissenters. The *Voluntary Church Magazine*, a publication of the Scottish Voluntaries, was glad to report in 1834 of a meeting in England at which clear Voluntary resolutions were passed.[4] William McKerrow and George Hadfield, two Manchester Dissenters who were prominent militants in the middle decades of the century, both looked back to a public meeting of Nonconformists in Manchester on 5 March 1834 as one of the first fruits of the new era. That meeting led to a petition to the Commons 'for the separation of Church & State' which received 34,000 signatures.[5]

Local Voluntary associations were formed in various English towns during the 1830s and already in 1830 the first of the national societies came into being – the Society for Promoting Ecclesiastical Knowledge.[6] The work of this society was purely to encourage the publication of literature articulating the case against church establishments and, starting in 1835, one way it undertook this task was by publishing the *Ecclesiastical Journal*. The first article of its first issue was entitled 'What is Meant by the Separation of Church and State?'[7] People who – in the years upon which this study is focused – would be considered moderates such as Dr Raffles of Liverpool and J. A. James of Birmingham were on the committee of this society with people who would emerge as prominent militants such as the Baptist ministers J. P. Mursell and F. A. Cox.[8] As the decade drew to a close two new organisations were formed: the Evangelical Voluntary Church Association (founded on 4 December 1839) and the Religious Freedom Society (first annual meeting, 7 May 1840). The first of these was narrower than the latter, restricting its membership to 'Evangelical Christians holding the Voluntary principle' and its activities to reasoned argument (as opposed to the tactics of pressure group politics).[9] Nevertheless, there was an overlap

---

[3] Supplement to the *Liberator*, 1 June 1865, p. 99.

[4] *Voluntary Church Magazine*, II, XVII (July 1834), p. 316.

[5] Hadfield, 'Personal Narrative', p. 125. See also J. M. McKerrow, *Memoir of William McKerrow, D.D.*, London: Hodder and Stoughton, 1881, pp. 37–47.

[6] *The Second Annual Report of the Society for Promoting Ecclesiastical Knowledge*, London: Harjette & Savill, 1831.

[7] *Ecclesiastical Journal*, January 1835, pp. 1–7.

[8] *The Third Annual Report . . .* , London: Harjette & Savill, 1832.

[9] John Burnet, *The Church of England, and the Church of Christ*, London: J. Dinnis, n.d. The rules of the Association are printed on the first page.

between the committees of the two societies with people such as Sir Culling Eardley Smith (later known as Sir Culling Eardley Eardley), Dr F. A. Cox and Dr Thomas Price offering their services to both of them.[10] All three of these organisations, from the perspective of mid-century militant Dissent, were more or less moderate and more or less ineffective. None of them survived for long the founding of the Anti-State Church Association in 1844. Nevertheless, the 1830s marked the beginning of church disestablishment as a public movement amongst nineteenth-century Dissenters.

In the mid-1840s the growing desire in England to protest against religious establishments was moulded into an organised national movement. This change was in no small measure due to the work of one man – Edward Miall. An Independent minister in early adulthood, Miall's political consciousness was significantly intensified after he moved to Leicester in 1834 in order to become the minister at Bond Street Chapel. By the middle of the century, Edward Miall had emerged as the undisputed leader of militant Nonconformity in general, and the dis-establishment movement in particular.

Miall's occupation from 1841 onward was to edit the *Nonconformist*, a Dissenting political journal which he founded in that year. Its advertisement identified the *Nonconformist* as 'an organ of advanced ecclesiastical and political opinions'.[11] On more than one occasion the Anti-State Church Association had to explain to an irate subscriber or even a member of its own Executive Committee that it could not be held responsible for what was said in Miall's newspaper.[12] Matthew Arnold, in his cultural critique of Nonconformity, seemed to suggest that the *Nonconformist* was an official organ of the Independents. The journal answered back that not only did it not represent such a vast body but also it 'never knew any committee of management, and its editor alone is answerable to the public for what may appear in its columns'.[13] The fact that Miall was more radical than most of his fellow Dissenters was reflected in the journal's strong support for the National Complete Suffrage Union.

But even if the *Nonconformist* was not a journal which necessarily spoke for most Dissenters on every issue, it certainly did speak to a significant number of them. A correspondent wrote to the paper in 1855, 'I was gratified, on perusing the Parliamentary Stamp Returns of 1854 to

[10] *Report presented at the First Annual Meeting of the Religious Freedom Society*, London: W. Tyler, 1840. *Evangelical Voluntary Church Association*, n.p., n.d.
[11] *Nonconformist*, 1 December 1852, p. 946.
[12] See, for example, Liberation Society Papers, A/LIB/1, 22 August 1850, minute 227; 23 December 1852, minute 962.
[13] *Nonconformist*, 10 July 1867, p. 557.

find the circulation of the *Nonconformist* was over 161,000, and exceeded that of any other Dissenting paper.'[14] Opinions varied on the value of Miall's paper depending on the political and religious convictions of the speaker. The *Wesleyan Methodist Association Magazine* regarded it as 'eminently deserving the confidence and support of all true-hearted dissenters', but the same organ inspired a conservative Churchman to note that 'a political religious newspaper is as great a pest as is a religious novel, and more mischievous'.[15] The nature of the *Nonconformist*'s influence could be questioned, but the fact of its influence was indisputable.

Edward Miall's greatest contribution to the cause of disestablishment was not the founding of the *Nonconformist* in 1841, but rather the creation of the British Anti-State Church Association in 1844. This society (known as 'the Liberation Society' after a name change in 1853), led the attack on the Church Establishment from its birth onwards. Miall successfully harnessed enough of the Dissenting unity and political consciousness generated by the fight against the education clauses of Sir James Graham's Factory Bill of 1843 to make the new society viable.[16]

Nevertheless, much of the Dissenting world, and particularly many of its more respectable and prominent leaders, initially stood aloof from it. John Blackburn's *Congregational Magazine* opposed the new Association unequivocally, speaking out against the founding conference of the society in order 'to prevent any such misconception of the conference, as might lead to the supposition, that it really represented the opinions of the large portion of the body to which we belong'. Its own calculation was that 'only about one-tenth of our congregations in London, and about one-twentieth of our congregations in the country, had any connexion with this conference'. It also noted that 'the Congregational Union has not given the slightest aid, encouragement, or approval'.[17] Indeed, the *Eclectic Review* was still complaining in 1847 that the 'The Congregational Calendar' (the *Congregational Year Book*) would not even include the Anti-State Church Association in its list of societies.[18] Even the elderly and venerable Dr John Pye Smith, principal of Homerton College, one of the few distinguished Congregational ministers of

---

[14] *Nonconformist*, 14 March 1855, p. 199.
[15] *Wesleyan Methodist Association Magazine*, February 1848, p. 70. John Pulman, *The Anti-State Church Association and the Anti-Church Rate League, Unmasked*, London: William Macintosh, 1864, p. 239.
[16] Skeats and Miall, *Free Churches*, pp. 493–4.
[17] *Congregational Magazine*, n.s. VIII (1844), pp. 472–4. (See also pp. 392–4.)
[18] *Eclectic Review*, n.s. XXII (July–Dec. 1847), p. 772. This complaint, however, was satisfied in the following year: *Congregational Year Book* for 1848, p. 248.

London to endorse the society at its birth, was asked by the committee of the institution he served to severe his connection with the Association. He was secure enough to flout their wishes, but their wishes are nevertheless indicative of respectable feeling in that denomination.[19] J. A. James used his considerable influence to foster a 'suspicion and dislike' of the society.[20] The Anti-State Church Association did not have a honeymoon period with the great and the good of Congregationalism.

Nevertheless, the Association steadily conquered the hearts, minds and wills of the Dissenting community. The Baptists gave it good support even at its founding: several regional Baptist associations sent official delegates, as did the Baptist Union itself.[21] Robert Eckett, the dominating personality amongst the Wesleyan Methodist Associationists, took part in the founding conference and therefore it is no surprise to read in that denomination's magazine in 1848: '*We recommend the Anti-State-Church Association to Christian Dissenters.*'[22] Moreover, within a few years of its founding some of the distinguished Congregationalists who had previously kept their distance began to drift into the fold. In 1847, Edward Baines the younger joined the Association as did other noted Congregationalists in Leeds, including the venerable minister, R. W. Hamilton.[23] By 1850 the great philanthropist Samuel Morley was also on board.[24] A conversion testimony from an Association meeting in Bristol in 1850 typifies the way in which the current was moving:

> The Rev. Thomas Winter, who appeared for the first time on that platform, acknowledged in a very manly way, that he had acted wrong in keeping aloof from the Association for fear that it would assume too political an aspect for him as a minister; but, that now, after mature deliberation, he felt that "he should not really act out his character as a Christian minister, if he did not appear publicly to declare himself connected with the Institution."[25]

Two events in the 1850s facilitated the establishment of the society as the rallying point for Dissenters on the issue of disestablishment: the

[19] John Medway, *Memoirs of the Life and Writings of John Pye Smith*, London: Jackson and Walford, 1853, pp. 471–2.
[20] A. W. W. Dale, *The Life of R. W. Dale*, London: Hodder and Stoughton, 1898, p. 140.
[21] Liberation Society Papers, A/LIB/275, *First Conference* (1844), pp. 157–61.
[22] *Wesleyan Methodist Association Magazine*, January 1848, p. 4.
[23] *Ibid.*, June 1847, pp. 278–80. *Congregational Year Book* for 1848, p. 226. W. H. Stowell, *Memoir of the Life of Richard Winter Hamilton*, London: Jackson and Walford, 1850, p. 404.
[24] *Christian Witness*, VII (1850), p. 293.
[25] *British Banner*, 6 February 1850, p. 101.

name change in 1853 to the Society for the Liberation of Religion from State Patronage and Control (thereafter commonly called 'the Liberation Society') and the launching of its journal, the *Liberator*, in 1855. The name change had the psychological effect of decreasing the impression that it was a bitter, destructive movement. The effectiveness of this is ironically illustrated by the fact that the enemies of the Society persisted in using the old name.[26] The journal provided a non-threatening way for Dissenters to become familiar with the work and views of the Society. It received favourable notices in the Dissenting press and this, in itself, was a new way it which a signal of approval could be sent in regard to the whole movement. The *Primitive Methodist Magazine*, for example, considered political and controversial matters outside its mandate, but reviewing the *Liberator* proved a useful way for it to slip Anti-State Church views into its pages. Here is one of a whole series of such notices:

> This unpretending serial has done and is doing an important work. The spirit in which it is conducted is the best guarantee for its future usefulness in a cause which, we believe, must assuredly triumph.[27]

By 1857, the *Baptist Magazine* felt free to declare of the Liberation Society: 'No voices are now lifted against it, and even those whose disposition leads them to abstain from active co-operation with it, wish it success.'[28] Others, of course, who had initially endorsed the Association later withdrew from it, but the momentum was on the side of its growing acceptance as the unrivalled champion of the Dissenting desire for disestablishment.

The Liberation Society was committed to one goal – the removal of all state endorsement of and preference for particular religious bodies and their members. Therefore, although the Society was dominated by Nonconformists, it nevertheless welcomed the support of all those wanting to pursue this same object, regardless of their creed. This was the society's policy from the very beginning. For example, the Unitarian Dr John Bowring was a welcome figure at its founding conference. It was sometimes awkward for the Society to balance the fact that its sub-scribers were primarily motivated by religious zeal and were convinced that they were supporting a holy cause with its official neutrality in matters of faith. When the *Liberator* reported that 'before the commencement of the public proceedings, a number of the delegates

---

[26] Pulman, *Anti-State Church Association*, for example, was written a full decade after the name change, and the author was well aware of it.
[27] *Primitive Methodist Magazine*, XLII (1861), p. 43. For an example of praise at an earlier date see XXXVIII (1857), p. 679.
[28] *Baptist Magazine*, June 1857, p. 370.

assembled to ask the Divine blessing on the deliberations', it was trying to express the spirit of the conference without violating the letter of its laws.[29]

Churchmen derided the irreligious nature of the Society. Archdeacon Hale wondered how militant Dissenters could call his Church's alliance with the state unholy when they would freely join forces with Unitarians.[30] *The Church-and-State Handy-Book of Arguments, Facts, and Statistics Suited to the Times* (1866) claimed that the Liberation Society was an alliance between Infidels, Voluntaries, and those envious of the Church's wealth.[31] Dissenters themselves sometimes had qualms about choosing their comrades based on their politics rather than their religion. John Blackburn had offered this as one of his central reasons for rejecting the Association at its birth, and John Campbell revived this objection in his attacks in 1850.[32] Moreover, the historian J. P. Ellens has recently supported these arguments.[33] Nevertheless, contrary to such assessments, the Society's constitution can be seen as an effort by religious men to embrace the principle of religious equality and a mature political strategy, rather than as the fall of once religious men into the snares of compromise and secularisation.

The overwhelming majority of militant Dissenters were deeply religious people and their spiritual convictions were a central motivation behind their political ones. The *Nonconformist* declared in 1864:

> The Liberation Society is strong, simply because its members, in the main, believe that they are doing God's work, and do it in the spirit of faith, hope, love and prayer. They believe, moreover, that God is working with them; and that while they, in obedience to His will, compass Jericho seven times, and blow their rams' horns, the walls of the city will fall because He has determined it. This is the secret of their energy, confidence, and perseverance. Theirs is pre-eminently a religious movement, and Churchmen will not know how to deal with it until they recognise it as such.[34]

In 1884, the Congregational historian John Stoughton tried to unveil this motivation to those misled by the public coalitions of militant Dissenters:

[29] Supplement to the *Liberator*, June 1862, p. 105.
[30] W. H. Hale, *The Designs and Constitution of the Society for the Liberation of Religion from State Patronage and Control, Stated and Explained*, London: Rivingtons, 1861, p. 6.
[31] George F. Chambers, *The Church-and-State Handy-Book of Arguments, Facts, and Statistics Suited to the Times*, London: William Macintosh, 1866, p. 93.
[32] *Congregational Magazine*, n.s. VIII (1844), p. 393. *British Banner*, 24 April 1850, p. 275.
[33] Ellens, *Religious Routes*, see, for example, pp. 91, 118.
[34] *Nonconformist*, 11 May 1864, p. 361.

Men, who from simple secular motives aimed at disestablishment
– motives, which, compared with those whose movements have
just been described, were wide as the poles asunder – might
openly scoff or secretly smile at the profession of evangelical
religion; but that evangelical religion was really the secret spring
of the enterprise, of which the originators had not reason to be
ashamed, who took the word of God as the star to guide their
course.[35]

The disestablishment campaign cannot be adequately understood without exploring its theological underpinnings.

The primary area of theology which impinged upon this debate was
ecclesiology. A distinctive understanding of the church was the *raison
d'être* of Congregationalism. The Savoy Declaration, a major statement
of Congregational beliefs in the seventeenth century, had declared:

> By the appointment of the Father, all power for the Calling,
> Institution, Order, or Government of the Church, is invested, in
> a supreme and sovereign manner, in the Lord Jesus Christ, as
> King and Head thereof.[36]

This common tenet of Congregationalism (a view of ecclesiology also
held by Baptists) had direct bearing on the establishment debate because
the Church of England recognised the royal supremacy over its affairs
and sometimes even referred to the earthly sovereign rather than the
divine one as the Head of the Church. Congregationalists, therefore,
came to see the alliance between Church and state as achieved at the
staggering price of usurping the place of Christ and demeaning his
church. This teaching was not created by mid-Victorian militant Dissenters, but rather was a genuine component of a longer tradition of
Congregational convictions. In 1808, either David Bogue or James
Bennett wrote in their jointly-authored *History of Dissenters* in the
section on 'Reasons of Dissent': 'The fundamental principle on which
I build the whole of my system is, "That Jesus Christ is the sole head of
the church."' In the next section, 'Particular Reasons of Dissent', the
author goes on to say as his primary point: 'As I acknowledge no head of
the church but Jesus Christ, I cannot accord with the church of England,
which owns the king for her head.'[37] It was the strength of this
theological tradition which made it natural for the Baptist Dr F. A.

---

[35] John Stoughton, *Religion in England, 1800–1850*, II, London: Hodder and
Stoughton, 1884, p. 272.
[36] R. W. Dale, *History of English Congregationalism*, London: Hodder and
Stoughton, 1907, p. 386.
[37] David Bogue and James Bennett, *History of Dissenters*, I, London: Printed for the
Authors, 1808, pp. 292, 312.

Cox to justify the need for the Anti-State Church Association at its founding conference by saying that the Church Establishment had 'robbed [Christ] of his power' and that it was the duty of its members to plead the case of 'an insulted Saviour'.[38]

This religious line of reasoning resonated with a wider constituency than just those who embraced Congregational polity. The *Methodist New Connexion Magazine*, for example, denied in 1848 that the Bible taught Congregationalism – leaning instead toward Presbyterianism – but agnostically arguing: 'It does not appear to us that any particular mode [of church government] is either prescribed or exhibited in the New Testament.'[39] Nevertheless, it was clear on the theological errors of the Church Establishment, concluding a description of its ecclesiastical arrangements (written in the same year) with the words: 'Thus the sceptre of Christ is transferred to a secular hand . . . Can those who love the Church of God desire to see her thus degraded and enslaved?'[40] Likewise, a correspondent wrote to the Quaker journal, the *Friend*, of the need to:

> distinguish between a *Church* according to the Acts of the Apostles, and a *Church* according to the Acts of Parliament, the one holding Christ as its only Head, the other holding that the head of the State is head of the Church also.[41]

Nevertheless, Congregational views of ecclesiology provided a uniquely rich theological tradition for a critique of church establishments. Congregationalism was founded on the principle that local churches should not be subject to any outside, human control and therefore the idea of the state 'establishing' the church by its power was particularly foreign to its distinctive theological vision. Experiments with Congregational establishments in the early history of America were more in spite of, than because of, the principal tenets which distinguished this denomination from other branches of the Christian religion. Again, the incompatibility of Congregational ecclesiology with the notion of an Established Church was recognised before Miall was even born. In 1808, Bogue and Bennett quoted a scholar approvingly as saying:

> We speak now indeed, and this has been the manner for ages, of the Gallican church, the Greek church, the church of England, the church of Scotland, as of societies independent and complete in themselves. Such a phraseology was never adopted in the days of the apostles. They did not say the church of Asia, the church of Macedonia, but the churches of Asia, or Macedonia. The

---

[38] Liberation Society Papers, A/LIB/275, *First Conference*, p. 9.
[39] *Methodist New Connexion Magazine*, 51 (1848), p. 33.
[40] *Ibid.*, p. 446.
[41] *Friend*, Ninth Month [September] 1847, p. 175.

plural number is always used when more congregations than one are spoken of, unless the subject be the whole commonwealth of Christ.

This argument leads them to conclude: 'the common idea of a national church, composed of all the congregations in a kingdom, is thus exploded as unscriptural'.[42] Robert Vaughan said of church establishments in 1862:

> Why, a Congregational Dissenter, from the very essence of what is distinctive in his profession, must be opposed to it. If there be a State endowment of religion, there must be State influence and control in relation to it. . . . But it is of the very essence of our Independency to resist all such interference. In the nature of things, therefore, Congregationalists can never be parties to a State religion. They would cease to be Congregationalists if they submitted to a State Establishment. . . . All grades of Nonconformists hold this view – Mr. Edward Miall and Robert Vaughan alike.[43]

In other words, Miall's disestablishment campaign had an impeccable theological motive from the viewpoint of Independent Dissenters. In 1860, the *Eclectic Review* ran a long article on 'Congregational Principles' which identified them as 'the two principles of self-support and self-government'.[44] In this light, when the non-sectarian Liberation Society declared that the principles it stood for were 'Ecclesiastical self-rule and self-support' it was articulating a public policy which was extraordinarily compatible with the private theological convictions of English Congregationalists.[45]

'Voluntaryism' was the name given to the general principle advocated in contrast to the Establishment principle which was dependent on an element of compulsion – the arm of the State. This idea also found its original setting in explicitly religious thinking which pre-dated the agenda of mid-Victorian militants. It drew on the Congregational tradition of a gathered church – people who freely chose to join in fellowship with one another – in contrast to a territorial one which assumed a person belonged to a certain church merely because he or she happened to live in a geographical area it had claimed as its sphere. A national church, in contrast to a gathered one, was based on the

---

[42] Bogue and Bennett, *Dissenters*, I, p. 124.
[43] Quoted in John Waddington, *Congregational History*, V, London: Longmans, Green, and Co., 1880, p. 346.
[44] *Eclectic Review*, n.s. III (Jan.–June 1860), pp. 416–33.
[45] Liberation Society Papers, A\LIB\3, 19 September 1862, minute 117.

territorial principle, a notion which according to the *Nonconformist* had divested the Church of England of:

> one of the chief characteristics of a scriptural Church, and has made it a great aggregation of individuals, in which no distinction between the converted and the unconverted is attempted . . .[46]

By contrast, in 1804, the Congregationalist John Pye Smith took part in the forming of a new congregation. The founding members all signed a covenant which incorporated a statement of faith. It began, 'We, whose names are voluntarily subscribed to this Solemn Covenant . . .'[47] The *Christian Witness* contrasted the two views of ecclesiology on this matter in 1862:

> *The Church of England* says – The church and the world, in this country at least, are co-existensive and identical – there is no member of the church who is not also a member of the commonwealth, neither is there any member of the common-wealth who is not also a member of the church. The entire nation is regarded as the church.
> *Dissenters* say – That a church is a voluntary society of believers . . . [48]

As with the argument regarding the headship of Christ, this argument resonated wider than merely in Congregational-Baptist circles. The *Wesleyan Methodist Association Magazine*, for example, declared of the Christian Church in 1849:

> From the very nature of the case, this Church is in the highest sense of the term a Voluntary Society. No man can be compelled to be one of its members. Every man in becoming a member, follows the conviction of his mind and the inclination of his heart . . . [49]

The church of Christ, it was argued, was ordained to advance by willing hearts through persuasion, and therefore all use of compulsion – the power of the State – was contrary to a right understanding of ecclesiology. For numerous Evangelical Dissenters, their calls for disestablishment were grounded in their understanding of the nature of the church.

The fact that religious convictions underpinned the case against state churches is illustrated by the spiritual benefits which many Dissenters believed disestablishment would unleash. Indeed, there was almost a

---

[46] *Nonconformist*, 26 November 1851, p. 937.
[47] Medway, *John Pye Smith*, p. 126.
[48] *Christian Witness*, XIX (1862), p. 208.
[49] *Wesleyan Methodist Association Magazine*, January 1849, p. 32.

millenarian quality to some of the more wildly sanguine speculations which this inspired. D. A. Hamer has noted that a Victorian committed to pressure group politics often 'attached an exalted significance to the reform for which he was struggling'.[50] This dynamic can certainly be seen in the rhetoric of Evangelical Dissenters working for disestablishment. The moderate Baptist Noel anticipated that the destruction of the union between the Church and the state would lead to a revival of religion in the parish churches.[51] The *Methodist New Connexion Magazine* expressed this same conviction in the negative, claiming:

> that great revivals of religion have for the most part been begun and been carried on by men, either unconnected with State influence, or who have acted independently and irrespectively of that influence.[52]

Even the Dissenting Deputies expressed a hope that once Christianity had been emancipated from 'the awfully disastrous control of secular dominion and statecraft' a gracious Providence would gloriously illustrate true religion 'in all its divine purity, simplicity and power, by the recovery of a lost world to Himself'.[53] Another common assertion was that the ecumenical vision held by some was thwarted by the existence of a national church. A writer quoted approvingly in the *Liberator* went so far as to imagine that disestablishment would be 'the most effectual method of promoting true union [amongst the denominations] and healing the animosities of centuries'.[54] Handel Cossham of Bristol, with a more precise calculation of what was at stake, once suggested that the 'State-Church was the cause of nine-tenths of the disunion between Christians'.[55] When it came to the more extreme situation in Ireland the *Nonconformist* apparently felt that even the tithe which Cossham had left to be attributed to other sources was too cautious a calculation and simply asserted that the Church Establishment was 'the prolific source of all religious feuds and ecclesiastical animosities in that country'.[56] Although undoubtedly disestablishment would have removed some bitterness between Dissenters and Churchmen, the divisions between the denominations were resting on a far broader base, as the

---

[50] D. A. Hamer, *The Politics of Electoral Pressure*, Hassocks, Sussex: Harvester Press, 1977, p. 1.
[51] B. W. Noel, *Essay on the Union of Church and State*, London: James Nisbet, 1849, p. 601.
[52] *Methodist New Connexion Magazine*, 51 (1848), pp. 446–7.
[53] Dissenting Deputies Minutes, vol. 12, 'Report for the year 1848', 19 January 1849, p. 27.
[54] Supplement to the *Liberator*, 1 June 1865, p. 111.
[55] *Ibid.*, June 1862, p. 109.
[56] *Nonconformist*, 1 March 1865, p. 161.

American experience (a favourite comparison for Victorian Nonconformists) should have amply testified. A quotation from the *Eclectic
Review* will serve to sum up and illustrate some of the spiritual wishful
thinking indulged in by Dissenters:

> the withdrawment of all State patronage and control from all
> religious bodies whatsoever, would confer immense good upon
> our country – would benefit the Church as much as Dissenters –
> would tend to a great increase of public morality – would open
> the way for real, practical union between all Evangelical Chris-
> tians – would immensely increase the benevolent activity of all
> sections of the Church of Christ, and inaugurate the most
> glorious era ever witnessed in our country's history . . . [57]

Theological motivations were a vital component behind the campaign for
disestablishment. When a speaker at the young men's conference held by
the Liberation Society in 1867 inspired his youthful audience by telling
them they were participating in a 'Second Reformation' he was merely
dramatising the fact that for many sober men and women disestablishment was a religious crusade embarked upon for reasons of piety.[58]

Disestablishment was also advocated on the more general basis of
equality and justice. Nonconformists came to believe that religious
discrimination by the state was morally, as well as theologically,
indefensible. The argument from fairness, from the duty of the state to
treat its citizens equally, was ubiquitous in Dissenting political thought in
this period. Even the *British Quarterly Review* claimed of 'all evangelical
nonconformists':

> Their maxim is, that where a community embraces all these
> classes [Roman Catholics, Presbyterians, Episcopalians, etc.], the
> government, to be just, should endow all or none – endow all, if
> the principle of endowment be a just one, endow none, if it be not
> just. Whatever is realized by general taxation, should be applied,
> not to any sectional, but, as far as may be, to the general
> interest.[59]

Moreover, militant Dissenters, seeking to gain the support of English
society as a whole for their political goals, chose to develop this rhetoric
and to emphasise it in discussions and writings addressed to the wider
public. The *Eclectic Review*, for example, in the introduction of one of its
articles, candidly expressed its desire to arm Nonconformists with a

---

[57] *Eclectic Review*, n.s. IV (July–Dec. 1860), pp. 373–4.
[58] Supplement to the *Liberator*, 1 February 1867, p. 34.
[59] *British Quarterly Review*, VI, XI (August 1847), pp. 120–1.

wider range of arguments than those which would appeal only to their co-religionists:

> We propose to show why the connexion [between Church and state] should be severed and the emancipation effected, and in doing so, we shall labour to advance secular rather than theological arguments, to touch as slightly and briefly as possible upon topics already familiar to intelligent Dissenters.[60]

The Liberation Society, which claimed theological neutrality, emphasised the egalitarian facet of its supporters' convictions. The *Liberator* claimed that historians were in agreement that 'the priesthood of a State Church are [sic] invariably the opponents of liberty'.[61] In fact, its instincts for fair play were so fully developed that it could quote approvingly from the Indian paper *Rast Gafter*'s articulation of the struggle of Hindus against the civil imposition of the gospel, and – the Evangelical convictions of its committee members notwithstanding – go on to comment censoriously: 'The bigoted may have as consolation that the obstinate heathen who refused to swallow the doctrine of Christianity is made to pay for the maintenance of its preachers . . .'[62] Due to their egalitarian convictions, many militant Nonconformists wanted to distance themselves from bigots as well as Erastian Churchmen.

The *Nonconformist* claimed that it was marching to victory under the banner 'Justice to all Churches – favour to none' and frequently argued the case for its proposals on the grounds of equal treatment for every group in society.[63] Edward Miall, when speaking at the young men's conference sponsored by the Liberation Society, did not lose his audience when he shifted his argument from religious to egalitarian grounds:

> Our one great object in this Society is simply this, to give to Christianity a clear stage and no favour. (Cheers.) Nay, we go farther than this – to give not to Christianity only, but to every man, a clear stage and no favour for the dissemination of those religious principles and views which he holds. (Cheers.)[64]

Militant Dissenters, who were fond of extolling the American model, could have echoed that nation's Declaration of Independence, feeling

[60] *Eclectic Review*, n.s. VI (Jan.–June 1864), p. 467.
[61] *Liberator*, 1 September 1861, p. 148. This rhetoric also appealed to a strain of anti-clericalism which resonated beyond the bounds of Congregational ecclesiology: Eugenio F. Biagini, *Liberty, Retrenchment and Reform*, Cambridge: Cambridge University Press, 1992, chapter 4.
[62] *Liberator*, 1 August 1861, pp. 126–7.
[63] *Nonconformist*, 12 July 1854, p. 573.
[64] *Liberator*, 1 February 1867, p. 40.

that civic equality for all was such a fundamental belief for them that they considered it 'self-evident'.

Many Dissenters sought to demonstrate the sincerity of their commitment to a policy of the government acting with even-handedness toward members of all religious communities by agitating against the government's habit of giving money for distribution amongst members of their own denominations. The *Regium Donum* was an annual gift, originally from the crown and from 1804 from Parliament, which was awarded in small sums to secretly chosen, poor Dissenting ministers. As long as such grants had existed, there had been some Dissenters who objected to them on principle. Dr Daniel Williams, the early eighteenth-century Dissenter who left Dr Williams's Library as his legacy, for example, was one such person.[65] Dissenting unease over the *Regium Donum* became increasingly widespread beginning in the 1830s. The Congregational minister George Clayton wrote a conspiratorial letter to John Blackburn, leaking to him an extract from the minutes of the Dissenting Ministers of the Three Denominations which signalled the approaching campaign against the grant.[66] By the start of the period under consideration, the leading Dissenting bodies – the Congregational Union, the Baptist Union and the Dissenting Deputies – were actively opposing the grant. The Dissenting Deputies, for example, in their report for the year 1848 were already discussing it in the kind of language which they used for issues of long-standing concern: 'Your Committee trust this annual grant will never be made without renewed discussion until it is abandoned.'[67] The Anti-State Church Association adopted this abolition cause wholeheartedly, taking charge of orchestrating the pressure on Parliament to end the grant.[68] Dissenters increasingly felt that ending the *Regium Donum* was essential if they were to campaign with integrity against government grants to other religious bodies such as the one to the Irish Roman Catholic seminary, Maynooth College, or indeed the Church Establishment itself.

As the campaign grew in strength the Dissenting community became more and more frustrated with the handful of men in their midst who continued to be willing to distribute the grant and particularly with one

---

[65] K. R. M. Short, 'The English Regium Donum', *English Historical Review*, LXXXIV, CCCXXX (January 1969), pp. 59–78.
[66] Blackburn Papers, L52/5/73, George Clayton to John Blackburn, 14 February 1837.
[67] Dissenting Deputies Minutes, Ms. 3083, vol. 12, 'Report for the Year 1848', 19 January 1849, p. 8.
[68] Liberation Society Papers, A/LIB/1, 3 April 1851, minute 441; 17 April 1851, minute 458. These minutes reveal the Association's efforts to find an MP to move the withdrawing of the grant in the House. They secured the services of John Bright.

distributor, Dr Pye Smith, who was indisputably a venerable Noncon-formist and who, as a member of the Executive Committee of the Anti-State Church Association, was expected to see the matter differently. The Congregational Union went so far as to mention Smith by name in one of its resolutions and even his hagiographic biographer makes it clear that he was wrong on this issue.[69] John Campbell in the *Christian Witness* made a direct appeal to Smith and, with his usual sense of proportion, went so far as to label the distributors 'enemies of the cross'.[70] Smith, for his part, with the immunity that comes with age, stubbornly and publicly defended the *Regium Donum* as compatible with Dissenting principles throughout these final years of his life.[71] Dr Pye Smith, however, was merely an embarrassing anomaly. There was a widespread dislike of the grant amongst English Dissenters. One of the most prominent Unitarian theologians of the Victorian age, James Martineau, who was no friend of militant Dissent, resigned as the minister of a congregation in the 1830s and placed himself and his family in great financial risk rather than accept money from the much larger and more general Irish *Regium Donum*.[72] Militants successfully capitalised on this concern in order to highlight the contours of their worldview. Parliament found itself in the bizarre and untenable position of persisting with an expenditure which the communities who received it were petitioning to have stopped. In 1851, the government announced that the grant would not be included in the budget for the following year and militant Dissenters rejoiced that they could articulate an egalitarian political philosophy with the confid-ence that their own house was now in order.[73]

Nonconformists considered general arguments regarding fairness as a ground of belief separate from, but complementary to, their explicitly religious convictions. The *Liberator* felt that the anti-transubstantiation declaration forced on civic officials was outrageous 'on the ground of Christian feeling – to say nothing of civil right'.[74] In other words, an appeal could be made to the consciences of its readers either way. The *Nonconformist* referred to those who 'firmly hold the principle of religious equality as one founded in reason and taught by revelation'.[75] In fact, 'reason and revelation' became a catch phrase which the journal

---

[69] Medway, *John Pye Smith*, pp. 213–15.
[70] *Christian Witness*, VI (1849), pp. 22–6.
[71] See, for example, his letters to the *Eclectic Review*, n.s. XXV (Jan.–June 1849), pp. 135–6, 397–8.
[72] James Drummond and C. B. Upton, *The Life and Letters of James Martineau*, London: James Nisbet, 1902, I, pp. 64–8.
[73] *Nonconformist*, 23 July 1851, p. 577.
[74] *Liberator*, 1 September 1867, p. 165.
[75] *Nonconformist*, 4 October 1865, p. 793.

used to indicate the twin roots of its case in egalitarianism and religion.[76] The disestablishment campaign was at least partially motivated by both a general sense of justice and fairness and a specific sense of the nature of the church and the rights of its divine head.

Militant Nonconformists were often careful to insist that the only criticism of the Church of England they were making was of its established position. Charles Vince, a Dissenting minister in Birmingham, referred to this as 'the distinction which they drew between the Church as a spiritual institution and as a political establishment'.[77] The point of this distinction was to condemn the Establishment without imputing the spirituality of its members, the ministry of its clergy or the validity of its religious work. An article in the *Eclectic Review* in 1849, for example, offered a typical disclaimer:

> We are not now, of course, speaking of the motives of those who belong to the Church, nor of the religiousness of that Church, in so far as that exists in the true and excellent portions of its Articles, and its Liturgy; in the piety and virtue of its bishops, its clergy, or any of its members. We confine ourselves to the idea of the *State-connexion* of that Church.[78]

Miall was fairly diligent in his effort to concentrate on the political point alone, and the Liberation Society was founded on this basis, the sprinkling of clergymen amongst its subscribers serving as practical illustrations of its singular focus. This too was part of an effort by militant Dissenters to find a discourse which would reach wider than their co-religionists. Officially, the campaign for disestablishment was waged entirely on the issue of separation of Church and state.

Groups, however, do not always adhere to their theories. Internal controversies in the Church of England offered a tempting potential for exploitation which Dissenters did not always resist. In practice, suspicions that the Established Church was deviating from sound theology and practice proved to be a compelling way to reinforce the argument for disestablishment. A person might know intellectually that it was unjust for the government to support any form of religion, but hearing that his or her tax money was being used to promote doctrines which were an offence to God gave the matter a fresh urgency.

Anglo-Catholic impulses within the Establishment were sometimes attacked in disestablishment writings and speeches, as were latitudinarian tendencies. In the 1860s, the shocking comments about the Scriptures made in a book by J. W. Colenso, bishop of Natal, the innovative

---

[76] *Ibid.*, 26 July 1866, p. 593; 15 August 1866, p. 649.
[77] *Christian Witness*, XX (1863), p. 272.
[78] *Eclectic Review*, n.s. XXV (Jan.–June 1849), p. 651.

approach to traditional doctrines contained in *Essays and Reviews*, and the seemingly inadequate responses to these events which the Church was able and willing to make, exposed her to vehement attacks. The decisions concerning the latter publication tempted the theologically neutral Liberation Society to remark: 'Never since the day when the "Liberation" movement was commenced has it had a greater advantage given to it than it has now.'[79] Nevertheless, this was a rare slip. Far more typical was the time when a minister recommended to the Society that it sponsor a course of lectures on 'Eucharistic errors in England' and the Executive Committee responded by intimating to him that 'the Committee are precluded by the Society's constitution from complying with his request'.[80]

Those not under the same constraints as the Liberation Society could speak even more freely. The Birmingham Congregational minister, R. W. Dale, declared in 1862, the bicentenary year of the Great Ejection:

> The organised agitation against the Established Church has been directed to the one great question of her alliance with the State. I really think that Liberation Society, which, by its constitution, is bound to deal exclusively with this element of the controversy, deserves the warmest gratitude of all Churchmen who heartily love the Prayer Book; for owing very much to the lead of that society, which has this for its solitary object – the liberation of the Church from State-patronage and control – we have been almost silent for many a year about baptismal regeneration, priestly absolution, and the presumed salvation even of ungodly and irreligion men if they die in communion with the Church. But we have been silent long enough . . . [81]

Dale's comments were greeted with cheers by his Dissenting audience, but this kind of playing to the home crowd always ran the risk of undermining the disestablishment coalition.[82] When, in this heated bicentenary year, a speaker at the Liberation Society's triennial conference spoke too freely about the internal flaws of the Church, a delegate who was a Churchman felt compelled to respond, and Miall himself had to step in to smooth over the situation by setting the first speaker's words in a highly charitable light.[83] Militant Dissenters claimed that they opposed the Established Church in principle, irrespective of its

---

[79] *Liberator*, March 1864, p. 42.
[80] Liberation Society Papers, A/LIB/2, 21 September 1855, minute 437.
[81] R. W. Dale, 'Nonconformity in 1662 and in 1862', in Central United Bartholomew Committee, *The Willis's Rooms Lectures*, London: W. Kent & Co., [1862], p. 69.
[82] Supplement to the *Nonconformist*, 8 May 1862, p. 405.
[83] Supplement to the *Liberator*, June 1862, pp. 110–11.

theology and practices, but Nonconformists did have religious objections to the kind of church which had been established, and these provided an emotive subtext to their campaign.

As the 1850s drew to a close, some Churchmen had become sufficiently rattled by the increasingly prominent disestablishment campaign to begin to form Church Defence Associations as an organised response.[84] So many local organisations had sprung up across the country that by 1865 the *Liberator* could refer to 'the Church (Establishment) Defence Associations, whose name is legion', apparently finding the new societies comparable to an unwelcome host of demons.[85] In the *English Churchman* (a publication which the *Nonconformist* referred to as 'a journal characterized by High Churchmanship and low manners') there appeared an article entitled 'The Church Defence Movement: An Answer to the Question "What is it?"'. The author stated the aim of the Liberation Society to be: 'TO DEPRIVE THE CHURCH OF ALL HER PROPERTY, AND TO DEGRADE HER TO THE POSITION OF A SECT'. His answer to the title question was: 'The object of the Church Defence Movement is simply to counteract and defeat the political intrigues of the Dissenters, and their guiding star, the Liberation Society.'[86] The movement was simply a recognition of the fact that Dissenters were organising to implement their agenda and therefore those with a competing political vision needed to develop a co-ordinated response.

Churchmen who stumbled on to the literature of political Dissenters were sometimes so shocked by what they read that they felt it must have been hidden from them hitherto by some sinister design. Nonconformists such as Miall, who had been doing everything in their power to make their views more widely known for decades, were always frustrated by the accusation of secrecy. Church defenders who researched the topic more thoroughly were forced to reconcile their personal sense that the story was an exposé with their growing realisation that they were only commenting on a matter of extensive public record. Archdeacon Hale attempted to bridge this gap with the linguistically trying observation that 'conspiracy is not less conspiracy, because openly avowed . . .'[87]

[84] M. J. D. Roberts, 'Pressure-Group Politics and the Church of England: the Church Defence Institution, 1859–1896', *Journal of Ecclesiastical History*, 35, 4 (October 1984), pp 560–82.
[85] *Liberator*, 1 August 1865, p. 137.
[86] *Nonconformist*, 2 September 1863, p. 698. The article was later published as a pamphlet: George F. Chambers, *The Church Defence Movement: An Answer to the Question "What is it?"*, London: Wertheim, Macintosh and Hunt, 1862.
[87] W. H. Hale, *The Designs and Constitution of the Society for the Liberation of Religion from State Patronage and Control Stated and Explained*, London: Rivingtons, 1861.

Churchmen were awakening to a realisation of the Nonconformist vision for civic society.

Beyond their antidisestablishmentarianism, Church defenders held other stances in opposition to the militant Dissenting agenda, or their perception of it. Particularly, they sought to expose a hidden alliance between the cause of manhood suffrage and that of disestablishment. Miall's interest in the former movement, particularly in the 1840s (the *Nonconformist* even becoming the official organ for the short-lived National Complete Suffrage Union) did not make the connection difficult to demonstrate. Richard Masheder, a fellow of Magdalene College, Cambridge, wrote an entire book dedicated to showing the connection between the two movements: *Dissent and Democracy; their Mutual Relations and Common Object: An Historical Review*. Masheder evaluated Dissenters in the light of the alleged godlessness of the Chartists. It was difficult for him to imagine supposedly Christian ministers associating with a group that would march under a banner saying 'More Pigs and less Parsons'.[88] Masheder's book was only providing a more thorough presentation of a common Church defence theme. Archdeacon Hale simply said that opposing the Liberation Society was the duty of everyone 'who dreads democracy'.[89]

If liberationists could sometimes make themselves believe that disestablishment was a panacea which would usher in a millennial age of ecumenical warmth and widespread revival, Church defenders were equally capable of imagining that it would be a calamity of almost apocalyptic proportions. Pulman (who fought Dissenters with their own weapon – the case study of America – by claiming that the raging civil war in that nation was the direct result of 'politico-religious sectarianism') predicted that after disestablishment 'instability would reign triumphant' and 'everything' would be 'uncertain and unstable'.[90] Masheder, however, with greater ambition, turned the entire Dissenting vision on its head by arguing:

> Whenever the Church of England be separated from the State, then will burst out anew the flames of persecution. That separation will proclaim, not perfect equality, but the savage domination of the sword, and fanaticism, and democracy, all blended together.[91]

The Church Institution did not, during the period under discussion, generate the degree of support which the Liberation Society enjoyed.

---

[88] Richard Masheder, *Dissent and Democracy*, London: Sauders, Otley & Co., 1864, p. 90.
[89] Hale, *Designs*, p. 39.
[90] Pulman, *Anti-State Church Association*, p. 201.
[91] Masheder, *Dissent*, pp. 310–11.

Church defence tracts sometimes ended with an acknowledgement of this fact made in a half pleading, half scolding tone. For example, George Chambers wrote in 1862: 'The present annual income of the London Church Institution is hardly *one-fourth* (think, *one-fourth*, whereas it ought to be at least *fourfold*,) that of the Liberation Society.'[92] M. J. D. Roberts' study of the Church Institution confirms Chambers' contemporary perception of its relative weakness.[93]

Nevertheless, this is not the entire story. The new suspicion of Dissenting political goals which the Church Defence Associations reflected and augmented was far more significant than the direct support acquired by these groups betrays. When the Executive Committee of the Liberation Society reported in 1862 on their work over the past three years, it was forced to admit a sharp decline in legislative advances and placed the blame on the emergence of an organised opposition.[94] The campaign for disestablishment was met from the late 1850s onward by the campaign for Church defence.

Since the founding of the Anti-State Church Association there was always a small number of Churchmen who supported the disestablishment campaign. Moreover, even amongst Churchmen who abhorred Dissenting theology and politics there was sometimes a strange affinity (but certainly not affiliation) on this issue. In particular, some Tractarians occasionally flirted with disestablishment. Although Congregationalists engaged in frequent and vehement attacks on the theology of the Oxford Movement, they shared with its members a pre-occupation with ecclesiology which resulted in a shared dislike for Erastianism. The degradation of the Church having to submit to the decisions of a Parliament composed of men whose religious convictions might be far from orthodox, made disestablishment look tempting to the High Churchman W. F. Hook in the 1840s. Not flinching at disendowment as well, he declared, 'Give us liberty and we will pay the price – our property.'[95] R. I. Wilberforce gave as his reason for joining the Church of Rome the Established Church's submission to the royal supremacy.[96] Dissenters did not have a monopoly on yearnings for the liberation of the Church from state control.

Occasional public hints regarding the attractiveness of disestablishment by some leading High Churchmen might be contrasted with the lack of such comments by the leadership and organs of opinion of a body

---

[92] Chambers, *Church Defence*, p. 8.
[93] Roberts, 'Pressure-Group Politics'.
[94] Supplement to the *Liberator*, June 1862, p. 105.
[95] W. R. W. Stephens, *The Life and Letters of Walter Farquhar Hook*, London: Richard Bentley & Son, 1881, p. 409.
[96] For Dissenting reaction to Wilberforce's convictions, see *Christian Witness*, XI (1854), p. 541.

outside the Church's walls – Wesleyan Methodism. Unlike Tractarians and Congregationalists, Wesleyans did not regard issues of ecclesiology as crucial points of sound doctrine and therefore the theories and practicalities of a church establishment had few hooks on which to catch their attention. The annual address of the Wesleyan Conference for 1848, for example, noted:

> If Christian brethren of some other denominations solicit us as Ministers to join them in their organized opposition to the continued union of the Church of England with the State, our reply is this: . . . In our view Christianity is a system of absolute TRUTH and LAW, as well as of goodness and mercy; and therefore we regard with complacency both the national or legal acknowledgment of its claims, and the private or voluntary extension of its influence.[97]

The *Watchman*, in the midst of the American Civil War, announced its eccentric opinion of that conflict's underlying cause:

> In our minds the conviction is deep and strong than when the Church of England perishes, the greatness of England dies with it. We wish to make no ungenerous reflections; but we cannot avoid the contrast with another country where our own Protestant faith is professed, and where the want of a state church, with its independence in the pulpit, and in every walk of ministerial life, may in this gloomy hour of civil war and national distress, be distinctly traced.[98]

The official voices of Wesleyanism not only refrained from endorsing the campaign for disestablishment, but actually sought to bolster the State Church.

Evangelical Churchmen had fewer qualms about the Church's alliance with the state than their High Church colleagues, but the few who did were of more use to the Nonconformist agenda because, if they defected, it was to Dissent rather than Rome. Baptist Noel and Christopher Nevile were the two most influential cases. The aristocratic Baptist Noel, who had established a notable reputation for himself within the Church, created a sensation when he renounced the Episcopalian ministry at the end of 1848. His Christian name proved prophetic, and he continued to minister in Bedford Row, but in a Baptist instead of a proprietary chapel.[99] Noel's parting shot at the Church was a book which militant

[97] *Wesleyan Methodist Magazine*, October 1848, p. 1131.
[98] *Watchman*, 1 January 1862, p. 3.
[99] For Noel's life see D. W. Bebbington, 'The Life of Baptist Noel: its setting and significance', *Baptist Quarterly*, XXIV, 8 (October 1972), pp. 389–411.

Dissenters zealously read and recommended entitled *An Essay on the Union of Church and State.*[100] Unquestionably he was firmly convinced that disestablishment would be a development which would benefit the Church, but his argument is most poignant when he is deriding the pains of conscience which the Thirty-Nine Articles and other positions of the Church caused for some of the Evangelicals in her fold. Noel offered a series of theological criticisms of the Church which he had come to believe separation from the state would somehow help remove. His essay catered to both the political and religious convictions of the militant Nonconformists. Nevertheless, Baptist Noel was not willing to maintain an on-going association with the political campaign against the Establishment, let alone with the Liberation Society. His aloofness was mourned by militant Dissenters who, in the heady months surrounding his conversion, had thought they had found a lifelong comrade and friend.[101]

Christopher Nevile, who became an heroic figure for Nonconformists in 1862 by resigning from his two family livings, proved to be a more enduring ally. It is true that in 1864 he made a point of saying he was not a member of the Liberation Society or 'of any party against the Church' and refused to speak from its platforms, but this assertion appeared to be a somewhat technical distinction which ignored a close association.[102] As early as 1861 Nevile was writing letters for publication in the *Liberator* and by the following year he was attending the triennial conference as an observer who felt comfortable enough to enter into the debate.[103] His very statement denying a direct association was contained within a book in which he blamed 'religious Dissenters' for the harm done by the Establishment because of their sins of omission.[104] One wonders if the distinction was still alive in his mind when he gave a dinner address at the seventh triennial conference of the Liberation Society in 1865.[105] As with his fellow pilgrim, Baptist Noel, Nevile's passions seemed most aroused by the theological faults which he perceived in the National Church. These doctrinal concerns led them, and a very few others, on to a belief in

---

[100] Noel, *Union.* For an example of Dissenting interest see *Eclectic Review*, n.s. XXV (Jan.–June 1849), pp. 251–65; XXVI (July–Dec. 1849), 649–64.

[101] Their disappointment can be sensed in C. S. Miall's remarks about Noel in which he still feels a need to comment on why his decision was based on 'very illogical' and 'unsound' thinking even though he was writing about it four decades later. Skeats and Miall, *Free Churches*, pp. 510–11.

[102] *Nonconformist*, 16 March 1864, p. 201.

[103] *Liberator*, 1 June 1861, p. 102. Supplement to the *Liberator*, 1 June 1862, p. 111.

[104] *Nonconformist*, 16 March 1864, p. 201. (C. Nevile, *Political Nonconformity*, London: Arthur Miall, 1864.)

[105] Supplement to the *Liberator*, 1 June 1865, p. 100.

the value of disestablishment and sometimes even into Dissent, and Nonconformists were always ready to welcome these converts with open arms.

Although the removal of a national church in England was high on the list of goals of the militant Dissenters and a prominent theme in their political journals, it was not proposed in Parliament during the period under consideration. When a zealous liberationist began to stir up the troops in 1864 for a direct attack on the Establishment in Parliament, the *Nonconformist* used its front page to denounce the strategy, noting:

> True, a David with a sling and a stone may bring a Goliath clad
> in complete armour to the ground. But, at least, let us be certified
> that he is a David, and that God is with him.[106]

English disestablishment was a long-term ambition for militant Nonconformists, but it was not politically feasible during these decades.

Liberationists had to content themselves with occasional bits of legislation concerning religious establishments outside England. One area of particular interest was the colonies. They derived the most pleasure from the Canadian Clergy Reserves Bill of 1853, in which Parliament consented to the wish of the Canadian legislature to be free to apply land set aside for religious purposes for secular uses. Miall, who was a member for Rochdale at the time, was a strong advocate of the bill, feeling that it was representative of disestablishment principles, but undoubtedly its passing had more to do with relationships with the colonies than the strength of the English liberationists. The *Nonconformist* ranked the bill as 'the great triumph of the session', claiming that it 'surrenders the very principle of State establishments of religion'.[107]

The colonies, as a general rule, were less sympathetic to religious establishments than the mother country. Liberationists paraded them as case studies in the power of Voluntaryism and as signs of its inevitable advance. When the royal assent was given to the bill gradually to end the use of government money for ministers' salaries in New South Wales, the *Nonconformist* felt that their religious struggle in the colonies was assured of ultimate victory:

> We are in no fear now as to the future of these new nations. They
> have grasped and throttled the serpents hid in their cradles.
> Canada is free – South Australia is free – New South Wales is
> free – British Columbia is free – and wherever Anglo-Saxons
> organise themselves into new communities, we are warranted by
> sufficient facts in concluding that within a few years, at the

[106] *Nonconformist*, 26 October 1864, p. 857.
[107] *Ibid.*, 24 August 1853, pp. 669–70.

utmost, the State will leave religious bodies to their appropriate work . . . [108]

The *Liberator* viewed the scene with similar satisfaction, 'In the colonies religion is almost, or altogether self-supported, and Episcopalians are comparatively free.'[109] Militant Dissenters in England gained some vicarious pleasure in their pursuit of disestablishment through the decline of the establishment principle in the colonies.

Closer to home, an opportunity ripe for exploitation was the situation in Ireland. Because the vast majority of its population were Roman Catholics, considering Episcopalianism the nation's religion was, at best, the product of a certain amount of fiction and, more to the point, an insult to the general populace and a source of injustice. Already in 1849 the *Nonconformist* was predicting that the issue of the Irish Church would be the wedge liberationists needed to hold open the door to disestablishment in England: if this issue was aired the 'spell which has hitherto imposed silence in regard to the first principles of Church Establishments will be dissolved'.[110] Edward Miall himself had brought the issue of the Church Establishment in Ireland before the House as early as 1856. Moreover, his action seems to have had the sympathy of the Dissenting community. The *Wesleyan Methodist Association Magazine* began its favourable review of Miall's speech on the Irish Church with the words, 'The Irish Establishment is one of the greatest grievances of which Ireland has to complain.'[111] Even the *Primitive Methodist Magazine* pronounced it a 'calm and able speech'.[112] By the middle of the next decade a new religious settlement in Ireland was widely viewed as a political necessity. The liberationists did their part to fan the flames and to ensure that the right response was made. The Dissenting Deputies, for example, passed this resolution:

> That in the judgment of the Deputies, the Endowment of any religion by the State is opposed to the teaching of the New Testament; that the Irish Church Establishment is peculiarly a grievance to the people of Ireland, it being the Establishment by the State of a form of religion opposed to the belief of a large majority of the people of that country; that the proposal to buy off the opposition to the disendowment of the Irish Church Establishment by offering a share of the revenues of that

---

[108] *Ibid.*, 26 August 1863, p. 677.
[109] Supplement to the *Liberator*, June 1862, p. 107.
[110] *Nonconformist*, 3 October 1849, p. 777.
[111] *Wesleyan Methodist Association Magazine*, August 1856, pp. 386–9.
[112] *Primitive Methodist Magazine*, XXXVII (1856), p. 546.

Establishment to other sects appears to this meeting most objectionable and should meet with strenuous opposition.[113]

J. G. Rogers, a Congregational minister and militant Dissenter who grew up in Ireland, bent his own rule against bringing his politics into his pulpit and used a sermon to allay any fears of Irish disestablishment. At the end of his life he reflected, 'So far as I can remember Nonconformists were perfectly united upon this question.'[114] The Wesleyan body was naturally not included in the term 'Nonconformist'. The *Wesleyan Methodist Magazine* opposed Irish disestablishment and grumbled that English Dissenters had become 'the allies of the Popish party'.[115]

The Liberation Society had fostered relations with Irish leaders in the 1850s and, as it became clear that Parliament was ready to tackle this issue in the mid-1860s, it revived these efforts. The Society actively supported several bills by Sir Colman O'Loghlen, member for Clare, which relieved Irish Catholics of various disabilities.[116] It renewed its warm relationship with the Irish leader O'Neill Daunt and its secretary made a visit to Ireland.[117] As early as 1866 the Society's Parliamentary Committee had met with Sir John Gray, member for Kilkenny City, and other members, and 'had agreed on the terms of the proposed motion on the Irish Church Establishment'.[118] When Lord Russell called for a Royal Commission into the Irish Church in the following year, the Society was vigilant, seeing it as a possible prelude to concurrent endowment, rather than their chosen option of disestablishment.[119] Indeed, prominent members on both sides of the House toyed with the idea of concurrent endowment. The failure of the coalition of Voluntaries and Anti-Catholics to end the Parliamentary grant to the Irish Roman Catholic Maynooth College amply shows that many members did not find the idea of government money going to the Church of Rome in Ireland unbearably repugnant. J. S. Newton has shown the important part the militant Nonconformists played in the settlement of the Irish Church issue.[120] Numerous historians have noted that the power and stance of the English Dissenters was the reason why

---

[113] Dissenting Deputies Minutes, Ms. 3083, vol. 13, 31 July 1867, p. 393.
[114] Rogers, *Autobiography*, pp. 131, 204.
[115] *Wesleyan Methodist Magazine*, June 1867, pp. 552–4.
[116] Liberation Society Papers, A/LIB/3, 8 February 1867, minute 430; 30 August 1867, minute 536a.
[117] *Ibid.*, 4 October 1867, minute 549a; 25 October 1867, minute 563a.
[118] *Ibid.*, 2 March 1866, minute 661.
[119] *Ibid.*, 5 July 1867, minutes 505a, 506a and 507a.
[120] J. S. Newton, 'The Political Career of Edward Miall, Editor of the *Nonconformist* and Founder of the Liberation Society', Ph.D. thesis, University of Durham, 1975, chapter 4.

concurrent endowment was not the solution to the Irish Church problem in the 1860s, even if they do not always agree on how significant this achievement was.[121] Without the wooing they did in Ireland and the pressuring they did in London, it is probable that the solution adopted by Parliament would not have been the one of pure disestablishment (including the ending of the Maynooth grant and the Irish *Regium Donum*) which was, with the benefit of their efforts, enacted under Gladstone's guidance in 1868. Moreover, this is not a small achievement or an isolated observation. If the strenuous campaigning of the Voluntaries had not been part of the whole political equation in mid-Victorian England, it is probable numerous efforts would have been made to meet the challenges of growing religious pluralism through extending endowments to more and more religious groupings. Voluntaryism won in Ireland, as in many of the colonies but, despite the hopes of militant Dissenters, these victories were not foreshadowing an imminent repetition of this solution in England.

To many Nonconformists disestablishment was the most important political goal they were pursuing. They saw all the Nonconformist practical grievances and even other issues such as national education within the context of the campaign for the separation of Church and state. Even the Dissenting Deputies could resolve at its annual general meeting in 1849:

> That the evils under which Dissenters suffer arise from the connexion of Church and State and this meeting desires to enter its solemn protest against such Union and to hope that the time is fast approaching when it will be dissolved.[122]

When the Qualification for Offices Abolition Bill and the Parliamentary Oath Bill were assured of victory in 1866, the Liberation Society admitted that the grievances they addressed were 'slight' but hailed them none the less as establishing an 'important principle'.[123] 'Principle' was a rallying word for militant Nonconformists. Alexander Hannay, given the task of instilling Liberation Society ideals into a new generation, began his address with the words, 'It is good to get down to principles', and informed his young audience that this pleasing act should be 'a man's first concern'.[124] This line of thinking was part of an already existing

---

[121] Machin, *Politics and the Churches, 1832–68*, pp. 356–8. Thompson, 'Liberation Society', p. 235. John Vincent, *The Formation of the British Liberal Party, 1857–68*, Harmondsworth, Middlesex: Penguin, 1972 [originally 1966], p. 264. Chadwick, *Victorian Church*, II, pp. 428–9.
[122] Dissenting Deputies Minutes, Ms. 3083, vol. 12, 19 January 1849, p. 4.
[123] Supplement to the *Liberator*, 5 May 1866, p. 90.
[124] *Ibid.*, 1 February 1867, p. 34.

tradition in Dissenting religious thought. T. S. James said of his father, the venerable Dissenting minister, J. A. James, 'In matters of right and wrong, he was always governed by abstract notions, and habitually endeavoured to bring everything to first principles . . .'[125] This was so ingrained as a Dissenting virtue that it even gained a place in Nonconformist accounts of good deaths. The Congregational minister, John Ely, was reported to have sent a message of encouragement to the 1847 autumnal meeting of the Congregational Union from his death bed, 'Keep to great principles, and on no account abandon or compromise them.'[126] Edward Baines the younger performed the traditional death bed interrogation on a noted minister in Leeds, R. W. Hamilton, asking, 'You hold all your principles clear and firm to the last?' To which the dying Congregationalist replied: 'O yes, my principles! If those principles fail, everything fails. I have always relied on principle!'[127] Indeed, some saw a commitment to principle as Nonconformity's *raison d'être*. James Bennett claimed in 1833 that Dissent was 'founded solely on principle'.[128] The *British Quarterly Review* argued that Dissent could not survive without its commitment to principle:

> An established system, especially if it be wealthy, may readily degenerate into a round of unreflecting worldly observances; but a religion which is left to be self-sustained must have principle in it of some kind – principle which has been more of less reasoned out, and which is appreciated for its own sake.[129]

If commitment to principle was a virtue, the vice which befell those who did not have it was decisions based on shameless compromise and expediency. This mindset was maintained when religious Dissenters began to reflect on the political arena and to develop their political philosophy. The Victorian biography of Sir Titus Salt, a wealthy Congregational textile manufacturer and politician, claimed of his subject:

> As for mere expediency, either in politics or religion, his soul abhorred it. . . . calmly he felt his way, amid conflicting opinions, until he found the rock of principle, and on this his foot was planted.[130]

---

[125] Dale, *James*, p. 573.
[126] Waddington, *Congregational History*, IV, p. 592.
[127] W. H. Stowell, *Memoir of the Life of Richard Winter Hamilton*, London: Jackson and Walford, 1850, p. 431. *Congregational Year Book* for 1848, p. 228.
[128] James Bennett, *The History of Dissenters*, second edition, London: Frederick Westley and A. H. Davis, 1833, p. ix.
[129] *British Quarterly Review*, VI, XI (August 1847), p. 129.
[130] R. Balgarnie, *Sir Titus Salt, Baronet: His Life and Its Lessons*, London: Hodder and Stoughton, 1877 (reprinted: Settle, Yorkshire: Brenton, 1970), p. 171.

The blending of the two is well illustrated in an article on 'Christian Politics' in the *Wesleyan Methodist Association Magazine* which noted: 'A temporizing policy may always plead for compromise of principle, but the man who adorns the Gospel in all things will endure, as seeing Him who is invisible . . .'[131] 'Voluntaryism' was literally a principle which was claimed as both explicitly religious, and generally political. John Stoughton listed it as their key principle as Protestant Dissenters in his address as chairman of the Congregational Union in 1856, but the non-sectarian Liberation Society could also refer to its supporters as 'the friends of Voluntaryism'.[132] The campaign for disestablishment thrived in this world, a world where an absolutist line of thought needed to be trumpeted and, if possible, applied no matter what the practicalities of the situation might suggest. Stoughton, from the perspective of the 1880s, explained the mental habits behind the mid-Victorian disestablishment movement:

> people accustomed to trace branches to their roots, and who thought more of principles than of practices lying on the top of them, did not feel satisfied with leaving matters just as they were. Right or wrong is not the question here; whether such persons are to be regarded as impracticable or not is a matter which leaves the simple fact untouched; namely, that between 1850 and 1880 there was a growing tendency in many quarters to look below the surface and penetrate to what is fundamental.[133]

Miall presented his disestablishment campaign as the march of a great principle and the Dissenting community received it as such. A journalist wrote of him in 1854, 'Yet that Miall has achieved what he has, shows how much may be done by the possessor of a principle; Miall is a principle, an abstract principle embodied . . .'[134] Dissenters saw disestablishment as a prime objective in a grand crusade to apply noble truths in their society, truths of equality and justice as well as Voluntaryism and pure ecclesiology.

Some Nonconformists, however, had trouble distinguishing between when a question deserved the high Victorian compliment of 'a matter of principle' and when the age's epithet of 'a mere abstraction' was more accurate. For some, there was an uneasy feeling that disestablishment, by itself, was of no practical importance. Dr Cox tried to pre-empt this

[131] *Wesleyan Methodist Association Magazine*, June 1847, p. 238.
[132] *Congregational Year Book* for 1857, p. 7. Liberation Society Papers, A/LIB/3, 15 September 1865, minute 575.
[133] John Stoughton, *Religion in England*, II, pp. 408–9.
[134] J. E. Ritchie, *The London Pulpit*, London: Simpkin, Marshall, and Co., 1854, p. 128.

accusation at the founding conference of the Anti-State Church Association:

> We are sometimes reproached as standing upon mere points of form, abstractions, and trifles. . . . But what is insignificant in the eyes of worldly men or political ecclesiastics, may be great in the view of God.[135]

In 1852, however, the *Nonconformist* was still trying to answer this frequent charge. An article in that year noted that many people had made the same complaint during the initial agitation for the great cause of free trade.[136] Samuel Morley withdrew from the Liberation Society after Irish disestablishment, feeling that it had largely accomplished what needed to be done.[137] Ironically, it was Morley who had revealed to the Lords' committee in 1859 that church rates were merely the tip of the militant Dissenting iceberg and thereby helped to provoke the 'ulterior objects' backlash of Church defenders. Numerous others, less prominent or politically aware, felt that disestablishment was an insignificant 'abstraction' when deprived of a practical grievance to plead its case.

Disestablishment, therefore, was paradoxically the most important political issue for many political Dissenters and yet, stripped of the cumulative grievances which brought harassment and injustice to religious minorities, some people felt an uneasy sense that there was nothing left of this cause to make a fuss about. When disestablishment was isolated from the context of the 'practical grievances' the whole notion of no longer having an 'established' church could seem little more than a symbolic squabble with little tangible import.

But such moments of introspection did not come often for most militant Nonconformists during this period. It is difficult today to imagine the passion which the issue of disestablishment aroused for numerous Victorian Christians. It was a goal held by the overwhelming majority of English Dissenters, no matter how reticent some of them might have been about exerting political pressure to see it accomplished. When the Liberation Society published a collection of 'Standard Essays on State-Churches' in 1867 it seemed to glory in including contributions (originally published elsewhere) from figures who were known to have been moderates such as Baptist Noel and J. A. James.[138] Undoubtedly, it did this in order to highlight the theological consensus within Dissent

---

[135] Liberation Society Papers, A/LIB/275, *First Conference*, p. 17.
[136] *Nonconformist*, 5 May 1852, p. 337.
[137] Edwin Hodder, *The Life of Samuel Morley*, third edition, London: Hodder and Stoughton, 1887, pp. 279–80.
[138] Liberation Society, *Standard Essays on State-Churches*, London: Arthur Miall, 1867.

which many of its supporters believed provided the rationale for its actions. Liberationists augmented these spiritual arguments which were generally affirmed by even the most respectable Dissenting ministers with a separate, complementary line of reasoning based on notions of justice, equality and fairness. Although they did not achieve their ultimate goal of English disestablishment, they did successfully awaken in their co-religionists a sense of its desirability. The issue of separation of Church and state was not just rhetoric; it was the focus of a large amount of time and money generously expended by the Dissenting community. For militant Dissenters, and the bulk of Nonconformity which followed them on this issue, disestablishment was a Christian duty, a just cause, a necessary consequence of their principles and the heart of their political agenda.

Chapter Four

RELIGIOUS EQUALITY

Nonconformists thought in terms of applying principles, and religious equality – by which was meant the equal treatment by the state of all citizens irrespective of their religious convictions – was the central, unifying principle which inspired the politics of the radical Nonconformists in the mid-nineteenth century. Moreover, the worldview of the militants, if not always their tactics, dominated Dissenting political thinking as a whole. Even the moderate *British Quarterly Review* paid homage to this principle and condemned church establishments on the grounds of its violation. Already in 1848 it noted:

> For many years past, the conviction has been everywhere strengthening in men's minds, that persecution or deprivation of civil rights, simply on religious grounds, is utterly wrong and unjust. It is merely might against right. . . . England has gone beyond most in abolishing religious distinctions, and protecting equally all its subjects, though it is yet reluctant to yield all that justice claims. Our established church is a great barrier to perfect civil equality.[1]

Likewise, the Quaker journal, the *Friend*, could opine in 1857, 'May Friends everywhere, in the firmness and dignity of the truth, maintain the rights of individual conscience, and of religious equality and liberty.'[2] Militant Nonconformists honoured those who supported their political agenda with the title 'friends of religious equality'.[3] Sometimes they even went so far as to impose upon their sympathisers in Parliament the collective label of the 'Religious Equality Party'.[4] Religious equality accurately reflected the genuine political convictions of the bulk of politically articulate Dissenters and was for them an orientating marker used for discerning the political divide. The noncontroversial *Congregational Year Book*, when reporting in 1864 on the preceding

[1] *British Quarterly Review*, VIII, XV (August 1848), pp. 252–3.
[2] *Friend*, Tenth Month [October] 1857, p. 183.
[3] See, for example, *Nonconformist*, 5 July 1854, p. 553.
[4] Liberation Society Papers, A/LIB/3, 1 July 1865, minute 563.

Parliamentary year, could lament that it 'has done nothing to advance the cause of religious equality', apparently secure in the assumption that the Congregational community acknowledged the validity of this political principle.[5] Once when John Bright was attacking Benjamin Disraeli in the Commons, he put into the Conservative leader's mouth the phrase 'we, the enemies of religious equality'.[6] A Dissenter who supported the goals of the Conservative party must unfortunately be lumped with Disraeli, but a Churchman could be just as much a 'friend of religious equality' as a true physical and spiritual descendant of one of the ejected ministers of 1662. Spiritual affinities were not at issue; religious equality was concerned with good politics based on sound principles.

For militant Dissenters, the recognition of the necessity of equality was the coming of age of political thinking concerning religion. It exposed the inadequacy of past calls for mere religious 'liberty' or 'toleration'. The founding meeting of the Anti-State Church Association in 1844 had rooted the ideology of the movement it was forming in the call for religious equality. In the opening paper Dr Cox repudiated any lesser goal, arguing that 'toleration itself is but a permission on the part of a worldly policy to do something under favour, which the rulers of mankind have no authority whatever either to refuse or compel being done'.[7] Samuel Martin, revered minister at Westminster Chapel, London, and a figure not notably associated with radical Dissent, presumed to articulate the convictions of his co-religionists when he was chairman of the Congregational Union in 1862:

> We desire not the destruction of other churches of Christ; we should mourn over it as a fearful catastrophe. But we do want perfect liberty – we do want complete equality . . . To be tolerated is to be insulted. To be patronized by the dominant sect is to be degraded.[8]

The militant Dissenter J. P. Mursell likewise used his address as chairman of the Baptist Union just a few years later to exhort the members of his denomination:

> it is for us to hold fast the liberties we have won, to use all peaceful means to sweep away the petty tyrannies that remain, to substitute equality for toleration in all that relates to conscience and to right . . .[9]

[5] *Congregational Year Book* for 1864, Appendix, p. 25.
[6] Trevelyan, *Bright*, p. 391.
[7] Liberation Society Papers, A/LIB/275, *First Conference*, p. 11.
[8] *Congregational Year Book* for 1863, p. 19.
[9] *Baptist Magazine*, May 1864, p. 232.

The *British Quarterly Review* argued in 1865:

> As a beginning, as an instalment, the Toleration Act was a great boon and a great gain to the Nonconformists. As a final thing it was a great mistake, and a great injustice. . . . Our cry is now – 'Toleration['] no longer, but 'equality.'[10]

For radical Dissenters, this distinction became a kind of ideological litmus test which was used to reveal a person's true political allegiance. In preparation for a general election in 1852 the Anti-State Church Association instructed its followers:

> Candidates who, in general terms only, express their attachment to "religious liberty," should be called upon to state what they include in that phrase; and whether they are favourable to "religious equality" also.[11]

The more mischievously minded of their followers could even agitate for their principles by purchasing placards bearing the slogan 'No more "Religious Liberty"!'[12] The traditional slogans of 'liberty' and 'freedom', however, were never meant to be stigmatised literally, and they continued to be used and cherished by many advanced Nonconformists. Conversely, Josiah Conder, a less radical but true friend of religious equality, despite using the term himself in the past, became frightened of how it might be interpreted and therefore denounced it in 1853 in favour of the older term 'religious liberty'.[13] Nevertheless, Dissenters (and not least *Patriot* readers) were no longer content to be simply free from harassment. They now asserted their right to be treated with equity.

Religious equality was a sincere and grand political philosophy. It was not simply a way of marketing the aspirations of a special interest group, but rather it was a political theory which transcended loyalty to people with similar religious affiliations or personal gain. 'A clear stage and no favour' was a phrase militant Dissenters used to describe what they believed the government should offer to all religious groups, including their own.[14] The fairness of this position sometimes made boasting irresistible. Edward Miall, while a candidate for Parliament in 1867, declared:

[10] *British Quarterly Review*, XLI, LXXXI (January 1865), p. 73.
[11] Liberation Society Papers, A/LIB/1, 19 June 1852: loose letter 'The General Election'.
[12] *Ibid.*
[13] Conder, *Political Position*, pp. 46–8. The Religious Freedom Society which he founded in the 1830s was conceived as 'a general union for the promotion of religious equality'. Conder, *Conder*, p. 284.
[14] See, for example, Miall's chapter of this title: Edward Miall, *The Politics of Christianity*, London: Arthur Miall, 1863, chapter 6.

I have never sought through political agency to assert that my religion is better than yours. I do not arrogate to myself any superiority either in the power to judge or in feeling to love the truth that I hold. What I claim for myself in these respects I am most willing to give to others. The question is not whether your religion or my religion be the better one, but the question is, What is the fair position on which both religions should stand in regard to the Legislation?[15]

The *Nonconformist*, while reporting with joy the increased number of Dissenters in Parliament after the 1865 General Election, was also careful to note, 'PARADOXICAL it may seem to say it, yet one of the last things we should wish to see is a Parliament composed exclusively of Nonconformists.'[16] Fair representation and participation was the goal, not domination. Although the attitudes of Dissenters specifically toward Roman Catholicism will not be dealt with until the final chapter of this study, it is worth noting for the sake of the general principle that the *Patriot* bragged in 1847 that Dissenters 'alone, as a body' combined theological criticisms of the Church of Rome 'with the unreserved recognition of the claims of the Roman Catholics to perfect civil equality and protection without patronage'.[17] Indeed, Nonconformists sometimes noted that their campaigns regarding practical grievances were not the pleadings of a special interest group, but rather an application of this egalitarian principle. The militant Congregationalist J. G. Rogers claimed of efforts to remove religious tests at the ancient universities:

The question was not a Dissenter's question. What they asked was that the rights of religious equality should be recognised; and this was a question for them, not as Dissenters, but as citizens, and above all as Christians.[18]

Even the *British Quarterly Review* argued on egalitarian grounds – in a way which must have seemed vexingly mischievous to some Churchmen – that Nonconformists must pursue the complete abolition of church rates rather than accept a compromise solution which would have exempted them:

Of course, the ordinary plan of exemption is inadmissible to Dissenters, on the other main aspect of their principle, that it confers civil privilege on the ground of religious belief. The application is no doubt novel, treating the Dissenter as one of a favoured faith, and so relieving him from a public burden. He

---

[15] Miall, *Miall*, p. 271.
[16] *Nonconformist*, 26 July 1865, p. 593.
[17] *Patriot*, 7 January 1847, p. 12.
[18] Supplement to the *Liberator*, May 1866, p. 84.

cannot, without violating his most cherished convictions of duty, accept it . . . [19]

Through the principle of religious equality Nonconformists sought to rise above the merely selfish interests of their own groupings.

This political doctrine was built upon a philosophy which assumed that equality was essential to justice. Joseph Sturge justified his political convictions to the electors of Nottingham in 1842 by explaining that 'as all men are equal, they are entitled to an equality of civil, religious, and political privileges'.[20] The fact that this argument seems a trifle circular, or appears to beg the question, only serves to illustrate how deeply this way of thinking was ingrained into the psyche of the radicals. The *Nonconformist* felt in 1848 that the necessity of treating Jews with full equality was 'too obvious for argument' and therefore: 'One might almost as well attempt to expand into eloquence, proofs of the proposition that two and two make four.'[21] When it found itself still having to deal with this issue three years later when David Salomons was not allowed to take his seat in the Commons, the paper was reduced in exasperation to running an article entitled ' "Fudge!" "Pish!" ' The article explained by analogy, 'When a person tells you that . . . he cannot sit down to dine with a party of thirteen, you do not argue . . .' (you say 'Pish!').[22] Likewise the *Eclectic Review* claimed that the right of Jews to sit in Parliament was 'so obvious, that some difficulty is experienced in arguing it at length'.[23]

The truth of their position on philosophical grounds was viewed by militant Nonconformists as a kind of general revelation which complemented the special revelation which was offered in their theological arguments (which are examined below). The philosophical and theological were two, equally true, separate lines of argument. This is well illustrated by a telling book published in 1860: *The Ultimate Principle of Religious Liberty. The Philosophical Argument: with a review of the controversy, as conducted on grounds of Reason and Expediency, in the writings of Locke, Warburton, Paley, Dick, Wardlaw, Gladstone, Martineau, and Miall.* This work appeared anonymously and its author is not revealed in published guides to anonymous literature or noted at the British Library or Dr Williams's Library. Nevertheless, the author is given as 'John Rippon, Esq.' in the 'Congregational Literary Register for

[19] *British Quarterly Review*, XXXV, LXIX (January 1862), p. 231.
[20] Stephen Hobhouse, *Joseph Sturge: His Life and Work*, London: J. M. Dent, 1919, p. 76.
[21] *Nonconformist*, 9 February 1848, pp. 84–5.
[22] *Ibid.*, 23 July 1851, p. 577.
[23] *Eclectic Review*, n.s. XXIII (Jan.–June 1848), p. 10.

1861'.[24] Whilst no biographical details concerning Rippon have been discovered, the listing of this work in this register means that he was a Congregationalist. The 'Esq.' indicates that he was a layman – one of only four in the entire list for that year. One can also safely assume that Rippon was either English or at the very least resident in England – particularly as his book was published in London. What is interesting about this book for the purposes of the discussion in hand is that the author deliberately and explicitly chose to avoid biblical arguments, not because he did not believe them, but in order to attempt to influence a wider audience including the 'philosophical politician' of the not very religious variety.[25] Moreover, Rippon's effort to articulate this argument was praised widely in the Dissenting press, including denominational journals.[26] Religious thinkers were seeking a discourse which could be used in the wider public arena rather than just at conferences of the faithful.

It would be erroneous to suppose that secular language or arguments were used because they were more deeply felt by these Dissenters than religious ones. R. W. Dale, one of the most respected Congregational ministers and theologians of the Victorian era, wrote privately to the Liberation Society in order to request that it attempt to gain sympathy for its goals in fresh circles by offering a course of national lectures 'bearing expressly on the philosophical & political aspects of the Society's principles'.[27] It would hardly be credible to suggest that he was personally only superficially interested in the scriptural or religious aspects of these same subjects. Radical Dissenters were thoroughly convinced as to the truth of the philosophical rationale for religious equality and it sometimes served their interests to let this argument stand alone.

Most Nonconformists were suspicious of government interference. Edward Miall, who was a more systematic political thinker than most Dissenters, occasionally expressed this instinct by attempting to articulate a view of the role of government. For example, he wrote in the first issue of the *Nonconformist* (speaking on behalf of the paper) that 'we ask nothing more from the State than *protection*, extending to the life and liberty, the peace and property of the governed'.[28] For the *Nonconformist*, government involvement was usually seen as a warning sign of

[24] *Congregational Year Book* for 1862, p. 358.
[25] Anon. [John Rippon], *The Ultimate Principle of Religious Liberty*, London: Ward & Co., 1860, pp. vii–ix.
[26] For examples, see the *United Methodist Free Churches' Magazine*, November 1860, pp. 697–9; *Baptist Magazine*, November 1860, pp. 708–9; *British Quarterly Review*, XXXIV, LXVIII (October 1861), pp. 553–4.
[27] Liberation Society Papers, A/LIB/3, 10 November 1865, minute 604.
[28] Miall, *Miall*, pp. 51–2.

potential danger ahead. In 1866, it published a letter and sample petition composed on behalf of the Anti-Compulsory Vaccination League – an organisation endeavouring to thwart a bill which, according to the letter, 'covertly aims to establish a medical inquisition'.[29] Likewise the *Patriot* in 1847 damned a scheme for sanitation reform on the grounds that it was rooted in 'the Socialist principle, that the people are to be done for by the State'.[30]

However, because interference is inevitably a question of degree, it was difficult to find that position of pure principle which Dissenters so loved to occupy. The *Leeds Mercury* might object bitterly to people's 'infatuated thirst for governmental interference', but it could also celebrate the success of the national postal service without reservation.[31] Apparently, it is one thing to publish condemnations of government programmes, but quite another to get them delivered. Because government non-interference could not be established as an absolute principle, it was an area in which differences of political philosophy between Dissenters could and did arise. The *British Quarterly Review*, for example, did not adhere to this doctrine. Whilst Miall could expound the role of the state under the title 'The Sword Bearer', Vaughan's journal argued:

> To lay it down as a principle, in relation to any community the world has yet seen, that its government should be an institute for protection and nothing more, would be to write one of the sheerest pieces of nonsense that could be put upon paper.[32]

Although this cleavage was made manifest in debates over a few areas of public policy during the years of this study – notably state education – in general, the instinct for non-interference reigned throughout this period, only to be sweep away as it came to a close and a new day of Dissenting politics began to dawn. In the middle of the century, the dominant influence was suspicion of government control. Perhaps it was predictable that after generations of civil discrimination most Dissenters would be wary of the government. Moreover, the attractiveness of *laissez-faire* arguments and their belief in the virtue of voluntary action reinforced their unmistakable aversion to government interference.[33]

---

[29] *Nonconformist*, 25 April 1866, p. 325.
[30] *Patriot*, 13 June 1850, pp. 372–3.
[31] *Leeds Mercury*, 31 May 1851, p. 4; 28 April 1857, p. 2.
[32] Miall, *Politics of Christianity*, chapter 5; *British Quarterly Review*, XXI, XLI (January 1855), p. 289.
[33] Moreover, it has recently been shown that this instinct belonged to the wider world of popular Liberalism: Eugenio Biagini, *Liberty, Retrenchment and Reform*, Cambridge: Cambridge University Press, 1992, especially chapter 2.

116

The vast majority of Nonconformists who made their views publicly known were fervent anti-corn law free traders. Richard Cobden had said in 1838 of the abolitionist case, 'It appears to me that a moral and even a religious spirit may be infused into that topic, and if agitated in the same manner that the question of slavery has been, it will be irresistable.'[34] Largely without the help of the Established clergy, Nonconformist ministers and the people of their congregations proved Cobden right. By the end of 1841 the General Body of Ministers of the Three Denominations – a group which was not known for its rashness – had passed a resolution supporting free trade.[35] A conference of 645 abolitionist ministers was held in Manchester in that year – only two of them were clergymen of the Church of England (two others were from the Church of Scotland).[36] In the biographies and autobiographies of prominent Victorian Nonconformists, sections on the subject's free trade efforts are well-nigh ubiquitous. It would be wearisome to list all the notable Dissenters beginning with their most prominent leader on this issue, John Bright, who joined in the struggle. Indeed, six of the seven founders of the Anti-Corn Law League were members of the congregation of the militant Dissenter William McKerrow.[37] Perhaps this point might be illustrated by noting that even the General Baptist entrepreneur Thomas Cook was sufficiently carried away by the free trade cause to found in 1846 a short-lived paper entitled the *Cheap Bread Herald*.[38] The elderly Congregational scholar and divine, Dr John Pye Smith, was so enraptured by the cause that he enthused like an idealistic youth: 'I would sell my books even most highly prized, or undergo any other supportable self-denial, rather than be wanting to God and my country at this crisis.'[39] George Hadfield started his list of the principles which had motivated him in politics by saying, 'I advocated absolute religious freedom, free trade . . .'[40] Indeed, at some points one could even wonder how essential this order was. In 1852 the Anti-State Church Association decided not to place pressure upon Parliamentary candidates to pledge themselves to religious equality measures on the grounds that the 'next General Election will chiefly turn on the question of

[34] John Morley, *The Life of Richard Cobden*, London: T. Fisher Unwin, 1903, p. 126.
[35] Raymond G. Cowherd, *The Politics of English Dissent*, London: Epworth Press, 1959, pp. 134–5.
[36] *Report of the Conference of Ministers of all denominations on the Corn Laws*, Manchester: J. Gadsby, 1841.
[37] J. M. McKerrow, *Memoir of William McKerrow*, London: Hodder and Stoughton, 1881, p. 288.
[38] Robert Ingle, *Thomas Cook of Leicester*, Banor, Gwynedd: Headstart History, 1991, p. 45.
[39] Medway, *Pye Smith*, p. 447.
[40] Hadfield, 'Personal Narrative', p. 127.

Parliamentary Reform and Free Trade'.[41] The mass of Dissenters were unwavering on this issue during the crucial years of this fight. John Bright was their political hero and free trade was their cause.

Moreover, abolition of the corn laws did involve a great principle. The virtue of *laissez-faire* economics and the evil of monopolies rolled several core instincts of Dissenters into one large truth. Hatred of established churches, suspicion of government interference, the virtue of Voluntaryism could all find shelter under this broad canopy. Anti-monopoly became a deeply rooted stance which was repeatedly applied in new areas. The Dissenting newspapers were predictably against the 'taxes on knowledge' which inflated their price.[42] Josiah Conder opposed the idea of a national railway service in 1853 on the grounds that all monopolies were bad and government ones were the worst of all.[43] Moreover, this principle had much wider implications. Anti-monopoly and free trade became metaphors for religious equality. The Established Church was a monopoly. Religious discrimination, like the corn laws, artificially rigged the market. The result was that the system benefited an elite, but did not adequately meet the needs of the masses. The Liberation Society, when it was disturbed by some apparent set-backs in 1861, encouraged itself by rehearsing its own convictions:

> Law should not, and shall not place us, under social disadvantage on account of our religious faith and practices. We decline to be dealt with as inferiors. We stand upon equality of citizenship . . . We have the same right in justice, though not in law. . . We claim to be on equal footing with them. We will tolerate no monopoly. . . . [This is] the key note of our music. . . . What we want is not that every verse should treat of the same topic, but that to every verse there should be the refrain – "No monopoly".[44]

In such a climate, the patent on printing the Authorised Version of the Bible became a focal point for Dissenting principles, desires and fears. Only three publishers (the Queen's printer and the two ancient universities) could legally print it in England. Dissenters denounced this 'Bible monopoly' and demanded that it be replaced by a 'free trade in Bibles'. This had already happened in Scotland, thus providing a useful precedent. The *Patriot* offered statistics on the resulting drop in price and increase in circulation of Bibles which it announced in advance

[41] Liberation Society Papers, A/LIB/1, 12 February 1852, minute 707.
[42] The *Leeds Mercury* was pleased to be able to become a daily at the start of 1862 due to the removal of the paper duty: 1 January 1862, p. 2.
[43] Conder, *Political Position*, p. 12.
[44] Liberation Society Papers, A/LIB/2, 27 September 1861, minute 1206.

would give 'a demonstrative proof – perhaps the most remarkable that can be referred to – of the value of the principle of Free-trade in all saleable commodities'.[45] This monopoly was particularly emotive. The corn laws inflated the price of bread, but the Bible monopoly made more scarce the 'Bread of Life'. Dr Campbell reasoned, 'Is it not high time to cheapen the Bread of Life to the millions of England's poor peasantry and distressed artisans?' This was the most precious commodity: he recommend that the government tax the wind in our sails and the light from the moon 'but oh! leave, and leave, untaxed, the MANNA as it descends'.[46]

The campaign against the Bible monopoly was primarily and peculiarly a Nonconformist fight. When *The Times* announced that it was in favour of renewing the patent the *Nonconformist* was outraged. Who would have thought, it wondered, that after the monopolies of cork-cutters, ribbon-weavers, hop-growers, paper-makers and brewers had been destroyed and 'just as this process is coming to a close, and Protection is all but extinct' *The Times* would become protectionist?[47] Dr Adam Thomson, a Scottish Voluntary who led the fight against this monopoly, claimed that those who wanted its removal were mostly Dissenters.[48] Moreover, it was championed by militant Nonconformists. Thomson's attention had been drawn to this cause by John Childs of Bungay – the celebrated church rate martyr.[49] These two men were seen as the most important leaders of the movement, with Dr Campbell providing valuable support in the press in the early years. Thomson himself was a prominent agitator on behalf of Voluntaryism.[50] Both men had helped Miall to establish the *Nonconformist* and both men had attended the founding conference of the Anti-State Church Association.[51] Dr Campbell, although he argued the case on the anti-monopoly principle, gave up the fight when lower prices had been secured, much to the annoyance of his erstwhile comrades-in-arms, Thomson and Childs, and the embarrassment of his sympathetic biographers, Ferguson and

---

[45] *Patriot*, 5 September 1850, p. 563.
[46] Robert Ferguson and A. Morton Brown, *Life and Labours of John Campbell, D.D.*, London: Richard Bentley, 1867, pp. 183–6.
[47] *Nonconformist*, 15 April 1860, p. 301.
[48] Leslie Howsam, *Cheap Bibles: Nineteenth-Century Publishing and the British and Foreign Bible Society*, Cambridge: Cambridge University Press, 1991, p. 115.
[49] P. Landreth, *Life and Ministry of the Rev. Adam Thomson, D.D., Coldstream, and his Labours for Free and Cheap Bible Printing*, Edinburgh: Andrew Elliot, 1869, p. 412. Childs was himself a printer and Howsam implies, not unconvincingly, that he had a personal motive for wishing to see the monopoly ended. Howsam, *Cheap Bibles*, p. 114.
[50] Landreth, *Thomson*, pp. 343–6.
[51] Miall, *Miall*, pp. 40–3, 257.

Brown.[52] Thus the leadership of the cause was left completely to
architects of the contemporary militant movement. The Liberation
Society took the campaign for abolition firmly in hand, although one
could argue it had little direct relationship to its stated *raison d'être*. In
1859, when the patent was due for renewal in the following year, the
Society went so far as to place this issue on its list of test questions for
Parliamentary candidates.[53] As with some of the practical grievances, the
Society undertook the responsibility of finding a member of Parliament
who would advocate their position in the Commons. It succeeded in
securing the services of Edward Baines.[54] Archdeacon W. H. Hale
illustrated the power of the Liberation Society by noting, 'The scheme
for doing away with any authorised printing of the Holy Scriptures is
their scheme.'[55] Hale was not being alarmist; the militants won this fight
as well and the patent was not renewed.

Dissenters had no doubt that giving all printers the freedom to publish
the Bible would be good for England. *Laissez-faire* had no dark shadow
for them. When Dr Thomson, after years of championing abolition, was
finally allowed to print the Scriptures in Scotland, he nearly went
bankrupt due to the flood of cheap editions which the goaded Bible
societies simultaneously released onto the market. However, instead of
Dissenters allowing this to cripple them with second thoughts, they
simply let Christian Voluntaryism make up for what market Voluntaryism lacked, raised a subscription, and saved Dr Thomson from ruin to
fight another day.[56] Free trade principles and sound religious principles,
although already firmly bound together in the minds of most Dissenters,
were given further occasion for joining forces through the anti-Bible
monopoly agitation.

Churchmen did not fail to condemn what they perceived to be the
vulgarisation of religion by associating it with trade and the market. A
prominent Evangelical clergyman, Dr J. C. Miller, in a polemic against
militant Dissenters, claimed that what they called Voluntaryism was in
fact 'the *Commercial*, system'.[57] The *English Review* protested in 1848, 'It

[52] Landreth, *Thomson*, p. 406; Ferguson and Brown, *Campbell*, pp. 197–201.
[53] Liberation Society, *The General Election. Hints to Electors*, London: Reed and
Pardon, 1859.
[54] Liberation Society Papers, A/LIB/2, 15 June 1859, minute 964.
[55] Hale, *Designs*, p. 32.
[56] The subscription had widespread support. See, for example, *Wesleyan Methodist
Association Magazine*, December 1847, pp. 563–4; *Methodist New Connexion
Magazine*, 50 (1847), pp. 615–16. Dr Campbell, perhaps feeling pains of guilt
about his own desertion, went out of his way to association himself with the
appeal: *Christian Witness*, VI (1849), pp. 335–8; VII (1850), p. 445.
[57] John C. Miller, *A Lecture on Churchmen and Dissenters*, second edition, Birmingham: Benjamin Hall, 1862, p. 13.

is impossible to conceive of anything more wretched than this application of the "free-trade" principle to religious truth.'[58] Moreover, an
impressive array of influential historians have echoed this opinion. Elie
Halévy perceived the abandonment of a truly spiritual vision: 'free trade
become a religion or rather perhaps a religion whose sum and substance
was unqualified free trade'.[59] Norman Gash sees free trade in religion as
'an extreme as well as a nakedly utilitarian view'.[60] Owen Chadwick
instinctly feels that it is at odds with true spirituality.[61] Nevertheless, free
trade was a public stance which was at least partially nurtured by a
theological vision which Victorian Churchmen did not share – or even
understand – and which historians have not fully explored.[62]

Free trade in religion was simply another term for religious equality
and, at their core, radical Nonconformists believed in religious equality
for theological reasons. Voluntaryism as a theological idea pre-dated the
rise of the Anti-Corn Law League. One of the reasons why Dissenters
latched on to the rhetoric of free trade was because they recognised it as
a persuasive, secular line of thinking which would help them communicate their political goals to people who did not share their theological
vision. Indeed, one could look at the rise of free trade as an application
to economics of a distinctly religious conviction that the sovereign
Creator had providentially established and faithfully oversees all the
forces of the world.[63] Mid-Victorian Dissenters held a deep faith that –
by the will of the Almighty – what was true and right would always
ultimately prevail. This is not a dulled religious instinct, but rather the
kind of faith Elijah had when he called for a free competition between
his theological vision and that of the prophets of Baal. The Congregational minister, John Ely, for example argued that the Voluntary system
was better than church establishments from this position of spiritual
faith:

> Leave all to the God of truth, and to the instrumentality which he
> has instituted for the support of truth, and who can doubt the

---

[58] Quoted in the *Nonconformist*, 18 October 1848, p. 785.
[59] Elie Halévy, *A History of the English People in the Nineteenth Century*, IV,
London: Ernest Benn, 1951, p. 184.
[60] Norman Gash, *Reaction and Reconstruction in English Politics, 1832–1852*,
Oxford: Clarendon Press, 1965, p. 64.
[61] Owen Chadwick, *The Victorian Church*, Part I, London: Adam & Charles Black,
1966, p. 4.
[62] An important exception is G. I. T. Machin, who does acknowledge the religious
components in this line of thinking: *Politics and the Churches*, p. 100.
[63] This idea is explored in Boyd Hilton, *The Age of Atonement: The Influence of
Evangelicalism on Social and Economic Thought, 1785–1865*, Oxford: Clarendon
Press, 1988.

issue? Give the state the right of interference, and truth may be repressed, and error forced on the community.[64]

The backdrop of the Dissenting Deputies' work on behalf of religious equality was a millennial hope grounded in their view of what the Almighty had revealed in his Word:

> We must therefore labour more earnestly and hopefully in our high calling, not doubting but that religious freedom shall at length prevail, because we have the promise that pure, free Christianity, recognizing only its unseen but Almighty Head, shall eventually and universally triumph.[65]

The *United Methodist Free Churches' Magazine* countered the Church defence cry of 'Church in danger' with sound doctrine: 'That Church, purchased by the blood of Christ, and destined to be the eternal reward of His redeeming love, IS not, and CANNOT be, in danger.'[66] The *British Quarterly Review* ridiculed the Papal Index of Prohibited Books as betraying a lack of faith:

> Clearly the Popes do not believe their own doctrines; they have no confidence in their own system; they are devoid of trust in Providence; they declare that error, if fairly matched against truth, will gain the victory, or that, what they call truth, they hold to be error.[67]

It was because they were part of a religious community which was accustomed to taking into account the decisive role played by unseen forces in the spiritual realm that militant Dissenters could see any help the state would try to offer to the advance of the kingdom of God as, to put the case at its most mild, superfluous. It is true that Victorian society as a whole was pervaded by an optimistic sense of progress, but this again was arguably the adoption into secular thinking of convictions which originally arose in a religious vision. The *British Quarterly Review* believed it knew the roots of this thinking and therefore labelled it the 'rational notion of a millennium' or 'the political millennium'.[68] As to the views of militant Dissenters themselves, Dr Price understood the spiritual convictions of his hearers when he argued that the Liberation Society's agenda of religious equality – of free trade in religion, if one wishes to put

---

[64] *Christian's Penny Magazine*, I (1846), p. 69.
[65] Dissenting Deputies Minutes, Ms. 3083, vol. 11, 20 December 1847, 'Report of 1847', p. 442.
[66] *United Methodist Free Churches' Magazine*, January 1867, p. 11.
[67] *British Quarterly Review*, XIV, XXVII (August 1851), p. 143.
[68] *Ibid.*, p. 13.

it that way – was right on these grounds: 'Truth is always more powerful than error, and requires only "a clear stage" in order to overcome it.'[69]

All that was said in the preceding chapter regarding ecclesiology also nurtured the Dissenting notion of religious equality. Most Nonconformist denominations believed that the church should be gathered rather than territorial. R. W. Dale expressed the convictions of the founders of Independency this way in a speech in 1854:

> They thought that a true Church was "a congregation of faithful men," not an institution including the godly and the godless, and stretching over an entire nation. They thought that when a church gathered, those who wished to enter it, should promise to live and worship according to the laws of Christ . . .[70]

Therefore, when in the mid-nineteenth century Dissenters began to make new efforts to forge their political philosophy, they did not see the institution of the church as one which should be structured as a kind of national service for all people – like a national postal system – and they did not see the truths which the church taught or even the specific rules which it asked its members to live by as something which the state should attempt to force upon all citizens. The government dealt with the whole population, and Dissenters were willing to work politically with all people, despite the indignation of some Churchmen who claimed they were in league with infidels. Dissenters, by contrast, were affronted by the Church's willingness to view the whole populace – even its most notorious sinners – as members of the Church. The religious census of 1851 was a census of who gathered, but when Churchmen wanted to have a census by profession in 1861, Dissenting ecclesiastical views were outraged by the idea that Churchmen would want to count as belonging to their number people who never actually gathered with them:

> We might have thought that no sect would be willing to descend so far as to eke out its apparent numbers by claiming persons as belonging to their organizations who never act with them, or meet with them.[71]

Religious equality meant that the affairs of churches were decided by their members and not by the state and it meant that the church imposed its beliefs and standards on its members and not the citizens of the nation indiscriminately. The church, they believed, extended its influence by spiritual power through persuasion, not by government power through coercion. These values were in tune with Dissenting ecclesiology.

---

[69] *Methodist New Connexion Magazine*, 50 (1847), p. 47.
[70] Dale, *Dale*, p. 103.
[71] *British Quarterly Review*, XXXII, LXIII (July 1860), p. 232.

These theological principles, which were not shared by Churchmen, made it possible for Dissenters to embrace the principle of religious equality. Nevertheless, they also drew on wider theological resources which they shared with other Protestants, other Evangelicals and other Christians generally. As to Protestantism, Dissenters saw their political philosophy as an extension of the Protestant principle of the right of private judgement. George Legge, in his address as chairman of the Congregational Union in 1859, argued:

> When, however, the Reformation proclaimed the right of private judgment, and referred every man for his faith to the Word of God, there ought to have been an end at once of statecraft and of priestcraft.[72]

As to Evangelicalism and Christianity generally, Dissenters saw religious equality as an application of the equality of human beings which is revealed through the Almighty treating all people without discrimination. The Evangelical idea that every single human being – rich or poor, female or male, kind or mean, churched or unchurched – needed to undergo a conversion experience in order to secure salvation reinforced this spiritual principle. Militant Dissenters applied this notion to the political realm. As the *Eclectic Review* put it, 'The man who admits the equality of souls cannot refuse the doctrine of the equality of men.'[73] A journalist who wrote a sketch on Miall in 1854 claimed that he derived his principles from the Bible, illustrating this with the idea: 'If all are equal before God, surely they should all be equal before man.'[74] The militant Dissenter and orthodox Presbyterian minister, William McKerrow, explained his political motivations in this way:

> The political principles which I have always held have been founded, I trust, on the practical precepts of the New Testament, – on its justice, and mercy, and benevolence, on the universal brotherhood which it reveals, and the equality of all men in the sight of God.[75]

Religious equality, for many Dissenters, was an attempt to model in their political behaviour the egalitarian ways of the Almighty.

While 'equality', 'justice' and 'fairness' might seem like secular notions today, to a Victorian Dissenter an awareness of these concepts was secured through the revelation of a God who was just and who would

---

[72] *Congregational Year Book* for 1860, p. 42. The motto of the *Wesleyan Methodist Association Magazine* was: 'The right of private judgment in the reading of the Sacred Volume.'
[73] *Eclectic Review*, n.s. XXIV (July–Dec. 1848), pp. 176–7.
[74] Ritchie, *London Pulpit*, p. 128.
[75] McKerrow, *McKerrow*, p. 225.

judge every person without partiality or favouritism. Moreover, while he would certainly, in their view, judge people harshly who clung to false religions after they had been exposed to the light of Christianity, he had forbidden his servants to persecute anyone. Instead, they were called to love even those who persecuted them and all uses of coercion to further the gospel were contrary to the Almighty's holy will. Joseph Sturge once explained when he was running for Parliament that 'his political creed was based upon the Scriptural injunction, "Whatsoever ye would that men should do unto you, do ye so unto them."'[76] That text alone, if taken seriously, as indeed it was, could lead a man to seek to abolish slavery, unjust corn laws and religious discrimination. The golden rule embodied the spirit of the principle of religious equality for militant Dissenters. Here, for example, is a report of a speech Miall made in 1867:

> He himself started from the general principle on which he had been accustomed to base all his moral and political conclusions – a principle of Divine authority: 'Whatsoever ye would that men should do unto you, do ye likewise unto them.' That was the foundation on which the political edifice must rest – justice.[77]

The *Eclectic Review* explained why government should be based on the principle of religious equality in this way:

> A very obvious limit to the religious responsibility with which the administration of civil government has to do, is, that it should preserve a perfect equality of treatment between the different religious parties of the state. . . . In dealing with our own religious interests we have to follow the personal convictions of our own conscience in the matter; but in dealing with religious interests of others, we have to respect their conscientious convictions, just as we desire ours to be respected. This is surely right and Christian. We can quote for it the universal command – 'All things whatsoever ye would that men should do to you, do ye even so to them.' We can confirm our particular application of this command by the apostolic rule of judgment – 'Conscience, I say, not thine own, but of the other; for why is my liberty judged of another man's conscience?'[78]

Theological arguments, therefore, were central to Dissenters embracing religious equality. Philosophical arguments and rhetoric from the world of economics were consciously developed as a way of engaging a wider audience and were seen as complementary to religious ones to the point

---

[76] These are Sturge's words as recollected by Charles Vince: Henry Richard, *Memoirs of Joseph Sturge*, London: S. W. Partridge, 1864, p. 328.
[77] Miall, *Miall*, pp. 270–1.
[78] *Eclectic Review*, n.s. XXIV (July–Dec. 1848), p. 756.

where guidance on subjects as diverse as economics and ecclesiology was provided – in their minds – by a single, overarching worldview. For militant Dissenters, their case was supported by both 'reason and revelation'. It remains in this chapter to explore the degree to which Dissenters delivered on their rhetoric of religious equality when specific cases of discrimination against non-Christians were brought to the attention of mid-Victorian society.

The most pressing issue of religious equality in England during the mid-Victorian era was whether or not Jews should be given the right to be members of Parliament without having to swear to the standard oath which included the words 'upon the faith of a true Christian'. This issue clearly reveals the cleavage between the political agenda and philosophy of Dissenters, most of whom were Evangelicals, which was based upon the principle of religious equality, and that of many other Christians, including the Wesleyan body and their fellow Evangelicals in the Establishment. In 1848, the *Wesleyan Methodist Magazine* claimed that a measure for allowing Jews into Parliament should be viewed 'with regret and alarm' on the grounds that it would undermine the Christian nature of the Legislature.[79] J. P. Westhead, member for Knaresborough, felt obligated when he decided to vote in favour of Jewish emancipation, to use a good portion of his speech in Parliament in order to explain his actions to his friends in the Wesleyan community.[80] Wesleyan Methodists generally left it to others to concern themselves with getting Jews into the House of Commons, choosing instead to concentrate their energies exclusively on trying to get them into the household of Christ. As for Churchmen, the fight against such measures in the Commons was led by two Evangelicals: Lord Ashley and Sir Robert Inglis. Lord Ashley is remembered in history by his subsequent title of the Seventh Earl of Shaftesbury. He was the leading Evangelical layman of the mid-Victorian age and is still celebrated as a model of Christian, and particularly Evangelical, political activity.[81] Nevertheless, his political vision was quite distinct from that of Evangelical Dissenters and did not include the principle of religious equality. On the issue of admitting Jews to Parliament he prophesied bitterly in 1847:

[79] *Wesleyan Methodist Magazine*, April 1848, p. 463.
[80] *Hansard*, XCVIII, 617–31 (4 May 1848).
[81] Numerous biographies of Shaftesbury have been written. The standard Victorian one is Edwin Hodder, *The Life and Work of the Seventh Earl of Shaftesbury, K.G.*, 3 vols., London: Cassell & Company, 1887. For a scholarly work of more recent origin, see G. B. A. M. Finlayson, *The Seventh Earl of Shaftesbury, 1801–1885*, London: Eyre Methuen, 1980.

Some years ago they stood out for a Protestant Parliament. They were perfectly right in doing so, but they were beaten. They now stood out for a Christian Parliament. They would next have to stand out for a white Parliament; and perhaps they would have a final struggle for a male Parliament.[82]

Likewise Charles Goring, member for Shoreham and a Protectionist, felt that the religious argument was settled by the clear teaching of the Bible in 2 John ix–x:

He that abideth in the doctrine of Christ, he hath both the Father and the Son. If there come any unto you and bring not this doctrine, receive him not into your house . . .[83]

A large majority of bishops continually voted against Jewish emancipation in the House of Lords, and members for both of the ancient universities (whose constituents were exclusively Churchmen) were in the front line of the resistance in the Commons. Inglis, member for Oxford University, could approach the friends of religious equality brandishing a petition opposing the admission of Jews from the venerable institution which he represented.[84] Churchmen, and not least the Evangelicals in their ranks, led the fight against religious equality for Jews.

Dissent, however, was overwhelmingly and publicly in favour of their admission. The hegemony of the political philosophy of militant Nonconformists is clearly demonstrated by the support which the Dissenting community as a whole gave to the political aspirations of their fellow citizens in the Jewish community. Despite its *raison d'être* as a defender of the rights of Protestant Nonconformists, the agenda of the Dissenting Deputies in 1847 was dominated by its efforts on behalf of Jews. The wording of the relevant petition by that body demonstrates that it embraced a wider political vision:

That your Petitioners are and ever have been the friends of civil and religious liberty and that they are as anxious that its blessings should be extended to all their fellow countrymen as well as to themselves . . .[85]

Congregational voices were apparently invariably in favour of the measure. Even Campbell's *British Banner* saw the issue in terms of the distinctive political vision which Dissenters had to offer. It contrasted

---

[82] *Hansard*, XCV, 1278 (16 December 1847).
[83] *Ibid.*, XCVII, 1215 (3 April 1848).
[84] *Ibid.*, XCV, 1260 (16 December 1847).
[85] Dissenting Deputies Minutes, Ms. 3038, vol. 11, 20 December 1847, p. 432.

Churchmen, who try to evangelise Jews, but wish simultaneously to deprive them of 'social equality, political justice', with:

> Dissenters, on the other hand, . . . [who] stand nobly forth, and say, "Is the Jew a man? He is bone of my bone, and flesh of my flesh, my fellow; and he shall not, if I can prevent it, be a slave! I demand for him equal rights and privileges, and a place within the pale of the Constitution!" Let all the people say, Even so, AMEN![86]

The *Congregational Year Book*, which limited its opinions to the consensus of Congregationalism, claimed that the measure for the admission of Jews was 'fraught with justice' and blamed its failure in the 1848 session on Churchmen:

> The High-Church prejudices of many, and the fears of others, especially of the Lords Spiritual, were excited; and, consequently, notwithstanding the noble majority of the Commons, the bill was defeated.[87]

In 1831 T. B. Macaulay had supported the removal of Jewish disabilities with a comment that would later be often quoted for purposes of criticism: 'We hear of essentially Protestant governments and essentially Christian governments, words which mean just as much as essentially Protestant cookery, or essentially Christian horsemanship.'[88] The *Patriot* admitted that it could not endorse this sentiment, but it nevertheless supported the cause in which it had been enlisted. It argued that it would be just as opposed to it as anyone else, 'If we did not deem it a Christian act, to admit our Jewish fellow-citizens into the Legislature, – an act in perfect accordance with Christian principles, and adapted to recommend and promote the Christian faith'.[89] In other words, Macaulay is wrong if he is saying religion has nothing to do with the matter, since we are supporting this cause for theological reasons. The organs of Congregational thought, even those deemed more moderate, supported the measure.

Baptists, as could be anticipated, were of the same mind as Congregationalists. The wealthy metropolitan world of a Jew like Baron Rothschild, whose desire to sit in Parliament was central to the agitation, was not so far removed from that of Yorkshire Baptists to prevent them

---

[86] *British Banner*, 24 May 1848, p. 374.
[87] *Congregational Year Book* for 1848, p. 269.
[88] Lord Macaulay, *Critical and Historical Essays*, London: Longmans, Green, and Co., 1884, p. 135. (This article was originally published in 1831 in the *Edinburgh Review*.)
[89] *Patriot*, 25 October 1847, p. 716.

from taking up the cause of Jewish emancipation.[90] Moreover, denominations less associated with militant Dissent raised their voices on this issue as well. For example, the *Methodist New Connexion Magazine* unequivocally called upon the people of the denomination it represented to play a full part in the agitation on behalf of the Jewish Disabilities Bill: 'We trust that the members of our congregations will not be backward in signing any local petitions that may be got up in favour of this additional tribute to the principles of genuine liberty.'[91] Even the Quaker journal, the *Friend*, believed that the bill established the important principle 'that a man's religious opinions are no criterion of his fitness for political offices'.[92] Josiah Conder noted approvingly in 1853 that on the last occasion when members of Parliament had an opportunity to vote for the removal of Jewish disabilities 'an honourable unanimity was manifest' with not one of the Evangelical Nonconformists voting against it.[93] The Dissenting community – informed by a conviction that the principle of religious equality was a just one – embraced Jewish emancipation.

Lord John Russell introduced a bill for the removal of Jewish disabilities in 1847. Pressure was increased for such legislation by the election of Baron Rothschild for the City of London alongside Russell. The Whig Prime Minister's speech on this occasion was a virtual rehearsal of the ideas of religious equality held by Dissenters. He spoke of 'a question of principle', of 'a matter of right' and of 'a claim to justice' and even made mention of the 'principles of Christianity' which taught 'to do unto others as you would that others should do unto you'.[94] Surely Sir R. H. Inglis had a point when he replied that Russell 'proves too much for his more immediate object'.[95] Most arguments against the admission of Jews followed one of two lines. The first of these was a nationalistic argument which claimed that Jews were not fully integrated into England or were hampered in their patriotism by a divided loyalty (the other part belonging to either world-wide Jewry or an awaited future state of Israel).[96] The nationalistic argument was given a ready-made illustration in Baron Rothschild's 'foreign title'.[97] Inglis said bluntly that the Jews in England were 'strangers . . . whose very

[90] C. E. Shipley (ed.), *The Baptists of Yorkshire*, Bradford: Wm. Byles & Sons, p. 303.
[91] *Methodist New Connexion Magazine*, 51 (1848), p. 47.
[92] *Friend*, Tenth Month [October] 1858, p. 185.
[93] Conder, *Political Position*, p. 66.
[94] *Hansard*, XCV, 1234–48 (16 December 1847).
[95] *Ibid.*, 1252.
[96] For an examination of Jewish life in England during these years, see Bill Williams, *The Making of Manchester Jewry, 1740–1875*, Manchester: Manchester University Press, 1985 [originally 1976].
[97] Lord Stanley was one of the speakers who used this phrase: *Hansard*, XCVIII, 1396 (4 May 1848).

names and titles prove them to be un-English' and as far as he was concerned they 'never can be English'.[98] One cannot help but wonder if he counted in their number his colleague with the un-English name who was destined to be the leader of his party. Perhaps it was to avoid such logical snares that the second line of argument was most often employed – that the admission of Jews would 'unchristianise the legislature'.[99]

In essence, the whole debate boiled down to a religious scrap. Benjamin Disraeli, who supported the bill, summed it up well when he explained that on one side they were promoting 'the principle of religious liberty' while on the other they were defending 'the principle of religious truth'. However, as a good Dissenter might, he claimed that he was also motivated by a concern for religious truth and, in words which would have made any Voluntary proud, he added, 'I have that faith in Christian principles, that I think they will make their own way, and must make their own way, by their own essential power.'[100] Such a comment could tempt one to try to sign him up for disestablishment. Like Russell, he too was forced to prove too much. A few opponents revived the old charge that the Jewish people were collectively responsible for Christ's death, but just as many explicitly repudiated it. It was more typical to accuse them of currently rejecting or hating Jesus Christ. The bishop of St David's, Connop Thirlwall, one of the minority of prelates who supported Jewish emancipation, noted that a Jew could love and respect Jesus without ascribing divinity to him, just as a Unitarian did – an argument which anticipated theological developments of the following century but failed to impress his fellow peers.[101] A. J. Hope, Conservative member for Maidstone, perhaps sensing that anti-Catholicism was more emotive than anti-Semitism, explained to the Commons that the Jews were 'in fact a religious order' which 'recruited itself in every country'.[102] Nonconformists had answers for all of these arguments but, in Parliament, it was usually left to government ministers and the more prominent members to articulate the case for emancipation.

An occasional complaint of those against the admission of Jews which is particularly relevant to this study was the accusation that this change would pave the way for future Dissenting attacks upon the Church. Inglis warned that 'Jew legislation in these walls will be a new argument for the separation of Church and State.'[103] Viscount Mahon, member for

---

[98] *Hansard*, XCV, 1263 (16 December 1847).
[99] C. L. Cumming Bruce, member for Elgin and Nairn Counties, for example, used this phrase to express his opinion: *Ibid.*, XCVII, 1215 (3 April 1848).
[100] *Ibid.*, XCV, 1321–28 (16 December 1847).
[101] *Ibid.*, XCVIII, 1361 (25 May 1848).
[102] *Ibid.*, XCV, 1364–5 (16 December 1847).
[103] *Ibid.*, 1265.

Hertford, felt that when evaluating the bill it was only right also to examine 'the secret and ulterior motives of some of its supporters' who had signed petitions on its behalf on the ground that 'it would finally lead to a separation between the Church and the State'.[104] In the Lords, the bishop of Oxford, Samuel Wilberforce, was even clearer. He revealed to the House that he:

> had looked at the petitions which had been laid upon their Lordships' table, and he found they were almost exclusively from people who belonged to a certain league, which had for its object, . . . destroying the relation between the Church and the State.

He further warned that passing a bill for the relief of Jewish disabilities would sooner or later lead on to that question.[105]

Of course, such people had good reason to be suspicious. They were butting against a worldview propagated by Dissenters who embraced the principle of religious equality and were far from finished applying it. Richard Gardner, member for Leicester, gave a blunt speech which aroused the anger of some of his fellow members. He made it clear that he supported the bill because he supported religious equality and, he claimed, because:

> I think I see in the success of this measure – as successful I have no doubt it will be – a fresh shock to that *quasi* ecclesiastical character of the Government of this country, against which I, for one shall always protest.

He denied that all Christians should rally in opposition to the alleged onslaught upon them, claiming that it was 'in the main a Church of England question'. Quite to the contrary, it appeared to him that the argument in favour was based 'on the cardinal Christian virtues of charity and humility'. He comforted himself with the thought that:

> At all events, I know that out of doors at least, the lamp of Nonconformity has not quite gone out, and that Englishmen have not altogether banished from their minds that principle of immortal truth, that the civil magistrate has no power or jurisdiction in matters of religious belief – a principle which I take to be fatal to the institution of an Established Church, but upon which, and which alone, I found my hearty support of this Bill.[106]

Like so many other issues of particular interest to Dissenters, the right of Jews to sit in Parliament was delayed by a refractory House of Lords.

---

[104] *Ibid.*, XCVIII, 652 (4 May 1848).
[105] *Ibid.*, 1381 (25 May 1848).
[106] *Ibid.*, XCVII, 1219–27 (3 April 1848).

When resistance became untenable a compromise was proposed and adopted whereby each House could decide for itself whether or not it would accept Jewish members in its midst. The Commons acted promptly, devised an alternative oath, and on 6 June 1859 Baron Rothschild and two other Jews who had been elected to the current Parliament duly took their seats.[107] M. C. N. Salbstein's doctoral thesis on the admission of Jews to Parliament, although it focuses on efforts within the Jewish community, is right to admit in the concluding paragraph that 'Jews in Britain won Emancipation as another branch of religious dissent from the Anglican Establishment, rather than as a national minority.'[108] Nonconformists were unwavering friends of Jewish emancipation. When it came to the rights of Jews, militant Dissenters passed the test. Religious equality proved to be more than a euphemism for the interests of Protestant Nonconformists.

The other major issue involving religious equality for non-Christians during this period concerned the treatment of the inhabitants of India. There was a particular focus on this issue once the Indian Mutiny had begun in 1857 and during the couple of years thereafter when the British government needed to settle on the kind of government and policies which it would establish in its aftermath. When examining the sources, it is essential to realise that Nonconformists were pre-occupied, even when using the language of religious equality, with two issues which concerned them as devout Christians: first, the way in which prior to the mutiny the colonial government had actually supported non-Christian religions through policies such as agreeing to undertake the management of Hindu temples and the collection of some Hindu religious taxes; and secondly the way in which it had restricted the religious freedom of Christians by policies which discouraged Britons from proselytising and Indians from converting. Naturally, this was the side of the difficulty which interested the *Wesleyan Methodist Magazine*. With all the questions of conscience which were raging in the subcontinent, its sensibilities were inflamed by the story of 'The One Christian Sepoy', an Indian soldier who was apparently discouraged from converting to Christianity.[109]

No passionate Christian would want to see the government place his

---

[107] *Ibid.*, CLIV, 19 (6 June 1859).
[108] M. C. N. Salbstein, 'The Emancipation of the Jews in Britain, with Particular Reference to the Debate Concerning the Admission of the Jews to Parliament, 1828–1860', Ph.D. thesis, University of London, 1974, p. 434. A revised version has been published: M. C. N. Salbstein, *The Emancipation of the Jews in Britain: The Question of the Admission of the Jews to Parliament, 1828–1860*, London and Toronto: Associated University Presses, 1982.
[109] *Wesleyan Methodist Magazine*, December 1857, pp. 1083–8.

or her religion at a disadvantage. Nevertheless, many Dissenters were also genuinely seeking to create a level playing field and raised their voices for religious equality for Hindus as well. Emotions ran deep over events in India. Some Dissenters were painfully aware of the unjust way in which that country had been treated in the past. When the mutiny occurred, Joseph Sturge felt that an enquiry should be made into the grievances of the population. He made plans to go to India and undertake the project personally before he capitulated to the advice of his friends that it would not be safe to go at that time.[110] On the other hand, Dissenters, like other Britons, were outraged by the atrocities perpetrated by the mutineers. Therefore there was a tendency to want to support British rule in its time of trial. Edward Miall felt, in the words of his son, 'that British supremacy in India should be maintained and retained at any cost'.[111] R. W. Dale, in a series of anonymous articles for the *Eclectic Review* managed to capture both of these moods and with them probably the general opinion amongst radical Nonconformists. In 'The India Mutiny' (December 1857) he offered strictures on the native population, but he also warned against responding in a way that would unleash a domineering established church on the subcontinent. In words familiar from other issues of religious equality, he reminded his audience that:

> All we have a right to ask for Christianity – all she really needs to secure her triumph – all it would be well for her to have – is a fair and open field, and no hindrance from Government.[112]

The Liberation Society did not fail to raise a voice for religious equality in India. In a published letter entitled 'Special Minute on the Future Government of India' dated 18 November 1857 it made its views publicly known. It is worth quoting from it at length. After noting that the government must ensure the protection of Christian organisations, it went on to say:

> But the Government, having thus cleared the stage for the unrestricted pursuit, by Christian societies of every denomination, of their spiritual purposes, should carefully abstain from officially identifying itself with any of them – and neither by contributions from public funds, by grants of public land, by appointment to ecclesiastical office, nor by establishment of ecclesiastical law, should it give countenance to the idea, that to convert the natives to the Christian religion, or to control the efforts of those who within the proper limits of the law seek their conversion, is any part of the business of the State. . . . It will

---

[110] Richard, *Sturge*, pp. 523–8.
[111] Miall, *Miall*, p. 219.
[112] *Eclectic Review*, December 1857, p. 543.

equally devolve upon the Government to guarantee the fullest liberty of worship, teaching, religious celebration and moral efforts to proselytise, to the natives of British India, whatever faith they may profess . . . and to abstain from offering to them any civil or official advantage as an inducement to abandon the faith of their forefathers.[113]

Nor was this a purist stance by the Society which was not echoed in other Dissenting quarters. The *British Quarterly Review*, of all publications, actually praised the Society's statement (which had been published in various newspapers) and did a remarkable job of singing from the same political hymn sheet:

we also contend that the Government should abstain from identifying itself with any society whatever. Neither . . . should the British Government in India give countenance to the idea that to convert the natives to the Christian religion . . . is any part of the business of the Indian Government. The British native in India, no matter what creed he professes, should have full liberty to profess and celebrate it, to teach it, and if he will, to proselytize others to his views. We will go the length of saying, too, that the natives of India should be protected from all insult and injury on account of their religious belief.[114]

The *Baptist Magazine* printed in its correspondence columns a model petition on India, which was, if anything, a stronger statement of religious equality than the Liberation Society's minute:

That your Petitioners deprecate any attempt whatever, on the part of the civil power, to put down, or even to restrain, the idolatries of India . . .
That your Petitioners deprecate any attempt to enforce the Christian Religion upon the inhabitants of India . . . Because, any such act on the part of the British Government in India would be unjust . . .
Your Petitioners, therefore, pray your Honourable House, to adopt such measures as in its wisdom may seem meet, to relieve the Government of India from the responsibility of interfering with religious belief or worship, and invest it with powers definite and adequate to the protection of all civil rights belonging to citizens or the community: and to relieve the inhabitants of India from all such vexations and injuries, as are, and must be produced by the interference of Government with religion . . .[115]

[113] Liberation Society Papers, A/LIB/2, 18 November 1857, inserted, printed item: 'Special Minute on the Future Government of India'.
[114] *British Quarterly Review*, XXVII, LIII (January 1858). p. 219.
[115] *Baptist Magazine*, January 1858, p. 42.

Dissenters even gave some of their time and energy to defending the right to religious equality of the non-Christian population of India.[116]

The application of religious equality was a continuum. The most radical and consistent Nonconformists did not shirk from admitting that their principles could rightly be applied to all citizens, even if they happened to be Hindus, Moslems, Mormons or atheists. However, practical cases which would have tried the strength of these assertions most sorely (like a Moslem being elected to Parliament) did not arise, and those who were reticent to embrace such possibilities even in the abstract could simply plead the implausibility of such occurrences and carry on preaching liberty. Still, it took a certain level of courage for the more militant ones to let their liberal views be known even in regard to hypothetical dilemmas; yet they still did. Lord Ashley, when speaking against Jewish emancipation, slid further down his imagined slippery slope, beyond the inclusion of people from other races and of women into the legislature, to reveal that 'according to the principle laid down . . . not only Jews would be admitted to Parliament, but Mussulmans, Hindoos, and men of every form of faith under the sun of British dominions'.[117] The *Eclectic Review*, however, refused to balk at this spectre:

> Now we are not disposed to deny the fairness of this inference, so far as the principle it involves is concerned. The case put is not likely to become a practical one, but we should not shrink from the principle, even were it otherwise. Electors, we maintain, are the only proper judges of the qualifications of those who represent them in parliament, and should the improbable case ever arise, of their electing a Mussulman, or a Hindoo, our voice would be raised in defence of their right to do so.[118]

John Locke's thoughts on religious liberty, although written in the seventeenth century, were still ahead of the times in the mid-Victorian era. Nevertheless, the Congregationalist, John Rippon, in his work much praised by Dissenting journals, *The Ultimate Principle of Religious Liberty*, chided that great champion of tolerance for depriving atheists

---

[116] This stance on behalf of religious equality by at least some major Dissenting voices is not acknowledged in a recent, relevant article by Ainslie T. Embree and by making 'Evangelical Christians of all denominations' the coercive villains of the piece the opposite is implied: Ainslie T. Embree, 'Christianity and the state in Victorian India: confrontation and collaboration', in R. W. Davis and R. J. Helmstadter (eds), *Religion and Irreligion in Victorian Society*, London: Routledge, 1992, pp. 151–65.

[117] *Hansard*, XCV, 1278 (16 December 1848).

[118] *Eclectic Review*, n.s. XXIII (Jan.–June 1848), p. 382.

of the benefits of his generosity.[119] Religious equality for all was the Dissenting ideal.

Nonconformists in this period were spared the full challenge of religious pluralism. Without question, a more diverse environment would have complicated the situation and more than likely would have altered their thinking in some ways. It is also without question, however, that in the environment which they did inhabit they became the active defenders of the civil rights of others. As bodies, the Established Church, the ancient universities, the House of Lords and the Conservative Party emerged all too often as the defenders of religious discrimination. The other House and the other great political party were at least sporadically sympathetic, but there was no major force in the land which was more a friend of religious equality than Protestant Nonconformity.

[119] [Rippon], *Ultimate Principle*, p. 44.

Chapter Five

STATE EDUCATION

Educational provision in England, like so many other British institutions, became what it was not through the implementation of a visionary plan upon a tabula rasa, but by the continual adaptation of existing structures. After the founding of the British and Foreign School Society in 1809 and the National Society for Promoting the Education of the Poor in the Principles of the Established Church in 1811 (henceforth referred to as the British Society and the National Society respectively), concerned individuals had nationally organised channels through which their zeal for popular education could flow. Nevertheless, these societies did not have resources equal to the enormity of the task and therefore an ever increasing number of people began to advocate government intervention. In response to this demand, Parliament ventured into the field of education in 1833 with a grant of £20,000 which was distributed the following year to schools associated with either the British or the National Society.[1] Another step in the direction of state education was the establishment in 1839 of a committee for the on-going distribution of the annual grant – the Committee of the Privy Council for Education.[2] Government involvement in education continued to increase (save a time of retrenchment for budgetary reasons during the 1860s) and finally culminated in the Education Act of 1870. Increased Parliamentary involvement was a direct response to a widespread conviction that only the government could adequately meet the need. The middle decades of the nineteenth century were marked by the leavening power of a belief in government aid for education, until by the late 1860s it had transformed even most of its fiercest opponents, as our study of the Nonconformists will show.

[1] Francis Adams, *History of the Elementary School Contest in England*, London: Chapman and Hall, 1882 (reprinted: Brighton, Sussex: Harvester Press, 1972), pp. 87–8.
[2] Sir James Kay-Shuttleworth, *Four Periods of Public Education*, London: Longman, Green, Longman and Roberts, 1862 (reprinted: Brighton, Sussex: Harvester Press, 1973), pp. 179–83.

Several abortive efforts were made prior to the years of this study to legislate for a more interventionist government plan than merely awarding grants to private, charitable societies. Conflicting ideas about the kind of religious instruction and control which would or would not be permitted was central to the failure of these schemes. Those which avoided the Scylla of Dissenting hostility were driven into the Charybdis of opposition from the Established Church. Decisively for the attitude of the Nonconformist community at mid-century, the education clauses of Sir James Graham's Factory Bill of 1843 erred on the side of appeasing the Established clergy. His scheme had several key clauses which guaranteed that the educational provision it would create would be controlled by Churchmen. Dissent surprised itself with the force of its own agitation against this measure. Nonconformists across the denominations mobilised their forces as did, crucially, the Wesleyan body. Roman Catholic voices joined the chorus of protest as well. The bill, in its original version, was denounced by a staggering 13,369 petitions containing 1,920,574 signatures and its amended form produced a smaller, but comparable number.[3] For the Congregational denomination particularly – but by no means exclusively – this experience awakened a suspicion of government interference to the point where many of its leaders came to reject the very idea of state education as unsound in principle. Vaughan's *British Quarterly Review* (which did not endorse this trend) observed in 1845:

> The history of Sir James Graham's attempt in the way of peace-making on this question, has placed protestant nonconformists in a new position with regard to it. They have not only declined the overture made by the state in the form proposed, but, as the effect of discussion, have become much more decided than previously in their opposition to state interference with the education of the people in any form.[4]

In other words, the need to articulate a public response sent Dissenters in search of a principle to apply to this matter.

The result was the application of Voluntaryism to education. Its advocates argued that the Scylla and the Charybdis could be avoided because the very journey toward state provision for education was an unnecessary one. The *Nonconformist*, in a typical statement, claimed in 1851 that 'education is no more a part of the business of government, general or municipal, than trade on one hand or religion on the other'.[5]

---

[3] J. T. Ward and J. H. Treble, 'Religion and Education in 1843: Reaction to the "Factory Education Bill"', *Journal of Ecclesiastical History*, XX, 1 (April 1969), pp. 79–110.
[4] *British Quarterly Review*, II, III (August 1845), p. 144.
[5] *Nonconformist*, 28 May 1851, p. 417.

Educational Voluntaryism, although it was not a hardened choice of militant Dissenters prior to 1843 and would be rapidly abandoned by the late 1860s, was in the intervening period a principle which was vehemently defended by many of Dissent's prominent political figures.

The leading Nonconformist champion of educational Voluntaryism was Edward Baines the younger. Baines was a political voice of the same order of eminence amongst Dissenters as Edward Miall and he had the added advantages of an influential family name and newspaper as his inheritance, a clear local base of support, and the ability to get faithfully re-elected to Parliament. The member for Leeds (as he was from 1859 to 1874) was so central to the cause of state non-interference that Voluntaryists were sometimes referred to as 'the Baines party'.[6]

As editor of the family-owned *Leeds Mercury*, Baines had a respected forum for his convictions already to hand. By 1847, Baines had already been in control of the paper for decades and its circulation was at nine thousand copies weekly.[7] This number was a new high for the publication and represented a considerable rise from when the family had bought it at the start of the century as a floundering paper struggling to sell 800 copies weekly.[8] In 1861 the paper was confident enough to capitalise on the abolition of the paper duties and become a daily. It was pleased to report that even though this bold step had been made 'in the worst season of the year' the result was that 'circulation has increased by nearly threefold'.[9] As a general newspaper, readers were offered articles such as 'The Mysterious Glasgow Poisoning Case' and 'Look Under Your Beds. – A Caution to Travellers', and as a local newspaper items of regional interest such as 'Industrial Museums. Their Value and Importance' were included along with items aimed more directly at the town's residents such as an account of 'The Leeds Bachelors' Ball'.[10] Undoubtedly such a publication had its articles on Voluntaryism and other topics of Dissenting interest read by people who would never have thought to buy the *Patriot* or the *Nonconformist*.

Statistics were Baines' political weapon of choice. He approached more than one political opponent with a mountain of figures which he claimed proved his case. When he wrote a series of open letters to Lord John Russell on state education in 1846 no one could accuse him of not

[6] Derek Fraser, 'Edward Baines', in Patricia Hollis (ed.), *Pressure from Without*, London: Edward Arnold, 1974, p. 198.
[7] *Leeds Mercury*, 2 January 1847, p. 5.
[8] *Ibid.*, 4 January 1851, p. 4. For an account of the Baines family's *Mercury* in the first half of the nineteenth century, see Donald Read, *Press and People, 1790–1850*, Westport, Connecticut: Greenwood Press, 1975 (originally 1961), pp. 108–36.
[9] *Leeds Mercury.*, 1 January 1862, p. 2.
[10] *Ibid.*, 11 July 1857, p. 4; 21 August 1863, p. 3; 24 October 1862, p. 2; 15 February 1862, p. 7.

attempting to fulfil his introductory promise: 'I shall pave my way with facts.'[11] When Robert Vaughan, a fellow Congregationalist, criticised these letters, he felt that Baines' reputation as a statistician was sufficiently established that he needed to use his introductory remarks to undermine the faith of 'some zealous believer in Mr. Baines' infallibility on a question of figures'.[12] An article in *The Times*, whose author presumably had the added advantage of not having to mingle with Baines at Congregational Union meetings, commented less deferentially: 'A great arithmetical genius is surprising the provinces.'[13] Armed with a pile of facts, figures and statistics which could tempt an opponent to surrender from sheer exhaustion, Baines advocated the case of purely Voluntary education.

The overwhelming majority of the great and the good of Congregationalism followed Baines' lead, with prominent parts being played by Samuel Morley, Edward Miall and R. W. Hamilton. The Congregational Board of Education became a vehicle for articulating the theory and attempting the practice of educational Voluntaryism, and the Congregational Union itself passed resolutions endorsing this stance.[14] When a young R. W. Dale questioned the validity of the notion that state education was wrong in principle at a Congregational Union meeting in 1861 he found that 'the recognised leaders, almost to a man, were arrayed against him'.[15]

Moreover, this idea proved attractive in many other Dissenting quarters as well. Because Congregationalists were clearly leading this fight, historians have wrongly assumed that hardly anyone else was following them. Richard Johnson, for example, has claimed that Lord John Russell's Minutes on Education of 1846 (which further expanded the role of the state in education) 'received overwhelming support from a majority of religious educators, extreme High Churchmen and Congregationalists apart'.[16] This judgement is particularly misleading because even some Dissenters who did not sustain a commitment to educational Voluntaryism raised their voices against these Minutes because of their failure to be based on the principle of religious equality and their bias

---

[11] Edward Baines, *Letters to the Right Hon. Lord John Russell, First Lord of the Treasury, on State Education*, London: Simpkin, Marshall, & Co., 1846, p. 38.
[12] Robert Vaughan, *Popular Education in England*, London: Jackson & Walford, 1846, p. 5.
[13] *The Times*, 9 April 1847, p. 4. J. R. Lowerson, 'The Political Career of Sir Edward Baines (1800–90)', M.A. thesis, University of Leeds, 1965, p. 151.
[14] Albert Peel, *These Hundred Years: A History of the Congregational Union of England and Wales, 1831–1931*, London: Congregational Union, 1931, pp. 179–83.
[15] Dale, *Dale*, pp. 267–8.
[16] Richard Johnson, 'Educational Policy and Social Control in Early Victorian England', *Past and Present*, 49 (November 1970), pp. 96–119.

toward denominationalism in general and (allegedly) the Church in particular. The Dissenting Deputies, for example, made opposing them its central pre-occupation in 1847 and even went to the extent of including this issue as a test question for Parliamentary candidates in the General Election of that year.[17] Even Robert Vaughan, the leading Congregational supporter of state education, condemned the Minutes.[18]

Michael Watts has recently claimed that educational Voluntaryism was embraced by 'fewer than half of the politically aware Nonconformists'.[19] This assessment, however, crucially depends on his including the Wesleyans in this term. It is difficult to assess the degree to which he believes this statement would hold true if this large, anomalous body was excluded. Watts does quote a passage from the *British Quarterly Review* claiming that the opposition was left to Congregationalists and Baptists, but this journal was a hostile source and an investigation of the opinions held by members of some other denominations does not confirm its judgement. To the extent which Vaughan's journal was speaking the truth, it was concerning the ability of various denominations to mobilise a pressure group response, rather than the views expressed by their organs of opinion. The *Wesleyan Methodist Association Magazine*, for example, fully endorsed the ideology of exclusively Voluntary education. It pronounced on Russell's Minutes in 1847: 'Consistent voluntaries will regard it as inconsistent with their principles to accept the aid thus offered.'[20] Within a few years it could look back on the opposition to these Minutes as formative for the whole approach of Nonconformity to this question: 'At this time, the subject of governmental education was thoroughly investigated, and by the great majority of Dissenters it was declared to be unsound in principle.'[21] The *Methodist New Connexion Magazine* opposed the Minutes vehemently, grounding its stance in its opposition to government control of education generally, and claiming that Dissenters who accept them 'abandon their principles'. For the magazine's own part, it was counselling war:

> Let Dissenters then of every name, let our own Denomination in particular, which has so long and so often boasted of its love of freedom and its hatred of tyranny, unite in one determined course of opposition to a measure fraught with evils of such formidable magnitude.[22]

---

[17] Dissenting Deputies, Ms. 3083, vol. 11, 22 January 1847, p. 360; 19 February 1847, p. 362; 20 December 1847, 'Report of 1847', p. 423.
[18] *British Quarterly Review*, V, X (May 1847), pp. 540–51.
[19] Watts, *Dissenters: Volume II*, p. 551.
[20] *Wesleyan Methodist Association Magazine*, March 1847, p. 128.
[21] *Ibid.*, April 1851, p. 153.
[22] *Methodist New Connexion Magazine*, 50 (1847), p. 192.

Even the *Primitive Methodist Magazine*, which had as its stated policy to avoid all issues of controversy, found ways to lend its support to the agitation. It reprinted a long article by Baines which had appeared in the *Leeds Mercury*, the editor even daring to insert a call to agitation as a postscript:

> We may add that the members of the Primitive Methodist general committee residing in London, deplore, as a whole, the steps now taken by her Majesty's Government on the question of Education, as they appear unfriendly to civil and religious liberty. Such of our friends as view the case in the same light as we do will bestir themselves to petition the House of Commons to leave the education of British youth to the voluntary efforts of parents and the generous public. Most likely, ere these remarks can have reached our readers, the form of a petition will have been sent to our different stations, and have called forth the signatures of tens of thousands of our members and scores of thousands of our hearers.[23]

This stance was maintained in the decade which followed. In a review of a polemic by Baines on the subject of state education, the magazine confided 'without wishing to commit our Connexion to the views of the author, we have no hesitation in stating that our *personal* views on the subject of education are in harmony with his'.[24] Educational Voluntaryism was certainly not bereft of Methodist supporters.

A focal point for educational Voluntaryists in denominations other than Congregationalism was the Voluntary School Association, founded in 1848.[25] Baptists, who of course agreed with Congregationalists on this issue, found this association particularly needful 'prevented as we are from cooperating with the Congregational Board of Education'.[26] The *Baptist Magazine* believed, 'This association is most important . . .'[27] Prominent Baptists who supported it include William Brock, Morton Peto, Dr Cox, J. H. Hinton and Charles Stovel. An examination of the Voluntary School Association also reveals that educational Voluntaryism was attractive to some influential Quakers as well. Indeed, the animating force behind it was a Quaker: G. W. Alexander.[28] Although

[23] *Primitive Methodist Magazine*, XXVIII (1847), pp. 232–40.
[24] *Ibid.*, XXXV (1854), p. 365.
[25] Apparently none of the Association's own records have survived. Its activities, however, can be traced through reports in the press.
[26] This statement was made by William Brock: *Baptist Magazine*, January 1852, p. 43.
[27] *Ibid.*, June 1851, p. 378.
[28] Alexander was chairman at the Association's first annual meeting. *Christian Witness*, VI (1849), p. 257.

his official position in its leadership was treasurer, he was undoubtedly the dominating influence. Alexander was a veteran of the campaigns to abolish slavery and, indeed, continued during this period to serve as the treasurer of the British and Foreign Anti-Slavery Society as well. It is perhaps not surprising that Joseph Sturge – a Friend who frequently went where many other Quakers would not tread – supported the Association; but he was not alone.[29] The *Friend* defended its decision to include a report on a conference of the Voluntary School Association by saying:

> Notwithstanding the great difference of opinion which exists in the present day on the subject of the general education of the people, and . . . even amongst members of our own Society, we believe there is a large number by whom the operations of this Association will be regarded with interest, and to whom they will present a powerful claim.[30]

This report mentions the names of several Quakers including Edward Smith and the journal's own editor, Joseph Barrett. The Congregational peace advocate, Henry Richard, was the honorary secretary of the Voluntary School Association. His friend and biographer, C. S. Miall, provides a generalisation in keeping with the evidence given here, claiming that the Association was supported by 'prominent members of the Baptist body and the Society of Friends', and mentions specifically another influential Quaker, Stafford Allen.[31] The notion of educational Voluntaryism gained notable support from some key publications and figures across a wide spectrum of Dissent.

Educational Voluntaryism was undergirded by several convictions and concerns. One of these was a general suspicion that state education was connected with state religion. The campaigns to remove Dissenting grievances and to achieve disestablishment both bombarded Nonconformists with a hostile image of the work of the government and offered them a frame of reference which could be applied to education. Naturally, the *Nonconformist* would see the education debate through the grid of the disestablishment question, but it was far from alone.[32] Baines himself believed that 'the connexion between State-Religion and State-Education is very intimate'.[33] The *Wesleyan Methodist Association Magazine* was quick to suspect an Anglican conspiracy:

---

[29] Richard, *Sturge*, p. 547.
[30] *Friend*, Twelfth Month [December] 1851, pp. 229–30.
[31] C. S. Miall, *Henry Richard, M.P.*, London: Cassell & Company, 1889, p. 21.
[32] *Nonconformist*, 28 May 1851, p. 417.
[33] Baines, *Letters to Russell*, p. 3.

Already we have been informed, by some of the dignitaries of the Established Church, that they are prepared to avail themselves of the means which the Government scheme will afford of increasing the number of the clergy, by admitting schoolmasters to deacons' orders![34]

The haunting image of the state Church frightened some Dissenters away from state education.

Moreover, as has already been shown, many Dissenters during this period embraced a political philosophy which dictated a narrow role for government. One of Baines' favourite rhetorical techniques was to let his imagination slide down the slippery slope which he believed government grants for education to be. Something as seemingly benign as school inspections could cause him to speak of MPs who:

love Government *surveillance* for its own sake; or at least who have got so much of the *police spirit* that characterizes the statesmen of Germany, as to not be satisfied without something like a universal *espionage* . . .[35]

Baines argued tirelessly that a desire to place education under the aegis of government was a despot's dream and he felt that the logic involved must inevitably lead to state control over the pulpit, the press, and industry as well.[36] Therefore, as far as he was concerned, even if a particular instance of government aid appeared harmless it was not to be trusted. Baines warned, 'When Governments offer their arm, it is like the arm of a creditor or a constable, not so easily shaken off: there is a handcuff at the end of it.'[37] The *Methodist New Connexion Magazine* seemed to see taking a government school grant as almost as dire an action as Adam and Eve eating the forbidden fruit:

if Dissenters can so far forget themselves as to accept of this Government pelf, they must make up their minds to the self-degradation to which they will sink. By so doing they will become dependent on Government patronage, and subject to Government influence. They thus sacrifice their independence, they renounce their freedom, they abandon their principles. Self-reliance, and self-control are the very elements of political and religious freedom, and the moment that we surrender these important prerogatives, that moment the spirit of freedom will

[34] *Wesleyan Methodist Association Magazine*, April 1847, p. 163.
[35] *Leeds Mercury*, 13 February 1847, p. 4.
[36] For examples, see Baines, *Letters to Russell*, pp. 82, 119; *Leeds Mercury*, 13 February 1851, p. 4.
[37] Baines, *Letters to Russell*, p. 137.

expire, and the dignity of our position be exchanged for one of servile debasement.[38]

Many Dissenters believed that educational grants would be the first peep into the Pandora's box of state interference.

Religious Voluntaryism was a fundamental conviction of nearly all Protestants outside the Establishment save some Wesleyans and Unitarians. Many Dissenters were tempted to apply this principle to the question of educational provision. This link had already been made at a conference of influential Congregationalists which met to oppose Sir James Graham's bill in 1843:

> That this meeting, utterly repudiating on the strongest grounds of Scripture and conscience, the receipt of money raised by taxation and granted by Government, for sustaining the Christian religion, feels bound to apply this principle no less to the work of religious education . . . [39]

This connection was only strengthened by Russell's expansion of state involvement beginning in 1846. The *Eclectic Review* commented on this:

> the government scheme has compelled a reference to first principles. Dissenters have been driven home by the force of circumstances to the great radical truth of religious voluntaryism.[40]

Many Dissenters applied their Voluntary convictions regarding the church to the school: the Voluntary Church Associations were the inspiration for the Voluntary School Association.

Critics claimed that only the systematic work of the state could adequately met the educational needs in the country, but Churchmen also said the same thing about the nation's spiritual needs. This was an old war and therefore Dissenters were well used to the weapons and tactics of their opponents. For example, S. R. Maitland, a clergyman from Gloucestershire, wrote a book in the 1830s entitled *The Voluntary System* which endeavoured to show that a ministry adequate to the needs of the people could not be created and maintained without an established church.[41] Therefore, one of the reasons why many Dissenters held to the notion of educational Voluntaryism so tenaciously is that they came to

---

[38] *Methodist New Connexion Magazine*, 50 (1847), p. 192.
[39] The delegates included, besides the younger Edward Baines himself, prominent figures such as Thomas Raffles, J. A. James and John Kelly: Waddington, *Congregational History*, IV, pp. 566–7.
[40] *Eclectic Review*, n.s. XXI (Jan.–June 1847), p. 636.
[41] S. R. Maitland, *The Voluntary System*, second edition, London: J. G. & F. Rivington, 1837.

believe that a concession on this point might be to admit the inadequacy of a 'free church' as well as 'free education'. As the *Eclectic Review* put it:

> And, of course, we could as easily append hereto a number of conclusions we deem quite as just; as that ridicule of voluntary-ism *in re* education is much more appropriate *in re* religion; or that the theory of government which suffers state interference in one, is equally constrained to suffer it in both . . .[42]

The *Baptist Magazine* seemed to fear that to slur educational Voluntary-ism might be to impute the divine plan:

> It should never be forgotten, that when our Lord cast the support of Christianity upon the spontaneous offerings of his people, it was not an arbitrary law, having no reason but his own author-ity. He adopted it because it was, in its own nature, the principle best adapted to the end in view.[43]

Many Nonconformists looked to the driving beliefs of the chapel when considering how best to promote the school.

Chapel, by instilling a sense of duty, inspired people to support charitable endeavours voluntarily. Many Nonconformists felt that there were vital spiritual reasons which demanded that social under-takings should be performed on this basis. They believed that to accept one's duty was a sanctifying, Christian act, while to help someone to shirk theirs was to be a stumbling block. Therefore, Dissenters were keenly committed to establishing whose 'duty' education was. The *Leeds Mercury* felt that the whole education muddle was produced by the adoption of the erroneous principle that '*it is the duty of Government to teach the people*'.[44] Instead, the paper argued it was the duty of parents to provide for their children's schooling.[45] The *Eclectic Review* spoke of 'the primary law of nature, which constitutes the parent the responsible guardian of the child', adding:

> Not only should domestic ties be held sacred, but the obligations and responsibilities of the family should be developed and strengthened rather than infringed or neutralised. It is the parent's duty to provide education for the child . . .[46]

Government education, according to this view, would undermine the moral order by severing parents from one of their natural duties.

G. R. Searle has recently made the seminal observation that the

[42] *Eclectic Review*, n.s. XXIII (Jan.–June 1848), p. 118.
[43] *Baptist Magazine*, February 1847, p. 97.
[44] *Leeds Mercury*, 5 June 1847, p. 4.
[45] *Ibid.*, 30 April 1862, p. 2.
[46] *Eclectic Review*, n.s. XXII (July–Dec. 1847), p. 591.

generous way which some wealthy and middle-class Congregationalists supported efforts to educate children from the lower classes was inconsistent with some of the rhetoric of educational Voluntaryism.[47] Whilst Searle concentrates on the logic of free trade, this point could be made in regard to the duties of parents as well. Indeed, the Baptist minister, J. H. Hinton, who represented the educational Voluntaryists before a Parliamentary committee in 1853, conceded this point, arguing that 'efforts to promote popular education on the voluntary principle have erred by excess of benevolence'. More practical minds, less preoccupied with theological niceties, did not have much time for his objection to education paid for by a local rate:

> Why do you put things out of the order of God's Providence? You make me provide that for myself by a rate which God meant I should provide as a parent for my children by a different state of feeling.[48]

The damage done to the case of the Voluntaryists by conceding that philanthropists could also deprive parents of their duty could be minimised by highlighting another pillar which upheld the divinely-designed social order: the duties of the rich. Naturally, Nonconformists were not blind to the fact that some parents were not unwilling but simply unable to finance their children's schooling. It was at this point of genuine need where assisting the poor became the duty of those who were more fortunate. Nevertheless, it would not be a solution to provide for the education of these children through taxation because this would upset the moral economy. As Edward Miall put it:

> No moral change can happen to a man calculated more extensively to affect his destiny, than that which removes him from the sphere of "you ought" to that of "you shall". It brings the growth of his character under subjection to an entirely opposite set of conditions.[49]

Nonconformists like Miall believed that the voluntary fulfilment of the duty of the better off toward the poor was a divinely established relationship which preserved the stability and health of a society. Therefore:

---

[47] G. R. Searle, *Entrepreneurial Politics in Mid-Victorian Britain*, Oxford: Oxford University Press, 1993, pp. 243–4.

[48] J. H. Hinton, *A Review of the Evidence taken before a Committee of the House of Commons in relation to the Scheme of Secular Education*, London: J. Haddon & Son, 1854 (reprinted: Manchester: E. J. Morten, 1972), pp. 18–19.

[49] Edward Miall, 'On the Non-Interference of the Government with Popular Education', in Congregational Board of Education, *Crosby-Hall Lectures on Education*, London: John Snow, 1848, p. 148.

> To take education into the hands of Government, would be rudely to break the ties which are thus uniting and harmonizing the different classes of society.[50]

Advocates of public education, Voluntaryists argued, had not adequately calculated the disastrous consequences which would flow from depriving the rich of their traditional role as philanthropists and benefactors.

The current campaign for national education was, to them, a flight from duty which did not bode well for the future. Miall confessed, in keeping with Boyd Hilton's portrait of the old-style Victorian Evangelical:

> I augur no lasting good to society from the very general disposition of the present age to merge individual responsibility into that of civil government, and to perform our duty to our neighbour by a sort of public proxy, – thus attempting to evade the penalties of our own indolence and selfishness, by purchasing a joint-stock substitute for fulfilling our solemn trust.[51]

Baines, with apocalyptic fervour, saw the destruction of the moral economy which Voluntaryism had hitherto sustained as 'one of the greatest moral and social calamities that could happen to the nation'.[52]

Consequentially, if a choice had to be made between a more systematic provision of education and the continuation of Voluntaryism, Miall knew where his priorities lay: 'Increased sense of duty is more to be desired than increased knowledge.' He would not accept 'this novel and overstretched claim' that 'the poor man has the luxury of demanding the education of his offspring as a right rather than a boon'.[53] The *Patriot* also feared the day when 'education would come to be regarded as a favour conferred upon [sic] the State, instead of a duty which every parent is bound to perform to his children'.[54] R. W. Dale, whose instincts often lay in the sensibilities of the future, would seize the moment of the turning tide to argue in 1867 that children had a 'right' to education, but in the preceding decades his ministerial colleagues were overwhelmingly committed to the language of 'duty'.[55]

An exploration of the ideas and actions of Nonconformists would help to illuminate the discussion of education as a means of social control which has been pursued by some historians. Richard Johnson, for

---

[50] Baines, *Letters to Russell*, p. 132.
[51] Congregational Board, *Crosby-Hall Lectures*, p. 151. Hinton, *Age of Atonement*, pp. 256–60.
[52] Baines, *Letters to Russell*, p. 119.
[53] Congregational Board, *Crosby-Hall Lectures*, pp. 159, 146.
[54] *Patriot*, 30 April 1858, p. 276.
[55] *English Independent*, 7 March 1867, pp. 310–11.

example, has made an impressive case for the proposition that proponents of national education were seeking to by-pass parental authority in order to control the emerging generation.[56] The educational Voluntaryists, by rejecting state involvement, exempted themselves from this charge. Social control can of course be attempted through private as well as public institutions. Nevertheless, the distinctive position of the educational Voluntaryists – who were the majority of Dissenting voices on this issue – does not fit well even into this more general category. Historians of social control, however, although they have occasionally noted more subtle differences between Dissenting and Anglican educators, have thus far failed to mention this much more sweeping difference.[57] It is possible that some scholarship has been hampered by the premature adoption of an assumption that Evangelicalism is virtually synonymous with social control. Therefore, it is important to highlight this neglected observation: the other side of the coin of the insistence by educational Voluntaryists that education was the duty of parents was their assertion of the right of parents from the lower classes to control the socialisation of their own children. J. H. Hinton was completely unequivocal on this point in his evidence to Parliament:

> I do not wish popular education to be (as Sir Kay Shuttleworth phrases it) "in the hands of the religious communions." On the contrary, what I wish to see is the self-education of the working classes, or parents everywhere attending to the education of their own children; and under such circumstances I should be most happy to witness the dissolution of all the educational societies which religious communions have formed, and which, for the time, have been of such great advantage.[58]

One of his chief recommendations to the Committee was that parents from the lower classes should have more control over the schools in their communities, believing that a serious error 'has been committed in excluding the poorer classes entirely from the management, and from all share in the management, of the schools provided for their children'.[59] Moreover, one of the principle concerns of the educational Voluntaryists themselves was that educational provision by the government would be used as a means of social control. A question from the *Baptist Magazine* is a typical expression of their apprehensions: 'Who shall assure us that

[56] Johnson, 'Educational Policy and Social Control'.
[57] None of the essays in a major volume on this subject explores the possibility that the educational Voluntaryists might not fit the social control model in some significant ways: Phillip McCann (ed.), *Popular Education and Socialization in the Nineteenth Century*, London: Methuen & Co., 1977.
[58] Hinton, *Review*, p. 27.
[59] *Ibid.*, p. 19.

the school will not be made the means of training the people in political subserviency, and thus prove a mighty bulwark against the advances of liberty?'[60] Those who employ the concept of social control have an unhelpful tendency to find it everywhere, and perhaps especially wherever Evangelicals can be found.[61] Nevertheless, it cannot be applied in an unqualified way to the work of the numerous mid-Victorian Evangelical Dissenters who were educational Voluntaryists.[62]

Educational Voluntaryism, grounded ideologically in the sensibilities already discussed such as suspicion of the state and the moral virtue of freely choosing an appropriate option, was also advocated on the basis of some practical concerns. Particularly, educational Voluntaryists claimed it was unwise to embark on a plan for national education because the costs would prove prohibitive. They could only continually point back to their original prediction as government expenditure on schooling rose year by year. The *Leeds Mercury* observed in 1857:

> SIR JAMES SHUTTLEWORTH informs us that the Education Grant in this year is to be £540,000: last year it was £450,000: the year before £350,00; and a few years before £100,000. This is a pretty rate at which the Committee of Council are throwing about the public money.[63]

This was unquestionably a phenomenal progression from the original grant of £20,000 for 1834, and it would continue to rise by hundreds of thousands in the following couple of years. Moreover, to some Nonconformists much of this expenditure could be viewed as so much wasted money. Edward Baines had warned the nation early in the game, in a delightful dovetail of Nonconformist pre-occupations: 'Public money is held as in the trembling hand of a drunkard, whereas private money is held with the steady grasp of a teetotaller.'[64] The educational Voluntaryists argued that, literally as well as spiritually and morally, the nation could not afford state education.

Finally, a considerable portion of the debate surrounding the choice between voluntary and state provision for schools revolved around assessing the existing situation. Edward Baines unleashed his full statistical powers in an effort to prove that a surprising number of

---

[60] *Baptist Magazine*, February 1847, p. 98.
[61] F. M. L. Thompson has written a telling critique of the way this concept tends to become all-embracing in the minds of its users: 'Social Control in Victorian Britain', *Economic History Review*, 2nd series, XXXIV, 2 (May 1981), pp. 189–208.
[62] Michael Watts has also critiqued the sweeping way the activities of Dissenters are judged by historians of social control: Watts, *Dissenters: Volume II*, pp. 627–8.
[63] *Leeds Mercury*, 10 February 1857, p. 2.
[64] Baines, *Letters to Russell*, p. 111.

children were already receiving some schooling or had a local option available and therefore the remaining challenge was not so insurmountable as to warrant government intervention. Much of this was based on a comparison of how many pupils existing schools could accommodate with how many children should be receiving an education. In 1847, he calculated that England and Wales were short 'a mere 61,345 school places *at most*', a gap which private initiatives could undoubtedly fill when one realised that 'there has been an increase of school accommodation to the enormous extent of 50 per cent. within the short space of thirteen years!'[65] The *Leeds Mercury* claimed in 1851 that Manchester had more schools places than '*could by any possibility be used*' and by 1854 it had extended this to the whole nation, claiming that the quantity of school accommodation was 'positively beyond the demand'.[66] Such calculations brought Baines to the conclusion that, as he declared it afresh in 1857: '*There is no need for any legislative interference on behalf of education.*'[67]

Many contemporaries rose up to dispute Baines' calculation of school places. Moreover, even if his statistics had been reasonably accurate, larger questions would have still remained such as: Were not the surplus school sittings in cities whilst numerous rural children were deprived of any facilities? Could parents afford to send their children to the existing schools? What was the quality of education the existing schools were offering? The last question was particularly thrust upon Baines because it was felt that he was allowing 'schools' which did not actually educate to swell his figures. He responded glibly:

> It is said that dame schools are mere places for keeping children out of mischief. If it were so, according to the recollection I have of myself and my early contemporaries, this would be no small achievement . . .[68]

But the issue could not be dismissed with a quip. Moreover, by arguing so passionately about the statistics the Voluntaryists tacitly conceded that they did not completely believe that their notions of duty and principle should, at any price, come before education and therefore, as their wishful thinking became increasingly exposed, it was not completely unpredictable that they would re-evaluate their position. However, that day of reckoning did not come for Baines until 1867. Throughout most of the middle decades of the mid-nineteenth century the editor from Leeds claimed – on behalf of the Voluntaryists – that the national outcry

---

[65] *Ibid.*, pp. 34, 39.
[66] *Leeds Mercury*, 21 April 1851, p. 1; 21 January 1854, p. 4.
[67] *Ibid.*, 3 March 1857, p. 2.
[68] Baines, *Letters to Russell*, p. 55.

over the state of schooling was seen to be unduly alarmist when examined in the light of the facts.

Although the extent of the influence of educational Voluntaryism has been underrated, it would be just as unhelpful, in an effort to correct this impression, to fail to highlight the views of those who did not accept this ideology. Dissenters had hoped that the Wesleyan body would join with them in opposing the government's educational plans in 1847 just as it had done in 1843 in response to the educational clauses of Sir James Graham's Factory Bill. The *Leeds Mercury* wrote on 13 March 1847 regarding the pending meeting of Wesleyan leaders to discuss the denomination's educational policy: 'we confidently anticipate a very strong opposition to the Government measure'.[69] The paper's confidence was ill-founded. The Wesleyan minister, Thomas Cutting, writing to Jabez Bunting on the very same day, articulated the opinion which the denomination would adopt:

> I trust that there will be no pandering in this instance to the Anti-Church and State, alias purely Dissenting, objects of the party who are decrying the *government new scheme*! I myself conceive that its *main* principles are *sound*, and such as (if generally understood and adopted) *will prevent in future years* the possible introduction of a *purely secular*, alias semi-infidel, movement. I believe also that the *general* arrangement (if approved and employed by us) will prove itself *permanently* advantageous to *Methodism*, and not antagonistic, as some suppose, and Mr. Baines would have us to believe.[70]

When the Nonconformists learned that the largest body outside the Establishment had rejected pure educational Voluntaryism many of them were bitter. The *Eclectic Review* was so livid that it feared it could not discuss the position of the Wesleyans 'without speaking in terms which may be deemed discourteous and condemnatory to the leaders of the methodist body'.[71] When the actual situation was made public all the *Patriot* could do was offer vague threats: 'The strange conduct of the Wesleyan leaders, in connexion with the Government Scheme of Education, will not soon be forgotten.'[72]

---

[69] *Leeds Mercury*, 13 March 1847, p. 4.
[70] Thomas Cutting to Jabez Bunting, 13 March 1847: W. R. Ward (ed.), *Early Victorian Methodism: The Correspondence of Jabez Bunting, 1830–1858*, Oxford: Oxford University Press, 1976, p. 349. For a public explanation of their position, see *Wesleyan Methodist Magazine*, May 1847, pp. 499–506.
[71] *Eclectic Review*, n.s. XXI (Jan.–June 1847), p. 641.
[72] *Patriot*, 3 May 1847, p. 293. The position of the Wesleyan body in regard to state education has been explored in detail by David Hempton in his article, 'Wesleyan Methodism and Educational Politics in Early Nineteenth-century

Even in 1847 Wesleyans were not the only people outside the Establishment to reject educational Voluntaryism. Particularly, many Unitarians supported government aid for schools. The *Inquirer*, a Unitarian journal 'devoted to Truth, Freedom and Charity', wrote sympathetically about Baines' educational writings early in 1847, feeling that he had many legitimate concerns. However, when the rigidity of his position was fully comprehended the paper broke ranks, baffled that 'the clamour of a portion of the Dissenters has veered round to a protest against any Government assistance at all'.[73] When the backlash from the *Patriot* and the *Nonconformist* started to mount, the paper patiently tried to explain its position. It did believe in Voluntaryism but 'the principle of our Voluntaryism in Religion does not of necessity carry us to Voluntaryism in Education'. Nevertheless, it demanded that religious equality be guarded and that charitable efforts be encouraged and government only be permitted to interfere when absolutely necessary. However, that time had arisen, for the paper noted, with a side poke at Baines' statistical argument about school accommodation: 'How anybody can at all pretend to be satisfied with popular education as it is, we can hardly understand.'[74] Unitarian opinion on this issue was closer to that of the Wesleyan body than that of most of the leaders of Congregationalism.

Even some Dissenters within the ranks of the Congregationalists opposed educational Voluntaryism. Robert Vaughan – the well-respected president of one of the denomination's institutions for ministerial training, Lancashire Independent College – ruffled the feathers of many of his co-religionists by publicly criticising Baines' opinions. Vaughan could not swallow the extreme position in which adherence to principle was leaving Congregationalists:

> It was one thing, also, to reject the agency of the state in popular education, when proffered after the manner set forth in Sir James Graham's Factory Bill; and it is another to resolve on rejecting all aid from that quarter, though based on principles of the strictest equality, and tendered in a manner which may warrant us in believing that the overture proceeds from just and patriotic intentions.[75]

Thus freed from the dogma colouring the perspective of his peers, he went on to launch an attack on the validity of Baines' statistics. On the

England', *History of Education*, 8 (1979), 3, pp. 207–221; and in chapter six of his *Methodism and Politics in British Society, 1750–1850*, London: Hutchinson, 1987 (originally 1984).
[73] *Inquirer*, 6 March 1847, p. 147.
[74] *Ibid.*, 20 March 1847, pp. 177–8.
[75] Vaughan, *Popular Education*, p. 7.

constructive side of the argument, he hinted at the potential viability of a more secular model for national education, arguing that it was time to learn to distinguish 'between man as a citizen and man as a Christian'.[76]

Other Congregationalists counter-attacked. Baines liked to refer to Robert Vaughan and W. F. Hook, a High Church vicar with his own educational plan, in the same breath as 'the two Doctors', thus discreetly emphasising the fact that Vaughan was not in step with his own religious community.[77] Many leaders of Congregational opinion found Vaughan's stance particularly annoying because it allowed their opponents to pretend that their community was deeply divided, when in fact the president of Lancashire Independent College had few troops behind him. The frustration behind the *Baptist Magazine*'s question is readily apparent:

> we feel authorised to ask, How far has Dr. Vaughan a moral right to wound voluntaryism by his incautious judgments, and to use the British Quarterly as the exponent of his views?[78]

The *Eclectic Review* gave full support to the *Patriot*'s vehement attacks on Vaughan:

> we think 'The Patriot' justified, and we give honour to it for its courage, in charging upon Dr. Vaughan all the discord, with the consequent weakness and reproach, experienced by evangelical dissenters in this matter.[79]

The Congregational minister, J. G. Rogers, remembered in later life the Congregational Union meeting at York in 1847:

> At one of the pleasant supper-parties which we had during that interesting week, I happened to be amongst a number of leading Dissenters, and I was surprised to hear the way in which they attacked Dr. Vaughan and his views, of which, I believe, I was the only defender present.[80]

Vaughan indeed was a lonely voice. In the crucial years in the 1840s, when the denomination's policy was formed, influential Congregationalists who agreed with him publicly could probably be counted on one hand. The *Eclectic Review* exposed the fact that a Vaughan-led 'Meeting

[76] Vaughan, *Popular Education*, p. 18.
[77] For example, Baines, *Letters to Russell*, p. 67. For Hook's views, see W. R. W. Stephens, *The Life and Letters of Walter Farquar Hook*, London: Richard Bentley & Son, 1881, pp. 262–7, 345–8, 403–8.
[78] *Baptist Magazine*, February 1847, p. 100.
[79] *Eclectic Review*, n.s. XXIII (Jan.–June 1848), p. 106.
[80] J. G. Rogers, *J. Guinness Rogers: An Autobiography*, London: James Clarke & Co., 1903, p. 195.

of Friends of Popular Education, resident in Manchester and Salford' which released a statement in favour of government education actually consisted of only thirteen people, one acting as chairman and all the rest having to either move or second one of the six resolutions passed. Moreover, some of them had quickly recanted.[81] The editor of the *British Quarterly Review* was forced to admit that his opinions were shared by 'some half-dozen public-spirited men'.[82] A few other scholarly Congregationalists affirmed the possibility of state education: Vaughan's colleague at Lancashire Independent College, Samuel Davidson, and Henry Rogers at Spring Hill College.[83] Thomas Binney was another Congregationalist of particular note who did not endorse the ideology of educational Voluntaryism.[84] R. W. Dale, who wished it had been otherwise, defined the relative strength within Congregationalism of the two sides of this controversy in this way:

> A few of the leaders – Mr. Binney, for example, and for many years Dr. Vaughan – held out against the prevailing opinion; but they were in a small minority; and denominational feeling, as represented by Mr. Edward Miall in the *Nonconformist*, denied their right to speak for the Congregational churches in general.[85]

And so Congregationalists largely fell in line with Baines' stance. The *British Banner*, for example, began the period under consideration open to the possibility that a national scheme of secular education might be devised which could be acceptable. Before it was far into 1848, however, it announced that the paper had 'after much meditation and long delay, made up our minds to merge our differences as to the subject of secular tuition, and to unite heart and hand with the Congregational Board of Education'.[86] By the end of the year it had moved from resisting the dogma of educational Voluntaryism to boasting that it had been in the forefront of bringing these great principles before the people.[87]

By the autumn meeting of the Congregational Board of Education in 1861 even Vaughan himself had had enough. He used the occasion

---

[81] *Eclectic Review*, n.s. XXII (July–Dec. 1847), pp. 494–5.
[82] *British Quarterly Review*, VI, XII (November 1847), pp. 536–7.
[83] Anne Davidson, *Autobiography and Diary of Samuel Davidson*, Edinburgh: T. & T. Clark, 1899, pp. 29–30. R. W. Dale, *History of English Congregationalism*, London: Hodder and Stoughton, 1907, p. 669. The *Eclectic Review* noted that, of the thirteen men at Vaughan's Manchester meeting: '*Four* of these gentlemen consisted of two tutors, the secretary, and the treasurer of Lancashire Independent College.' *Eclectic Review*, n.s. XXII (July–Dec. 1847), pp. 494–5.
[84] *Ibid.*, XI, pp. 261–8.
[85] Dale, *Dale*, p. 267.
[86] *British Banner*, 23 February 1848, pp. 129–30.
[87] *British Banner*, 29 December 1848, preface to the index for the year.

publicly to join the educational Voluntaryists. Vaughan joked that he was 'one of the repentant sinners' mentioned by a previous speaker and cleverly gave as the justification for his action the one feature of the debate which had actually changed, claiming (according to the *Nonconformist*) that 'it never entered his mind' in the 1840s that so much public expenditure would eventually be drained into schooling. Who would have thought, he wondered, that the curriculum would have spiralled out from its original brief of reading and writing and perhaps a little arithmetic to include such subjects as astronomy and botany? Vaughan now claimed, with the zeal of a new convert, that no 'graver or a more important question' faced Dissenters and Englishmen than 'the question of how we were to get rid of this entire system'. He closed with an appeal to those who 'looked at this subject as he had to look at it again as he had done'. The *Nonconformist* went on to report that when the freshly vindicated Edward Baines addressed the gathering he 'commenced by expressing the pleasure he had experienced in listening to the speech of his friend Dr. Vaughan'.[88]

Little did Vaughan imagine that if he could have held on for just a few more years it would be his opponents who would have looked at the subject again. But as Vaughan capitulated, others rose to take his place. R. W. Dale, who was still in his first year at Spring Hill College when Vaughan had endured so much opposition in 1847, rose just minutes after the editor of the *British Quarterly Review* to say that he supported government aid for schools and therefore did not subscribe to the Congregational Board of Education or its 'great abstract principle'.[89] Dale represented a new generation which had been convinced by the arguments in favour of disestablishment and religious equality, but were unconvinced by the arguments for government non-interference. Dale himself made this point when discussing opposition to educational Voluntaryism:

> Many of the younger Congregationalists were wholly dissatisfied with the theory that the State has no other function than to protect the subject against force and fraud. They had taken their degrees at the London University, which was partly supported by a Parliamentary grant . . .[90]

These unnamed men, however, were apparently, until the second half of the 1860s, either unwilling to raise their voices or lacking in the power to be heard when they did. And this alleged support is a point which easily could be overplayed. J. Guinness Rogers, one of the very few members of

---

[88] *Nonconformist*, 16 October 1861, pp. 827–9.
[89] *Ibid.*
[90] Dale, *English Congregationalism*, p. 669.

this younger generation of Congregationalists whose opinion during those years is known, imbibed the ideology of educational Voluntaryism, despite being a student at Vaughan's Lancashire Independent College.[91] Nevertheless, state non-interference was not a pure principle, and the weight of Congregational opponents to the prevailing opinion on this issue has no counterpart during these years in regard to issues such as disestablishment and Jewish emancipation.

Lord John Russell's Minutes on Education of 1846, which set the tone for government policy throughout the period under discussion, dealt with the religious problem by granting money to qualified schools, irrespective of whether their religious instruction was Anglican, Dissenting, Wesleyan or (eventually) Roman Catholic. Congregational and Baptist educational Voluntaryists objected to this, amongst other reasons, on the grounds that it was indiscriminate endowment – their tax money was going to support the teaching of doctrines which they did not approve.[92] One alternative to this would be some kind of generic religious instruction which would have been inoffensive to the vast majority of the population. This option, however, was rarely championed by Dissenters during these years. Nonconformists generally felt that it was either impossible in practice or a violation of either the principle that the government should not support religion or of the religious equality of excluded minorities such as Secularists.[93] The notion of the state introducing a national system of secular education, however, was attractive to a significant number of influential Dissenters. We have already noted that Vaughan was hoping for this, as did the *British Banner* before it bowed to the pressure of the educational Voluntaryists. Campbell's newspaper declared in 1848:

> In a word, then, we stand prepared for a system of Secular Education that shall be truly national, – a system in which neither Catholicism nor Protestantism, Church nor Dissent, shall appear . . .[94]

This dream was not new in Dissenting circles. As far back as 1839, the Congregational divine, John Pye Smith, had confided to Samuel Morley: 'My own opinion is decidedly in favour of a national measure of purely secular education, which millions would cry down as *infidel and*

---

[91] Rogers, *Rogers*, p. 194.
[92] *Eclectic Review*, n.s. XXI (Jan.–June 1847), p. 513.
[93] An effort had been made in Liverpool, in imitation of an Irish scheme, to find a generic Christianity which would be acceptable to both Protestants and Roman Catholics: James Murphy, *The Religious Problem in English Education: The Crucial Experiment*, Liverpool: Liverpool University Press, 1959.
[94] *British Banner*, 23 February 1848, pp. 129–30.

atheistic.'[95] And although opinions narrowed and hardened in the decade which followed, this sentiment was not entirely snuffed out. The Congregational Union's annual report for 1847 noted that on the issue of state education its meetings had:

> re-affirmed, without alteration or addition, the recorded declaration of the Educational Conference held in London in 1843; namely, that our churches cannot combine to promote any education, which shall not so include religious teaching as must exclude State assistance. Neither meeting gave any judgment on the abstract question, "Whether it be possible for Government to aid merely secular education?" It is likely that neither meeting would have been unanimous on that point . . ."[96]

Dissenters who believed that this was the way forward had a focus for their energies once the Lancashire Public School Association had been founded in 1847 (becoming the National Public School Association in 1850). The Association argued that its secular scheme was the only one in keeping with perfect fairness:

> As all should contribute to the support of public schools, so all should have the right of admission to them. And in order that none may be directly or indirectly debarred from the exercise of this right, nothing should be taught in the schools which would practically exclude any. All catechisms and creeds should, as a measure of simple justice to all, be strictly excluded.[97]

Moreover, this Association received its lifeblood from Dissent. It was conceived by a group of Dissenters literally in the vestry of Lloyd Street Chapel. This Presbyterian congregation's minister, William McKerrow, was himself a founder and key supporter of the Association as well as being a militant religious Voluntary. This meeting also included prominent Quakers: Jacob Bright and Samuel Lucas.[98] Vice-presidents of the Association included Unitarians such as William Scholefield, MP for Birmingham, and William Briggs of Leicester.[99] Moreover, even a number of prominent Congregationalists supported it. For example, the Association's correspondence reveals the support of the cotton master, Elkanah Armitage, and the member of Parliament, James

---

[95] Hodder, *Morley*, p. 68.

[96] *Congregational Year Book* for 1848, p. 20.

[97] Anon., *A Plan for the Establishment of a General System of Secular Education in the County of Lancaster*, London: Simpkin and Marshall, 1847, p. 4.

[98] J. M. McKerrow, *Memoir of William McKerrow*, London: Hodder and Stoughton, 1881, p. 155.

[99] National Public School Association, *Report of the Executive Committee . . . 1855*, Manchester: Alexander Ireland and Co., 1855.

Kershaw.[100] A hand-written invitation list for a breakfast meeting to be hosted by Kershaw and addressed by Richard Cobden comprises twenty-one names including McKerrow's and Cobden's himself, but also the Congregationalists Samuel Davidson (who other sources reveal was an active supporter), Robert Vaughan and Dr Robert Halley.[101] Edward Swaine, a regular figure on the committee of the Congregational Union, supported the National Public School Association and even went so far as to publish a pamphlet defending its views against the attacks of the *Eclectic Review*.[102] A not inconsiderable minority of influential Dissenters pursued the goal of secular state education.[103]

Educational Voluntaryists, in response to this option, argued that religion was a vital component in a child's education. The *Patriot*'s response to the Lancashire Public School Association was typical of many:

> The Scriptures have failed; try history and geography, music and mathematics! O ye wise men of Lancashire! is this, indeed, your nostrum for the removal of popular ignorance, crime, and social disorder?[104]

This pose, however, was easy to strike for those who did not even feel the need to find an acceptable form of state education.

A central reason why some Dissenters endorsed the idea of secular education was because they saw it as the best way to uphold the principle of religious equality when endeavouring to meet the educational needs of the country. Removing religious teaching from the curriculum guaranteed that government money would not be used to support a particular religion and that no child would be subjected to religious influences which undermined the convictions of his or her parents – however unrepresentative of the thinking of most Englishmen and women those beliefs might be. The clergyman, W. F. Hook, who was one of the more liberal voices in the educational debate from within the Established Church, nevertheless was fundamentally opposed to religious equality for Secularists. He wrote in 1850:

---

[100] Manchester, Manchester Central Library, Local Studies Unit, National (Formerly Lancashire) Public School Association Papers, M136/2/3/4, letter from Elkanah Armitage, 23 October 1848; M136/2/3/1949, letter from James Kershaw, 20 October 1848.

[101] *Ibid.*, M136/2/3/1951, 'Copy and List: Mr Kershaw's Breakfast', 17 January 1851. Davidson, *Davidson*, p. 29.

[102] *Wesleyan Methodist Association Magazine*, March 1852, pp. 118–20.

[103] The history of the National Public School Association has been discussed in Anthony Howe, *The Cotton Masters, 1830–1860*, Oxford: Clarendon Press, 1984, pp. 215–29.

[104] *Patriot*, 27 January 1848, p. 60.

Now you will observe here that infidelity has taken a new shape. It is a sect, demanding to be tolerated. . . . And if we do not look about us, depend upon it, we shall have secular schools established by Government and controlled by the ratepayers, to which we shall be denied access. If *we* had moved first, our offer might have been liberal, but we should have gained control of the schools.[105]

Dissenters who supported secular education, by contrast, were sensitive to the rights of Secularists. Dr McKerrow, for example, felt that the plan of the National Public School Association was needed because under the existing system:

> those who are opposed to Christianity, those who do not wish that the schoolmaster should meddle with doctrinal subjects, or the religious instruction of children, and those who have not in the locality in which they reside any denominational school harmonizing with the sentiments they entertain, if they would have their children instructed at all, must send them where opinions which they do not agree with are inculcated.[106]

Those Dissenters who supported secular education did so, not because they did not value religious instruction, but because they valued religious equality.

Moreover, religious equality was central to the thinking of the educational Voluntaryists as well. Apparently, no historian has ever highlighted this point and some have argued the opposite. For example, Francis Adams, the Victorian father of historians of English educational provision, claimed that the educational Voluntaryists were fighting for 'the control of education by religious denominations'.[107] Elie Halévy saw a great deal of spiritual pride in the position of the Dissenters, but was blind to their concern for religious equality.[108] One of the reasons why objections to the Minutes of Education of 1846 was so widespread in Dissent – wider than the camp of the educational Voluntaryists – was that, by making religious instruction a condition of receiving government grants, it violated the principle of religious equality by excluding Secularists. R. W. Hamilton noted this point in his address as chairman of the Congregational Union in 1847:

> Though we might not agree to an absolute unanimity on certain abstract and residuary points, – as it [the plan established by the Minutes] was declared to be designedly and necessarily a scheme

---

[105] W. F. Hook to W. P. Wood, 3 December 1850: Stephens, *Hook*, p. 490.
[106] Hinton, *Review*, p. 26.
[107] Adams, *Elementary School*, p. 129.
[108] Halévy, *English People*, IV, p. 129.

160

of religious education, we have, it is believed, with one voice, repudiated it.[109]

This was not a purely theoretical concern: the Manchester Model Secular School was forced to introduce religious elements into its teaching in 1861 as it could no longer sustain itself without accepting government aid.[110] Educational Voluntaryists maintained their concern for the plight of Secularists in regard to national education throughout this period. It is extraordinary that the first comment the *Congregational Year Book* made about the government's Revised Code for educational policy in 1861 concerned what it did not change: 'This document makes no alteration in the religious condition of the present system – the teaching of religion in the school is necessary in order to obtain aid . . .'[111] This preoccupation with religious equality even for Secularists was maintained right to the end of educational Voluntaryism. When Dissenters were ready to find a way out of the cul-de-sac where this application of their principles to matters of public policy had landed them, Baines confided to the secretary of the Committee of Council on Education, Sir James Kay-Shuttleworth:

> I believe Mr Morley & many of our leaders will make it a condition of their adhesion to the Minutes, that the rule confining aid exclusively to religious schools shall be relaxed . . . My firm conviction is that the admission of Secular Schools . . . would remove the objection felt both by Nonconformists & Secularists to the Minutes . . .[112]

There was a greater consensus amongst Dissenters that the principle of religious equality needed to be applied to educational policy than the principle of Voluntaryism.

The purity of the idea of educational Voluntaryism greatly simplified the position of its advocates in the debate over national schooling. They did not need to make difficult decisions about which scheme to adopt or how to adapt a plan in order to accommodate the special interests of a particular group. Instead, every piece of legislation which sought to promote state education could be simply dismissed *in toto*. At the start of this period the *Leeds Mercury* raged against plans for government aid for schools: 'If this infamous measure should succeed, the cause of Liberty is doomed in England.'[113] The passing of a decade served to temper the

[109] Stowell, *Hamilton*, p. 405.
[110] D. K. Jones, 'Socialization and social science: Manchester Model Secular School, 1854–1861', in McCann, *Popular Education*, pp. 132–5.
[111] *Congregational Year Book* for 1862, Appendix, pp. 369–70.
[112] Leeds, West Yorkshire Archive Service, Baines Papers, Ms. 52/11, Edward Baines to Sir James Kay-Shuttleworth, 19 October 1867.
[113] *Leeds Mercury*, 20 February 1847, p. 4.

rhetoric and add a note of weariness, but the simplicity of the approach remained:

> This is another of those well-meant but injudicious projects, which have been so often inflicted upon the country of late years, for the purpose of educating the people by Act of Parliament and public taxation.[114]

Nonconformists such as Baines spent much of the middle decades of the century on constant alert, ready to oppose every plan to extend national education. The *Leeds Mercury* could be powerfully aroused by a government plan as apparently innocuous as one allowing Mechanics' Institutes to receive books, maps and diagrams at a 40% discount.[115] If Parliament during this period was, as the clergyman Francis Close described it, 'a great cemetery for the interment of defunct Education Bills', the educational Voluntaryists felt they all deserved to be buried without honour.[116]

One government measure, however, was not treated in such a cursory way by the educational Voluntaryists. The Revised Code of 1861, motivated by a desire for retrenchment in order to curb public expenditure, was given their qualified welcome. Therefore it is an overstatement to say, as Mary Sturt has explicitly done and other writers seem to imply, that the Revised Code was 'hated by all concerned in or for education'.[117] It was certainly disliked by all those who had a vested interest in the existing system of government grants. The Wesleyan body, for example, petitioned against it, feeling that the changes caused 'peculiar discouragements' to their educational work.[118] And it certainly did curtail government spending: from a trend of rapid extension before the Code educational expenditure did not reach the 1861 level again until 1869.[119] For the educational Voluntaryists, however, any decrease in government interference was good news. Edward Baines, for example, agreed to support the measure as a step in the right direction.[120] The weaknesses of the Revised Code included a radical narrowing of the curriculum (one has to be particularly grieved that church history was abandoned), but for many Dissenters the solution to such difficulties would have been a

---

[114] *Ibid.*, 28 February 1857, p. 4.
[115] *Ibid.*, 31 January 1857, p. 4.
[116] Brian Simon, *Studies in the History of Education, 1780–1870*, London: Lawrence & Wishart, 1960, p. 341.
[117] Mary Sturt, *The Education of the People*, London: Routledge and Kegan Paul, 1967, p. 26.
[118] *Minutes of the [Wesleyan] Methodist Conferences*, XV, CXIX (1862), pp. 393–4.
[119] Gillian Sutherland, *Elementary Education in the Nineteenth Century*, London: The Historical Association, 1971, p. 26.
[120] *Nonconformist*, 16 October 1861, p. 828.

further withdrawal of government interference which would have left schools unfettered to teach whatever they saw fit.

Educational Voluntaryism died suddenly in 1867. Baines chose the Congregational Union Conference on Education in October 1867, of which he was chairman, for his announcement. The conference met in Manchester; the city which inspired Kay-Shuttleworth to champion education on behalf of the government, the city where Vaughan lived when he called for state aid for schools, the city that produced at least three of the most popular schemes for state education, was the setting for some of the last remaining opponents of government interference to concede defeat. Admitting that the Voluntaryists had 'overstrained a religious scruple' Baines the statistician bowed out:

> To violate any sacred principle would be unworthy of us as Christians; but also to shut our eyes to experience would expose us to the same ridicule as the theorist, who, being told that the facts were against his theory, replied "So much the worse for the facts!"[121]

Nonconformists could not pretend any longer that they could compete with government schools by their private efforts nor, for that matter, could they continue to ignore the fact that state efforts were producing good fruits. A few ministers rose to defend the old line but Samuel Morley agreed with Baines, and almost everyone else of consequence also knew that educational Voluntaryism was a weight holding them down. The wheel had continued to spin so that now the papers could report that 'The Rev. Dr. Vaughan said he could not express the pleasure with which he had listened to the paper the Chairman had read.'[122]

The *Baptist Magazine* noted at the start of this period, in 1847, that 'the argument for a voluntary education on the one hand, or for a national education on the other, seems for the present to have resolved itself into a question of statistics'.[123] Arguably, by choosing to fight in this way, Baines tacitly conceded that state education was not inevitably a violation of some sacred principle and therefore the educational Voluntaryists were always vulnerable to a presentation which seemed to show that the facts were against them. Already in 1853 the *Manchester Examiner and Times* reported on Dr McKerrow's testimony before a Parliamentary Committee on Education:

> But the strongest part of the Doctor's evidence, or at least that which pressed most by the accumulation of facts on facts, was

---

[121] *Leeds Mercury*, 12 October 1867, p. 7.
[122] *Ibid.*
[123] *Baptist Magazine*, February 1847, p. 93.

that portion wherein he showed statistically the utter and decided failure of the voluntary system even among the voluntaries themselves.[124]

Every year that passed it was that much more difficult for Dissenters to keep raising money to support their schools as well as their chapels, ministers, missions and other charities; it was that much harder for a school's board to refuse money from the government that it desperately needed; and the government system and the schools which it supported were that much more entrenched.

This general explanation, however, still leaves unexplained why 1867 was the year which tipped the balance. The answer to this must lie partially in all the reasons which made this year the terminus date for this study: the nation was expecting change, Palmerston was dead, Gladstone's star was rising, a Reform Bill was inevitable and the general hope that many previously deadlocked issues would now be addressed was in the air. Baines listed as one of his reasons for recanting the fact that Edward Miall had abandoned the camp earlier in 1867.[125] Miall did this in an election speech – indicating that perhaps its erstwhile supporters thought that educational Voluntaryism would be a liability, distraction or unwelcome source of division in the forthcoming General Election – and he justified it by an apparent reference to Parliamentary reform:

I have not therefore been favourable to what is called Government education; but Government is passing away now – passing away from one class chiefly into the hands of another class.[126]

Clyde Binfield has suggested that Baines' conversion was induced by the facts and men to which he was exposed through his work on a Royal Commission on secondary education, the Taunton Commission.[127] This theory explains the timing very well: the Taunton Commission reached the stage of attempting to write its findings down toward the end of 1866 and published its results in 1868, thus placing Baines' change of heart after he had been exposed to the full weight of these facts and before he needed publicly to defend his old position in the light of them.[128] The

[124] McKerrow, *McKerrow*, p. 178.
[125] *Leeds Mercury*, 12 October 1867, p. 7.
[126] Miall, *Miall*, p. 273.
[127] Clyde Binfield, *So Down to Prayers: Studies in English Nonconformity, 1780–1920*, London: J. M. Dent & Sons, 1977, pp. 89, 112.
[128] Baines Papers, Ms. 58, contains his personal notes on the work of the Commission. At their meeting on 6 November 1866 the tasks of attempting to write the chapters of their final report were assigned. Baines' last note on the meetings of the Commission is dated 10 January 1868.

end of the period under discussion marked the end of educational Voluntaryism.

Some individuals, of course, had jumped ship earlier. John Bright, for example, although he supported educational Voluntaryism in 1847, had by 1854 consented to address a meeting of the National Public School Association.[129] Nevertheless, a sizeable block of educational Voluntaryist opinion remained intact until its disintegration in 1867. The Primitive Methodists, for example, entered 1867 like the Congregational Board of Education – still refusing to take government money for their schools.[130] There is, of course, scant evidence of any private doubts which the educational Voluntaryists might have been having prior to this year, although one imagines that these must have prepared the ground for such a sweeping reversal. One example, as early as 1855, comes from J. A. James, who confided to a pro-state education clergyman who also resided in Birmingham:

> On no subject do I feel so much perplexity. I see and lament the evils you so accurately describe and so feelingly deplore; and I am often inclined, in spite of my theoretic difficulties, to say, 'Let us have some parliamentary measure, for we cannot meet the case without it.' . . . I need not say I write only for your own eye.[131]

In 1867, sentiments likes these were strengthened and finally placed before the public eye.

The educational Voluntaryists have often been castigated by historians for thwarting the advance of popular education. One could argue that it was the intransigence of the Church which forced so many of the leaders of Nonconformity into such a hardened position, but excuses such as this, although true enough on a certain level, ring hollow in a less religious age. The truth is that no excuse is ultimately satisfactory, as the Nonconformists themselves came to realise. Nevertheless some other parts of the picture also need to be maintained in order to keep our portrait of the Nonconformists in proper balance. Particularly, the high value which Dissenters placed on education must be remembered. Educational Voluntaryism was not a dogma intended to retard the spread of literacy, but rather a banner beneath which thousands of

---

[129] *Nonconformist*, 25 January 1854, p. 69. Bright privately confessed the temptation to join the secular state educationalists as early as 1848: Baines Papers, MSS. 1–41, John Bright to Edward Baines, dated 1 February 1848 and marked '*private*'.

[130] *Primitive Methodist Magazine*, XLVIII (1867), pp. 191–2.

[131] J. A. James to J. C. Miller, 28 April 1855: R. W. Dale, *The Life and Letters of John Angell James*, London: James Nisbet, 1861, p. 556. Dale, of course, also desired a state education system and therefore his publishing this letter in 1861 was probably intended to encourage defectors.

people gave sacrificially of their time and resources to people who were strangers to them, and often from a different class and religious grouping, in order to improve their quality of life. The Congregational Board of Education raised £173,677 between 1843 and 1859: this might be a small figure when compared to the need, but it was a large amount for a minority community with many other daunting financial responsibilities freely to contribute for the general welfare of society.[132]

It is not without reason that when the historian of Anglican educational efforts, Henry Burgess, wanted to praise the Church of England he credited it for achieving 'its great work for the education of the poor, through the agency of voluntary bodies' and that Mary Sturt communicates the worth of her hero, the champion of state education, Sir James Kay-Shuttleworth, by showing him bravely establishing a training college out of his personal income.[133] Even A. P. Wadsworth, who is deeply scathing about educational Voluntaryism which he claimed was 'one of the least edifying chapters in the history of Nonconformity', could nevertheless speak of 'that spirit of voluntary service and voluntary organization which is perhaps almost the best thing the nineteenth century bequeathed to us'.[134] One of the chief reasons why Dissenters were drawn to educational Voluntaryism was because of their deep desire to have a national life based on religious equality. Their experiment proved faulty in part due to an idealised estimate of the benevolent instinct in humanity which was shown to be overly optimistic. Educational Voluntaryists were just as much led astray by a naive do-goodism as by the logic of free trade. One could catch the flavour of this doomed idealism in J. H. Hinton's answer to the question put to him by a Parliamentary Committee at whose expense the education of the people was to be paid: 'At my own; others would join with me.'[135] Only religious or political visionaries think this way; almost everyone else preferred to make sure that they did not pay more than their neighbours by establishing a local rate. Finally, to their credit, the stance made by the educational Voluntaryists was one against government social control and for religious equality. Their vocal concerns undoubtedly helped to ensure that the kind of state education which was eventually established respected the political and religious convictions of the people.

So as the period under consideration drew to a close, Nonconformists

[132] Dale, *English Congregationalism*, p. 662.
[133] Henry Burgess, *Enterprise in Education: the story of the work of the Established Church in the education of the people prior to 1870*, London: SPCK, 1958, p. ix; Sturt, *Education*, p. 109.
[134] A. P. Wadsworth, 'The First Manchester Schools', in M. W. Flinn and T. C. Smout (eds), *Essays in Social History*, Oxford: Clarendon, 1974, pp. 117, 119.
[135] Hinton, *Review*, p. 15.

were finally faced with all the hard questions about how best to implement national schooling which educational Voluntaryism had allowed so many of them to avoid. Baines and Morley wanted government aid for various denominational efforts, while Miall and Vaughan sought a more uniform national system which would therefore need to be secular. The *English Independent* (successor to the *Patriot*) seemed to toy with the generic Protestant option, but quickly let its commitment to religious equality lead it down the secular path:

> If there is to be any great extension of public education, whether
> by Government grants or by local rates, it must be secular only.
> . . . In demanding this justice for all Congregational Dissenters
> will henceforth be foremost.[136]

Even Baines, although he was committed to religious education, would not allow religious equality to be sacrificed. If the great champion of Dissenting interests could no longer lecture about educational Voluntaryism, this grand theme did endure: 'we cannot presume to impose our own views upon others'.[137]

---

[136] *English Independent*, 23 May 1867, pp. 685–6; 20 June 1867, pp. 815–16; 1 August 1867, pp. 1006–7.
[137] *Leeds Mercury*, 12 October 1867, p. 7.

Part III

ANOTHER GOSPEL?

Chapter Six

MORAL REFORM

The picture which has been painted so far – one of Nonconformists as friends of religious equality, conscientiously defending the rights of others – bears scant likeness to some other portraits which have been made. The politics of Nonconformity has been represented as paternalistic and coercive. Victorian Dissenters are sometimes accused of being a crowd of legislative kill-joys who sought to impose their restrictive mores on the rest of society. Above all, prohibition and Sabbatarianism are the features which are highlighted in this type of portrait. Undoubtedly, the 'Nonconformist conscience' of the latter part of the century – coined as this term was during an effort to entangle issues of personal morality with matters of public policy – is a major contributor to this perception. John F. Glaser has vividly articulated this image: 'Liberalism in the 1890's appeared to many working-class voters as a Crotchet Castle, from which dreary teetotaling Dissenters launched raids on pubs, music halls, and politicians cited in divorce cases.'[1] Moreover, this spectre is projected backwards through time to haunt the decades of this study.[2] But how faithful a rendering of Dissent during these years is this portrait? Undoubtedly, some of the features of it do exist as part of any accurate picture of the activities of some Nonconformists in this era; but, perhaps upon a careful examination, it might prove that the pictures of mid-Victorian Dissent which have given prominence to these features are gross distortions rather than a genuine likeness.

Firstly, a detailed examination of prohibition is in order. The most important point which needs to be made at the outset of this study is that during the period under consideration, the majority of Dissenters, and particularly those articulating Dissenting politics, were against prohibition. For example, Samuel Morley and Edward Baines, both temperance advocates with a weak spot for Evangelical passions and both fine

---

[1] John F. Glaser, 'English Nonconformity and the Decline of Liberalism', *American Historical Review*, LXIII, 2 (January 1958), p. 359.
[2] Owen Chadwick, *The Victorian Church*, Part I, London: Adam & Charles Black, 1966, p. 464.

representatives of mainstream opinion among political Dissenters, were actually officially opposed by prohibitionists at the polls: Morley was deemed unacceptable by them in his 1868 election contest at Bristol and prohibitionists actually ran a candidate against Baines in 1874, a factor which he felt might have caused his defeat.[3] Before exploring the aloof response to prohibitionists by the bulk of the leaders of Dissenting political thought during this period, however, it would be helpful to look at the questions which it immediately raises: Who then were the prohibitionists and why did the Nonconformists in their midst deviate from the political attitude of the majority of their co-religionists on this issue?

An ideal person with which to begin such a study is the formidable prohibitionist minister, William McKerrow. Although he made his adult home in Manchester, McKerrow was Scottish. Moreover, being a Presbyterian, he was not associated with one of the more influential denominations in England. Nevertheless, it is too easy a game to explain why everyone who does not fit into a theory is atypical; for, in many ways, McKerrow was a quintessential leader of political Dissent in England. In Manchester, he was at the forefront of the attack on church establishments, the campaigns for the removal of Nonconformist grievances and the insistence on the connection between the two. He helped to found the Voluntary Church Association in Manchester (a precursor to the Anti-State Church Association) and was reputedly the first minister to agitate for the repeal of the corn laws.[4] Nevertheless, McKerrow was also amongst the first ministers to support the leading prohibitionist organisation – the United Kingdom Alliance (UKA).

The Alliance was launched in 1853, having been inspired by the so-called 'Maine Law' which had pioneered the idea of prohibition legislation in the United States. The legislative proposal of the UKA was not to make the possession or consumption of alcoholic beverages illegal, but rather the 'suppression' of the 'drink trade'. It was the *sale* of alcohol (for consumption as a beverage) which they desired to prohibit. Alliance supporters saw the drunkard as more of a victim than a villain. Much like views common today of drug dealers, they saw the publican as the real menace to society because he made a profit by enticing people to their ruin. For example, Jabez Burns, a prominent General Baptist New Connexion minister who supported the UKA, preached his annual

---

[3] Brian Harrison, *Drink and the Victorians*, London: Faber and Faber, 1971, pp. 240–1, 256. L. L. Shiman, *Crusade Against Drink in Victorian England*, Houndmills, Hampshire: Macmillan, 1988, p. 79.
[4] J. M. McKerrow, *Memoir of William McKerrow, D.D.*, London: Hodder and Stoughton, 1881, pp. 33–46, 58–59, 91.

temperance sermon in 1848 on 'delivering the victims of intemperance' and his reaction to a fellow minister who had fallen through drunkenness was: 'we can only feel profound pity for the victim, and equal contempt for the tempter on the occasion'.[5] The drink interest was their target. Home brewing, personal importing, private wine cellars and parties – were all to be allowed to go on unhindered. Moreover, in 1857, just a few years after it was founded, the concrete legislative goal of the UKA became the 'Permissive Bill'. It did not call for a national prohibition. Instead, it merely would have allowed localities to ban the drink trade in their jurisdiction if two-thirds of the ratepayers so desired.[6]

Working on behalf of the UKA, William McKerrow organised a national conference of ministers of religion interested in prohibition. It was held in Manchester in 1857. A careful examination of this 'Minister-ial Conference for the Suppressing of the Liquor Traffic' provides a way to unearth the nature of Nonconformist support for prohibition. This conference is an ideal window into this world; but as specific observa-tions arising from this source are made in the section which follows, they will be supplemented and qualified throughout by information from other sources.

McKerrow created this conference in conscious imitation of one of the great successes of his life: the ministerial conference for the repeal of the corn laws which he had organised in 1841. That impressive gathering had given an important impetus to an emerging movement which was destined to triumph. In 1857, McKerrow thought he had identified the new cause and he wanted to help put it on the map just as he had done with the last one. He failed. The moment did not prove ripe to harness any imagined groundswell of support for prohibition. The corn law conference had attracted 645 ministers – many of them some of the most influential figures within their denominations. Even the *Nonconformist* (no friend of the UKA) reported uncritically that the prohibition conference would be attended by 'from 500 to 600' ministers, but this proved to be based on wishful thinking on the part of the Alliance.[7] In the event, there were only 360 delegates; an embarrassment which the organisers attempted to disguise by publishing a list of everyone who 'responded favourably' to the address which included the invitation to the conference and merely placing an asterisk by those who had actually

---

[5] Jabez Burns, *A Retrospect of Forty-Five Years' Christian Ministry*, London: Houlston & Co., 1875, pp. 147, 149.

[6] This summary of UKA goals is derived from numerous primary and secondary sources. A useful introduction to the origin and goals of the UKA can be found in chapter one of A. E. Dingle, *The Campaign for Prohibition in Victorian England*, London: Croom Helm, 1980.

[7] *Nonconformist*, 29 April 1857, pp. 325–6.

attended – thus providing a single, grand list of 1,109 names.[8] Moreover, no criteria were given for 'responding favourably' and one suspects that a polite rejection of the invitation could have been easily misconstrued. Nothing could be done, of course, about the noticeable absence of notable divines.

Of these 1,109 ministers, 737, and 302 of those who actually attended, were resident in England. For Scotland, there were 29 delegates from 126 names; Wales sent 185 replies but only 18 men; and from the 61 ministers listed as living in Ireland 11 were present. However, the Scottish contingent was more significant than these number might indicate. Although they represented only 8% of the total delegates, they provided close to a quarter of the ministers who made substantive contributions to the deliberations.[9] More than one of these speakers took the opportunity to boast that Scotland had the Forbes Mackenzie Act (a strict measure passed in 1853 for closing the public houses on Sundays) and to recommend that England should catch up with her in this matter. It would seem that prohibition might have been received with more interest on the other side of Hadrian's Wall.

Over a third of the English delegates were from Lancashire; and Yorkshire had no serious rival for its position as the second most represented county. Together, these two great northern counties provided over half the delegates at the conference. Even more revealing is the fact that these two counties (in reverse order) are also the clear leaders when those who 'responded favourably' but did not attend are analysed. Middlesex sent only 10 delegates, while a modest 29 others from London's county 'replied favourably'. It is perhaps not very surprising that Cheshire could find almost three times as many ministers willing to travel to Manchester for the conference, but the fact that it could still almost match Middlesex's 29 non-attending replies must imply a variation in regional enthusiasm. Indeed, there is a rough correspondence between the two lists with, for example, UKA support reaching its nadir in places like Dorset and Berkshire, both of which sent only one delegate and one non-attending favourable reply. Dorset is particularly interesting, as this county was a bastion of Congregational strength. Likewise the great Baptist county of Bedfordshire sent no delegates at all, and only two 'favourable replies'. Buckinghamshire, Huntingdonshire

---

[8] *A Full Report of the Proceedings of the Ministerial Conference on the Suppression of the Liquor Traffic, Held at Manchester, in the Town Hall, on June 9th, 10th and 11th, 1857*, Manchester: United Kingdom Alliance, 1857.
[9] There were 63 such people in total, of whom 41 were English and 15 were Scottish. Substantive contributions include such items as speeches on the issues under consideration and proposing resolutions, but not making procedural or administrative points or seconding a resolution.

and Oxfordshire all sent only one 'favourable reply' and no delegates. Some places, however, do seem to indicate that factors like the inconvenience of the journey were involved. For example, seventeen ministers from the great Methodist county of Cornwall made it on to the list, but only two of them managed to attend the conference. Nevertheless, the general picture is clear: the strength of the English prohibition movement lay in the industrial north.

Four-fifths of the English delegates came from non-established churches and the dominance of Dissenters was more than merely numerical. In the listings, clergymen of the Church of England were identified as representing the 'Episcopal Church', thus providing a kind of rhetorical disestablishment. The complete denominational breakdown for the 302 English delegates was as follows: Independents, 98; Episcopal Church, 60; Baptists, 49; Wesleyan Associationists, 24; Primitive Methodists, 19; Wesleyans, 18; New Connexion, 11; Wesleyan Reformers, 10; United Presbyterian Church, 3; with one delegate each from the Bible Christians, Calvinistic Methodists and the Reformed Presbyterian Church, and seven other humble ministers defying even this admirable effort by the author of the official report on the conference's proceedings to acknowledge the manifold streams of Dissent. The relative strength of these various denominations at this conference can be compared and contrasted with their general numerical strength as indicated by the results on religious worship of the Census of 1851. It revealed that the body with by far the most attendees was the Established Church, a significant drop brought the second largest, the Wesleyans, then the Congregationalists, then the Baptists (which were not distinguished by their various denominations in the UKA data), then the Primitive Methodists, and after another major drop, four groups of Methodists clustered together: the Wesleyan Reformers, Wesleyan Associations, New Connexion Methodists and Bible Christians.[10]

A comparison of these census results with the conference list shows that the Church of England was underrepresented at the UKA event. This is not surprising, as Churchmen were slow throughout this period to accept even the virtues of teetotalism. Lord Shaftesbury, that most sober and earnest of moral reformers, never became a total abstainer, arguing that a great way to rebuild a broken relationship was over a glass of wine and that the British should 'never give up this convivial system'.[11] There

---

[10] *Census of Great Britain, 1851: Religious Worship. England and Wales. Report and Tables*, London: George E. Eyre and William Spottiswoode, 1853 (reprinted: *British Parliamentary Papers*, Population 10, Shannon, Ireland: Irish University Press, 1970), especially Table A, p. clxxviii.
[11] He made this comment in 1868: Edwin Hodder, *The Life and Work of the Seventh*

can be no doubt the Alliance conference was being led by Dissenters and that, as Brian Harrison's anaylsis reveals, Nonconformists were the backbone of the agitation for prohibition.[12]

The Wesleyans were closer in attitude to the Establishment than to most other Methodists on this issue, as is also plain in this comparative analysis which shows them as even more strikingly underrepresented. The Wesleyan Conference of 1841 actually passed measures to distance the society from the teetotal movement, most notably forbidding the use of chapels for teetotal meetings and the use of non-alcoholic substitutes for communion wine. Naturally, this was a disappointment and a continual embarrassment to the zealous total abstainers in their midst. One teetotaller appealed in vain to Jabez Bunting in 1848, noting that many Christians in other denominations 'cannot account for our apathy, not to say hostility' in this matter.[13] The leadership were well aware that their stance was not popular with everyone: the controversial resolutions of 1841 were not even published in the official minutes and ministers were encouraged to enforce them without actually citing them.[14] A reference to teetotalism which has been found in the *Wesleyan Methodist Magazine* during the period of this study was a passing shot at the excessive claims of total abstainers in a book review. This article concluded by reminding the targets of its exhortation of the verse 'Judge not, that ye be not judged' – a text which is hardly a suitable battle cry for a militant moral reform of the nation.[15] In this period, the Wesleyans, as a body, did not even make it past the usual first hurdle on the course toward prohibition. Moreover, the denominational breakdown makes clear that this is in contrast to some of the other bodies of Methodism, whose relative strength was adequately or even – in the case of the Associationists – disproportionately reflected at the conference. Indeed, these groupings, as bodies, were perhaps the most enthusiastic for prohibition. The *Primitive Methodist Magazine* even went so far in 1864 as to call for petitions on behalf of the Permissive Bill.[16] Likewise the *United Methodist Free Churches' Magazine* endorsed the Permissive Bill in 1860, arguing that the problems caused by drink could not be

---

Earl of Shaftesbury, K.G., popular edition, London: Cassell and Company, 1887, p. 672.

[12] Brian Harrison, 'The British Prohibitionists, 1853–1872: A Biographical Anaylsis', *International Review of Social History*, XV (1970), especially pp. 406–12. See also Harrison, *Drink*, pp. 225–6.

[13] Richard Tabraham to Jabez Bunting, 15 February 1848: W. R. Ward (ed.), *Early Victorian Methodism: The Correspondence of Jabez Bunting 1830–1858*, Oxford: Oxford University Press, 1976, pp. 362–4.

[14] James Allen to Jabez Bunting, 5 March 1845: *Ibid.*, pp. 328–9.

[15] *Wesleyan Methodist Magazine*, March 1848, p. 324.

[16] *Primitive Methodist Magazine*, XLV (1864), pp. 255–6.

solved merely with the tool of moral suasion.[17] Prohibitionism did find notable support in the Methodist family: the children rushed in where the parent body refused to tread.

Because it was a *ministerial* conference, its denominational breakdown does not even mention the one group of historic Dissenters which was most receptive to prohibition: the Society of Friends. The founder of the United Kingdom Alliance, Nathaniel Card, was a Quaker. Numerous prominent members of the Society were involved with the UKA.[18] The *Friend*, although it did not wish to be divisive, endorsed the movement as much as it dared. In the year of the conference, it remarked that in the light of the damage done by drink:

> We cannot, therefore, but rejoice in any tokens of success which may attend a great popular movement, that promises not merely to scotch but to kill the reptile – Intemperance. Whether the *Maine Law* is the weapon which is really to give the *coup de grâce*, it is premature yet to say; but if it should only be successful in crippling the monster, we may safely bid God-speed to those who are wielding it with such hearty energy and right goodwill as the United Kingdom Alliance. . . . we believe that the agitation for such a law has done, and is doing, much good. . . . we confess to a strong sentiment in favour of the experiment of attempting such a law for England.[19]

Nor was this a passing flirtation; comments in 1865 reveal a remarkably similar tact:

> Whatever slight difference of view may exist between us in regard to the ultimate form which the Permissive Bill or a similar measure should take, we are entirely of the mind that the present is not the time for disputing about details, but rather for joining heart and hand in the endeavour to enact the great principle, that ratepayers [should decide] . . . We hope the effort of the Alliance to raise a guarantee fund of £30,000 will be more than successful . . .[20]

Nevertheless, the letter columns of the *Friend* show that there were also Quakers opposed to prohibition, and even the necessity of personal abstinence. Such letters unfailingly provoked a torrent of militant replies. For example, one correspondent told the editor that he did 'not wish to

---

[17] *United Methodist Free Churches' Magazine*, February 1860, pp. 97–101.
[18] Elizabeth Isichei, *Victorian Quakers*, Oxford: Oxford University Press, 1970, p. 241, n. 1, provides a list of some of them.
[19] *Friend*, Fourth Month [April] 1857, pp. 70–1.
[20] *Friend*, Tenth Month [October] 1865, p. 215.

originate in your columns a "Maine-law" controversy', but he could not help but note in passing that:

> For my own part, I have never been able to see that we have any right to impose laws on others, even for their own good, in a manner to infringe personal liberty, where the safety or property of others is not concerned . . .

Letters in reply noted, amongst more substantive points, that the usual course to take when one does not wish to start a discussion on a subject is to avoid voicing one's own opinion.[21]

This tension between passionate convictions and Quaker freedom and politeness was a hallmark of the Society's internal debate. Edward Smith warned the Friends' Temperance Association in 1855 that their practice was one of 'carefully avoiding topics on which we may not be agreed' because he was aware that:

> some now present take a lively interest in the Maine Law question, and would desire that every suitable opportunity should be seized for advancing it in public opinion.

However, such a policy did not apparently preclude them from asking the American champion of the Maine Law, the Hon. Neal Dow, to address their gathering when he visited the country two years later.[22] The usual rule was to avoid direct confrontations. Indeed, while some prominent Friends felt that coercive measures were needed for society in general, they were adamant that the same was not true for their Society in particular. American citizens might have been right to use the decrees of the state to further the cause, but American Friends had taken matters too far by using the decrees of the Yearly Meeting to do the same. The *Friend* wrote in 1851 concerning total abstinence:

> We can come to no other conclusion, than that the adoption of it by the Yearly Meeting as a rule, or even as a strong advice, is far from being desirable . . . [it would be] a burden upon conscience, helping to make our little church appear as an association for the purpose of prescribing certain practices, rather than of uphold-

[21] *Friend*, Tenth Month [October] 1858, pp. 178–9; Eleventh Month [November] 1858, pp. 206–7. The continued existence of this controversy can be tracked throughout this period: Ninth Month [September] 1867, pp. 209–11, Tenth Month [October] 1867, pp. 241–7, Eleventh Month [November] 1867, pp. 267–72, Twelfth Month [December] 1867, pp. 295–300.
[22] Edward Smith presided at this occasion. This meeting was of the 'Friends' Temperance Union' but it seems most likely that this is what was called the 'Association' in 1855. It certainly was not a rival organisation. *Friend*, Sixth Month [June] 1855, pp. 105–6, Sixth Month [June] 1857, pp. 106–7.

ing principles, and laying the foundation for future weakness and disunity.[23]

While the issue did heat up over the following decades to the point where offering advice seemed in order, the vast majority balked at making it a matter for discipline. John Taylor did not presume too much when he said:

> As regards the action of the Yearly Meeting, I should deprecate any attempt to enforce "Total Abstinence" by a rule of Society. It is impossible to speak for every individual; but I may safely, for the great body of temperance Friends, and especially for the leaders, in saying that the only force they desire to use is, example, argument, and Christian persuasion. The influence of the Yearly Meeting was only invoked to obtain for this important subject the thorough and prayerful consideration of our members.[24]

Reform for Friends in this period still meant stamping out wickedness externally, but internally it was increasingly coming to mean loosing the rigid rules concerning personal habits which had once marked them out from their peers.

Prohibition, as has already been indicated, was not to the liking of most of the classic political Dissenters. John Bright, for example, the most significant Quaker in the political world, steadfastly refused to support it even in the latter part of the century.[25] In 1858, he refused even to write an endorsement for a temperance pamphlet on the grounds that – although his usual practice was to drink only water – he found alcohol useful for enhancing his general health and Continental tours.[26] When the idea of prohibition was mooted in 1855 the *Nonconformist* responded in a manner far removed from the stereotype of the conscience which is suppose to go with its name:

> We, however, – notwithstanding all this play upon our emotions, and this home-thrust at our will – must decline, not only to shut up public-houses, but to prevent their increase. We even think it would be better that the trade in alcoholic liquors should be free as the trade in bread.[27]

---

[23] *Friend*, Third Month [March] 1851, p. 50.
[24] *Friend*, Tenth Month [October] 1867, pp. 243–4.
[25] R. A. J. Walling (ed.), *The Diaries of John Bright*, New York: William Morrow, 1930, pp. 374–5; H. J. Leech (ed.), *The Public Letters of the Right Hon. John Bright*, second edition, London: Sampson Low, Marston and Company, 1895, pp. 203–10.
[26] London, British Library, Sturge Papers, II, B.L. Additional Ms. 43,723, John Bright to Joseph Sturge, 5 Fifth Month [May] 1858.
[27] *Nonconformist*, 10 January 1855, p. 31.

The paper never expressed any sympathy for the legislative goals of the UKA during this period. So who then were the supporters of prohibition in the denominational strongholds of militant Dissent? In order to attempt to uncover the answer to this question it is necessary to undergo a more detailed and systematic analysis.

The Baptists who attended the 1857 conference are an ideal case study for such an exploration. Baptists were notoriously amongst the most radical of Dissenters; they had been the only denomination to be officially represented at the founding conference of the Anti-State Church Association. However, they also provided the prohibition movement with one if its greatest leaders, Dawson Burns. Judging by the letter Burns placed in the *Baptist Magazine* inviting his follow ministers to attend the conference, he was not over-confident of their response. One might even think that the conference was going to discuss whether or not prohibition was wise rather than how it was to be achieved by his vague explanation that it would deliberate 'in reference to the liquor traffic of this country, and the policy to be pursued by the Christian Church regarding it'. Moreover, he gave no indication at all as to why such a debate might be necessary, not even a passing comment on the evils of drunkenness. In fact, the only reason for attending which he could muster was that while in town his colleagues could also visit the Art Treasures Exhibition.[28] Baptist ministers were not deemed natural prohibitionists.

In the event, only 49 Baptist ministers (including Dawson Burns himself) attended. Of the five Baptist ministers who were serving congregations in Manchester and Salford, only one attended; and none of the rest 'responded favourably'.[29] When perusing the list, the first thing one notices is the absence of the notable. The current president of the Baptist Union was not there, and the only former one in attendance was Dawson Burns' father, Jabez Burns – who was a prominent temperance reformer himself. This compares unfavourably with McKerrow's great Anti-Corn Law conference which had been attended by over three times as many Baptist ministers (178); and although the sitting president of the Baptist Union had been absent, four former ones were present, including such distinguished figures as F. A. Cox, J. H. Hinton and James Acworth.[30] Moreover, these four came from a potential pool

---

[28] *Baptist Magazine*, May 1857, p. 306.

[29] Ministers serving congregations in that year are recorded in the *Baptist Handbook* for 1857, pp. 5–31.

[30] *Report of the Conference of Ministers of All Denominations Held in Manchester, August 17th, 18th, 19th, and 20th, 1841* [by the Committee], Manchester: J. Gadsby, 1841. For a list of Baptist Union presidents see appendix one of E. A. Payne, *The Baptist Union: A Short History*, London: The Carey Kingsgate Press, 1958.

of only seven surviving former presidents (the Union having been formed only a decade earlier), while by the time of the UKA conference there were almost twice as many living former presidents; yet still only one chose to attend. There was no Baptist equivalent at the UKA conference to their fellow delegate, J. Julius Wood, D.D., Moderator of the General Assembly of the Free Church of Scotland.

A sketch of the life and labours of two-thirds of the Baptists ministers at the conference has been found, primarily obituary accounts in the *Baptist Handbook*. At least for this study, the motivations of the remaining third must remain as obscure as their lives. Nevertheless, relevant patterns can be discerned by examining the lives of the majority for which a record has been found. Many of the Baptist ministers present had energetically devoted themselves to the temperance cause and were intimately connected to it in some way. G. C. Smith, one of the oldest ministers there, had dedicated his life to advocating temperance, particularly through his ministry to sailors. He is reputed to have written the very first temperance tract.[31] Smith is a prime example of the kind of single-minded reformer who was more likely to have adopted a political position from an overriding specific concern rather than as a single component of a pattern of taking positions on public questions based on applying certain abstract principles. George Whitehead was a temperance missionary for 'the Ladies' Association for the Suppression of Intemperance' before he became a Baptist minister and in 1864 he resigned his pastorate to become a full-time lecturer for the United Kingdom Alliance.[32] John Compston spent three and a half years in the late 1870s as a full-time secretary for the Yorkshire Band of Hope Union and the author of his obituary notes that he was 'capable of vigorous declamation against the drink system'.[33] Dawson Burns himself, who was a founding member of the UKA and for thirty-seven years its full-time representative in London, can be placed in this category.[34] Others lived more obscure lives, like Peter Prount who, although he never held a notable post, is said to have been 'an ardent Temperance reformer' and no other cause is associated with his name, other than debating with unbelievers; or John Batey who gave his special attention to supporting temperance reform and chapel building.[35] There were also those who gave themselves to several causes, but had a very strong connection with temperance, such as Isaac Doxsey, who had the energy during a lifetime of service to be involved in the fights against church rates and

---

[31] *Baptist Handbook* for 1864, pp. 121–2; Harrison, *Drink*, p. 102.
[32] *Baptist Handbook* for 1879, pp. 328–30.
[33] *Ibid.*, 1890, pp. 115–17.
[34] *Ibid.*, 1910, pp. 476–8.
[35] *Ibid.*, 1888, pp. 113; 1892, pp. 119–20.

compulsory vaccination and to serve on school boards and the Board of
Guardians and even to become a Fellow of the Royal Statistical Society,
in addition to being a secretary for the National Temperance Society and
an editor of the *National Temperance Chronicle*; and it would be unfair to
limit John Mathew to teetotalism, but it would be foolish to ignore this
aspect of his life or to overlook his family connection with the celebrated
Roman Catholic temperance reformer Father Mathew.[36] A primary type
of Baptist minister which the UKA conference attracted was those who
were sufficiently concerned about the evils of drink to be willing to give
their lives to fighting it.

However, the conference also drew another distinct category of Baptist
minister beside the unsung and the single-minded. This other group
comprised those who were destined to emerge as leaders of the denomination in the decades which followed. C. M. Birrell was to be president of
the Baptist Union in 1871, J. P. Chown in 1883 and Charles Williams in
1886. Also Charles Stovel, who 'responded favourably' but did not
attend, was to be president in 1862 and again in 1874; and P. H.
Cornford, who did attend, went on to serve as the president of the
Baptist Union of New Zealand in 1887.[37] Certainly prohibition – and
therefore prohibitionists – was more popular in the latter part of the
century than in the middle and would therefore be more compatible with
gaining denominational approval. Nevertheless, what is particularly
interesting is that of these five men, four of them are not even identified
in their obituaries as personally committed to temperance, let alone
publicly championing the cause or supporting prohibition.[38] One might
argue that by the era of their deaths such convictions were more
ubiquitous and therefore less remarkable, but that would not account
for why their commitment to religious liberty, an even more predictable
trait, was often made explicit. It is hard to avoid the conclusion that
several of them gave themselves to religious equality issues with much
greater zeal, with Charles Williams in particular becoming a virtual
martyr for the cause when he 'overbalanced himself' in his chair and fell

---

[36] *Baptist Handbook* for 1900, pp. 212–214; 1899, p. 217.
[37] I am grateful to Douglas N. Dean, Curator of the Baptist Historical Society of
New Zealand, for this information concerning Cornford.
[38] *Baptist Handbook*, 1881, pp. 323–6 (C. M. Birrell); 1884, pp. 300–4 (C. Stovel);
1887, pp. 103–6 and *Freeman*, 16 July 1886, p. 464 (J. P. Chown); *Baptist
Handbook*, 1908, pp. 495–6 (Charles Williams); *New Zealand Baptist*, October
1901, p. 146 (P. H. Cornford). J. P. Chown is the one exception. His deeper interest
is reflected in the more prominent role which he played at the UKA conference.
Interestingly, a more recent sketch of his life does not mention prohibition or the
UKA at all, although it dwells upon his temperance work for the Band of Hope
Union: D. Milner, 'J. P. Chown, 1821–1886', *Baptist Quarterly*, 25, 1 (January
1973).

off a Liberation Society platform to his death.[39] Their interest in prohibition seems to have been either a passing or less deeply rooted one. One gets the impression of young talent looking for a way to make its mark. The generations before them had had their struggle against slavery, against the corn laws; they could speak with pride of attending McKerrow's great Anti-Corn Law Conference or perhaps the founding gathering of the Anti-State Church Association. Perhaps they wondered if it was their turn to launch a great moral crusade.

This theory is strengthened by noting the one name amongst the Independents on the conference list which is easily recognisable: R. W. Dale did not attend, but he did 'respond favourably'. Dale was a young man of no great reputation at this time. His letter was one of around a score which were read to the conference, but he was unique in being identified by something other than his place and position. After his name it was noted in parentheses 'colleague of the Rev. J. A. James' and it is clear that the conference would have preferred to have had the endorsement of the latter. Although Dale went on to become a chairman of the Congregational Union, whatever interest he might have had in either temperance or prohibition was not deemed significant enough for even a passing reference in the 750–page account of his life written by his son.[40] The man who published his first book, an obscure volume entitled *The Talents*, when he was just sixteen, ultimately did not decide to expend his prodigious talent on prohibition; and he was not alone.

Once again we need to remember that Baptist ministers who advocated prohibition were not in step with their denomination or political Dissent in general. *The Baptist Magazine*, although it was not afraid to address a wide variety of social and political issues, ignored this one. It did not even become a channel for promoting teetotalism, let alone government coercion. The first mention of the subject (at least during the period under consideration) is a favourable review in 1860 of *The Bible, Teetotalism , and Dr. Lees*. This book is an attack on some of the claims of teetotallers and an indictment of some of the advocates of this cause for their lack of civility. Dr Lees, who receives the brunt of it, was a leading prohibitionist.[41] The second and only other allusion to the subject in this period is also in the book review section. Of *The*

---

[39] *Baptist Handbook* for 1908, pp. 495–6. A more recent sketch of his life discusses his commitment to disestablishment at length, but only lists temperance as one of his interests without elaborating or mentioning any organisations, let alone prohibition, the Permissive Bill or the UKA: John H. Lea, 'Charles Williams of Accrington, 1827–1907', *Baptist Quarterly*, 23, 4 (October 1969).

[40] A. W. W. Dale, *Life of Dale*, London: Hodder and Stoughton, 1898. Much is made, however, of his work on behalf of religious equality.

[41] *Baptist Magazine*, February 1860, p. 108.

Temperance Dictionary by their very own Dawson Burns the magazine said in 1861:

> Everything and everybody that can by any means be connected with total abstinence are here catalogued and made to advocate it in some form or other.

This seems to imply a feeling of being led where they do not wish to go and a corresponding unease with the social and political agenda lurking behind the work. This review was immediately followed by one of *Scripture Claims of Teetotalism*. The author, the celebrated Dissenting divine Newman Hall, was described in a slightly detached way as 'a favourite with abstainers' and given the backhanded compliment: 'It is not always that temperance authors write temperately; Mr. Hall has done so.'[42] The picture the *Baptist Magazine* reveals of Dissenters is certainly not one of a mob of teetotallers and prohibitionists.

The *Nonconformist*, of course, could never be satisfied with a disdainful silence. Politics were central to its subject matter; it needed to voice an opinion on any social or political movement on the horizon. Miall's paper ran an article in 1855 entitled 'Wrong Ways to Right Ends' which condemned not just full prohibition, but even laws for complete Sunday closing of the public houses, editorialising:

> If we might presume to advise in such a case, we should certainly counsel instead abandonment of any further reliance upon law for bringing about great moral changes. We have always protested against it – we do so still. It is proverbially an unthankful office to interpose in quarrels between man and wife – it is not less unprofitable to call in the aid of the law to protect men from their own bad habits.[43]

The *Nonconformist* maintained a dislike of prohibition, despite occasional letters appealing for it to change its mind; notably in 1864 when it had the ineptitude or aplomb to reject proposed restrictions on the drink trade as 'over-legislation' while in the very same issue endorsed a proposed bill for the suppression of street music on the grounds that it was a nuisance.[44]

Even the *Patriot* was not carried away by the moral indignation of prohibitionists. It said flatly that: 'This would be to rule by a tyrannical majority with a vengeance' and that people 'must be persuaded into sobriety, not coerced'.[45] The only exception to this general editorial trend

---

[42] *Baptist Magazine*, September 1861, p. 569.
[43] *Nonconformist*, 8 August 1855, p. 597.
[44] *Nonconformist*, 22 June 1864, p. 501.
[45] *Patriot*, 26 January 1855, p. 51.

in the Congregationalist-Baptist world which has been found was that great editor, John Campbell, who did flirt with prohibition in these years.[46] Nevertheless, if some Dissenters were attracted to prohibition, it was more in spite of than because of the influence of their denominational leadership and the leading Nonconformist organs of political thought.

With the history that stands between us and the men of 1857, it is perhaps easy to forget that prohibition is not an inherently religious issue. Certainly the religious amongst its supporters often attacked the drink trade from a religious motivation, but that was equally true when they were opposing slavery or Corn Laws. Prohibition is not different in kind to today's laws prohibiting cannabis or campaigns to legislate against the tobacco industry. All such causes are argued on the effect to individuals and society as whole and none is more the private property of religious zealots than anyone else. In fact, there was a suspicion that teetotalism was anti-religious during the formative years of that movement. Even in the mid-1850s the prohibitionist minister William Reid felt a need to use a section in his *Temperance Cyclopaedia* in order to answer the charge: 'You are in Alliance with Infidels.'[47] In countering this accusation, Christian teetotallers and prohibitionists sought to baptise the cause; and they eventually became victims of their own success when society moved into a less religious age. William Lovett, no friend of traditional religion, was an early supporter of the UKA and he continued to advocate its cause. His participation reflected the roots of teetotalism in artisan culture. Chartists or working-class leaders such as George Howell, Ernest Jones, Patrick Brewster, Thomas Burt and John Fraser all supported prohibition.[48] When the Secularist paper, the *Yorkshire Tribune*, was founded in 1855 it listed prohibition as one of its political goals.[49] It is a misconception to view prohibition as the coercive face of Evangelical Christianity.

Therefore, although prohibition should rightly be considered as part of another political gospel from the one the *Nonconformist* preached, it was not religious equality which was violated (by a zealous band of Evangelicals trying to force others to adhere to their religious codes), but rather the principle of state non-interference. Whether or not consuming alcohol is actually harmful to people can be debated just as the possible

[46] See, for example, *Christian Witness*, IX (1852), pp. 269–71 and 413–16.
[47] William Reid, *Temperance Cyclopaedia*, second edition, Glasgow: Scottish Temperance League, n.d. [1856], pp. 642–3.
[48] Brian Harrison, 'Religion and Recreation in Nineteenth Century England', *Past and Present*, 38 (December 1967), p. 107; *Drink*, pp. 243, 255.
[49] Edward Royle, *Victorian Infidels*, Manchester: Manchester University Press, 1974, p. 187.

risks of smoking cannabis or cigarettes might be discussed. The fact that society might be divided or might later revise its opinion about how harmful a certain activity actually might be is neither here nor there. The pertinent point is that many prohibitionists were utterly convinced from the evidence they had seen that alcohol was a destructive force in society. Moreover, they were convinced not so much by biblical evidence as by the testimony of those whose lives had been ruined by drink.

Take, for example, the life of the Methodist Associationist, John Ashworth. Ashworth was, as the master of a house painting business, ultimately a member of the so-called 'labour aristocracy', but as a young man he had learnt first hand what debt was like and of the ubiquitous struggles and trials of the lower classes. As his personal financial position became less precarious, his well-respected ministry to 'the destitute' continued to exposed him to harsh realities. His diary is littered with entries like these:

> Parkinson's child come to ask for clogs; his father in prison, and his mother just come out; both drunkards; poor little thing.

> A woman cut her throat to-day; she is the mother of a large family; her husband a steady man, but she has been such a drunkard that she sold meat, coal, clothes, or anything that she could lay her hands upon for drink.[50]

Moreover, these were home truths as well: Ashworth's own childhood was clouded by his father's drink problem. His biographer is right to note:

> Mr. Ashworth's life-long hatred to the "accursed thing," as he termed it, and his unflagging efforts and advocacy in the cause of temperance, may, doubtless, be attributed to the remembrance of what he, and others dear to him, suffered in consequence of his father's besetment.[51]

This personal lesson from his immediate social world was rehearsed in adulthood. Ashworth recalled wistfully that of his eleven work colleagues from his first job: 'only one is now alive; all have died of drink, and very poor'.[52] Ashworth's own story can represent thousands of other 'strange tales', as he called them: an urge to root out the evils of drink need not signify that its possessor was a self-righteous prude or an ideologue. And once someone is convinced that an activity is harmful the discussion moves on to the role of the state in such matters. For those

---

[50] 18 March 1867 and 4 April 1867: A. L. Calman, *Life and Labours of John Ashworth*, Manchester: Tubbs and Brook, 1877, p. 135.
[51] *Ibid.*, p. 20.
[52] *Ibid.*, p. 32.

who believed the drink traffic was a serious threat and that the government is meant to intervene to promote the good of society, prohibition was a natural political consideration.

It is not a coincidence that William McKerrow was also in favour of national, compulsory education when much of Dissent was still committed to educational Voluntaryism. McKerrow, as we have seen, in addition to being a founding member of the United Kingdom Alliance, also helped to found the Lancashire Public School Association in 1847.[53] It is at least interesting to note that R. W. Dale, whom we have seen must have flirted with the UKA, was one of the few Congregationalists to be in favour of government involvement in education during this period. The *British Quarterly Review*, another key supporter of state education, made the connection between prohibition and rejecting government non-interference even clearer. Although this publication apparently did not go on record in support of the UKA or any of the specific measures it sponsored during these years, it was adamant that the state could rightly take on a much wider role than the political philosophy of the militants allowed. In an article criticising the minimalist view of the role of government espoused by Herbert Spencer, Vaughan's journal even speculatively endorsed a kind of social services which would have the power to send alcoholics into a compulsory detoxification programme:

> We have a strong feeling, for example, as if there might not only
> be nothing wrong, but even something capitally right, in an act –
> should ever society be in the true disposition for it – which should
> kidnap all the private drunkards in a community, and curtail
> them of at least that portion of their social liberties which has
> proved invariably to end in their getting drunk.[54]

Moreover, whilst these were minority voices amongst the leaders of Dissenting political thinking during this period, the defeat of educational Voluntaryism at the close of these years marked a decisive turning point in the decline of Nonconformist political thinking being based on a desire to preserve government non-interference. If it is accepted that the state can force some people to go to school and others to pay for it because it is for the good of the individuals concerned (whether they admitted it or not) and society in general, then it becomes harder to imagine what principle prohibition would be violating. Therefore, the watershed – if the play on words can be forgiven – on the issue of prohibition came at the same time as the one on education – in the late 1860s and early 1870s, although more gradually. John Ashworth's support for the UKA and the 'Maine Law' does not enter the published account of his life, with its

---

[53] McKerrow, *McKerrow*, pp. 153–5, 221.
[54] *British Quarterly Review*, XIV, XXVII (August 1851), p. 34.

excerpts from his diary, until 1868 – and his favourable comments at this time can be read to indicate that he is just coming to these views.[55] However, although temperance was a far bigger preoccupation, his sympathy for a larger role for the state in education is recorded already in 1866, when he confided to his diary:

> Sent three boys to the ragged school this morning; had their likenesses taken. I begin to think that a compulsory education will yet have to be given to these poor ragged children of drunken parents.[56]

The militant Dissenter George Hadfield first noted in his personal autobiographical record his support for the Permissive Bill in 1869.[57] By 1870, the Baptist Union was even willing to pass a resolution in favour of the Permissive Bill for the first time – and with little opposition.[58] The rise of prohibition in Nonconformist politics in the period following this one was at least partially a by-product of the decline of the instinct for state non-interference.

Moreover, even for militant Dissenters in the years before this shift in their political philosophy had begun in earnest, the Permissive Bill also had the added attraction of being implemented through the agency of local government. Nonconformists generally felt that local, collective measures were more palatable than national ones. Dale himself would later help lead the way to a so-called Municipal gospel in Birmingham. John Bright found the use of local government a very attractive feature of the Permissive Bill, so much so that his comments were sometimes misconstrued as supportive of prohibition.[59] The kind of rhetoric which the *Primitive Methodist Magazine* used to describe this bill was certainly tailored to resonate with the sensibilities of radical Dissenters – virtually couching it as a measure for decreasing state control:

> a law empowering the majority of a town or neighbourhood to veto the licensing of public houses, so as to put into the hands of the people a power which has been, to say the least, very indifferently used by the magistracy of the nation.[60]

A major fault line in Nonconformity over the issue of the suppression of the drink trade ran between those – the majority in this period – who

---

[55] Calman, *Ashworth*, pp. 152–7.
[56] *Ibid.*, p. 115.
[57] Hadfield, 'Personal Narrative', p. 267.
[58] J. H. Y. Briggs, *The English Baptists of the Nineteenth Century*, Didcot, Oxfordshire: Baptist Historical Society, 1994, pp. 336–7.
[59] Leech, *Letters of Bright,* pp. 203–10.
[60] *Primitive Methodist Magazine*, XLIV (1863), p. 759.

were instinctively against state intervention and those who were more in favour of it.

The second major moral reform issue of this period was Sabbatarianism. The majority of church-or-chapel-going Protestants in Britain believed that it pleased the Almighty to treat Sunday as a sacred day during which unnecessary secular work, and recreation as well, should be abandoned. Nonconformists could rival, if not surpass, the zeal of others in maintaining this habit of living. In the realm of political concerns, however, the centre of Sabbatarianism lay not with the Liberal, English Dissenters of this study, but rather with three (sometimes overlapping) groups of people which stand in contrast to them: Tories, Scotsmen and Churchmen. As to the Tories, many of the most vocal supporters of Sabbatarian legislation in the House of Commons were the very people who most vehemently opposed measures of religious equality for Dissenters and others–most notably Sir R. H. Inglis, who was very active in both causes, but as well many of the usual suspects like Richard Spooner and C. N. Newdegate; and even Benjamin Disraeli can be found dutifully listed amongst the supporters of Sabbatarian measures.[61] Conversely, the merry band of radicals who supported religious equality measures were usually anti-Sabbatarians; Sir Joshua Walmsley was their captain and W. J. Fox, J. A. Roebuck and Joseph Hume were included in this informal club.[62]

Secondly, the movement in England was controlled by members of the Established Church. The Lord's Day Observance Society (LDOS) was the organisation at the forefront of this cause; and Dissenters were explicitly ineligible to serve on its committee.[63] (The Liberation Society and the United Kingdom Alliance were models of ecumenism in comparison to this.) When Sabbatarians were sufficiently roused to action, a deputation would be sent to the powers that be, usually headed by the Archbishop of Canterbury and the Bishop of London, followed by a string of other Churchmen and perhaps some Scottish or Wesleyan representatives as well, with the occasional presence of a few token Dissenters being purely optional.[64]

The Scots were famous for their strict observance of the Sabbath. When the idea of opening the Royal Botanic Garden in Edinburgh on Sundays was mooted in 1862, Dr Thomson warned his countrymen that

---

[61] For example, see *Hansard*, CXII, 1190–1220 (9 July 1850).

[62] *Ibid.*; also CXL, 1054–1121 (21 February 1856).

[63] John Wigley, *The Rise and Fall of the Victorian Sunday*, Manchester: Manchester University Press, 1980, pp. 119–20.

[64] For example, the deputations sent in 1852 and 1856: George Mark Ellis, 'The Evangelicals and the Sunday Question, 1830–1860', Ph.D. thesis, Harvard University, 1951, pp. 229, 296.

this act would place them on a dangerous road for it would leave them with no defence against the evils which already infested the English metropolis:

> Why not have musical bands, as in Hyde Park? Why not have orange-women selling their wares to the thirsty promenaders? Why not have photographers, as in London, plying their vocation outside, and tempting the working-man and his wife to have their portraits taken when in their Sunday dress?

He denied the charge that strict Sabbath keeping was 'peculiar to Scotland'; however, his appeal to catholicity could enlist the support of only 'several hundred congregations' in both Holland and New England and possibly some more in 'the kingdom of Wurtemberg'; and his trump card was 'the great Wesleyan body everywhere'.[65]

The Wesleyans had the personal zeal of the strictest Nonconformists and the legislative zeal of the most earnest Churchmen on this matter. They were utterly thorough, taking great care to place a warning label on any activity which a less reflective mind might suppose was suitable for Sundays. Jabez Bunting, the ruling force in Wesleyanism for much of the first half of the nineteenth century, came to prominence partially through his opposition to teaching the secular discipline of writing in Sunday schools.[66] The *Wesleyan Methodist Magazine* ruled in 1854 that even the seemingly sacred and religious act of a Christian wedding ceremony should not be performed on a Sunday. It listed among the reasons for this advice the suspicion that the newly-weds might be tempted to skip the normal church service; and even if they did attend it would scarcely be much better since they would undoubtedly be 'ill able to worship as devoutly as after the excitement of the occasion may be passed away'.[67] For those who might be wondering what they were to do with themselves in between public acts of worship on Sundays, the *Wesleyan Methodist Magazine* helpfully suggested that the more literate might read aloud the *Wesleyan Methodist Magazine* and the rest could listen.[68] The Wesleyans, with their Committee for Promoting the Religious Observance of the Sabbath (or Lord's Day Committee) and its Sub-Committee 'to act on emergencies', were highly energetic in trying to preserve and enact Sabbatarian legislation. For example, in the years 1861 to 1863, which were subdued ones on this subject nationally,

---

[65] His speech is printed in the *Wesleyan Methodist Magazine*, December 1862, pp. 1087–9.
[66] David Hempton, *Methodism and Politics in British Society, 1750–1850*, London: Hutchinson, 1984, pp. 90–2.
[67] *Wesleyan Methodist Magazine*, October 1854, pp. 901–3.
[68] *Wesleyan Methodist Magazine*, November 1858, p. 984; January 1866, p. 3.

this committee was actively fighting threats to the Sabbath from excursion trains, park bands and public houses; and Conference was sufficiently concerned to pass resolutions on all of these matters, expressing a particular regret that the government would not prevent private bands from playing in the public parks of London on Sundays.[69] Those Churchmen who sought government action to protect 'the Lord's Day' found 'the great Wesleyan body' more than willing to lend a helping hand.

The Dissenting bodies, as will be shown, did not equal this zeal. Much of Nonconformity harboured a certain unease in regard to Sabbatarian legislation. Nevertheless, Dissenters often joined the various campaigns over specific, focused concerns which arose during this period. These were viewed by most of their Nonconformist advocates, however, not so much as seeking to use the government to promote the Sabbath as restraining it from promoting its desecration. The first move in this period was made by the anti-Sabbatarians. In 1849 Joseph Locke introduced a bill in Parliament to force railways in Scotland which were running postal trains on Sundays to provide passenger cars as well. Apparently the tyranny of the devout controllers of such matters was beginning to irk those not holding similar scruples. Scotland, of course, was more strict on this issue than England. In the same year, the English Wesleyans were fretting over the continual growth of Sunday train excursions. The committee, in its report to Conference, illustrated the drastic state the country was in by citing the case of 'a party of professedly religious persons' who were 'lately found on the Sabbath railway, going to hear a celebrated Preacher'.[70] Dissenters in the House of Commons, however, including John Bright and S. M. Peto, voted with the minority in favour of Locke's motion.[71] Peto's vote is particularly interesting, seeing that he was a Baptist of eminently respectable credentials not given to excesses of radicalism. One could argue that his personal interest in the success of railways might have overridden his pious sensibilities, but even if we took this ungenerous tack it would be most unjust to make it representative. Due to their high polemical and entertainment value, stories of Sabbatarians as hypocrites can be easily overplayed. In seeking a more balanced picture, if we take the issue at hand for example, the fact that the Pease family never ran a Sunday train on their great Stockton and Darlington Railway and Joseph Sturge resigned as a director of the London and Birmingham Railway when he could no longer curb its temptation to capitalise on the market for

---

[69] *Minutes of the [Wesleyan] Methodist Conferences*, XV (1861–63), especially pp. 322–3.
[70] *Wesleyan Methodist Magazine*, November 1849, p. 1210.
[71] *Hansard*, CIV, 831–849 (25 April 1849).

Sunday travel certainly demonstrate a costly scruple.[72] The subtlety of Locke's bill was that it did not require anyone to work on a Sunday who was not already doing so; tailoring it in this way seemed to be sufficient to alleviate the concerns of at least some, if not most, of the leaders of Dissenting political thought.

In fact, this bill induced the *Eclectic Review* to unleash such scorn and condemnation on the very notion of legislative Sabbatarianism that it is hard to imagine a political stance more completely in defiance of the Puritan stereotype sometimes imposed on Victorian Dissenters. It is worth quoting at length, for claiming that this respected Dissenting journal labelled existing Sabbatarian legislation 'evil' and 'blasphemous' might have to be seen to be believed:

> there is no doubt in our minds that it would have been infinitely to their own advantage, and for the honour of the Christian religion, if they [past legislators] had left the Sabbath to rest on its divine authority, and to be advanced without the aid of the secular arm. These laws are endurable, only because they are contemptible and forgotten. But the terms in which they are written, the rights they arrogate to earthly rulers, are offensive and blasphemous; and the penalties they affix, were they inflicted, would be the worst forms of tyranny. The whole system from which this legislation proceeds, is evil. We regard it with undisguised suspicion and dislike, as an attempt to appropriate the prerogatives of the Holy One, and overrule the dictates of conscience towards God. From the secular authorities we look for protection in our secular estate; but we shall neither invoke them, nor can we endure them, to use the sanctions of their authority and the resources of their power, in maintaining or inforcing Christian institutions.[73]

If there was another gospel which compromised a pure commitment to religious equality for the sake of moral reform, there was also zealots for the true faith who were on guard against this syncretisation.

In the year following Locke's bill, Lord Ashley sought to end the Sunday labour of some post office workers. This was an attractive idea to many Dissenters. They believed a day of rest was in the interest of labourers and sought to protect this benefit for all by seeing it widely distributed. They also decried the violation of the consciences of those workers who did have religious convictions regarding Sunday activities. According to these Nonconformists, as the situation stood, the government was actively promoting disregard for the Sabbath. In the light of these arguments, much of Dissent agreed with Lord Ashley, even if it did

[72] *Wesleyan Methodist Magazine*, March 1864, p. 277; Richard, *Sturge*, pp. 250–4.
[73] *Eclectic Review*, n.s. XXII (July–Dec. 1847), pp. 702–3.

not do so with the same energy as some others. The London Post Office was largely inactive on Sundays, unlike some of those in the provincial towns, but its plan to hold a special training day for its staff on an October Sunday in 1849 caused an outcry. The Baptist Board and the General Body of Dissenting Ministers both passed resolutions against it.[74] The Congregational Union also sent a memorial for the closing of post offices on Sundays in 1848.[75] Lord Ashley's bill was successful in a poorly attended House, but it was overturned within a matter of months. Bright was against it. He confessed:

> I do not think we can prescribe for each other the precise mode in which it is to be observed, and I doubt extremely the wisdom of endeavouring to press the Sabbath further upon the people by acts of the Legislature. It is too much the tendency of the human spirit to wish to *impose* on others what we deem essential for ourselves . . .[76]

Many Nonconformists, while agreeing with this sentiment, were not convinced that it was applicable in this instance: for them, this was not a case of imposing on others but of releasing employees from their labours for one day of the week and freeing the Sabbath-keeping Christians in their midst to follow their consciences.

Therefore, Dissenters generally supported Sabbath legislation which was for the purpose of preventing people from being forced to work on Sundays. The *Christian Witness* printed a letter which cited the case of 'an engine-driver on a railway, who is occupied constantly, sixteen hours a day, on the Sabbath as well as on the week days'.[77] The *Primitive Methodist Magazine* discussed the issue in terms of egalitarianism, 'And why should not the postmen of our provincial cities and towns, and of the rural villages also, have their Sabbath rest . . .'[78] The only reason which the Dissenting Deputies gave in their resolution against Sunday postal work was that: 'it will occasion to many Officers who are members of Dissenting and other religious bodies labors of the Sabbath day to which they conscientiously object'.[79]

If the logic of this was compelling for most of Dissent, the issue of Sunday trading was more of a grey area. Sellers were generally self-employed and therefore were freely choosing to work on the Sabbath.

---

[74] *Baptist Magazine*, November 1849, pp. 708–9.
[75] Albert Peel, *These Hundred Years*, London: Congregational Union, 1931, p. 201.
[76] Letter by John Bright to one of his constituents, printed in the *Nonconformist*, 25 July 1850, p. 592.
[77] *Christian Witness*, IX (1852), p. 527.
[78] *Primitive Methodist Magazine*, XLII (1861), p. 543.
[79] Dissenting Deputies Minutes, vol. 12, 22 October 1849, p. 68.

Therefore, legislation against this could only be argued, in strict Dissenting logic, on the grounds of protecting the sellers who would like to keep the Sabbath but who would be forced to work on Sundays in order not to give an advantage to the competition which could drive them out of business. The *Liberator* disapproved of this argument, but the *British Quarterly Review* disagreed:

> We have seen nothing to disapprove in the numbers before us, except in the leaning of what is said about the Sabbath question. One of the most malignant charges of the infidel press, in reference to Sabbath legislation, has been, that it is pushed on by traders who wish to be religious, but who would coerce their neighbours, so that their religion may cost them nothing. We are sorry to see something like an echo of this harsh injustice in the second number of the *Liberator*.[80]

The *Nonconformist* agreed with the line taken by the *Liberator* but the attitude taken by Vaughan's journal was probably more representative of Dissenting opinion.[81] The *British Banner* argued that Sunday trading restrictions were 'not for the purpose of coercing' but protecting the freedom of people to choose to use Sundays as a day of worship, if they so wished.[82] The *Wesleyan Methodist Association Magazine* claimed, 'We do not think that religion can be propagated by Acts of Parliament.' Nevertheless, it felt that legislation would be appropriate, highlighting the dire consequences of the present arrangement:

> shopkeepers who have been unwilling to open their shops on the Lord's Day, have, by those who have disregarded the day, thought themselves compelled to violate their consciences, in order to save themselves and families from ruin.[83]

The *Methodist New Connexion Magazine* resorted to satire to tackle this issue, printing a mock handbill entitled 'Six Special Reasons Why I Open My Shop on the Sabbath Day', the final of which was:

> Because I think Sunday is the best day in the week for a man like me to get money at the expense of other tradesmen – for, seeing I have my shop open when honest and conscientious tradesmen close theirs, I have thus a fine opportunity of depriving them of trade, and of getting rich by their losses.[84]

Nevertheless, this desire was close to the edge where one could fall off the high ground of religious equality because the drafting of such legislation

---

[80] *British Quarterly Review*, XXII, XLIV (October 1855), p. 605.
[81] *Nonconformist*, 23 May 1866, p. 1072.
[82] *British Banner*, 9 February 1848, p. 97.
[83] *Wesleyan Methodist Association Magazine*, November 1847, p. 507.
[84] *New Connexion Methodist Magazine*, 54 (1851), pp. 362–3.

could easily get hijacked by full-blooded legislative Sabbatarians. The *Baptist Magazine* quoted approvingly an article in the *United Presbyterian Magazine* which observed on the issue of Sunday trading: 'We are no great admirers of legislation respecting the Sabbath, nor are we sure that there is any living statesman to whom we would be prepared to trust the drawing of a bill on that subject.'[85] Nevertheless, whatever the practical difficulties, the theoretical position of most Dissenters was that although legislation to protect the Sabbath, enshrine its sacredness or compel its observance might not be acceptable, measures to ensure that workers were not pressured to continue their labours on Sundays were.

The rest of the contentious questions on this matter were primarily issues of recreation. Sabbatarians were particularly angered by the notion of the Crystal Palace being opened on Sundays – an idea which was first mooted in 1852. Although it had been recently privatised, the government's initial responsibility for it and its place as a national symbol made it a question of politics for many. Much of the Established Church, from the Primate of all England on down, was stirred to action. Much of Nonconformity followed suit. The *Nonconformist*, however, was actually sympathetic to Sunday opening; but it was not representative, nor even was the paper, in this instance, the keeper of a principle abandoned by the less arduous; it was just peculiar. The *Patriot* was agitating for continued Sunday closing and this led to a bitter exchange between the two Dissenting newspapers which seems to be at least partially due to a certain touchiness on the part of the *Nonconformist* due to an awareness of the unpopularity of the line which it was pursuing.[86] The *Baptist Magazine* printed a model petition in order to help others appeal for the Crystal Palace to stay firmly shut on Sundays and in the following year the Baptist ministers of London sent an address to its directors containing the same request.[87] The *Leeds Mercury* also spoke out against Sunday opening.[88] The *British Quarterly Review* carried an astute article which clearly argued against a Sabbatarianism which violated the separate spheres of church and state before rooting its opposition to the Sunday opening of the Crystal Palace in non-confessional arguments.[89] Likewise the *Wesleyan Methodist Association Magazine* was careful to attempt to maintain this balance: 'Although we do not approve of Governmental interference in matters of religion, we

---

[85] *Baptist Magazine*, September 1855, p. 568.
[86] *Nonconformist*, 10 November 1852, pp. 877–82; See the *Patriot*, 22 January 1855, p. 51, for an example of continuing concern over Sunday opening of the Crystal Palace.
[87] *Baptist Magazine*, November 1852, p. 700; February 1853, pp. 102–4.
[88] *Leeds Mercury*, 15 July 1854, p. 4.
[89] *British Quarterly Review*, XXI, XLI (January 1855), pp. 79–114.

do not see any reason why, as a Charter is solicited, the Government may not stipulate the terms on which the Charter may be granted . . .'[90] The *Primitive Methodist Magazine*, on the other hand, was not troubled by such nuances:

> To give legal sanction to open the Crystal Palace on the Sabbath, would be as plainly a sin as to legalize drunkenness, lying, and stealing. It would be to set God's law at utter defiance, to spurn his authority, and to upset his government.[91]

In the minds of most Dissenters, the proper stance to be adopted towards this proposal was crystal clear.

A similar reaction was provoked by suggestions of opening national institutions on Sundays, particularly the attempts of Sir Joshua Walmsley to pass legislation for the Sunday opening of such places as the British Museum and the National Gallery. Nonconformists like Frank Crossley, George Hadfield and Apsley Pellatt voted with the large majority who opposed such measures rather than with the minority of their radical friends.[92] Dissenters could oppose these kinds of openings on the same grounds that they opposed Sunday being a business day for the post office because one person's recreational facility was another person's place of employment. The *Baptist Magazine* noted that while Walmsley's measure:

> is treated as an extension of liberty, it is forgotten that it would be a diminution of liberty for all those who are bound by office to be at their posts in these institutions whenever they are open.[93]

Sunday openings of such places were also seen as an official endorsement of Sabbath breaking and opposed on those grounds. However, proponents like Walmsley argued that they were measures for the benefit of the poor whose only leisure time was on Sundays. True Sabbatarians, of course, did not believe that Sunday was the right day for leisure activities. Edward Baines expressed the difference between the two points of view succinctly when he said, 'I ask for a *holy day*, you for a *holiday*.'[94] Nevertheless, many Nonconformists fancied themselves as the friends of the poor and believed that the Sabbath was 'the poor man's day' which protected his rest against the selfish interests of hard-driving masters. Therefore, they were extraordinarily sensitive to this argument

---

[90] *Wesleyan Methodist Association Magazine*, November 1852, pp. 524–5.
[91] *Primitive Methodist Magazine*, XXXIV (1853), p. 167.
[92] *Hansard*, CXL, 1054–1121 (21 February 1856).
[93] *Baptist Magazine*, March 1856, p. 173.
[94] *Leeds Mercury*, 15 July 1854, p. 4.

and the corresponding charge that by their stance they were thwarting the well-being of the poor.

In order to prove their earnestness – as well as for other reasons – many Nonconformists threw themselves with dedication into the campaign for a half-day holiday on Saturdays and the Early Closing Movement. Therefore, although Owen Chadwick was discussing a single Sabbatarian movement encompassing Churchmen and Dissenters, it is unfair (from the perspective of the Nonconformist camp at least) to claim that their efforts on behalf of a half-day Saturday were 'lukewarm'.[95] The *Baptist Magazine* supported Early Closing already in 1850 (if not earlier) and continued to do so.[96] It was well aware that Sabbatarian restrictions on recreation might cause the poor to believe that the religious community was against them, but it found the following silver lining in such fears:

> We observe with pleasure that apprehensions of this kind have quickened the efforts of those who advocated a holiday for the working-classes on the Saturday afternoon.[97]

A favourable reviewer of 'the Prize Essay on the Early Closing Movement, Saturday Half-Holiday and Early Payment of Wages' remarked emphatically in 1860: 'How can masters blame their men for Sunday trading, when they do not receive their pay till late on Saturday night?'[98] The Congregational MP, Apsley Pellatt, praised these movements in the House and put forward amendments to Walmsley's bill which called for Saturday instead of Sunday opening.[99] The *United Methodist Free Churches' Magazine* hailed Early Closing as 'one of the most important movements of the present day'.[100] A journalist's sketch of the respected Congregational minister Samuel Martin, published in 1854, noted that the only causes he had allowed himself to be identified with were Ragged Schools and the Early Closing Movement.[101] The *Primitive Methodist Magazine*, which was also careful as to its associations, printed a long endorsement of the movement in 1855.[102] The *British Banner* was praising it at least as early as 1848.[103] The Dissenting community demonstrated a

---

[95] Chadwick, *Victorian Church*, I, p. 464.
[96] *Baptist Magazine*, April 1850, p. 223.
[97] *Baptist Magazine*, June 1857, p. 371.
[98] *Baptist Magazine*, December 1860, p. 779.
[99] *Hansard*, CXXXVII, 925–6 (20 March 1855); CXL, 1066–71 (21 February 1856).
[100] *United Methodist Free Churches' Magazine*, February 1861, p. 109.
[101] Ritchie, *London Pulpit*, p. 119.
[102] *Primitive Methodist Magazine*, XXXVI (1855), pp. 367–8. See also *Minutes of the [Wesleyan] Methodist Conference*, 1863, p. 573.
[103] *British Banner*, 5 April 1848, p. 254.

widespread enthusiasm for efforts to see workers freed from their labours on Saturday afternoons as well as Sundays.[104]

Others talked of opening some institutions in the evening, an option which the labouring classes themselves seemed to favour, but it was difficult to implement because the necessary lighting was a fire hazard.[105] The most fantastical solution was offered by a correspondent to the *Nonconformist* who proposed that the Christian community should fund and create an entirely new Crystal Palace at which 'the poor shall be admitted at every possible time on the week-day free of expense'.[106] Naturally the paper was right gently to suggest that this scheme was impractical, but the very thought is an apt illustration of the extent of Dissenters' anxiety to separate Sabbatarianism from class discrimination.

A more controversial question was the closing of public houses on Sundays. As a planned marriage between prohibitionism and Sabbatarianism, members of both families had their own views about their prospective in-laws. Sabbatarians who were not teetotallers might be reluctant to give prohibition a stepping stone; and conversely for anti-Sabbatarian prohibitionists. Moreover, prohibition purists like the UKA saw Sunday Closing as a half measure and therefore refused to support it on the conventional wisdom that all anti campaigns should be of the 'total and immediate' variety. Grass-roots prohibitionists, however, often supported Sunday Closing as an achievable first step toward their goal. The Friends' Temperance Association in 1855, for example, forbade discussion of total prohibition as too contentious, but freely endorsed the Sunday Closing Movement as a 'topic on which there will be no difference of opinion' amongst its members.[107] The *Friend* and some of its correspondents thought that it was a more moderate cause which their Society could respond to with a unified front.[108] The *Patriot*, in contrast, rejected the movement precisely because it was a form of prohibition.[109] The Wesleyans endorsed the movement for Sabbatarian reasons, despite their official distaste for teetotal zealots.[110] The Wesleyan Conference petitioned for Sunday Closing, but this task was in the domain of its Lord's Day Committee.[111] The *Christian Witness* entitled a

---

[104] W. R. Ward has also noted the breath of support for the neglected Early Closing Movement: *Religion and Society*, p. 208.
[105] G. M. Ellis, 'Evangelicals and Sunday', p. 318.
[106] *Nonconformist*, 1 December 1852, p. 946.
[107] *Friend*, Sixth Month [June] 1855, p. 105.
[108] *Friend*, Eighth Month [August] 1855, pp. 147–8; Ninth Month [September] 1855, pp. 166–7; Sixth Month [June] 1862, p. 140; Ninth Month [September] 1867, p. 216.
[109] *Patriot*, 26 January 1858, p. 60.
[110] *Wesleyan Methodist Magazine*, April 1863, pp. 356–7.
[111] *Minutes of the [Wesleyan] Methodist Conference*, 1861, p. 113.

letter with a model petition for Sunday Closing which it printed in 1848 'Sabbath Desecration'.[112] John Ashworth, the Wesleyan Associationist house painter and friend of the destitute, felt so strongly about this cause that he decided to run as a single issue candidate for Stockport in the General Election of 1868, withdrawing only after securing a relevant pledge from another candidate. Although he was clearly a concerned Sabbatarian, undoubtedly his life long battle with the evils of drink was a large factor in this decision.[113] The overlap of two distinct issues in the Sunday Closing Movement makes discerning the motivations of its popular supporters particularly difficult.

The final recreational issue which incensed Sabbatarians in this period was the playing of bands in public parks on Sundays. In 1856 Palmerston allowed military bands to play in Kensington Gardens and other London parks on Sunday afternoons. The experiment quickly attracted huge crowds and the ire of Sabbatarians. The latter saw it as the government actually enticing people to break the Sabbath. Much of Dissent took its place as vehement opponents of this innovation. Indeed, this incident, more than any other, tempted Nonconformists away from their usual concern that Sabbatarian legislation might violate the principle of religious equality. It reveals political Dissent at its least generous. This became particularly clear after Sabbatarians had quickly succeeded in forcing the government to stop the military bands only to have the anti-Sabbatarian National Sunday League immediately continue the experiment by engaging private bands to take their place. The *Leeds Mercury* felt that moral suasion had proved insufficient to stop them and it offered the rather strained argument that the bands violated the liberty of Sabbatarians who might unwittingly hear them from their homes though they did not wish to do so. It claimed that a comparable liberty would be Christians being allowed to read the Bible in a loud voice at the window of anti-Sabbatarians at all hours of the day and night, but a more apt analogy would have been the habit of street preaching which Dissenters were so quick to endorse.[114] The *Baptist Magazine* opposed the bands on the grounds that they would 'militate against the *religious* observance of the Lord's day' and many Dissenters were afraid that Sunday recreation would tempt people away from public worship and Sunday schools. Such talk sounds suspiciously like a plea for the preservation of a monopoly, a tendency which Nonconformity, in a more self-confident mood, liked to expose as an unjustifiable claim made

---

[112] *Christian Witness*, V (1848), pp. 177–8.
[113] Calman, *Ashworth*, pp. 146–8.
[114] *Leeds Mercury*, 16 July 1862, p. 1. It would be interesting to know the opinion of Sir Morton Peto. He lived at 12 Kensington Palace Gardens and so might have fitted the *Mercury*'s category of an unwilling listener.

by the Established Church.[115] Where had their faith in Voluntaryism gone? It seems it was easier to believe in the irresistible triumph of the gospel when it was struggling against a clever heretic rather than against a skilled trombonist. In the decades which followed, the Salvation Army would discover that this too could be enlisted in Christ's cause. Meanwhile, the Dissenters could not silence the Sunday bands, despite their best efforts.

None of this should mislead one into failing to notice the deep unease which Dissenters felt concerning Sabbatarian legislation. Already in 1837 the LDOS complained that it would have obtained more votes for a Sabbatarian measure if it were not that:

> at this time the dissenting denominations put forward with unusual prominence, as a fundamental principle, that it was wrong to legislate in regard to religion.[116]

This stance continued throughout the decades which followed. In the 1850s an emergency Metropolitan Committee was occasionally formed in order to enlist a wider support base than the Churchmen represented by the LDOS; but the Wesleyan leader Dr William H. Rule admitted that the Nonconformists mostly stood aloof because of 'their own principle of not accepting legal obligations to the performance of any religious duty'.[117] When in 1853 a Wesleyan surveyed the battle for the Sabbath in Britain, in addition to the infidels and papists, which he thought were the straightforward foe, he found a hybrid curiosity: 'Meanwhile there are bands of Dissenters who love the Sabbath, but disapprove of its protection *by law*.'[118] When a Sunday trading bill was being considered in 1860, the LDOS wanted it killed because it was a half measure; however, a representative of Nonconformity in the delegation to the Home Secretary which it had arranged opposed the bill on the somewhat different line that:

> among the Baptists and Independents, there was an unanimity of opinion that it would be well if the government would abstain from any legislation with regard to the Sabbath.[119]

Indeed, the gulf was particularly wide between the legislative Sabbatarians and the Dissenters on the Sunday trading issue. The LDOS wanted the sacredness of the Sabbath enshrined in law and therefore

---

[115] *Baptist Magazine*, June 1857, p. 371.
[116] Wigley, *Victorian Sunday*, p. 45.
[117] W. H. Rule, *Recollections of My Life*, London: T. Woolmer, 1886, pp. 230–1; G. M. Ellis, 'Evangelicals and Sunday', pp. 293–4.
[118] *Wesleyan Methodist Magazine*, April 1853, pp. 364–72.
[119] *Record*, 6 June 1860: G. M. Ellis, 'Evangelicals and Sunday', p. 325.

rejected every bill for restricting Sunday trading as falling short of this ideal. The slightly more practical *Wesleyan Methodist Magazine* admitted in 1855 that on this issue: 'We *desire* legislation which in terms acknowledges God, and refers to His holy commandment' – a political goal which would have made many Nonconformists cringe.[120] It is ironic that the great popular outburst of anti-Sabbatarianism in this period, the Hyde Park riots of 1855, was directed against a Sunday trading measure which the real legislative Sabbatarian zealots had disowned as too weak. Therefore, the riots do not really belong in the mainstream story of political Sabbatarians, except because of the indirect effect which they had of making Parliament gun-shy of Sabbatarian measures.[121] Most Dissenters seemed to have wanted some measure of protection for people from the need to work on Sundays, without grounding this custom in religious scruples. Sunday trading was complicated because, although the labouring classes needed the day of rest, they also needed to shop on Sundays, particularly for highly perishable food items. Dissenters wanted to help the poor, and they wanted to preserve the British tradition of a quiet Sunday, but they were not interested in using the government to enforce a religious concern.

The *Nonconformist*, as ever, had one of the clearest grasps of the position of principle which was being taken. When it received an angry letter reminding it of the importance of Sabbath observance, the editorial note pointed out that the author had failed to grasp that the paper was not against Sabbath keeping itself but merely invidious Sabbath legislation, and then went on to articulate the position of many political Dissenters:

> we have always done our best to support the principle of keeping Sunday as a day of rest from secular toil, and have resisted all proposals to infringe it. That is a question of civic polity. We are, also, as ready as our correspondent, to admit the benefits that flow from that day being set apart to Divine worship. But this is a matter of individual preference, not of State command. It seems to us impolitic, to say the least, to endeavour to compel people indiscriminately to observe the day according to our ideas, if not so inclined.[122]

The degree to which this mode of thinking was widespread amongst the leaders of Dissenting opinion is well illustrated by examining the *British Quarterly Review*. Extraordinarily (if one is predisposed towards viewing

---

[120] *Wesleyan Methodist Magazine*, July 1855, p. 644.
[121] The riots are discussed in Brian Harrison, 'The Sunday Trading Riots of 1855', *Historical Journal*, VII, 2 (1965).
[122] *Nonconformist*, 28 August 1867, p. 702.

these Dissenters with the Puritan stereotype in mind), this moderate organ provided one of the clearest articulations of how laws prohibiting Sunday work could be combined with the strictest standards of religious equality. It is worth quoting at length this thoughtful expression of a non-confessional basis for some Sunday restrictions:

> We do not invoke the government to legislate in this matter because the Christian Sabbath is to be kept, but as we should appeal to a Mohammedan or infidel government if the great body of its subjects were desirous of observing any festival or holiday. . . . we demand it as a right, because in this way it protects the great majority of its subjects in the exercise of their conscientious convictions, whilst it does not compel any one to do what conscience forbids. . . . On this ground we should not object, if residing at Lisbon or Madrid, to the law which compelled us to close our shops on a saint's day, even if we felt inclined to keep them open. Such regulations do not affect the rights of conscience. They compel no one to be religious, or to worship God against the dictates of their conscience, but simply require that the minority shall forbear from doing what must be injurious to the majority and to the general rights of civil society.[123]

Even the great Scottish theologian and defender of religious Sabbatarianism, Ralph Wardlaw, argued that legislative restrictions on Sunday activities could be valid only if successfully justified with secular arguments – to the great embarrassment of his sympathetic biographer who felt a need to attempt to expose the error of this thinking and to protect his subject by offering the groundless speculation that this portion of his otherwise excellent volume on the Sabbath must have been written 'hastily or perhaps under the depressing influence of feeble health'.[124] Perhaps a comment by the fatherly Congregational leader, John Angell James, might best represent the true feeling of Dissent on this matter. After appealing to the powers that be not to force postal staff to work on Sundays, he went on to say:

> I ask not for the interposition of your power to enforce or uphold the religious observance of the Sabbath. Men cannot be made pious by Acts of Parliament, nor compelled by statute to worship God. But legislation may, in my opinion, be righteously employed in protecting the poor man from oppression and from being robbed by the craving unsatisfied and remorseless

---

[123] *British Quarterly Review*, XXI, XLI (January 1855), pp. 105–6.
[124] W. L. Alexander, *Memoirs of the Life and Writings of Ralph Wardlaw*, Edinburgh: Adam and Charles Black, 1856, pp. 294–5.

spirit of trade, of his opportunity to give rest to his weary limbs, and to worship his Creator.[125]

Today's society is keenly sensitive to the rights of minorities. Looking back on Victorian Sabbath legislation, we cannot help but feel for the plight of fun-loving or workaholic Secularists, not to mention the Jewish community. Observers today might be quicker to view such legislation as inherently religious; but there is no clear divide between recognising and endorsing the habits of a people. Is the fact that Christmas is a public holiday throughout the western nations of the world today – however officially secular their governments might be – any different in principle from Victorian politicians bowing to the wish of a large portion of the community to have business cease on Sundays? It becomes harder to empathise now that Sabbatarianism has so gone out of fashion. To take an analogous problem, perhaps the restrictive dress codes of Islamic countries are a violation of the rights of non-Moslems, but some rules for public society are necessary, and western society has its own, albeit more diminutive, dress code. Dissenters saw a minimum of Sunday legislation as a kind of public dress code: a day of rest was socially useful for all and Sunday was the traditional day for it, though admittedly for religious reasons. However, when Nonconformists perceived that the religious freedom of non-Sabbatarians was at stake, many of their leaders of political opinion were ready to act.

The best example of this comes toward the end of this period. In January 1866 the anti-Sabbatarians began a series of Sunday evening lectures in St Martin's Hall. The topics were typically new scientific ideas. T. H. Huxley, the great populariser of Darwinism and the coiner of the term 'agnostic', was one of the speakers. However, the series did not last very long before some arch-Sabbatarians succeeded in stopping them by invoking a law from the reign of King George III which forbade charging admission to various events on Sundays. The free-thinking and progressive worlds were outraged. John Stuart Mill was one of those who thought that the case was so important that it needed to be resolved by Act of Parliament.[126] However, many political Dissenters were also concerned. The *Nonconformist* called the threatened suit 'a piece of gross injustice and an egregious blunder', claiming in a charitable application of Scripture:

It is just the old, old story over again – resenting as a crime to be punished the independence of those who "will not bow the knee to the image which the king has set up".

---

[125] J. A. James, *The Sabbath*, 1848, p. 400, in J. A. James, *Collected Works*, vol. 16, London: Hamilton Adams, 1862.
[126] *Hansard*, CLXXXVIII, 89–116 (19 June 1867).

Such comments were naturally made despite the fact that the paper had 'no sympathy' for the series of lectures or the doctrine which they allegedly espoused that because human beings were 'descended from a monkey ancestry, we have no spiritual nature to cultivate'.[127] The *Baptist Magazine* also strongly disapproved of the threatened prosecution, noting: 'It is in such cases of unmitigated mischief that Christianity may well desire to be delivered from the misguided zeal of its friends.'[128] John Bright voted with the minority which sought to amend the law so that the lectures could continue.[129] Religious equality was far from being completely drowned in Sabbatarian passions.

So where does all this leave the stereotype of the narrow-minded, coercive Dissenter with which we began? From where does such an image originate? Part of the answer lies in a tradition of cultural disdain for Nonconformity. This instinct is epitomised in the lectures Matthew Arnold gave in 1867 which eventually became his book *Culture and Anarchy*. His distaste for Dissent is palpable. He comments on the *Nonconformist* and Charles Spurgeon by name, but the whole ethos of Dissent is condemned as 'Puritanism'.[130] While one might expect little more from Arnold, it is more difficult to explain such a feeling in the political allies of Dissent. J. S. Mill's *On Liberty* also reeks of dislike for contemporary 'Puritans' and it takes as its particular targets the United Kingdom Alliance and Sabbatarianism. Despite the fact that it is a book in praise of dissent, dissenters and dissenters' rights, it completely ignores the on-going struggle and stances of Nonconformity, seemingly finding only narrowness there.[131]

Modern, secondary sources have not entirely succeeded in disentangling cultural habits from political goals either. Owen Chadwick, as we have seen, despite recognising that campaigns for legislative Sabbatarianism were led by Churchmen, still labels them as a manifestation of the emerging 'Nonconformist conscience'.[132] John Wigley, whose book is apparently the only secondary source to explore Victorian Sabbatarianism at length, admits that Nonconformists were not as eager for legislation as Churchmen, but he sees this as 'a valuable compromise' and 'a way out of their difficulties' rather than as fidelity to principle or a genuine expression of liberalism.[133] Moreover, the word

[127] *Nonconformist*, 31 January 1866, p. 81.
[128] *Baptist Magazine*, March 1866, p. 181.
[129] Wigley, *Victorian Sunday*, pp. 124–5.
[130] Matthew Arnold, *Culture and Anarchy*, popular edition, London: Smith, Elder and Co., 1897, pp. 17–20, 128.
[131] J. S. Mill, *Utilitarianism, On Liberty, and Considerations on Representative Government*, London: J. M. Dent and Sons, 1972, especially pp. 143–7.
[132] Chadwick, *Victorian Church*, I, p. 464.
[133] Wigley, *Victorian Sunday*, pp. 92, 104, 188.

'Fundamentalism' runs throughout his text like the word 'Puritanism' in Matthew Arnold's; and so beleaguered mid-Victorian Nonconformity sits, being identified with coercive movements from centuries which surround it, until it is all viewed as one, continuous whole.

This study is not the place to engage in a critique or defence of Nonconformist culture. However, it is worth noting that the more narrow that Dissenting culture is shown to be the more remarkable does Dissenting politics become. For example, many Sabbatarians believed that widespread Sabbath breaking would bring the judgement of God on the nation. It is staggering to imagine a culture where people seriously believed, as the *Wesleyan Methodist Magazine* claimed to, that Constantinople fell to Moslem invaders because its theatre was open on Sundays.[134] Dissenters were by no means immune to such thinking. John Angell James hinted darkly that the Almighty might inflict Britain with famine, pestilence, a financial crash or war if she was not careful to observe the Sabbath.[135] However alien such logic might be to minds today, it is necessary to remember that those who took it seriously would have been sorely tempted to compel the nation to comply with the divine requirements. Special powers are often justified in the face of an imminent national danger (real or imagined). The political Dissenters largely resisted this temptation.

In fact, they occupied a unique position in this debate by distinguishing their personal convictions from their political objectives. Typical supporters of the National Sunday League rejected Sabbatarianism personally and did not accept the theological arguments which underpinned it. This coincidence of private and public convictions disqualified them from displaying a disinterested or altruistic liberalism in these matters. By contrast, Arthur Miall, the son of Edward Miall, tells how his father sinned in his youth by a lack of sufficient discrimination in his Sunday reading without any sense that he was evoking a quainter age or that his father in later years (or he himself) might have abandoned such convictions concerning the Sabbath.[136] Miall vigorously attacked the legislative Sabbatarians who wanted 'every tavern and tea-garden shut – every vehicle prohibited – every avenue to pleasure barred', but he nevertheless did shut up himself on the Sabbath: throughout his adult life he kept a quiet Sunday at home after attending morning worship.[137] The Miall who felt inhibited from enjoying the pleasures of a tea-garden in the cool of a Sunday evening

---

[134] *Wesleyan Methodist Magazine*, January 1856, p. 65.
[135] J. A. James, *The Sabbath*, pp. 411–12.
[136] Miall, *Miall*, pp. 8–9.
[137] Edward Miall, *The British Churches in Relation to the British People*, second edition, London: Arthur Hall, Virtue & Co., 1850, p. 114. Miall, *Miall*, p. 359.

was the same Miall who was not interested in legislating against Sunday amusements; and if the former is judged severely as narrow the latter is shown to be all the more broad. Joseph Sturge's spiritually-motivated habits of personal austerity far surpassed those of Miall, but though his decision to resign his directorship from a railway company when it ran Sunday trains might appear distastefully sanctimonious in the eyes of some cultural critics, this also serves as a stark relief for his political views which were formulated so as to 'entirely preclude the idea of enforcing Sunday observance by legislation'.[138] These Dissenters occupied the unique position of valuing the Sabbath without resorting to Sabbath legislation.

There was another political gospel within Nonconformity which called for prohibition and legislative Sabbatarianism; but it was not the faith of the majority. Nonconformists did want moral reform, often passionately, but many felt that the government was not the agent for effecting such changes. If the Almighty was really poised to pour out wrath on the nation, then it was imperative that it put its house in order. But what did that mean? For example, were Sunday bands in the public parks tantamount to *national* apostasy or merely an expression of the banal fact that not everyone was religious? For Nonconformists to answer such questions they needed to address the most intractable problem of all for God-fearers with a political creed of liberty and equality: the question of national identity.

[138] Richard, *Sturge*, p. 251.

Chapter Seven

NATIONAL IDENTITY

National identity tends to become most apparent and self-conscious when a nation interacts with foreign influences. In political terms, issues of national identity are often revealed in the area of foreign policy. For many Dissenters at the start of the period under discussion, their instinct for government non-interference at home also had its counterpart abroad. Non-interference abroad (defined more as a desire to avoid becoming entangled in conflicts between other countries and a reluctance forcefully to impose Britain's will on other sovereign nations than as a rejection of perceived colonial duties) was one such principle. The *Leeds Mercury* affirmed it at the beginning of this period when, in an article entitled 'Non-Interference Policy' it claimed:

> no Government has a right to place thousands of its subjects in a position where their blood may be shed and themselves hurried into eternity, to decide a quarrel between other Powers. Be the injustice of any one Power towards another as great as it may . . .[1]

Likewise, toward the end of this period, in a long, serialised article entitled 'Patriotism; Or Our Fatherland' in the *United Methodist Free Churches' Magazine*, the author expounded seven national shames and then twelve legitimate matters of national pride. The former included such items as the level of alcohol consumption and the nation's part in the opium trade, but the first item on this list was the nation's failure to adhere to a policy of non-interference abroad: '*There is her often-repeated intermeddling in the internal government of other lands, instead of guarding and perfecting her own.*'[2]

Naturally, this principle was most clearly embraced when an intervention appeared imminent which did not capture the passions of the public. Dissenters were grateful in 1864 that their government ultimately resisted the temptation to become entangled in the dispute between the Danish and German governments. On that occasion, even the *Primitive Methodist Magazine* could not resist expressing a political opinion: 'Let us hope

[1] *Leeds Mercury*, 14 August 1847, p. 6.
[2] *United Methodist Free Churches' Magazine*, June 1866, p. 377.

England will keep her hands out of the fire.'[3] When Britain did manage to escape the flames, the *Nonconformist* crowed triumphantly:

> We believe the common-sense of Englishmen has finally settled that the foreign policy of the British Government shall be based in future upon the doctrine of non-intervention.

Moreover, with its usual candour, it expressed the general rationale for non-interference:

> We have been pained within this present hour – we often are – by the screams of an infant which an ignorant and brutal mother provokes by a discipline little short of cruelty. What are we to do? . . . [the *Spectator* argues] – at least if from the duties of a nation we may deduce the duties of an individual – that we should rush into the woman's domicile, interpose between the strong and the weak, and use the superior physical force which Providence has given us, to restrain the wrong-doer . . . Well, experience has taught us that, on the whole, the evil is not put down in this summary and high-handed way. It does no good. It does harm.[4]

The peace-loving George Hadfield recorded in his personal review of this year his relief that in Parliament both parties had declared 'in favour of the doctrine of non-intervention in the affairs of other countries which, I hope, will save us trouble and risk in future years'.[5] Non-interference abroad was a political doctrine to which numerous Dissenters professed loyalty, even if on certain occasions many failed to apply it.

A practical manifestation of this principle, along with other cherished and related ones such as peace and retrenchment, was an instinct to reduce or restrain the increase of military armaments, personnel and expenditure. In the late 1840s, loud calls came from the Dissenting camp decrying attempts by the Whig government to strengthen the military through measures such as a new Militia Bill and increased expenditure. The *British Banner*, a paper which was not on the squeamish end of the national identity spectrum, was so opposed to this plan that it considered the matter a test question for elections, ending an article entitled 'A Word to Electors':

> Stand or fall who may, no increase of Naval or Military Expenditure – no increase of Taxation – no Militia! Let the nation be saved![6]

---

[3] *Primitive Methodist Magazine*, XLV (1864), pp. 127–8.
[4] *Nonconformist*, 20 July 1864, p. 586.
[5] Hadfield, 'Personal Narrative', p. 232.
[6] *British Banner*, 23 February 1848, p. 128.

During these years the *Wesleyan Methodist Association Magazine* showed a recurring interest in this issue. An article in 1848 entitled 'Our National Defences' attempted to discredit the measures by expounding biblical admonitions to trust in the Almighty rather than in military superiority. The following year brought an article which discussed the expenditure for the Church of England along with that for the military as two examples of money wasted; and an article in 1852 drew attention to the shameful fact that the country spent more money on the armed forces than it did on missions.[7] The *Eclectic Review* ran an article in 1849 under the heading 'Unreformed Abuses' which included tables of the amount of national expenditure on war from 1688 onwards, the number of Britons slain in these conflicts and the national expenditure on the military since 1820 (showing a steady rise).[8] Dissenters during these years were undoubtedly partially influenced by a general middle-class instinct for retrenchment motivated by economic self-interest.[9] The *Methodist New Connexion Magazine*, for example, in addition to religious arguments such as 'Our best national defence will be secured by turning with all our hearts to God', could also speak fluent Cobdenism: 'Unrestricted commercial intercourse is a national defence.'[10] The question of defence spending came to prominence again in the 1860s when numerous Dissenting MPs were amongst those calling for a reduction in military expenditure.[11] Sir Morton Peto articulated this point of view in his book, *Taxation: Its Levy and Expenditure, Past and Present*, which was published in 1865.[12] Like the Dissenting desire for non-intervention abroad, the instinct for seeking to curb the size of the military is a recurring, though not continuous, one.

A prominent cause in the field of foreign policy was the peace movement. Indeed, it was a driving force behind the ones already discussed. During the late 1840s and the first years of the fifties, the Dissenting world was enchanted with the idea of maintaining the peaceful state of its own country and of creating a sustained, peaceful co-existence between the nations of the earth. Negatively, this meant

---

[7] *Wesleyan Methodist Association Magazine*, June 1848, pp. 262–3; April 1849, p. 185; March 1852, p. 122.

[8] *Eclectic Review*, n.s. XXV (Jan.–June 1849), pp. 739–41.

[9] For the wider context, see M. S. Partridge, 'The Russell Cabinet and National Defence, 1846–1852', *History*, 72 (1987), pp. 231–50; Searle, *Entrepreneurial Politics*, pp. 52–4.

[10] *Methodist New Connexion Magazine*, 51 (1848), pp. 93–4, 161.

[11] N. W. Summerton, 'Dissenting Attitudes to Foreign Relations, Peace and War, 1840–1890', *Journal of Ecclesiastical History*, 28, 2 (April 1977), pp. 163–4. Summerton mentions, amongst others, Edward Baines, Frank Crossley, George Hadfield and James Kershaw.

[12] Anon., *Sir Morton Peto: A Memorial Sketch*, London: Elliot Stock, 1893, p. 68.

opposition to war; and positively, it meant the encouragement of arbitration as a means of settling international disputes.

The hard core of the peace movement consisted of the Quakers, with their historic commitment to pacifism, and the Peace Society (founded in 1816), which was animated by the principles of the Society of Friends and the dedicated labour of some of its members. Nevertheless, there was a larger circle of goodwill toward the peace movement which at its most expansive point (in and around the year 1851) seemed to encompass most of Dissent. An expression of this achievement was the concept and popularity of International Peace Congresses. These gatherings attracted the support of a wider group than just those who could support the purist stance taken by the Peace Society. There were six in all: Brussels (1848), Paris (1849), Frankfurt (1850), London (1851) and, less successfully, Manchester and Edinburgh (1853). Favourable notices and reports on Peace Society meetings and publications and on the Peace Congresses pervaded the Dissenting press in these years.[13] The biographer of Henry Richard, the energetic secretary of the Peace Society and a Congregationalist, reveals that his subject wrote peace articles during these years for 'such periodicals as the *Eclectic Review*' and undoubtedly one of these was 'Arbitration Versus War' which appeared in that journal in 1849.[14] The peace movement found Dissent to be fertile ground, ready to receive its seeds.

The names of so many of the great and good of Nonconformity appeared in one way or another in association with the peace movement. One could spot, for example, Dr Jabez Burns speaking on a peace platform at Exeter Hall in 1848; Edward Miall and John Burnet addressing the Paris Peace Congress in 1849; J. A. James attending the one at Frankfurt in 1850; William Brock speaking at the one in London in 1851; the Congregational scholar, Dr Samuel Davidson, serving as a chairman and G. W. Conder speaking at the one in Manchester in 1853; the Wesleyan Associationist house painter, John Ashworth, attending the one in Edinburgh in 1853; and Samuel Morley expressing his approval of peace congresses and subscribing to a testimonial to Henry Richard in the light of the success of the one at Paris.[15] This must be set in the context of the largely apathetic response from the

---

[13] For example, *Baptist Magazine*, June 1847, p. 371; July 1847, p. 505; July 1851, p. 459; *British Banner*, 8 November 1848, p. 759; 23 July 1851, pp. 497–8; *Nonconformist*, 4 December 1850, p. 982.

[14] C. S. Miall, *Henry Richard, M.P.*, London: Cassell & Co., 1889, p. 89. *Eclectic Review*, n.s. XXVI (July–Dec. 1849), pp. 236–51.

[15] *British Banner*, 8 November 1848, p. 759; Miall, *Richard*, pp. 55, 57; *Nonconformist*, 4 December 1850, p. 982; *Baptist Magazine*, August 1851, p. 523; Calman, *Ashworth*, p. 289; Hodder, *Morley*, p. 451.

Established Church. Of the 194 ministers of religion from Britain at the London Peace Congress, 119 identified themselves as Nonconformists and 71 with the ambiguous designation 'minister', but only 4 as clergymen.[16] What is even more remarkable is that some eminent Dissenters (beside those within the Society of Friends) were willing actually to join the Peace Society – a move too radical even for the foremost peace advocate of the age, Richard Cobden.[17] For example, Dr Pye Smith, John Burnet, George Hadfield, William McKerrow, Robert Vaughan and Newman Hall all lent their support to the Society.[18]

However, what ultimately proved to be significant, was not the existence of some prominent figures who were ideologically dedicated to the cause of peace, but the way in which the peace movement created an atmosphere of enthusiasm for its cause which appeared to be successfully wooing the heart of Dissent. The *Baptist Magazine* printed an article in 1847 entitled 'Non-Resistance' which told the story of a Quaker ship captain who, because he allowed pirates to stop and board his vessel without a struggle, gave the intruders the mistaken impression that he must not be carrying any cargo and thereby prevented its loss.[19] Giving space to this anecdote in a denominational magazine typifies the kind of soft approval for peace principles which was circulating within Dissenting circles in these years. It is not surprising that the young Norwich Baptist J. J. Colman might enthuse in his private journal at the start of 1851:

> But oh! How vast the events of the first half of the nineteenth century . . . Men in it have learnt the meaning of the word liberty, and are beginning to appreciate the *glory (!) of war*. They have learnt that there is over all the world a bond of brotherhood, not a league of enmity.[20]

This last sentence appears to echo the title of another peace group, 'The League of Universal Brotherhood', an organisation which had branches in Britain, but had been founded by Elihu Burritt, an American peace advocate who was a friend of Joseph Sturge and a popular figure on the Dissenting peace circuit in England. Colman went to hear Burritt speak in 1849 and pronounced it 'a capital speech'.[21] The Colman of 1851

---

[16] Alexander Tyrrell, 'Making the Millennium: the Mid-Nineteenth Century Peace Movement', *Historical Journal*, 20, 1 (1978), p. 92.
[17] John Morley, *Life of Richard Cobden*, London: T. Fisher Unwin, p. 510.
[18] Miall, *Richard*, p. 29; Hadfield, 'Personal Narrative', p. 179; McKerrow, *McKerrow*, p. 141–2; Summerton, 'Dissenting Attitudes', p. 156.
[19] *Baptist Magazine*, March 1847, pp. 154–5.
[20] H. C. Colman, *Jeremiah James Colman: A Memoir*, London: The Chiswick Press (private printing), 1905, p. 62.
[21] *Ibid.*, p. 68.

typifies numerous Dissenters whose imaginations were excited around this time by notions emanating from the peace movement. In the autumn of 1853, when the peace movement itself was about to enter its own winter, John Campbell made the following comments which, because they came from him, capture best the extent to which within Nonconformist circles the peace movement had become – for a season – as ubiquitous as fallen leaves in autumn:

> I look upon the Peace Society as, of its class, by far the most important movement of the age. Next to Associations for Propagating the gospel, nothing, in my view, can be compared with it. And, indeed, as it relates to the kingdoms and empires of Europe . . . I assign to the Peace Society a place above that even of missionary societies.[22]

Then came the Crimean War. Looking back over the previous years, one could see that much of Dissent had been careful, at least occasionally, to distinguish its position from the more extreme one held by the Society of Friends that engaging in warfare is always a sinful act. Miall, with his usual thoroughness and bluntness, did publish a clear denial of pure pacifism in the *Nonconformist* during the late 1840s and thereby provoked a flood of letters in protest.[23] More typical, however, was the *Baptist Magazine* which, when the Peace Society published *Peace (Permanent and Universal) the Law of Christ* in 1847, gave it a favourable review, and even conceded the point that perhaps the Bible forbids self-defence, but it also deferentially affirmed that it was not wholly persuaded:

> While we give credit to the Peace Society, and its advocates, for the achievement of much good, in promoting aversion to war, in teaching men to regard it as one of the chief sources of misery and crime, and in urging the adoption of other measures for the settlement of national disputes, and while we wish to increase the circulation of the society's publications, as beneficial in their tendency, we cannot unite with it heartily and without reserve, as for many reasons we would wish to do, because we are not convinced that the employment of physical force in the defence of others is not in some cases a duty.[24]

The *Wesleyan Methodist Association Magazine* was even more discreet, simply noting, 'it contains some few statements to which we are inclined to demur' before pronouncing it to be 'on the whole . . . an excellent

[22] Miall, *Richard*, p. 97.
[23] Miall, *Politics of Christianity*, pp. 149–69.
[24] *Baptist Magazine*, October 1847, p. 707.

212

work'.[25] Such faint reservations, on the face of it, hardly seem to prepare one for the way so much of Nonconformity acquiesced in war with Russia.

Britain declared war on 28 March 1854 and the *British Banner* promptly announced its support for it the following day. Such eagerness came from a paper whose editor, John Campbell, had no more than eight months earlier claimed that the Peace Society embodied the most important movement of the age. Without any apparent unease, the paper argued that Russia's behaviour (bringing its army into the Danubian Principalities in order to exert pressure on Turkey) made the war necessary and that therefore Britain was not tainted by deciding to send its army to fight in a distant land, but rather she could enter this conflict with 'hands so clean'.[26] As we shall see, the rest of the Dissenting newspapers generally fell in line with the war effort and many influential Nonconformists did as well. For example, the prominent Unitarian minister, James Martineau, published articles about the conflict in which he painted Russia 'in the blackest colours' and wrote 'strongly in support of a vigorous prosecution of the war'.[27] The peace-loving J. A. James held aloof from the passionate mood in favour of the war, but he could not convince his colleague, R. W. Dale, to do the same. James turned down an offer to speak on behalf of the Patriot Fund and when Dale took it up in his stead, he suggested points the younger man might make 'without committing yourself to an *approval* of war'. Dale, however, was in no mood for such restraint and instead warned against declining 'the duty to assert by arms' the claims of liberty and justice.[28] Dale, Martineau and the *British Banner* were in tune with the feelings of the bulk of Dissenters.

Naturally, the unswayed rump of the peace party felt betrayed. Joseph Sturge, commenting to a Baptist correspondent already in December 1853 on the number of people who had previously been involved with the peace movement who were now infected by the epidemic of militarism, noted:

I am sorry to say that amongst these are some even of the Dissenting ministers. I may name one of your Body Mursell of Leicester.[29]

The *Friend* protested vehemently against the newspaper editors, states-men and ministers of religion who were fuelling the war spirit. Calling the

[25] *Wesleyan Methodist Association Magazine*, October 1847, p. 462.
[26] *British Banner*, 29 March 1854, pp. 216–17.
[27] Drummond and Upton, *Martineau*, I, pp. 271–2.
[28] Dale, *Dale*, pp. 129–30.
[29] Joseph Sturge to John Clark, 17 December 1853: Tyrrell, *Sturge*, p. 210.

latter 'blood-blinded', it wondered: 'Over how many *pulpits* of our land does this red mist hover?'[30] Richard Cobden, viewing Dissent from the outside, was particularly bitter. His letters during this period are sprinkled with outbursts against, amongst others, Edward Baines and the *Leeds Mercury*. At one point he wrote:

> I can forgive everybody but Baines, 'the Patriot', and the so-called 'Saint' party. *They* are doing their best to drag Christianity itself through the blood and mire of the field of Alma.[31]

Reprisals were being made from the other camp as well. Even after the war was over, the *Leeds Mercury* ran an article on the 'Decline and Fall of the Manchester School' in order to insist that Cobden and Bright could no longer be trusted because they were 'entirely wrong' on the war with Russia.[32]

Indeed, Baines was clearly a leader in the pro-Crimean War Dissenting camp, making Albert Peel's claim that he opposed this conflict inexplicable.[33] The *British Quarterly Review* agreed, from the opposite perspective, with Cobden's singling out of Baines, noting that when it came to the need to back the war effort: 'Mr. Edward Baines and the *Leeds Mercury*, have done eminent service in this respect.'[34] One of the longest and most literary of Baines' surviving letters from these years is one written to his wife from Portsmouth, gleefully recounting the grandeur of the fleet's departure for the Crimea. Here is but a small portion of it, focusing on the activities of the Queen:

> There they remained, the whole of the splendid fleet marching past her in succession, receiving & giving the loud & touching adieu. Thus every vessel of the squadron appeared to sail with the special charge & benediction of the Sovereign. Each as it passed gave three loud cheers, & the Queen looked & waved her farewell.[35]

By contrast, perhaps his shortest letter from these years was his one to the Quaker Joseph Sturge, a man whom he had warmly invited some years earlier to become a Parliamentary candidate for Leeds:

---

[30] *Friend*, Tenth Month [October] 1855, p. 185.
[31] Letter dated 16 October 1854: J. A. Hobson, *Richard Cobden*, London: Ernest Benn, 1968 (first edition, 1919), p. 113.
[32] *Leeds Mercury*, 25 April 1857, p. 4.
[33] Albert Peel, *The Congregational Two Hundred, 1530–1948*, London: Independent Press, 1948, p. 157.
[34] *British Quarterly Review*, XXIII, XLV (January 1856), p. 227.
[35] Baines Papers, Ms. 45/21, Baines to his wife, 11 March 1854.

My dear Sir,
I revere your motives, but my conscientious views on the War are
expressed in the *Mercury*.
I am Dear Sir,
Yours truly,[36]

Perhaps it would not be too mischievous to recall another letter of his,
from many decades earlier, when in his youth Baines wanted his father's
advice on his vocational path:

I wish to know if you think the Printing Business will be a good
one; will not 2 things hinder greatly the sale of Newspapers. 1*st*
The Peace that is made; as the cessation of War will take off
much of the curiosity of the Public concerning affairs of State . . .[37]

Baines and Cobden argued their opposing views at a public meeting in
Leeds; the native son of that town won easily and Cobden did not waste
his breath on another public gathering for the remainder of the conflict.[38]
Writing to Baines himself, Cobden concealed his bitterness and struck a
note of resignation:

For my own part, I have been for some time in the settled belief
that either the Country or I must be mad; & since it would be
presumptuous to suppose that Queen, Lords & Commons
deserve a straight waistcoat, I am modestly bound to believe
that I am in that predicament . . . But it has brought me to the
most complete state of political scepticism. I have no faith left.
Nothing will surprise me, or disappoint me, or displease or
greatly please me any more. Having lived to see realized the
greatest improbability of the age – the invasion of the Russian
Empire by 30,000 Englishmen, I can make up my mind to any
thing that may happen, even to a balloon attack on the moon![39]

Edward Baines was representative of the bulk of Nonconformity which
also backed the war.

There was, however, some opposition to the war within Dissenting
circles. The Society of Friends naturally held its long-cherished ground.
The Meeting for Sufferings passed an 'Address on the War' and had it
sent to every member of Parliament. It reaffirmed its position 'that all
War, on whatever plea of policy or of necessity, is unlawful under the

---

[36] London, British Library, Sturge Papers, B.L. Add. Ms. 43,845, 47, Baines to
Sturge, 19 January 1855.
[37] Baines Papers, Ms. 45, Baines to his father, 27 February 1815.
[38] Nicholas C. Edsall, *Richard Cobden: Independent Radical*, Cambridge, Massachusetts: Harvard University Press, 1986, pp. 277–8.
[39] Baines Papers, Ms. 1–41, Cobden to Baines, 11 December 1854.

Gospel dispensation'.[40] John Bright marshalled the full force of his eloquence in order to denounce the whole business.[41] George Hadfield opposed the war, as did the youthful Charles Spurgeon.[42] William Brock, J. A. James, Thomas Binney and Dr Robert Halley (chairman of the Congregational Union in 1855) were credited with attempting to restrain the war spirit.[43] After the war, when there was a great, popular dislike of Bright and Cobden, William McKerrow became a friend in need and publicly supported them in the difficult general election of 1857. In his mind, this was the first time he had ever associated himself with a political cause.[44] The light of peace was not entirely extinguished.

Nevertheless, what explanation can be offered for the discrepancy between the heightened peace rhetoric of the years preceding this crisis and the remarkable level of its collapse once it had arrived? One explanation is that the peace movement had schooled its disciples only in the necessity of seeking to prevent war. Little thought seems to have been given to the position one should take once a conflict had begun. Edward Miall, when war with Russia seemed highly likely, told his constituents:

> But then, gentlemen, if we are to have a war, my feeling is this: we must go at it vigorously. . . . It is of no use to hit, unless you can hit hard, and unless you can hit home.[45]

Dissenters were not just Dissenters, but also patriots. Perhaps during a time of war the proper course of action was to mobilise behind one's country. S. M. Peto distinguished himself by resigning his seat in Parliament in order to help the war effort by building a railway for the troops in the Crimea. He received a baronetcy for his public-spirited actions.[46] Quakers debated amongst themselves whether or not it was appropriate to subscribe to the Patriot Fund.[47] At the very least, it could be argued that those who held peace convictions should literally hold their peace until a moment when passions were less inflamed and British lives and national honour were not imperilled. *The Wesleyan Methodist*

---

[40] *Friend*, First Month [January] 1855, pp. 4–5.
[41] Trevelyan, *Bright*, chapters 10–11.
[42] Hadfield, 'Personal Narrative', pp. 180–3; Paul R. Dekar, 'Baptist Peacemakers in Nineteenth-Century Peace Societies', *Baptist Quarterly*, XXXIV, 1 (January 1991), p. 8.
[43] *Nonconformist*, 24 October 1855, p. 776. Brock's biographer says that his subject 'sought to raise himself and his people above the passions of the hour'. C. M. Birrell, *Life of William Brock*, London: James Nisbet, 1878, p. 211.
[44] McKerrow, *McKerrow*, p. 225.
[45] Miall, *Miall*, p. 190.
[46] Anon., *Peto*, p. 91.
[47] *Friend*, First Month [January] 1855, p. 11.

Association Magazine seems to have followed this policy. It did not have much to say during the war, but much afterwards. In May 1856, when the peace treaty was scarcely a month old, it ran an article entitled 'The Military Oath' which suggested that enlisting in the armed forces made one 'a practical atheist' because orders must be obeyed irrespective of conscience. A few months later, the magazine's lead article, 'A Time of War, and a Time of Peace', offered a strong condemnation of war. It claimed:

> a time of war is a period of gross inconsistency. The inconsistency is that of professedly Christian men going to war at all . . .
> War is opposed to the teaching of Christianity, and what a falling away from its mild nature do we witness when some of its teachers openly advocate it. A Christian cannot fight if he has right views of holy religion . . . and that which he cannot do himself, he is certainly not justified in hiring and encouraging others to do.[48]

These were unpopular sentiments in 1856. Perhaps they were not expressed in 1854 or 1855 due to a sense that, for the Christian patriot, there is not only a time for peace but also a time to keep silent.

However, this explanation is insufficient. It might explain the actions of those who were silent or those who dutifully supported the war effort, but it does not account for those who actually encouraged and enthusiastically embraced the possibility of fighting Russia. The *British Quarterly Review*, for example, was already warning in its August 1853 issue (i.e. over seven months before war was declared) that Britons must prevent the Czar from taking over Turkey 'to the last shot we can discharge, and to the last man who can mount the breach'.[49] What reason can be given for such a stance? In truth, the Dissenting peace movement had an Achilles' heel: unlike other Dissenting causes, it was not founded on the assertion and application of an absolute principle. Slavery and church establishments were always wrong but, for most Nonconformists, the same could not be said of wars. Cobden, who was himself no pacifist, admitted as much in 1853 when he wrote:

> In this Peace Conference movement, we have not the same clear and definable principle on which to take our stand, that we had in our [Anti-Corn Law] League agitation.[50]

---

[48] *Wesleyan Methodist Association Magazine*, May 1856, pp. 221–2; September 1856, pp. 401–2. However, there were two short extracts printed which seemed to be more sympathetic to militarism: June 1856, pp. 286–7; September 1856, pp. 444–5.
[49] *British Quarterly Review*, XVIII, XXXV (August 1853), p. 260.
[50] Cobden to McLaren, 19 September 1853: John Morley, *Life of Richard Cobden*, London: T. Fisher Unwin, 1903 [originally 1879], pp. 608–9.

Nonconformists were moralistic and highly susceptible to passionate pleas for justice to be done or merciful assistance provided. The Dissenting mind was given to thinking in terms of absolute right or wrong. In a confusing world, the sure guide of clear principles set a course on the issues of the day through the compromises embraced by lesser minds. When such a principle was lacking, Nonconformists were not well-suited to the more subtle task of discerning the lesser of two evils or the more humble plan of pursuing what would be presently useful or achievable rather than what is ultimately just or ideal. Attempting to right a wrong or thwart an injustice – even by means of war – was more in keeping with the Dissenting imagination than dispassionate analyses about the imprudence of an undertaking. In the late 1840s and early 1850s Nonconformists did not want to see their nation stumble into a war with France and therefore they energetically promoted the cause of peace, but the peace movement was ill-prepared for the passionate case which was suddenly made for war with Russia.[51] If some wars could be justified, then Dissent was left to evaluate each potential conflict on its merits; and its discernment was heavily influenced by its passionate soul.

In short, the abstract goal of peace, however enthusiastically it might be championed, was not a very secure protection against the heightened emotional appeals which accompany a state of war. Peace rhetoric, even if sincere, was not reliably applicable. The *British Banner* explained its position during the Crimean War:

> we beg explicitly to say, that we are thoroughly with the Peace Society in its general principles and general objects. But every rule has exceptions; and we claim one for the special purpose of resisting the march of NICHOLAS in his fearful project of over-running Europe . . .[52]

The days ahead were littered with exceptions. In 1857 came the Indian Mutiny. It inflamed even greater passions. Military action to suppress the uprising won the support of the Dissenters who had backed the Crimean War and some, like C. H. Spurgeon, who had not.[53] Even John Bright wrote:

> Does our friend Southhall think our govt. should rest quiet & allow every Englishman in India to be murdered[?] I don't think so. They must act on their principles, seeing that they admit no

---

[51] Richard, *Sturge*, pp. 420–1 and 433, offers comments on the role of attitudes toward France.
[52] *British Banner*, 24 May 1854, p. 371.
[53] Brian Stanley, 'Christian Responses to the Indian Mutiny of 1857', in W. J. Sheils (ed.), *The Church and War* (Studies in Church History 20), Oxford: Basil Blackwell, 1983, pp. 277–89.

others. I have never advocated the extreme non-resistance principle in public or private. I don't know whether I could logically
maintain it. I opposed the late war, as contrary to the national
interests & the principles professed & avowed by the nation & on
no other ground. It was because my arguments could not be met
that I was charged with being for "peace at any price" . . .[54]

The Baptists gained a new appreciation for militarism from the Indian
Mutiny because one of their own, Sir Henry Havelock, died serving his
country and rose again in the public imagination as a national martyr-
hero.[55] The *Baptist Magazine* was so proud that it placed a special,
costly engraving of General Havelock in the issue which included his
memoir.[56] William Brock, who had stood aloof from the passions of the
Crimean War, was destined to write the popular hagiography of
Havelock.[57] The ever more influential image of the Christian soldier
which the Baptist general embodied was a long way from the attitude of
the *Methodist New Connexion Magazine* back in 1848: 'The work for
which a soldier is designed, the discipline to which he is subjected, and
the circumstances in which he is placed are all unfavourable to true
morality.'[58] But imperialists could not afford to be pacifists. When poor,
kind, idealistic Joseph Sturge wrote to the legendary missionary, David
Livingstone, fishing for an endorsement of peace principles from so
popular a Christian, he received an extraordinarily rude reply in which
the explorer argued that such theories were nonsensical to anyone who
had lived in some parts of Africa – where a gun was essential kit for
dealing with some people:

this is the place where your principles ought to be tested, not
where the people are friendly or where the policeman keeps the
peace. . . . I can never cease wondering why the Friends who
sincerely believe in the power of peace principles don't test them
by going forth to the heathen as missionaries of the cross.[59]

The Civil War in the United States tempted others to support military
action, finding in this instance their absolute principle in the desire to
eradicate slavery. Even Charles Sturge, Joseph's brother and a loyal

---

[54] Sturge Papers, II, B.L. Add. Ms. 43,723, Bright to Joseph Sturge, 24, 9 [September]
1857.
[55] Olive Anderson, 'The growth of Christian militarism in mid-Victorian Britain',
English Historical Review, LXXXVI, CCCXXXVIII (January 1971), pp. 46–72.
[56] *Baptist Magazine*, February 1858, p. 112 (announcing that the engraving would be
in the April issue).
[57] Birrell, *Brock*, pp. 212–16.
[58] *Methodist New Connexion Magazine*, 51 (1848), p. 157.
[59] Sturge Papers, B.L. Add. Ms. 43,845, David Livingstone to Joseph Sturge,
December 1858.

Quaker, expressed his support for the North's war effort.[60] Peace rhetoric continued to have a place within Dissent after the Crimean War, but it did not provide immunity from a desire to support specific military actions.

National identity has its domestic issues as well. In the Victorian era, the suffrage question – defining who was to be recognised as a full participant in the politics of the nation – was a recurring concern. Dissent was not fully tested on this point because none of the decisions which this period demanded could match the heady atmosphere of the years which preceded it. In the early 1840s, Joseph Sturge and Edward Miall had founded the National Complete Suffrage Union, a movement which sought to unite the efforts of working and middle-class reformers. In early 1842 it adopted all six points of the People's Charter.[61] For numerous reasons, including the extreme nature of its radicalism and its overtly political purpose, the Union never became a movement which was strongly supported by Dissenters. Also, it is worth recalling that Edward Miall was in his very first years as editor of the *Nonconformist* and the Anti-State Church Association had not yet been founded, so his personal influence was not yet what it would become – and Joseph Sturge's Quakers were one of the least likely of Dissenting groups to be attracted to meddling in so purely political a question. The Union officially floundered on whether or not the People's Charter should be adopted *by name*, but the underlying issues included a conflict of personalities between the middle-class Dissenters and the Chartist leadership.[62] Essentially, the Chartist leadership did not want to be marginalised or patronised and the Dissenters did not want to be associated with unrespectable elements and, more particularly, with advocates of violence. The two groups fell out at a conference in late 1842 at which the controversial Chartist leader, Feargus O'Connor, had determined to assert his influence over the new movement. Trouble had begun even before the conference was held. Thomas Cooper later claimed that two celebrated Dissenters, J. P. Mursell and the 'church-rate martyr' William Baines, would have been in the four-member delegation to the conference from Leicester if they had not withdrawn when they realised that disagreeable characters like himself would also be involved.[63]

[60] Tyrrell, *Sturge*, p. 243.
[61] Richard, *Sturge*, pp. 302–5, 316.
[62] Alex Tyrrell, 'Personality in Politics: The National Complete Suffrage Union and Pressure Group Politics in Early Victorian Britain', *Journal of Religious History*, 12, 4 (December 1983), pp. 382–400.
[63] Thomas Cooper, *The Life of Thomas Cooper*, Leicester: Leicester University Press, 1971 [originally 1872], pp. 220–1.

This backdrop set the stage for Dissenting attitudes within the period under consideration. It was not uncommon for Dissenters to express a sympathy for the cause of working-class enfranchisement or even for the principles embodied in the Charter. Titus Salt, one of the greatest industrialists of the age, publicly expressed sympathy for Chartism, as did the Congregational minister Newman Hall.[64] Even the wealthy and respectable Samuel Morley wrote to the influential Congregational layman, Joshua Wilson, in April 1848, when a Chartist riot seemed hours away:

> Do not be needlessly alarmed at the present aspect of events. While everything tending to a breach of the peace must be put down, and the violence of misguided men must be met by force, depend upon it the aristocracy will never give up the prey on which they have always been disposed to fatten, till their fears are excited. I am far removed from being a Chartist, but I have the deepest sympathy with the working classes . . .[65]

In the same month of agitation, the *Nonconformist* ran an article entitled 'The People's Charter and the Chartists' which baldly reasserted the desire of some radical Dissenters to embrace the former whilst repelling the latter. It claimed that in all the excitement 'the great principles contained in the People's Charter have been overlooked' and asked in the document's defence, 'who will say that it is not founded on reason and justice?' However, it also faulted the men behind it, mentioning Feargus O'Connor by name, and in a follow-on article, spoke of 'the palpable unfitness and inconsistency of the Chartist leaders'.[66] Although the *Nonconformist* was probably more extreme on the matter of political reform than most of Dissent, it was certainly not acting alone. For example the *British Banner* can be found taking a strikingly similar line:

> In the Charter itself, considered merely as a documentary exhibition of principles, we see much, very much to approve, and very little to condemn; in the conduct of its principle advocates we see much, very much to condemn, and very little to approve.[67]

The *Leeds Mercury* was at least willing in 1847 to carry a report of a Complete Suffrage meeting on its front page, and it must have not found its principles overly alarming because it also felt free in that year to endorse the Parliamentary candidatures of Joseph Sturge and Edward

---

[64] Reynolds, *Salt*, pp. 79, 135; Hall, *Autobiography*, p. 108.
[65] Hodder, *Morley*, p. 109.
[66] *Nonconformist*, 19 April 1848, p. 275.
[67] *British Banner*, 19 January 1848, pp. 48–9.

Miall, both of whom were running for seats within the *Mercury*'s Yorkshire.[68] Some influential Dissenters and Dissenting organs were willing at least to flirt with the extremely radical end of the franchise debate.

The heated, stark choices of the 1840s gave way to the tepid, hedged options of the 'Age of Equipoise'.[69] Dissenters were generally content during most of the years of this study to express their desire for an extension of the franchise, without necessarily committing themselves to exactly how far it should be extended. The Wesleyans, by contrast, were not vaguely in favour of expanding the electorate, but vaguely against it. *The Wesleyan Methodist Magazine* hinted throughout this period that franchise reform might place the steering of public policy in untrustworthy hands and thereby produce unwanted results. For example, in an article in 1857 which was an unusually blatant attempt to influence the way its readers would vote in the forthcoming general election, it warned:

> we maintain that questions of *suffrage*, for example, are so to be dealt with as not to imperil the interests of the very persons whom it is proposed to benefit; . . . Representatives necessarily share the qualities of those whom they represent: a godless population will return a godless Parliament. . . . we must study to uphold due representation of those middling classes among whom chiefly flourishes the enlightened piety which is the distinguishing glory of these lands.[70]

Likewise John Angell James' son confessed concerning his father, 'I know he held in perfect dread any extension of the suffrage'; but such sentiments were not typical of Dissent as a whole.[71] Unlike the Wesleyans, many Dissenters convinced themselves that a larger electorate would be more sympathetic to their favourite political causes. The Liberation Society was willing to slacken its own campaigns when it thought electoral reform might take centre stage, and when an extension of the suffrage finally did come it was convinced that it spelt good news for its goals.[72] Even prohibitionists imagined that more political power in the hands of the masses would aid their cause.[73]

Nevertheless, what exactly did an extension of the franchise mean?

---

[68] *Leeds Mercury*, 20 February 1847, p. 1; 24 July 1847, p.1.
[69] The name given to the period between 1852 and 1867 by W. L. Burn's *The Age of Equipoise*, London: Unwin University Books, 1968 [originally 1964].
[70] *Wesleyan Methodist Magazine*, April 1857, pp. 361–2. A similar sentiment was expressed when reform became inevitable: June 1866, p. 551.
[71] Sketch of him by T. S. James printed as a supplement in Dale, *James*, p. 583.
[72] Liberation Society Papers, A/LIB/1, 12 February 1852, minute 707; A/LIB/3, 17 November 1865, minute 610; 30 August 1867, minute 536a.
[73] Harrison, *Drink and the Victorians*, p. 255.

Joseph Sturge could argue that justice demanded that all men should be treated with equality in the political system because they were all equal in the sight of God, but even he shied away from enfranchising women, despite their divine approval.[74] The *Leeds Mercury* was certainly opting for the road less travelled when it endorsed women's suffrage in 1867, J. S. Mill having raised the issue.[75] In fact, Edward Baines seems to have been mulling over the place of women in the electorate for some years. In 1861, Baines received a list of figures he had asked someone to compile on the number of female householders and the percentage of the total which these numbers represented. His source, apparently justifying the length of time he had taken, noted the novelty of this task, 'I never had to make a return showing the per centage of female occupiers . . .'[76] However, even if this scruple is set aside as unlikely to bother the consciences of most mid-Victorian leaders, one is still left with manhood suffrage as what justice demanded – if Sturge's theological logic was to be taken seriously. However, Dissent as a whole was not willing to put the case so unequivocally. The sound of squirming can almost be heard as the *British Banner* attempted to tackle the issue on one occasion: 'The subject of Universal Suffrage is much less simple than, at first sight, it may appear . . .'[77] When Campbell launched another newspaper, the *British Ensign*, in 1859 his announcement of its principles began very absolutist on this point: 'Manhood Suffrage *alone* can satisfy the demands of political justice. Every measure short of this will be but temporary. Why be afraid to do what is right?' This confident tone, however, soon lost its nerve and dissolved into a kind of millennial yearning which even the Wesleyan leadership could have endorsed:

> The mind of the millions once thoroughly replenished with Divine Knowledge, and properly trained in the school of Christian politics, there is nothing to be dreaded, but everything to be hoped, from such a suffrage. Evangelise the land, and all will be well; you may then enfranchise every man of twenty-one years of age.[78]

The *Eclectic Review* spoke sympathetically in the radical year 1848 of the idea of making 'the Christian doctrine of the equality of souls a reality, by enfranchising all consciences alike', but it was forced to be more

---

[74] Stephen Hobhouse, *Joseph Sturge*, London: J. M. Dent & Sons, 1919, pp. 64–5, 94–5.
[75] *Leeds Mercury*, 22 May 1867, p. 2.
[76] Baines Papers, Ms. 60, Christopher Heaps to Baines, 18 February 1861.
[77] *British Banner*, 8 November 1848, p. 751.
[78] From a prospectus for the *British Ensign* attached to the end of vol. 61 (1858) of the *Methodist New Connexion Magazine*.

explicit and less grand in a subsequent paragraph, reducing the pool of relevant consciences to 'every man of mature age, sound mind, unstained by crime, and of a fixed residence'.[79] Moreover, it had argued even more narrowly in the very issue before this one for the boundary to be set at male tax payers.[80] Despite the recurring temptation to employ a sweeping rhetoric, the true theoretical stance of most influential Dissenters was probably that of Samuel Morley when he wrote, 'The franchise is not a right to every man, but a trust committed by the nation to each capable and qualified citizen.'[81]

If manhood suffrage was a principle which justice demanded, then anything short of it would be a sinful compromise. In that case, one could no more accept a partial extension of the franchise than a partial abolition of slavery. However, if the matter could not be asserted quite this boldly, then it belonged back in the land of what is expedient or obtainable. In short, once again Dissent found itself lacking an absolute principle. Therefore, it did not have the intellectual and emotional resources with which to rally a coherent campaign. John Bright felt, like most Dissenters, that it was the kind of issue in which compromise was acceptable. In language unlike anything he would have uttered concerning his Anti-Corn Law activities, he wrote in defence of his half measure for franchise extension:

> I am not working for failure, but for success, and for a real gain, and I must go the way to get it. I am sure . . . putting manhood suffrage in the Bill is not the way. This has been done by the Chartists, and by the Complete Suffragists, but what has become of their Bills?[82]

The eminent Congregational businessman, Titus Salt, was equally pragmatic in the 1850s, hinting that he would like much more, but declaring a readiness to take whatever portion of the loaf could be obtained.[83] In the early 1860s, Edward Baines and John Bright were sufficiently practical and confident to propose specific reform schemes of their own, but these were not the kind of legislative attempts which the Dissenting community could collectively endorse through favourable resolutions by such bodies as the Congregational or Baptist Unions, the Dissenting Deputies, the Ministers of the Three Denominations or the Liberation Society. In the years between the radical campaigns of the 1840s and the Reform Act of 1867, Dissenters were generally content to

---

[79] *Eclectic Review*, n.s. XXIV (July–Dec. 1848), pp. 114–16, 120.
[80] *Ibid.*, n.s. XXIII (Jan.–June 1848), p. 639.
[81] From undated notes: Hodder, *Morley*, p. 445.
[82] Bright to Joseph Sturge, 25 February 1858: Trevelyan, *Bright*, p. 270.
[83] Reynolds, *Great Paternalist*, p. 202.

prod the politicians toward greater reform – being unable to mount a passionate campaign of their own for any precise demand. The advanced ideas of the 1840s were still applicable enough in 1867 to tempt a plagiarist to endeavour to enhance his reputation by running an entire series of Miall's old Complete Suffrage articles.[84]

National identity also had religious implications. Was it right to consider Britain a Christian and Protestant nation? What did such affirmations mean? In Victorian Britain, Roman Catholicism was the only serious, organised alternative to Protestant Christianity. Europe offered only two alternatives: Protestant nations and Catholic ones. The United States offered the intriguing possibility that perhaps a country could be Protestant without the government having to mention it (as did, increasingly, some of the colonies), and France had once hinted at the dark spectre that a country might become atheist, but usually the conceivable options were confined to two, with the American experiment, if taken into account at all, being considered a variation on one of them. It is needless to say that Victorian Dissenters preferred to live in a Protestant country rather than a Catholic one.

For the Wesleyans, as David Hempton has shown, their religious objections to 'Popery' and their conviction that Protestantism was the only safe foundation for the state, were translated directly into the politics of anti-Catholicism during the period under discussion.[85] For example, in 1857 the *Wesleyan Methodist Magazine* gave this reminder to electors:

> Neither may it be forgotten that we are a free and Christian nation, unlike those that submit to Papal bondage; and that the next Parliament should consist of such as will understand their duty, and perform it, in opposition to Rome.[86]

Nonconformists, however, despite agreeing with the theological critique of the Church of Rome and wishing to live in a Protestant nation, extended their vision of religious equality before the law to include the Catholics in their midst. As with the peace movement, a moment of tremendous crisis must be dealt with – in this instance the Papal Aggression agitation of 1850–1 – but it would present a false picture if focusing on this event obscured the continuity of this theme. The *Leeds Mercury*, at the start of this period, rebuked the Wesleyans for their desire for legislation which would have provided government money for their own schools while blocking Catholic ones from receiving it as well

---

[84] *Nonconformist*, 22 May 1867, p. 418.
[85] Hempton, *Methodism and Politics*, ch. 5 and pp. 183–5, 229–30.
[86] *Wesleyan Methodist Magazine*, April 1857, p. 362.

with the words, 'For ourselves, we declare that the exclusion of the Roman Catholics would only be an additional reason for opposing this insidious measure.'[87] Similarly, at the other end of this period, in 1867, the *Leeds Mercury* remarked clearly:

> The Protestant public have only got half rid of the idea that the Roman Catholics are disloyal and dangerous men. They have only got half rid of the idea because they feel in their hearts that the Roman Catholics have only too much reason to be discontented . . . To give them equal rights with their Protestant fellow-subjects is the only way to make them equally devoted to the maintenance of the Government which secures them in the possession of those rights.[88]

In between these dates, Dissenters often offered not just their goodwill but also their energy to the cause of extending the political rights of Roman Catholics. The *Patriot*'s boast in 1847 that Dissenters made an 'unreserved recognition of the claims of the Roman Catholics to perfect civil equality and protection' was supported by action taken by Dissenters in the following decades.[89]

This commitment went beyond merely not excluding Catholics from general statements of religious equality to fighting actively for the removal of disabilities which applied only to Catholics. The Liberation Society provides ample evidence for this. In the mid-1850s, it was seeking to establish a united front with Roman Catholics for the establishment of religious equality for all, to the point where in 1856 it had 5,000 extra copies of the *Liberator* printed 'to send to the Roman Catholic Priesthood in Ireland, and elsewhere'.[90] A working rapport was established in this year with the Irish Catholic politician, O'Neill Daunt, which continued intermittently for the rest of this period.[91] The Society invariably gave its public support to the Roman Catholic Oaths Bill and other measures which sought to remove Catholic political disabilities, including one which sought to remove an anti-transubstantiation declaration, Protestant disgust for this doctrine notwithstanding.[92] When the Society learned in 1865 that Protestant Dissenters on the Isle of Wight were not intending to support the Liberal candidate in the forthcoming general election on the grounds that he was a Roman Catholic, they sent H. S. Skeats to investigate and then G. W. Conder

---

[87] *Leeds Mercury*, 10 April 1847, p. 4.
[88] *Leeds Mercury*, 1 March 1867, p. 2.
[89] *Patriot*, 7 January 1847, p. 12.
[90] Liberation Society Papers, A/LIB/2, 9 June 1856, minute 593.
[91] *Ibid.*, 8 September 1856, minute 611; A/LIB/3, 25 October 1867, minute 563a.
[92] *Ibid.*, 24 March 1865, minute 508; 8 February 1867, minute 430.

literally to lecture them on religious equality. The man was duly returned, making him the only Catholic occupying an English seat in the Commons at that time and, on the estimation of the Executive committee, 'the result is one with which, to a large extent, the Society may fairly be credited'.[93] The Liberation Society had a unique burden of consistency to maintain, but its support for political equality for Catholics was not out of step with Nonconformist attitudes. The more moderate Protestant Dissenting Deputies petitioned in favour of the Roman Catholic Oaths Bill, despite their name and special interest *raison d' être*.[94] The editor of the *Methodist New Connexion Magazine* argued in 1848 that even though Popery was error, 'since the papist is a British subject he has a right to share with other British subjects all the immunities of the State'.[95] Despite its populist tone, the *British Banner* boasted in 1854 (just a few years after the Papal Aggression agitation) that it 'endeavoured fairly and fully, to represent the just and generous views of Protestant Dissenters on the subject, contending for the same civil rights and privileges on behalf of the Papists as for ourselves'.[96] Samuel Morley tried to do his bit for equal treatment by hiring whomsoever was deemed suitable to work in his business even if the person happened to be Roman Catholic.[97] Dissenters had a political vision for religious equality which did not exclude those faithful to the Church of Rome.

A contentious issue throughout this period was the government grant to Maynooth College, an Irish institution for the training of Catholic priests. Catholics were grateful for the yearly allowance, while extreme anti-Catholic Churchmen wanted it stopped. Nonconformists opposed the grant from their Voluntaryist position that no religious body should receive government money and that no government money should go toward education, particularly religious education. Because they conscientiously refused to receive any grants themselves, they were naturally annoyed to see their tax money used to support the propagation of a religion which they profoundly abhorred.

However, Nonconformists were concerned to distinguish their Voluntaryist rationale for opposing the Maynooth grant from the sectarian motivations of others, including the Churchmen who were leading the campaign in Parliament. In 1845, the militant Dissenters, inspired by the recently founded Anti-State Church Association, broke away from a united anti-Maynooth conference to form their own meeting which

---

[93] *Ibid.*, 1 July 1865, minute 563.
[94] Dissenting Deputies Minutes, vol. 13, 3 April 1865, p. 336.
[95] *Methodist New Connexion Magazine*, 51 (1848), p. 449.
[96] Supplement to the *British Banner*, 27 December 1854, p. 913.
[97] Hodder, *Morley*, p. 200.

would ground its objection in Voluntaryism. This break-away gathering released an 'Address to the Roman Catholics of Ireland' which promised: 'We are ready to contend by your side for the attainment of an equal participation in all rights, ecclesiastical, political, and social.' The Dissenting press backed it in full, leaving the old-style moderate, John Blackburn, feeling bitter and alone.[98] Even the newly founded organ for moderate opinion, the *British Quarterly Review*, gave its qualified, retrospective blessing to the separate, Voluntaryist approach to this agitation.[99] When it was rumoured in 1848 that the government wanted to pay Roman Catholic priests in Ireland, the *Baptist Magazine* claimed that Nonconformity had learned some lessons from the agitation against the bill in 1845 which had placed the Maynooth grant on a permanent footing:

> it has afforded us pleasure to find the conviction general, indeed almost unanimous, that the opposition will be conducted most effectively if instead of combining in one association, the dissenters conduct their opposition on the principles which belong exclusively to them . . . A combined movement was attempted in reference to the Maynooth bill, but the result did not leave on the minds of those who were most active in it an impression that it was desirable to adopt the same course a second time.[100]

In 1847, the Dissenting Deputies patiently rehearsed the distinctive position of Nonconformists for the benefit of confused observers in the government:

> Protestant Dissenters were conscientiously opposed to Romanism but without hostility to Romanists. They resisted endowments to the Roman Catholic Priesthood on the same ground of its general injustice as they would resist endowments to any other Class of Religionists. They wished for no relief to themselves nor any civil immunity which they would not willingly share with all their fellow subjects. They had petitioned for the removal of Roman Catholic disabilities . . .[101]

Nevertheless, Dissenters disagreed and vacillated during this period on whether or not to join wider movements for repealing the Maynooth grant. In 1852, the *Nonconformist* was delighted to hear that the

[98] John Blackburn, *The Three Conferences held by the opponents of the Maynooth College Endowment Bill . . . containing a Vindication of the Author From the Aspersions of the Dissenting Press*, London: Jackson & Walford, 1845. (The quotation is from p. 23.)
[99] *British Quarterly Review*, II, III (August 1845), pp. 108–9.
[100] *Baptist Magazine*, October 1848, p. 628.
[101] Dissenting Deputies Minutes, vol. 11, 19 February 1847, p. 362.

Dissenting Deputies had declared that it would no longer fight the Maynooth grant as a separate issue along with the Protestant Alliance, but only as a part of a campaign against all government grants to religious bodies. The paper noted:

> An isolated assault upon it, and *it exclusively*, can only be interpreted now as an assault upon Romanism *as such* – an assault which we think the *Legislature* of this empire would do most unrighteously as well as unwisely to make.[102]

In 1853, Josiah Conder regretted that Dissenters in Parliament were so divided on this issue, with some supporting the anti-Catholic Churchman, Richard Spooner, in his motion for repeal, others voting against him and still others abstaining. Nevertheless, he was gratified to think that they were all agreed on the 'general question relating to State Endowments for religious purposes'.[103] In 1855, the Liberation Society agreed to support Spooner's motion: 'care being taken to indicate the broad ground on which the Society takes action'.[104] By 1857 the *Nonconformist* had reversed itself, as had Edward Miall, who had been one of those voting against Spooner's motion. The paper confessed that Catholics might well wonder why they were picking on their little grant when the whole Irish Church Establishment remained intact, but it explained apologetically that the strength of resistance to disendowment had 'compelled the Voluntaries to consider whether it was possible to get at the citadel without helping to capture one of the outworks, and whether it would not be wise to lend their strength against the weakest'.[105] Meanwhile, about the same time, the Wesleyans were rallying the troops in the other camp, instructing electors not only to 'exact an unequivocal pledge' in favour of repeal from candidates, but also warning them that the 'general question of church endowments is not to be confounded with this', lest they do the right thing for the wrong reason.[106] Given the unquestionable grounds of principle and fairness on which Nonconformists could oppose the Maynooth grant, as exemplified by their own refusal to receive government money, it is a testimony to their deep recognition of the necessity of religious equality for Roman Catholics that they even considered holding aloof from a campaign to oppose it.

On 29 September 1850 Pope Pius IX changed the structure of the leadership of the Roman Catholic Church in England from the Vicar

---

[102] *Nonconformist*, 21 April 1852, p. 297.
[103] Conder, *Political Position*, p. 66.
[104] Liberation Society Papers, A/LIB/2, 13 April 1855, minute 357.
[105] *Nonconformist*, 21 January 1857, p. 41.
[106] *Wesleyan Methodist Magazine*, April 1857, p. 362.

Apostolic system, befitting a missionary situation, to the Church's preferred hierarchical system, complete with bishops bearing territorial titles. The tremendous national anti-Catholic fervour which stemmed from this event, the so-called 'Papal Aggression' agitation, culminated in the passing into law on 1 August 1851 of the Ecclesiastical Titles Bill: an act which prohibited the use of territorial titles by bishops and other church officials in Britain (excluding Ireland) from bodies other than the Established Church and the Protestant Episcopal Church of Scotland. The agitation was fuelled between these opening and closing events by several significant intervening ones. In Catholic churches on the Sundays of 20 and 27 October a pastoral letter was read which had been written from the Continent by the still absent Catholic leader, Nicholas Wiseman, who had been appointed 'Archbishop of Westminster' in the new hierarchy. The language of the letter might have been inspiring when read to the faithful at mass, but it sounded arrogant and threatening to many Protestants who read it in the press. On 4 November the Prime Minister, Lord John Russell, threw his reputation as a friend of religious toleration to the wind and wrote an alarmist letter in which he claimed that the actions of the Pope were 'inconsistent with the Queen's supremacy'.[107] Meanwhile, the next day was the fifth of November and the significance of Guy Fawkes celebrations was not lost on an aroused Protestant population.[108] The Papal Aggression agitation had been ignited, and the flames from a night of bonfires would not quickly die down.[109]

Churchmen busied themselves defending the royal supremacy: the Queen was the supreme temporal and spiritual authority in the land; the Pope was a would-be usurper, a foreign invader. Dissent was left in a quandary. It had always vehemently denied the doctrine of royal supremacy, but many Nonconformists felt a deep need to find a way to reassert the protest in their Protestantism. Those who resisted the whole agitation made the most of the difficulty created by its being couched as a defence of the royal supremacy. The *Nonconformist* spent

---

[107] The letter is reprinted in E. R. Norman, *Anti-Catholicism in Victorian England*, London: George Allen and Unwin, 1968 pp. 159–61. For the background to Russell's stance on this issue, see G. I. T. Machin, 'Lord John Russell and the Prelude to the Ecclesiastical Titles Bill, 1846–51', *Journal of Ecclesiastical History*, XXV, 3 (July 1974), pp. 277–95.

[108] Russell's letter, however, was not published until after Guy Fawkes Day.

[109] A detailed summary of the unfolding events from the Catholic perspective is given in Wilfrid Ward, *Life and Times of Cardinal Wiseman*, 2 vols., London: Longmans, Green and Co., 1897, chapters 16–20. Walter Ralls has identified some of the underlying forces which were influencing Protestants: 'The Papal Aggression of 1850: A Study in Victorian Anti-Catholicism', *Church History*, 43 (1974), pp. 242–56.

much time trying to place the matter in the right light for Dissenters, but its appeal, 'Let us look at the matter coolly', was not heard by those who were already heated.[110] Bristol Quakers took the unusual step of preparing an address explaining why they would *not* memorialise: the address to the Queen was based on a belief in the royal supremacy.[111] The Yorkshire Baptist Association passed a similar resolution. It explained:

> as Baptists have always denied the lawfulness, in a religious point of view, of the Queen's supremacy in the Church, equally with that of the Pope, they dare not, by sustaining the former against the latter, even seem to admit the one claim to be better than the other.[112]

Even the *British Banner*, in the early days of the agitation, was sensitive to the problem. On 6 November it claimed that:

> Dissenters, in this matter, having nothing positive to ask of the Government . . . If, by memorialising the Government, they could obtain on interdict tomorrow on the present movement, no such memorial, we are satisfied would proceed from them. We further conclude, that they will enter into no confederacy with the clergy of the English Church for the agitation of this question . . .

It saw the royal supremacy and the papal supremacy as both errors and, in true Dissenting fashion, its solution was:

> Sever the Church from the State, the Catholics from Rome, place all sects on the same foundation, without patronage of one or persecution of another, and leave them in quiet to conduct their own wars, so long as they do not interfere with the laws of the land and the peace of society.[113]

But the wave had not yet reached its full crest. Within a month, J. P. Mursell, that great friend of religious equality, had rallied to the Queen's defence on the grounds that the new hierarchy 'audaciously impinges on the civil supremacy of our only and rightful sovereign'.[114] In his mind, and increasingly in the minds of many other Dissenters, this was an issue of national, not religious, loyalty. As Josiah Conder would later state it, 'The Supremacy of the Crown is, in reference to all foreign jurisdiction,

---

[110] *Nonconformist*, 4 December 1850, p. 969.
[111] *Friend*, Twelfth Month [December] 1850, pp. 222–3. It was signed by fifty-three Friends and the *Friend* endorsed it.
[112] Passed on 20 December 1850: *Nonconformist*, 1 January 1851, p. 4.
[113] *British Banner*, 6 November 1850, p. 748.
[114] *British Banner*, 4 December 1850, p. 815; *Nonconformist*, 18 December 1850, pp. 1009–10, 1020–1.

but another name for the National sovereignty.'[115] The *Nonconformist* could argue that Dissenting ministers take the ecclesiastical title 'reverend' without the permission of the Queen, Wesleyans created territorial jurisdictions in England without royal consent, Anglican bishops nurture an Episcopal hierarchy in the United States without creating an uproar over sovereignty, and numerous other such points, but it was not enough to stop the wave of patriotic Protestantism which was engulfing many Dissenters. 'Church in danger' never impressed them, but 'crown in danger' struck a nerve.[116]

Dissent divided and then divided again. It split between those who agitated and those who refrained, and those who agitated scattered in different directions. Should they create a united front with Churchmen? What exactly was their objection to what the Pope had done? The stakes were high. The *Nonconformist* in one corner felt that joining in the agitation might show that the friends of religious equality had been found wanting in their hour of testing, while the *Patriot* in the other corner thought that what was being tested was their Protestantism and patriotism and it shuddered to imagine Dissent failing these tests. Therefore, the *Patriot* tried to rally Dissent to meet the moment. Its article, 'Protestant Dissenters – A call to Union' ended with the words, 'The option lies between Popery and Protestantism; and, in such an alternative, neutrality is treason.'[117] It ran a fierce campaign against the stance the *Nonconformist* was taking, speaking of 'the Nonconformist - Papal party' and claiming the Miall was allied with the new Catholic bishops, demonstrating that 'Extremes meet'.[118] Each side was nervously trying to save Dissent from committing a grave error.

What side did the bulk of Nonconformity take? The great Victorian diarist, C. C. F. Greville, the clerk to the privy council, wrote in his entry for 21 November 1850: 'The Dissenters have I think generally kept aloof and shown no disposition to take an active part.'[119] John Bright, a little more narrowly, claimed in the House of Commons:

---

[115] Conder, *Political Position*, p. 65.
[116] In light of the heightened desire to protect the Queen from offence, it was unfortunate that the delegates of the Ministers of the Three Denominations confused their date for presenting an address to the Sovereign and thereby caused Her Majesty to wait in vain for their arrival: *Baptist Magazine*, March 1851, p. 173.
[117] *Patriot*, 18 November 1850, p. 732.
[118] *Patriot*, 28 November 1850, p. 756; 18 November 1850, p. 732.
[119] Henry Reeve (ed.), *The Greville Memoirs*, VI, London: Longmans, Green, and Co., 1896, p. 377.

In the north of England the Dissenters have unanimously held aloof from the roar that has been got up in reference to this question.[120]

The *Nonconformist*, in far less sweeping language, argued that in the provinces the proportion of Dissenters who were not involved was greater than that in London.[121] George Hadfield claimed that the Congregationalists in Manchester were abstaining from the agitation, but Robert Vaughan went into print to dispute this.[122] There were indeed things happening outside London to cheer the hearts of people like Miall and Bright. On 11 December 1850 a town meeting in Birmingham voted down a proposal to send a memorial to the Queen requesting action to defend her prerogative. The personal influence of Joseph Sturge seems to have secured this result, despite J. A. James siding with those who were in favour of the plan.[123] The Congregationalists and Baptists of Leeds called a meeting in December explicitly to show that Dissent was not impressed with the agitation. On this occasion, G. W. Conder and numerous other men spoke against the uproar. Edward Baines presided at the meeting. He remarked in the opening address:

> We are Protestant Dissenters . . . Claiming religious liberty ourselves, we will never deny it to others (applause). We will be tolerant even to the intolerant. The view of most of those with whom I am acquainted is, that, much and loyally as we are attached to the Queen, we cannot on this occasion address her Majesty, because we do not recognise her ecclesiastical character as the head of the Established Church (hear, hear, and applause). Neither can we ask from Parliament any measure in the slightest degree restricting the civil rights or religious liberties of the Roman Catholics. Our reliance, then, is upon the truth, and upon the God of truth.[124]

Newman Hall, who was at this time a minister in Hull, lectured against joining the agitation and had his addresses printed. He was blatantly defiant, 'I shall not join in the "No Popery" cry. Neither shall I, by avoiding the subject altogether, give occasion to any suspicion of indifference . . .'[125] London might have been preoccupied with the

---

[120] *Hansard*, CXIX, 252 (7 February 1851).
[121] *Nonconformist*, 2 April 1851, p. 257.
[122] *British Banner*, 2 April 1851, p. 294.
[123] Richard, *Sturge*, pp. 412–13.
[124] Reprint from the *Leeds Mercury*: *Nonconformist*, 1 January 1851, p. 2.
[125] Newman Hall, *Dissent and the Papal Bull, No Intolerance: a response to the cry of "No Popery"*, London: John Snow, 1850, p. 6.

'Protestantism of the Protestant religion', but the provinces did not forget the 'dissidence of dissent'.[126]

However, such snapshots of a day in the life of provincial Dissent do not tell the whole story. As the agitation showed no sign of abating, more and more Nonconformists were tempted to join it. Before the Ecclesiastical Titles Bill finally received the royal assent on 1 August 1851 more than one Dissenter who had initially stood aloof had joined the clamour. The Dissenting Deputies typify this journey. Its records of the matter begin with a sub-committee recommendation that the body had no reason to join the agitation and end with it passing a resolution expressing its conviction that the Ecclesiastical Titles Bill was too weak a measure.[127] Miall and Bright's efforts to highlight the provinces were in reaction to the Deputies' decision to add their weight to the agitation. Both of them tried to discredit the body; Miall claimed 'the representative character of these deputies is the veriest pretence'.[128] Of course, they were not acting unanimously. Samuel Morley, who was a Deputy, opposed the agitation to the end – and he was not alone. His failed amendment at the late date of March 1851 said:

> They therefore regret the attempt . . . in the Commons House of Parliament to interfere by Legislative enactment with the discipline and organisation of the Romish Church because they believe it to be a violation of religious liberty . . .
> . . . they earnestly call upon all Protestant Dissenters . . . not to compromise their principles by recognizing the right of the state to interfere with the organization of any religious body whatever.[129]

Still, the collective actions of the Deputies were a sign of which way the currents were drifting.

A few months were also a long time for the *Eclectic Review*. In December 1850, it saw the issue as primarily a matter between 'two rival hierarchies' and it quoted at length and with approval Cardinal Wiseman's *An Appeal to the Reason and Good Feeling of the English People, on the Subject of the Catholic Hierarchy* in order to refute the various charges such as that the Queen's supremacy had been violated: 'The fallacy of this charge he demonstrates in very few words.' More-

---

[126] These two phrases together comprise a quotation from Edmund Burke which was adopted by the *Nonconformist* as its motto.
[127] Dissenting Deputies Minutes, vol. 12, 18 November 1850, p. 141; 31 March 1851, p. 168.
[128] *Nonconformist*, 2 April 1851, p. 257; John Bright made the same point: *Hansard*, CXIV, 252 (7 February 1851).
[129] Dissenting Deputies Minutes, vol. 12, 31 March 1851, p. 170.

over, it claimed that it would be 'inconsistent and disgraceful' for Dissenters to seek 'the interference of the Legislature in an ecclesiastical dispute' and, more than that, Dissenters must not even settle for 'a silent neutrality' but rather fight against the religious persecution of Catholics. Its conclusion is that having an Established Church is the real danger because Papists might take it over, inspiring it to leave its readers with the dramatic maxim: 'THE WAY TO EXTERMINATE TIGERS, IS TO BURN THE JUNGLE.'[130] Several months after this, however, it was ready to announce what kind of legislation it wanted from Parliament. The first article of its proposed four-point bill was, 'We would have the bull of September the 24th disallowed, and its reception into this country prohibited', and the second was, 'all appointments under such bull should be forthwith cancelled'. Although it had enough of a memory of its former way of thinking to add to the first point this virtually incomprehensible proviso:

> it being at the same time distinctly notified that no interference is contemplated with the appointment of purely ecclesiastical officers of whatever grade.[131]

Henceforth, the *Eclectic Review* was essentially on board with the agitation in general and the Ecclesiastical Titles Bill in particular.[132] The *British Banner* swiftly moved from the restrained position quoted previously, ending up, like the Dissenting Deputies, complaining that the measure was not tough enough.[133] Baines might have made a great speech in December, but by March (admittedly quite late in the game) the *Leeds Mercury* was in favour of legislation. At least it had the dignity to run an introspective article the month before in which it confessed that it honestly did not know whether the papal bull represented a serious danger or not.[134] Desertion was rife in the religious equality camp.

Of course, not everyone deserted but, as with the peace party during the Crimean War, some of those who remained might have read the public mood and decided it was a time to keep silent.[135] Newspapers do not have such a luxury, but people and denominational monthlies have

---

[130] *Eclectic Review*, n.s. XXVIII (July–Dec. 1850), pp. 739–63.
[131] *Ibid.*, XXIX (Jan.–June 1851), pp. 247–54.
[132] *Ibid.*, pp. 378–87, 502–11, pp. 632–4.
[133] *British Banner*, 19 February 1851, p. 120.
[134] *Leeds Mercury*, 1 February 1851, p. 4; 22 March 1851, p. 4. D. G. Paz does not note that Baines was slow to join the agitation and underrates his commitment to religious equality for Catholics after this event: *Popular Anti-Catholicism in Mid-Victorian England*, Stanford, California: Stanford University Press, 1992, pp. 215–21.
[135] The Executive Committee of the Liberation Society had an 'extended conversation' on the new hierarchy, but did not take any position concerning the matter: Liberation Society Papers, A/LIB/1, 14 November 1850, p. 301.

more latitude.[136] Various eminent Nonconformists can be found opposing the agitation at one point or another but, in the light of the
documented shifts of opinion, it is difficult to predict whether they
maintained this position to the end or not. J. H. Hinton, for example,
preached against the agitation and had the sermon printed, but that
address was delivered at the early date of 2 November. Although it is
probable that Hinton – like Miall, Bright, Morley, Newman Hall and
others – held his ground to the end, one doubts very much that he could
have still claimed in the spring of 1851 that he was speaking on behalf of
his congregation.[137] Snapshot evidence provides a glimpse of only one
moment in a shifting scene.[138]

When it became clear that the country would not be satisfied until
there was legislation, some Dissenting friends of religious equality tried
to find a scapegoat to offer up for this sacrifice. They all thought that the
real villain was church establishments in general, but they were aware
that this was not the hour when this point would capture the public
imagination.[139] Therefore, the *Nonconformist* suggested that if Lord John
Russell must have a bill he should at least have a better one. It imagined
one for him which comprised four points: (1) ending the Bible printing
monopoly (a true Protestant knows that the Bible is what fights Roman
Catholicism) (2) removing the religious tests at the ancient universities
(this would help clear the air of the Romish spirit which pervades a
Tractarian bastion) (3) terminating grants of money for 'religious
teachers of various sects, in our colonies' (a little Voluntaryist measure
capitalising on public indignation regarding the few state-paid Catholic
priests) and (4) inspecting of religious houses. This last suggestion shows
how desperately the paper was groping around for some acceptable

---

[136] The *Wesleyan Methodist Association Magazine*, for example, refused to call for
legislation in an article entitle 'Papal Aggression' in February 1851 (pp. 69–74), and
resisted this temptation throughout, reprinting in April a twenty-four-year-old
theological critique of Roman Catholicism on the grounds that: 'The best means
of opposing Papal aggression is that of pouring the light of truth . . .' (p. 158).
Undoubtedly it was easier for a denominational monthly to follow a course like this:
as is shown by quotations elsewhere, the *Baptist Magazine* and the *Friend* also
successfully avoided calling for legislation.
[137] John Howard Hinton, *The Romish Hierarchy in England: A Sermon preached at
Devonshire Square Chapel, London, on the 2nd November, 1850*, London: Houlston
and Stoneman, 1850, pp. iii–iv.
[138] Conversely, S. M. Peto voted for the Ecclesiastical Titles Bill, but that piece of
information also reveals his position only at one point in the agitation: *Hansard*,
CXIV, 701 (14 February 1851).
[139] There was a suspicion in the air generally that the Church of England was
partially to blame for the rise of popery because of Tractarian activities. Lord John
Russell had made this point himself in his Durham letter. However, Dissenters were
not able to focus the agitation toward that quarter.

measure with which to pacify its enraged countrymen. When the fiercely Protestant Churchman, C. N. Newdegate, later mounted a campaign for the inspection of nunneries, the *Nonconformist* thoroughly denounced it.[140] The *Baptist Magazine* stood against 'the so called aggression of the pope' in a long article which ended with these faithful words:

> there must be a most vigilant watch kept on the government and legislature, lest a single landmark of our liberties be removed. Let the great truth be often urged on their attention, that the laws of the land should know no sect, no party of religionists whatever; but hold an even balance to all. While justice demands liberty for every man to worship God without let or hindrance as his conscience shall approve, liberty demands the equal exercise of justice in protecting all and favouring none.

Nevertheless, it was also looking for a convincing object for redirected attention. The article wondered if the introduction of the force of canon law into English Catholicism, which was a by-product of the new hierarchy, was not the real issue, and even if perhaps its prohibition was an appropriate action for Parliament to take. However, it confessed with a refreshing note of caution: 'we do not feel at present competent to decide'.[141] The *Friend* never wavered in its opposition to the agitation and the Ecclesiastical Titles Bill, supporting the *Nonconformist* by name. Its own suggestion was:

> we do not hesitate to acknowledge that the laws relating to bequests of property from individuals at the point of death, made under priestly influence, as well as to the regulation of monastic establishments, now so much on the increase in this country, claim the attentive supervision of the legislature.[142]

The passions of the day were so high that even the most faithful friends of religious equality were resigned to the inevitability of some anti-Catholic legislation.   ·

Some of the reasons why so many Nonconformists – the self-declared friends of religious equality – gave in to this agitation have already been exposed. They were simply pulled along by the strong, passionate currents of the hour. Dissenters had always had an unflinching and emotive religious objection to Roman Catholicism. The Wesleyans had a particular obsession with popery. Not being friends of religious equality, it goes without saying that they fought for a place in the forefront of the Papal Aggression agitation. While the *Friend* bolstered its stance by

[140] *Nonconformist*, 15 January 1851, p. 41; 8 March 1865, p. 181.
[141] *Baptist Magazine*, January 1851, pp. 11–20.
[142] *Friend*, Tenth Month [October] 1851, p. 187.

reprinting an article from the *Nonconformist*, the *Wesleyan Methodist Magazine* reprinted from the *Church of England Quarterly Review*.[143] However, it must be remembered that even the most politically liberal Evangelical Dissenters protested vehemently against Roman Catholicism as a religious system. Even the *Nonconformist* had as the second half of its motto 'the Protestantism of the Protestant religion' and just a few months before the fateful papal bull, it had run a lead article ridiculing the Catholic Church entitled 'The Winking Madonna'.[144] In the midst of a great uproar, not everyone could maintain the *Nonconformist*'s balancing act of condemning Roman Catholic ideas as lethal on one hand, while defending their right to be propagated unhindered on the other. Secondly, as has been noted, most Dissenters did not even see it as a religious equality issue, but rather as one of national sovereignty. This observation is reinforced by the fact that Dissenters did not renege on their commitment to political rights for Roman Catholics. Even at its most strident period in the crisis, the *Patriot* paused to note that it still supported the Catholic Emancipation Act.[145]

A look at the diary of the Churchman, Lord Shaftesbury, helps to put these two points into a context wider than Dissent. Although he would shortly come to play a leading role in the agitation, on 25 October 1850 Shaftesbury wrote:

> We must be careful not to push this matter too far; it is an act of great annoyance and audacity, but not contrary to law, nor worth, in fact, a new law.

The lead he was giving not too long thereafter illustrates how passions mounted over time, sweeping so much into their current. His entry exactly one month later illustrates the way that nationalism was a driving force behind the movement:

> What a surprising ferment! It abates not a jot; meeting after meeting in every town and parish of the country. Vast meetings of counties, specially of York. At concerts and theatres, I hear, 'God save the Queen' is demanded three times in succession. It resembles a storm over the whole ocean; it is a national sentiment, a rising of the land! All opinions seem for a while merged in this one feeling.[146]

---

[143] *Friend*, Tenth Month [October] 1851, p. 185; *Wesleyan Methodist Magazine*, February 1851, pp. 153–8.

[144] *Nonconformist*, 3 July 1850, p. 529.

[145] *Patriot*, 21 November 1850, p. 740. Conversely, the *Wesleyan Methodist Magazine* did not need a national agitation to call Catholic Emancipation into question: November 1858, p. 1007.

[146] Edwin Hodder, *Life and Work of the Seventh Earl of Shaftesbury, K.G.*, vol. 2, London: Cassell, 1887, pp. 325, 328.

The emotional humanness and patriotic nationalism of Nonconformists go a long way toward explaining their actions. Their fault was that many of them were little better than most of their countrymen at this moment, despite the expectations of higher things which their own ideals and past actions had created.

However, there is another factor which needs to be taken into account: the old, liberal dilemma of how to treat the illiberal; the recurring bugbear that they will exploit the opportunities afforded by a liberal society in order to destroy it. In today's world, liberals in various nations sometimes wonder uneasily if radical Islamic groups will mount a systematic attack on all they hold dear from the safe harbour of liberal rights, liberties and protections. In Victorian Britain, the Church of Rome was seen as a persecuting, illiberal body. The Inquisition was its heritage, and the treatment of Protestants in Catholic countries was still thought to be despicable. It was assumed that if Catholicism ever came to dominate Britain again, religious liberty would be swept away. There was a long tradition of viewing Catholicism as a threat to the established government of the nation, with the Gun Powder Plot as just one link in its chain. To such liberal fears, past and present, the voice of calmness usually replies that their own values are firmly entrenched in the land and their opponents are only a minority; therefore liberalism can afford to treat them liberally. J. A. James' son remarked tellingly of his father:

> He was always for "Catholic Emancipation" circumstanced as the empire is; but he held that a Papist, on his own shewing, has no right to expect toleration from a man of any other faith, but is always to be regarded as the common enemy of human-kind; and he thought that Queen Pomare was right in sending the French priests away from her dominions.[147]

However, when passions are inflamed the threat can appear exaggerated. Such was the case during the Papal Aggression agitation. Most Englishmen were not in a mood to speak the double-edged words of response to Cardinal Wiseman which the *Nonconformist* tried to put in their mouth:

> "Whilst we wish to yield to you all that you can claim for your Church, and for her perfect organisation, we beg also to let you know that we are not ignorant of her true character, and that we abhor it as destructive of right, freedom, and charity, and will expose its villainies, past and passing, to the light of noon-day intelligence."[148]

The *Patriot* was more in keeping with the prevailing sense of alarm. It ran an article entitled 'The True Limits of Religious Liberty' in which it

---

[147] Dale, *James*, p. 583.
[148] *Nonconformist*, 27 November 1850, p. 949.

claimed that a broad line needed to be drawn between 'religious disabilities' which are certainly unjust and 'political restrictions, which are simply of a protective character'.[149] Many people believed that popery was gaining ground. Tractarianism in the Established Church, celebrated conversions to the Church of Rome and Irish immigration had been ominous signs, but the papal aggression had now begun in earnest.[150] The illiberal invasion seemed real and therefore many Dissenters were tempted to call for emergency measures.

Strong passions tend to dissipate. If popery momentarily seemed poised to conquer, that illusion was shortly dispersed. If the Ecclesiastical Titles Bill briefly seemed too weak, with the passing of a little time nothing further was desired. John Angell James wrote, barely a month after the bill had received royal assent, that 'the German mode of thinking' was the real threat to true religion:

> I am myself far more apprehensive of mischief from this source than I am from Popery . . . I have no fear at all of Popish ascendancy.[151]

When the Dissenting Deputies refused to fight the Maynooth grant along with the Protestant Alliance less than a year after the passing of the Ecclesiastical Titles Bill, the *Nonconformist* rightly concluded:

> We regard these as pleasing auguries of the rapid convalescence of the Dissenting body, so suddenly thrown into hysterics by the appointment of a Papal hierarchy in Great Britain and Ireland. The patient, so far as he was affected, is now coming around again, and will, doubtless, attain before long his wonted health and vigour.[152]

As has already been shown, Dissenters went on to support the Roman Catholic Oaths Bill in particular, and religious equality for Catholics in general, during the rest of this period.

D. G. Paz has provided a wealth of detailed information on the behaviour of Dissenters in this crisis, calculating, for example, that only 0.06% of Memorials to the Queen came from explicitly Nonconformist sources (as opposed to 26.97% from Churchmen) and, extraordinarily, 0.00% of Petitions to the Legislature (as opposed to 14.21%

---

[149] *Patriot*, 18 November 1850, p. 732.
[150] For an analysis of the numerical increase of Catholics in England through Irish immigration, see Philip Hughes, 'The English Catholics in 1850', in George Andrew Beck (ed.), *The English Catholics, 1850–1950*, London: Burns Oates, 1950, pp. 42–85.
[151] James to Dr Sprague, 18 September 1851: Dale, *James*, p. 545.
[152] *Nonconformist*, 21 April 1852, p. 297. For the Protestant Alliance and organised anti-Catholicism in general, see John Wolffe, *The Protestant Crusade in Great Britain, 1829–1860*, Oxford: Clarendon Press, 1991.

from Wesleyans).[153] Nevertheless, despite his study being a gold mine of data, his general evaluation underestimates the degree to which Dissenters resisted the agitation. His conclusion is, 'So, with but a few exceptions, Evangelical Nonconformity added its distinctive twang to the anti-Catholic bray.'[154] This assessment – and his analysis in general – has several weaknesses: notably, although both of these distinctions are sometimes made, Paz too often blends Wesleyans into Dissent and uses evidence of religious objections to Catholicism to serve to indicate an approval of political restrictions. Moreover, his own discussion shows that his 'few exceptions' include, for example, the Baptist denominations.[155] Nevertheless, if Paz has underplayed Dissenting resistance to this wave of politicised anti-Catholicism, the evidence which has been presented here clearly confirms that it can be safely said that the majority of Nonconformists backed the agitation. When weighing in the balance Dissenting attitudes toward Catholic rights, a just condemnation of the action of many during the Papal Aggression agitation must be tempered by a recognition that Dissenters did not whip up this hysterical reaction: the credit for that goes to the secular newspaper *The Times*, the friend of toleration Lord John Russell, and to some notable Churchmen. The country was in such an emotional frenzy that even some Roman Catholics such as Lord Beaumont backed the agitation. The Duke of Norfolk supported the Ecclesiastical Titles Bill and converted to Anglicanism, neatly making his peace with Rome on his deathbed.[156] Moreover, other mitigating points include: the brave way in which a prominent minority of Dissenting leaders and organs resisted it to the end, the nationalist light in which the issue was held, and most importantly of all, the proven commitment to religious equality for Catholics which was demonstrated before and after this incident. None of these points, however, should obscure the fact that this was a moment when the Dissenting community failed to live up to its own noble principles.

Although the leadership of the Catholic Church in England continued to use their new titles, no prosecution was ever brought under the provisions of the Ecclesiastical Titles Act. The Act was finally repealed in 1871, but such a move was already being seriously mooted in 1867. The *Baptist Magazine*, whose own hands were clean, spoke of the agitation which had produced it as 'a paroxysm of national frenzy' and noted wryly concerning the repeal movement:

---

[153] Paz, *Popular Anti-Catholicism*, p. 47 (Table 3).
[154] *Ibid.*, p. 195.
[155] *Ibid.*, pp. 153–95.
[156] 'Henry Charles Howard' (thirteenth Duke of Norfolk), *Dictionary of National Biography*, X, p. 37.

> History teaches us that it is the function of one generation to undo the follies generated by the passions and prejudices of the generation which preceded it . . . But in the present instance we have the example of repentance in the very same generation, and by the very same men who perpetrated the folly.[157]

The *Wesleyan Methodist Magazine* was predictably unrepentant. It saw the repeal movement as part of a Catholic plot 'towards the ascendancy at which they are systematically and unintermittingly aiming'; but this too just goes to show that everyone was back in their usual places.[158] The *Leeds Mercury* can serve to represent repentant Dissent. In 1867, it confessed that the bill had passed 'in a time of much fierce excitement' and attacked Orangemen for trying to block its repeal.[159] Despite all the shameful rhetoric that was uttered at the height of the agitation, the story of Nonconformist politics concerning Roman Catholics during this period remains foremost one of an unfolding campaign for the removal of Catholic disabilities.

Mid-Victorian Nonconformists were proud to be English, loyal to their nation, devoted to their Queen. Edward Baines' enemies might have liked to remind him of his call for 'Three Groans for the Queen' during the troubled days of the Reform Bill, but that was a youthful indiscretion.[160] The true Baines was the one who wrote poetry in praise of Her Majesty and anxiously endeavoured to find a channel through which he could have it officially presented to her:

> Mother of princes, trebly blest
> In Consort, children, land,
> Of history's queens the first and best,
> We own thy mild command.
>
> Still happier flow thy lengthened days,
> Their evening close serene!
> United England shouts and prays –
> *God bless and save the Queen!*[161]

J. P. Mursell, when he was president of the Baptist Union in 1864, said on behalf of his denomination in his presidential address:

---

[157] *Baptist Magazine*, May 1867, p. 310.
[158] *Wesleyan Methodist Magazine*, September 1867, p. 854.
[159] *Leeds Mercury*, 1 June 1867, p. 5.
[160] Fraser, 'Edward Baines', in Hollis (ed.), *Pressure from Without*, p. 185.
[161] Baines Papers, Ms. 1–41, Baines to Sir Charles Phipps, 1 September 1858, and loose draft. The Dissenting community was also allowed to taste Baines' royalist poetry: *Wesleyan Methodist Association Magazine*, July 1866, p. 455.

> We, as a body, in conjunction with other sections of the Dissenting community, yield to none in loyalty to the Queen, and in attachment to her dynasty, and shall not cease to offer our prayers at the throne of the heavenly grace for her prolonged happiness and for the continuance of her line – we honour and obey her as the head of the civil authority of the empire.[162]

The eighth triennial conference of the Liberation Society in 1868 was not adjourned until after three cheers has been given for Her Majesty and the national anthem had been sung.[163] The *Congregational Year Book* for 1857 (to take a volume at random) included in its calendar the birthdays of all ten members of the Queen's family, and Samuel Martin humbly told the Congregational Union in his chairman's address in 1862:

> Knowing that the sound cannot reach the royal ear, and bring upon us royal smiles, and secure royal favour, we can in all simplicity, and godly sincerity, and true concord, shout in this assembly, "God save our Queen!"[164]

Dissenters were not devoid of the national sentiments common to their countrymen.

Nevertheless, Nonconformists had their own convictions which sometimes set them apart from their fellow-citizens – and even the actions of their Queen. Moreover, as the disestablishment and religious equality campaigns reveal, Dissenters were often opposed to the very acts which Churchmen thought expressed their national identity as a Christian country with a Christian government. A case in point is royal proclamations of national days of humiliation and fasting or of thanksgiving. There was plenty of opportunities to contemplate the appropriateness of such proclamations during this period: a Fast Day in March 1847 in response to the Irish Famine, followed by a Thanksgiving Day for the harvest in October 1847, a Fast Day in April 1854 at the start of the Crimean War, a Thanksgiving Day in October 1854 for the harvest, a Fast Day in March 1855 due to the state of the war, a Thanksgiving Day for the ending of the war in September 1855 and a Fast Day in October 1857 in response to the Indian Mutiny.

Many Dissenters conscientiously objected to such proclamations on the grounds that they reflected an improper mingling of the state with religion. The Sovereign had no right to tell people to respond to God in a certain way. Repentance and gratitude were essential national reactions to the Almighty, but the state could not produce them by edict, nor was it right for it to make the attempt. Olive Anderson has offered a vital initial

[162] *Baptist Magazine*, May 1864, p. 281.
[163] Supplement to the *Liberator*, 1 June 1868, p. 106.
[164] *Congregational Year Book* for 1857, p. [vi]; for 1863, p. 52.

discussion of this subject.[165] However, her interest is in Dissenting attitudes toward the causes of the proclamations rather than toward the proclamations *per se*. Dissenters as patriots and believers in the power of prayer were naturally disinclined to let their protest be misconstrued. The more they felt solidarity with the sentiment which prompted the proclamation, the more cautious they might be tempted to be when objecting to it. The *Patriot* stood clearly against the proclamations of 1847 for ideological reasons. It even retold with delight the *Nonconformist*'s smirking remark that Dissenters should spend the Fast Day, not at solemn religious services, but at public meetings to protest against the government's education policy. However, its comments also indicate that the paper was not particularly concerned about the Irish famine at this stage.[166] Even the Methodist New Connexion was sensitive to this issue. Its magazine clarified its reservations regarding the Fast Day in 1847:

> Nor should we object to a day being set apart specially for such exercises, providing it were the voluntary and spontaneous act of the Christian Churches of the land. But the Royal proclamation *commands all* to fast . . . [167]

The enduring attitude of many Dissenters toward proclamations is nicely illustrated by the reaction of the *Friend* to the 1847 Fast Day. It briefly summarised Quaker objections to such days, ending with:

> the infringement of the rights of conscience in the imposition of religious exercised by the civil government, and the presumption of such an act in reference to Him who alone is Head and Ruler of his Church.

However, its main response was a dismissive suggestion that those interested could consult the decision of the Yearly Meeting on such matters which was given in 1833.[168] The firm ground of principle was beneath their feet. There was no need to reconsider their position every time there was a new royal proclamation.

Olive Anderson, in seeking to demonstrate attitudes toward the Crimean War, argues, citing the *Patriot* and the *British Banner*, that 'even voluntaryists observed the Fast Day' of 1854. However, her own quotation from the *Banner* makes it clear that they were explicitly not acquiescing in the idea of the appropriateness of royal proclamations as

---

[165] Olive Anderson, 'The reactions of Church and Dissent towards the Crimean War', *Journal of Ecclesiastical History*, 16 (1965), pp. 209–20.
[166] *Patriot*, 22 March 1847, pp. 178, 180; 14 October 1847, p. 692.
[167] *Methodist New Connexion Magazine*, 50 (1847), p. 192.
[168] *Friend*, Fourth Month [April] 1847, pp. 72–73.

such, but merely seeking to show their solidarity with the national mood.[169] This was a typical Dissenting response: join in prayer – which is always a good thing – but protest against the involvement of the state. Moreover, the newspapers she cites did not represent everyone. On this same day in 1854 when fasting was declared to be in order, a group of Nonconformists – including J. Carvell Williams, Henry Richard, Edward Miall and C. S. Miall – ostentatiously had a dinner party.[170] Of course some of these were against the war which occasioned the fast, as was John Bright, who wrote bitterly in his journal:

> Day of Humiliation and Prayer on account of war with Russia. It is wonderful what an amount of hypocrisy and ignorance there is in this proceeding. The Government secures the co-operation of the State Church and thus attempts to obtain the concurrence and sympathy of the "religious public" to their wicked policy.[171]

In 1854, the *Eclectic Review* registered its disapproval of both the proclamation of the Fast Day and the Thanksgiving Day, whilst making it clear that it was the secular source rather than the sentiment to which it objected.[172] Perhaps dining was not the summit of fast day protests. Thomas Binney did preach on the appointed Fast Day in 1855, but his address was defiantly entitled 'Objections to the royal Proclamations'.[173] Anderson notes that this Fast was unpopular for other reasons but, once again, this point must not obscure the conscientious objection which remained constant. Perhaps no event in this period more galvanised national sentiment than the Indian Mutiny; nevertheless the *Baptist Magazine* was not ashamed to write at that time:

> On two or three occasions within the last few years, it has happened that, under the pressure of some national calamity, actual or apprehended, the Government has appointed a day for fasting and humiliation. The recent disastrous events in India have given rise to a desire, expressed in many quarters, that such a day should be again appointed. As Nonconformists, we take a preliminary objection to any such action on the part of the Government, deeming any interference with religious rites to be an intrusion into a province which does not belong to it.[174]

---

[169] Anderson, 'Reactions of Church and Dissent', pp. 216–17.
[170] Miall, *Richard*, p. 103.
[171] Trevelyan, *Bright*, p. 234.
[172] *Eclectic Review*, n.s. XXXV (Jan.–June 1854), pp. 637–8; XXVI (July–Dec. 1854), p. 509.
[173] This address was published and the *Baptist Magazine* approved of it: May 1855, p. 298.
[174] *Baptist Magazine*, October 1857, p. 597. Moreover, this was written, not as a timely reminder to those who might waver, but merely as a topical way of beginning

Not all Dissenters, of course, were sensitive to this issue. C. H. Spurgeon, in a famous sermon on the Indian Mutiny Fast Day preached at the Crystal Palace to over 24,000 people, noted deferentially: 'mark, I am not the originator of it, as it is the Proclamation, and who am I that I should dispute such a high authority as that?'[175] Moreover, Dissenters did not always object to thanksgiving days, deprived as these were of the language in the fast day proclamations which declared what the Almighty might do if the Sovereign was not obeyed.[176] Nevertheless, despite their love of the Queen and their earnest desire to see their fellow-citizens respond appropriately to God, the attitude of many Dissenters toward royal proclamations concerning religious behaviour reveals political and theological concerns which served as a counterweight to unreflective patriotism even when it appeared to offer a reassuring extension of national piety.

Nonconformists wanted a Christian government and nation. This point was never in doubt, but it was so much a part of the air that they breathed that it usually took a time of crisis to elicit an explicit declaration of this conviction. The Papal Aggression provoked Josiah Conder to talk of foundations of the government which were taken for granted lest they be 'called upon to ignore all distinction between truth and error, and to make Christianity itself an open question'.[177] Even the most politically radical friends of religious equality within Dissent affirmed this. The *Nonconformist* asserted at the time of the Indian Mutiny:

> Ought the government of India in British hands, to be a Christian government? Is a question just now rife amongst us. Our answer, is Decidedly, it ought.[178]

If that could be said of India, Christian England could rest easy.

The label 'Christian government' was securely maintained, yes, but the real question is: What did it mean? This is a particularly relevant question for Voluntaryists who declared that it did not mean such

---

an article on the Christian practice of fasting. However, the magazine did receive a letter signed 'A Baptist Lawyer' which argued that the royal proclamations were not offensive on the grounds that they were not actually state commands to engage in religious activities, but only requests expressed in the traditional language used by a Sovereign: December 1857, pp. 778–9.

[175] C. H. Spurgeon, *Our National Sins: A Sermon*, London: Partridge & Co., 1857, p. 4.

[176] The *Congregational Year Book* for 1857, p. 19, reveals that the Congregational Union petitioned against the Fast Day, but offered no objections to the Thanksgiving one.

[177] Conder, *Political Position*, p. 67.

[178] *Nonconformist*, 14 October 1857, p. 801.

things as having an established church, teaching religious truths in state schools or proclaiming national fast days. Moreover, whatever it meant, did not the very label undercut the ideal of religious equality? When the meaning of 'Christian government' is explored, it becomes apparent that whereas many minds today might assume that a belief in religious equality and a desire for a Christian government would be eternally in tension, mid-Victorian Dissenters saw them as mutually reinforcing. For them, religious equality was a blessing which flowed from the application of Christian truth to the political sphere. The *Nonconformist*, in the very article in which it demanded a Christian government for India, explained unequivocally that what this meant is a government which is just – a standard which the Bible demands:

> the means by which the Government of India should show itself a Christian Government, and thus fulfil its ulterior Christian purpose, may be described in two words – *doing justice* . . .

The implications of this for religious equality were clear:

> We claim from law nothing more for the Christian, than for the heathen – but we claim as much. We demand ample protection for all – favour for none. As to the toleration of Mohammedan or Brahminical worship, it were well not even to assume the right to tolerate – but to recognise it as an indefeasible right . . .[179]

R. W. Dale wrote in the *Patriot* in 1863:

> I believe, indeed, in the possibility of a nation becoming Christian, as I believe in the possibility of railway companies becoming Christian. . . . let statesmen come from the sanctity of private communion with God to the great tasks of legislation and diplomacy, and without any formal profession of a national faith the national acts will be harmonious with the will of God.[180]

Likewise the *Eclectic Review* in 1847 hinted to a Churchman who thought that the Christian impulses of a righteous ruler demanded an explicitly Christian activism:

> it may be held at least possible that the Bible may tie a godly ruler's hands, rather than set them in motion, and teach that the most effectual manner in which he can show his care for the souls of his people is, *as a ruler*, to let them alone.[181]

According to some Dissenting views on Christianity and the state, sometimes less is more.

---

[179] *Nonconformist*, 14 October 1857, p. 801.
[180] Dale, *Dale*, pp. 375–6.
[181] *Eclectic Review*, n.s. XXII (July–Dec. 1847), p. 543.

Or even: more religious equality meant more influence for the spirit of Christianity. George Hadfield wrote in 1864:

> I hope that in all Christian countries there is arising a disposition to shake off State support and patronage of religion and that the bigotry of the dark ages will cease thus leaving a free course for the pure word of God, to run and be glorified.[182]

This quotation is a perfect jumble of reaffirming the idea of a Christian state while supporting the stripping away of state endorsements of religion; he anticipates not only that religious equality will flow from a Christian government, but also that the cause of Christianity itself will be advanced by the spread of liberalism. This is not a perception of incompatibility, but rather a vision of synergism. The *United Methodist Free Churches' Magazine* offered the same vision:

> England and America are the countries to which Continental orators and publicists refer, in order to support the liberal positions which they take, and point the arguments which they wield. And how is it that this vantage ground is ours? It is because the Bible is read and revered, more in these lands than it is in any other; it is because the Christianity found in its pages, has gradually acquired a certain hold of the national heart, and dictated, to a certain extent, the national career. . . . [Christianity] has drawn a broad line between the political and spiritual spheres. . . . Christianity has most distinctly asserted, the rights of *the individual*.[183]

Nor was this attitude confined exclusively to the latter part of the period under discussion or to the more radical Nonconformists. Already in 1847 the *Patriot* was defending its call for Jews to be allowed to enter Parliament with language which was not paradoxical to the Dissenting political mind:

> If we did not deem it a Christian act, to admit our Jewish fellow-citizens into the Legislature, – an act in perfect accordance with Christian principles, and adapted to recommend and promote the Christian faith, – we should be as strongly opposed to it as the Reviewer himself. And had we not regarded it as a Protestant act, flowing from Protestant principles, and worthy of a Protestant Government, to admit Roman Catholics into the Legislature,

---

[182] Hadfield, 'Personal Narrative', p. 231.
[183] *United Methodist Free Churches' Magazine*, August 1866, p. 527. Even the *Wesleyan Methodist Magazine* made a similar point, claiming, 'Men saw in the Bible their rights as human beings . . .' Nevertheless, typically, it twisted this observation into an anti-Catholic polemic: July 1859, p. 611.

we should have been not less strongly opposed to the repeal of the Catholic Disabilities.[184]

One imagines that even the Protestant Succession could have been seen by them as a hedge around liberal institutions rather than as a pandering to sectarianism.[185] Nonconformists believed that a Christian government was not an offence to the ideal of religious equality but rather its guarantor.

For Nonconformists, a Christian government was not so much marked by certain religious trappings as undergirded by certain principles and motivated by a certain spirit. A Christian government did not mean that a non-Christian could not participate in decision-making, but when they asked themselves why such a thing needed to be so, their answer was that their principles of justice were grounded in biblical revelation and Christian truth. If non-Christians founded their liberal principles on other sources that was neither here nor there. Dissenters were willing to work with atheists and agnostics, but the Nonconformist worldview was not limited to their secular arguments. As Josiah Conder tellingly noted:

> There are two ways of viewing and advocating the policy of [religious] non-interference on the part of the Civil Magistrate; the one an Atheistic, the other a Scriptural view.[186]

It did not trouble many Dissenters that their stance on a political matter might be identical to that of most Secularists; they knew that, in their own case, it was derived from their biblical and theological convictions. For Dissenters a liberal government was the product of a Christian government. This point might not always have great practical import when it came to building a liberal state with all people of goodwill, but it did matter when it came to the internal thinking of the Dissenting community. Many Nonconformists did not want a confessional state, but they were not ashamed to advocate a Christian one, name and all.

Ultimately, no piece of legislation or constitutional bulwark could make a nation Christian whose people were godless; and a truly Christian people would go a long way toward making overtly Christian acts by the government redundant. Joseph Sturge mused wistfully about a day when the politicians of the land would all be professing Christians, but that was a vision which was to be pursued by voluntary, spiritual acts, not by

---

[184] *Patriot*, 25 October 1847, p. 716.
[185] Even this, however, was not sacrosanct. John Campbell's most populist journal printed an article on Voluntaryism in 1846 which argued, 'Holding these views, we admit not into our vocabulary such phraseology as *a National Religion, a Christian Constitution, a Protestant Monarchy.*' *Christian's Penny Magazine*, I (1846), p. 68.
[186] Conder, *Political Position*, p. 54.

coercive politics.[187] A nation in which people feared God and prayed and lived righteously was a Christian nation indeed. Dissenters knew that it was not within the power of pressure group politics to deliver such a goal and therefore, ultimately, their hope for a truly Christian nation was not anchored in their political agenda. As one speaker prophetically declared at a Liberation Society meeting at the close of this period:

> They had so insisted on the doctrine of religious equality that those who legislated for them in high places imagined that religious equality was the only question about which they were interested. Now he need not say that they were far more interested in the freedom of Christian truth and Christian teaching than they were about the doctrine of religious equality; for though the latter comprehended the former, it was quite possible to have religious equality without religion, and he believed that that was the tendency of political thought and care in the present day.[188]

This utterance was not an anxious corrective from the fringe of the movement; the speaker was Edward Miall. He was protesting against latitudinarian attitudes in the Church of England. His point was that they had insisted that the government must not attempt to advance Christianity, not because this goal was not important, but because this task belonged exclusively to the church. Therefore, the church must not abdicate its role to stand for truth under a misguided desire to apply the principle of religious equality within its own voluntary society. Conversely, Dissenters must not abandon religious equality in politics to recoup ground lost to secularism, because the very gospel which they were seeking to advance demanded religious equality in the political sphere. Dissenters were genuine patriots. Their love for their country caused them to want the best for her which, according to their convictions, meant that she should be Christian and Protestant. This was the national identity which they sought. However, they knew that coercion did not produce a true conversion – whether of an individual or a nation. Therefore, politically, a Christian government was one which treated all its citizens with equity and justice. The God-given task of the government entailed providing religious equality. If the people of the land wanted 'religious equality without religion', that was a problem for the church, not the state.

[187] Tyrrell, *Sturge*, p. 188.
[188] *Liberator*, May 1867, p. 71.

CONCLUSION

One reason why this study has been necessary is in order to present a more accurate portrait of the politics of mid-nineteenth-century Dissenters to replace a distorted image which has continued to reappear. In that flawed picture, Nonconformists are painted as people who sought to use legislation in order to impose their religious convictions and standards of personal morality on the rest of society. Part of the reason for the origin and persistence of this inaccurate view is a failure to make three crucial distinctions: firstly, between the politics of this period and that of the eras which followed it, secondly, between the beliefs and codes of conduct which Nonconformists preached and practised and the goals which they sought to achieve through the agency of government and, thirdly, between the politics of Evangelical Churchmen and Wesleyans and those of Evangelical Dissenters.

For example, T. A. Jenkins, in an introduction to the diaries of Sir John Trelawny which he published in 1990, claims that despite the Parliamentary leadership which Trelawny gave to the struggle to abolish church rates, the member for Tavistock went against the Dissenting political agenda in other ways, citing legislation which he supported against the wishes of Sabbatarians, and the following:

> Nor was the other great cause with which Trelawny was associated during the early-1860s, the affirmations bill, proposing to allow atheists to give evidence in criminal cases, exactly designed to please the dissenters of Tavistock.[1]

Jenkins footnotes two passages in the diaries, one in which Trelawny complains of being called an atheist everywhere he goes, without stating the kind of people who are apt to make this charge, and another in which he remarks:

> Capital articles appear in the papers on my oaths questions – & I get many private letters of thanks. One Tory gentleman says I am an Atheist & ought to be hung. The Record very spitefully assails me.[2]

---

[1] T. A. Jenkins (ed.), *The Parliamentary Diaries of Sir John Trelawny, 1858–65*, London: Royal Historical Society, 1990, p. 14.
[2] Entry for 18 February 1861: *Ibid.*, p. 151.

The odds, however, are distinctly against the Tory gentleman having been a Nonconformist and the *Record* was a Church of England newspaper. Moreover, for Trelawny's attempt in 1863, there is a division list on the second reading. Although he lost this vote, Ayes 96 to Noes 142, all the Dissenters in the division voted with him, including such figures as the Quaker Charles Gilpin, the Unitarian William Scholefield and the Congregationalist George Hadfield.[3] When the Secularist leader, G. J. Holyoake, was fined after being summoned to serve on a grand jury because he refused to swear the religiously worded oath, the *Eclectic Review* cited it as 'a practical illustration of the gross injustice of the present state of the law on oaths' and placed the blame with 'the House of Commons, which threw out Sir John Trelawny's bill'.[4] In short, Jenkins's assumption that Dissenters would disapprove of Trelawny's actions is a false one, predicated on a basic and all too common misconception of the politics of Dissenters in this period.

Or to take another example, John Vincent in his classic study, *The Formation of the British Liberal Party, 1857–68*, notes rightly that the politics of John Bright were not a typical specimen of Dissenting views. Nevertheless, he attempts to establish this point by (amongst some other examples) citing a speech of Bright's in 1864 in which he failed to support the UKA's Permissive Bill and another one in 1867 in which he failed to use religious arguments in order to justify Sabbatarian legislation.[5] These stances, however, as this study has shown, in no way isolate Bright from broad currents in the Nonconformist political world during this period.

The period of this study begins at a time when a new departure was being made in Dissenting politics. The 1847 election was a turning point at which Evangelical Dissenters moved from entrusting their political agenda into the hands of Unitarians and sympathetic Churchmen to determining to send men of their own ilk, from their own ranks, to Parliament. Moreover, a corresponding change had already begun in their political worldview: they were moving from largely accepting the political world which they lived in as a fact, and trying to cull out a place of toleration and acceptance for themselves within it, to daring to develop and champion publicly a political vision in line with their own distinctive convictions.

A central, orientating mode of thinking in this political vision was an appreciation, assertion, and application of absolute principles. Evangelical preaching, with its fundamental truths of the gospel and the stark

---

[3] *Hansard*, CLXIX, Appendix, 'Division List on the Second Reading of the Affirmations Bill, Wednesday, 11 March 1863'.
[4] *Eclectic Review*, n.s. VI (Jan.–June 1864), p. 241.
[5] Vincent, *Formation of the Liberal Party*, p. 227.

contrasts between heaven and hell and light and darkness which it continually asserted were at stake, undoubtedly helped to create an intellectual climate in which the minds of orthodox Nonconformists were at home when great, sweeping consequences were claimed to flow from whether or not one grasped and applied certain basic propositions. Toward the end of the century, the Congregationalist John Stoughton described Dissenters during the years of this study as 'people accustomed to trace branches to their roots, and who thought more of principles than of practices lying on the top of them'.[6] This way of thinking was reinforced by the practical example of the absolutist rhetoric which was applied with such effect in the campaigns against slavery and the Corn Laws.

Contrary to the impression given by historians such as Eugenio Biagini, the political philosophy of these mid-Victorian Dissenters was rooted in their theology.[7] The specific principles which they wielded, however, were derived more from the distinctive theology within some of the Nonconformist denominations than from pan-Evangelicalism. R. J. Helmstadter has argued that Dissenting politics in this era was grounded in 'the theology of evangelicalism', focusing particularly on its emphasis on 'the salvation of individual souls'.[8] This theory fails to explain why those who were committed most to Evangelicalism were often those most divided on politics. There were not many greater polar opposites in the Commons of this period than, for example, the Tory, Richard Spooner, and the radical, George Hadfield, yet theologically they were both solid Evangelicals. Even if one sets aside the Evangelical Churchmen, one still finds a great political gulf dividing, for example, an influential Wesleyan minister like Dr Jabez Bunting from a prominent Baptist one like Dr F. A. Cox. It is possible, of course, for people to draw from the same principles contradictory conclusions on what course needs to be taken, but there is a more persuasive explanation of this cleavage than this vague observation.

The division between these two groups is quite comprehensible if one examines the various views held by these people of the church of Christ. Nonconformist politics was rooted in theology, but not in the soteriology of Evangelicalism, but rather in the ecclesiology of Congregationalism. Baptists and Congregationalists shared in common both their political views and their ecclesiastical views, but they were not always able to gain the political co-operation of those groups which held a different pattern of church government, notably the Wesleyans and the Unitarians (let

---

[6] Stoughton, *Religion in England*, II, pp. 408–9.
[7] Biagini, *Liberty, Retrenchment and Reform*, p. 16.
[8] R. J. Helmstadter, 'The Nonconformist Conscience', in Gerald Parsons (ed.), *Religion in Victorian Britain*, IV, Manchester: Manchester University Press, p. 66.

alone Churchmen). Congregationalists, as they began to assert themselves in the political arena, had as their heritage of thought their certainty – continually kept sharp by a need to justify themselves in the face of the rest of Christendom – regarding their theological distinctives. These distinctives focused on what a true church was, or at least ideally ought to be, namely a local body of believers who have voluntarily gathered together and who are collectively free from all outside human control or interference. The church is God's agent for accomplishing spiritual ends on the earth; particularly it is the carrier of the gospel of Jesus Christ which contains the power to regenerate sinful men and women.

For them, a church establishment was wrong first and foremost not because it was bad politics but because it was bad theology. Even the liberationists, with their pressure group, were not starting with political theory, whether liberalism, *laissez-faire* or some other doctrine. The very title of their organisation reveals a fundamental motivation of theirs: 'The Society for the Liberation *of Religion* from State Patronage and *Control*'. The starting point in their thinking was Congregational ecclesiology: it is wrong for the church to be controlled by outside influences. The reverse of this was also true: it is wrong for the state to attempt to undertake the spiritual task which has been given by Christ to the church. The work of the church, such as bringing the gospel message for the conversion of lost souls to the people, should not be attempted by governmental agency. A state church, therefore, meant that the church which was meant to be free was enslaved by government control and that the work of the gospel, which could be rightly done only by the divinely ordained spiritual agency of the church, was muddled, distorted and therefore ultimately hampered by the inappropriate, worldly agency of the state. Voluntaryism was an ecclesiological concept before it was ever applied by Dissenters to issues of public policy. It meant that the true church consists of those who have freely responded to the gospel and chosen to submit to the discipline of the communal life of the congregation as opposed to any notion of mandatory inclusion and participation established by coercion or by temporal incentives. When John Pye Smith joined with a handful of other Dissenters to found a church in 1804, they entered 'voluntarily' into a 'Church Covenant' which included commitments as specific as promising to have family devotions morning and evening every day.[9] As to society in general, however, the Baptist minister and theologian John Howard Hinton argued that it was not the state's responsibility to punish 'violations of morality' (such as lying), but only 'offences against society' which might incidentally also be

---

[9] Medway, *Pye Smith*, pp. 126–7.

breaches of the moral code (such as theft).[10] The true church was one which accomplished its ends by spiritual rather than carnal weapons.

All of this is in marked contrast to the Wesleyan body which took a far more pragmatic view of issues of church polity. It is hard to find a truly theological discussion of ecclesiology in mid-Victorian Wesleyan writings. Whilst an effort at systematic theology by a member of some other denominations might have naturally moved on from issues such as the Trinity and Christology to a section on ecclesiology which included a discussion of the competing claims of Episcopalianism, Presbyterianism and Congregationalism, Wesleyans rarely approached the subject so doctrinally. When the Wesleyan J. H. Rigg was provoked by attacks from some Congregationalists into writing his book, *Congregational Independency and Wesleyan Connexionalism Contrasted* (1851), the crucial contrast with which he begins is the relative importance the two communities place on this subject:

> A SYSTEM which claims for itself *Divine right*, is, of necessity, an exclusive and polemic system. Making such pretensions, it, of course, challenges and proscribes every other as unauthorised and anti-scriptural. . . .
> Now, such a system is that of Independency, as accepted and advocated by the more rigid of its adherents. . . .
> Wesleyans, on the other hand, have ever defended their system in a more modest tone and on less exclusive grounds.[11]

The Wesleyan body, not placing the same weight on issues of ecclesiology which many Dissenters did, also was not seduced in these years by the political philosophy and agenda being developed by their fellow Evangelicals outside the Establishment. Instead of seeking to implement the principle of religious equality in the public arena, Wesleyans officially adhered to another political gospel which sought to use the power of the state to pursue such explicitly religious goals as protecting the official Protestantism of the nation and the sacredness of the Christian Sabbath.

Congregational ecclesiology, however, did influence the United Methodist Free Churches – and the sympathy which this body had for the militant Nonconformist agenda rivalled that of the Congregationalists and Baptists themselves. Moreover, even those Dissenters who did not accept this form of church government were often susceptible to the general argument that having the head of state as the supreme governor of the church was demeaning to Christ and degrading to his people. The *Methodist New Connexion Magazine*, for example, was very animated by

---

[10] Hinton, *Review*, pp. 10–11.
[11] James H. Rigg, *Congregational Independency and Wesleyan Connexionalism Contrasted*, London: James Nichols, 1851, p. 7.

the truth that Christ was 'the only King of his Church' and therefore called for 'nothing less than the absolute extinction of those systems of ecclesiastical polity, which destroy freedom, tarnish the glory, and prevent the prosperity of the Church of Christ'.[12] In short, although its own church government was by no means Congregational, it nevertheless took ecclesiology seriously and fully imbibed the theological critique of the church being controlled by the state. Indeed, one could even argue that part of the glue in the alliance between the Nonconformists and Gladstone which was forged as the period under discussion drew to a close was a common pre-occupation with ecclesiology which produced a shared anti-Erastianism.[13] The Primitives do not seem to have been as concerned with ecclesiology as their fellow Methodists in the New Connexion and the United Methodist Free Churches, and their political views likewise fall between those of the Congregationalists and those of the Wesleyans: for example, following the former on educational Voluntaryism and the latter on legislative Sabbatarianism. Although it would be simplistic to make a crude correlation between ecclesiology and politics and to assert a reductionist theory along these lines, it is nevertheless necessary that this neglected theological theme be incorporated into any future attempts to identify the various factors which contributed to the development of Dissenting political thought during these years.

It was entirely natural that the theological vision held, in particular, by Congregationalists and Baptists should lead its adherents to adopt disestablishment as a central political goal, once they had gained the desire and confidence to develop and articulate their own views of government. The numerical rise of Dissenters in the first decades of the nineteenth century, the repeal of the Test and Corporation Acts, the bills for Parliamentary and then municipal reform, the official split with the Unitarians and disillusionment with the Whigs all contributed to Evangelical Dissent arriving in the 1840s at the point where it was ready to attempt to make its own distinctive mark on the political landscape. An Established Church was clearly labelled as bad politics and, in turn, the wider principle in which the single cause of disestablishment was said to be grounded was identified as religious equality. Because coercion was not the method the Almighty had ordained for spiritual advancement on earth, it was not the place of government to try to lend a helping hand to the church by using its worldly weapons in order to reinforce the church's efforts or to restrain those of its religious opponents. Religious

---

[12] *Methodist New Connexion Magazine*, 50 (1847), pp. 295–303; 51 (1848), pp. 17–21.
[13] D. W. Bebbington, 'Gladstone and the Nonconformists: a religious affinity in politics', in Derek Baker (ed.), *Church, Society and Politics* (Studies in Church History 12), Oxford: Basil Blackwell, 1975, pp. 376–80.

equality was a grand political worldview, an overarching principle, which took the politics of Dissenters beyond merely defending their own special interests and into offering a larger vision of the work of the state and its relationship to its diverse subjects. This political philosophy is a long way from Michael Watts's notion of Evangelical Nonconformists being captivated by an escapist spirituality which hampered a desire to benefit human beings through political and social reforms.[14] It had its flowering in the efforts Nonconformists made to overturn measures which discriminated against people from other religious traditions: the undivided support which Nonconformity gave to the campaign for Jewish emancipation is a tribute to the influence of this principle.

The militant Dissenting agenda was an application of theological convictions to the political arena. It is therefore misleading to try to divide 'religious' Dissenters from 'political' ones as if the latter were those who were drifting away from the religious orientation of the former into a more secular frame of mind. 'Political' Dissenters were typically deeply religious ones acting politically. Historians have sometimes neglected to highlight this point and therefore factual comments they have made might be misconstrued by some of their readers as supporting the division between 'religious' and 'political' Dissenters which contemporary writings by Churchmen misleadingly expounded. For example, D. M. Thompson remarks, when mapping out the various kinds of political stances held by Dissenters: 'Others eschewed political action altogether and formed the Evangelical Voluntary Church Association and were later involved in the formation of the Evangelical Alliance.'[15] Likewise W. H. Mackintosh observes, 'In 1846 the "more peaceful" Nonconformists participated in the founding of the Evangelical Alliance.'[16] Such phrasing might lead the uninitiated into imagining that those interested in promoting the doctrines of Evangelicalism went in one direction whilst those who wished to promote militant politics went in another. No such divide, however, took place: frequently the same men were committed to both causes. Moreover, Thompson's comment can even be easily overplayed on the specific point he is making regarding polarisation by organisation: one of the secretaries of the Evangelical Voluntary Church Association was F. A. Cox and its committee included such prominent figures in the world of mid-nineteenth-century militant Dissent as John Burnet and

[14] Watts, *Dissenters*, II, pp. 510–11.
[15] D. M. Thompson, 'The Liberation Society, 1844–1868', in Patricia Hollis (ed.), *Pressure from Without*, London: Edward Arnold, 1974, p. 213.
[16] W. H. Mackintosh, *Disestablishment and Liberation*, London: Epworth, 1972, pp. 34–5.

Thomas Price.[17] Cox wrote a book entitled *On Christian Union* in 1845 and the Scottish Voluntary, Ralph Wardlaw, contributed to a volume entitled *Essays on Christian Union* in the same year; Cox, Wardlaw and the leading minister in the Wesleyan Methodist Association, Robert Eckett, were all public champions of Voluntaryism, founding members of the Anti-State Church Association, and active supporters of the Evangelical Alliance.[18] There was no parting of the ways between those interested in Evangelicalism and those interested in radical politics; both causes were supported by the same communities and even sometimes actively promoted by work done for several organisations with various specific goals by the same individuals.

In a recent study, J. P. Ellens has argued that militant Dissent in this period marks a shift from the religious motivation of earlier Nonconformists toward a secular mentality and agenda. This theory is flawed. Ellens is led by the willingness of Dissenters to use non-religious arguments and language and to create non-religious organisations into imagining falsely that these Dissenters were themselves taking religion less seriously. In fact, these changes were actually marks of the increasing intellectual and political sophistication of Dissent; Nonconformity was no longer merely talking to itself and taking actions with a view toward influencing only its own constituency. The use it made of secular arguments does not imply a corresponding retreat from theologically informed thinking; it merely indicates a desire to persuade even those who were immune to such appeals. Ellens refers to the Liberation Society making 'an almost cynical attempt to gain the support of "religious Dissenters"', when it was suggested in the early 1860s that a tract on church rates 'of a high religious tone' be written 'for the use of what are called "religious Dissenters"'.[19] The Society, however, was employing the term 'religious Dissenters' ironically, in accordance with its use by Churchmen to refer to Dissenters who stood aloof from politics. This action was in no way cynical because the leaders of the Society themselves believed profoundly in such religious arguments. Different lines of reasoning could be articulated for different audiences: one for Churchmen, another for the non-religious, still another for Evangelical Dissenters. Nevertheless, the Evangelical Dissenters behind this flow of ideas believed them all: in their own worldview, the general, philo-

[17] Anon., *Evangelical Voluntary Church Association* [a tract explaining its purpose], n.p., n.d., p. 1.
[18] John Wolffe, 'The Evangelical Alliance in the 1840s', in W. J. Sheils and Diana Wood (eds), *Voluntary Religion* (Studies in Church History 23), Oxford: Basil Blackwell, 1986, pp. 333–46. For Eckett, see 'Anti-State-Church Association, and the Evangelical Alliance', *Wesleyan Methodist Association Magazine*, January 1848, pp. 1–7.
[19] Ellens, *Religious Routes*, p. 197 (n. 113).

sophical arguments were entirely compatible with the specific, biblical ones. It is interesting to note that one of the most prominent Congregational ministers and theologians of the latter part of the nineteenth century, R. W. Dale, attributed Miall's political dogmatism, not to the tyranny of secular ideology, but to the uncompromising grip of spiritual devotion: 'Instead of God living where he lived, he lived where God lived. . . . He looked upon the perpetual flux of human affairs from the everlasting hills.'[20]

More fundamentally, Ellens is led astray by not paying sufficient attention to Dissenting theology. He proclaims dramatically that the secularization and 'desacralization' of political theory and institutions which Nonconformists are said to have adopted in this period was in defiance of 'a millennium of tradition' and that it 'would have seemed incomprehensible to medieval Europe'.[21] This kind of language does indeed make it sound as though Dissenters were jettisoning their faith; in truth, however, it could be applied equally well to any distinctive doctrine held by Nonconformists, not least the Congregational theory of church government. Indeed, Protestantism in general, and Evangelical Dissent in particular, is a tradition in which religious veneers have repeatedly been stripped away for theological reasons; one could just as well view this tradition as 'desacralizing' marriage by denying it was a sacrament, 'desacralizing' the church building by stripping it of icons and religious symbolism, 'desacralizing' ministers by having them wear the same style of clothing as men in secular professions and on and on but, nevertheless, it would be hardly tenable to deny them any intrinsic theological motivation and logic in these matters. Indeed, perhaps it is chiefly people who are deeply committed to spiritual realities who care about such things. Perhaps a better case could be made for the preoccupation of Dissenters with disestablishment being a sign of the seriousness with which they took theology than that it was a sign of their abandonment of spirituality; their own contemporaries and subsequent history have amply proved that Englishmen and women whose thinking is truly secular more often than not respond to the cause of disestablishment with apathy.

Ellens does narrow his argument from the sweeping perspective of a thousand years of Christendom, claiming that the mid-Victorian Dissenters abandoned a more religious view of politics which was the historic tradition of Dissent and even the view of the generation of Congregationalists which immediately preceded them. 'Conservative Dissenters who favored spiritual over temporal activity' in the mid-Victorian period were, according to him, heirs to the true Dissenting

---

[20] Dale, *Life of Dale*, p. 369.
[21] Ellens, *Religious Routes*, pp. 5, 91.

tradition, keeping faith with men like John Angell James and John Pye Smith, the latter of whom is quoted approvingly for his politically naive suggestion that disestablishment would probably happen in the indeterminable future 'in a spontaneous way' (and this earlier attitude was later contradicted by his own support for the Anti-State Church Association). Ellens sees a dichotomy between spiritual and political efforts:

> The militant Dissenters who were becoming spellbound by the message of voluntaryism gradually replaced the passionate commitment to the transforming power of the Gospel that had earlier drawn them together with Evangelical Anglicans with an equally passionate devotion to the idea of liberty and the commitment to separate church and state.

And:

> it was an open question whether Dissent could retain its spiritual integrity while devoting its energies to a sustained political campaign for religious equality.[22]

Ellens takes as the symbolic moment when the forbidden fruit was bitten and the Fall came, the amending of the constitution of the Liberation Society in 1853 in order to remove language which implied its members were in agreement with Christian teaching, contrasting this unfavourably with the days when 'evangelical Dissenters and Anglicans had converged in Bible and missionary societies in the unity of the Christian gospel'.[23] All of this is riddled with false dichotomies. If political efforts betray a lack of faith in spiritual ones, then the previous generation would stand just as condemned in regard to its sustained campaign against slavery. Why might a campaign by Dissenters for religious equality subvert their spiritual integrity more than an arrangement in which the bishops of the Established Church are expected to give their sustained attention to the parade of legislation that comes before the House of Lords? Moreover, as Alexander Tyrrell has noted, the political activities of Dissenters were often fuelled by their spiritual expectations rather than a substitute for them.[24] Politics was certainly not replacing missions; both activities occupied the Dissenters of this era. Missions suffered no demotion whatsoever.[25] The two greatest speeches of J. P. Mursell's life were the one he gave at the founding of the Anti-State Church Association in 1844

[22] Ellens, *Religious Routes*, pp. 46–7, 85.
[23] *Ibid.*, pp. 117–18.
[24] Alexander Tyrrell, 'Making the Millennium: the mid-nineteenth century peace movement', *Historical Journal*, 20, 1 (1978), pp. 75–95.
[25] See, for example, Brian Stanley, *The History of the Baptist Missionary Society, 1792–1992*, Edinburgh: T. & T. Clark, 1992, chapters 3–7.

and his address for the Baptist Missionary Society anniversary in 1855, and he showed a sustained commitment to both organisations.[26] Mursell's sincere commitment to both political and missionary activity was typical of numerous Dissenters in this period. Or one might think of George Hadfield who gave a great deal of his public energy in the prime of his life to fighting for religious equality and against Unitarianism. The case of Hadfield illustrates a deeper commitment to fidelity to the principles dear to Congregationalists, whether in politics (disestablishment and religious equality) or doctrine (Evangelicalism and Trinitarianism), in contrast with the state of affairs amongst his older co-religionists in the initial decades of the century, when a desire to avoid conflict muted the assertion of a clear, distinctive and uncompromising voice in both these arenas.

Ellens is right to claim that the politics of Dissenters in this period had a different tone from that of the Congregationalists of the previous generation. He is wrong, however, to see this earlier view as the genuine voice of Congregationalism and the mid-Victorian message as a capitulation to secular forces. Actually, the previous generation represented a Congregationalism which had not yet fully developed or articulated a theology of the relationship between the state and the church. Men like John Blackburn were the last generation of nineteenth-century Congregational leaders to be content to leave political theory to others and humbly to accept the political structure of British society as a fact of life. The mid-century Dissenters dared to imagine and promote their own vision for the role of the state: they represent the maturing, indeed the flowering, of Congregational political thought. This vision was not the inevitable course which Dissenting thought had to take, but neither was it a detour from an imagined authentic course. With their numerical rise and increasing political influence, a question which had never before needed to be asked with such practical import now called for a thoughtful answer: what kind of government would and should a nation of Congregationalists and Baptists produce? In the days when Presbyterianism was the dominant expression of Dissent in politics, the principle of a state church could be maintained as part of the Dissenting political vision, but it was by no means natural that one would choose to establish as a state church a collection of congregations which had as its *raison d'être* the rejection of centralised authority and control. And why should Congregationalists be expected to aspire to such a thing? Experiments in New England with Congregational establishments were more in spite of, than because of, Congregational theory: more an imitation of models developed in other ecclesiological traditions than

---

[26] Mursell, *Mursell*, pp. 78–115, 207–60.

the fruit of a distinctive Congregational vision for civic life. Disestablishment, Voluntaryism and religious equality all flow legitimately from the theological convictions of Congregationalists and Baptists.

Better established concerns over Nonconformist grievances were successfully used by militants to enlist a wider base of Dissenters into their radical campaign and vision. The grievances served to extract the energy of Dissenters and the sympathy of Churchmen, whilst the goal of disestablishment and the ideal of religious equality provided an ideological framework which gave the politics of Dissenters a momentum and rationale. The adoption of the lead in the campaign to abolish church rates by the Liberation Society opened the door for many Dissenters to walk into the broad plain of religious equality and gave what could have been a petty squabble about minor sums a place of dignity and importance as an illustration of a point of principle within the context of a grand political vision. Norman Gash claims, 'Enough was said by the more extreme Dissenters to alarm; not enough was done to wound.'[27] The actual dynamic, however, was almost the exact reverse of this: enough was said to rally Dissenters to a great cause founded upon important principles, but not enough to prevent many moderate Churchmen from sympathising with their case. Similarly, Gash pronounces that disestablishment was 'a millstone round the neck of Dissenting political activity'.[28] This perspective does make sense if one views Dissenters as a special interest group – like publicans or landowners – and judges their political success by how quickly they won practical concessions for their own interests. If, on the other hand, one judges them by their success at building a coherent political worldview, then disestablishment was not a millstone, but a cornerstone. The fact that Dissenters were unable to make their political vision the view of the majority in the nation as a whole, does not invalidate it. Moreover, even if practical results become the criterion, the pure logic and noble cause which the friends of religious equality were able to offer to the Dissenting community did release resources, enlist support and motivate electors in a way which a focus on petty discriminations would have been unlikely to achieve. It is perhaps reasonable to imagine that less talk of disestablishment and religious equality could have secured the removal of some grievances earlier, but that estimate assumes that Nonconformists would have agitated just as forcefully as they did when mobilised by a wider vision. Perhaps without that vision they would have been closer in approach to the Wesleyans, and the government would have had insufficient incentive to disturb Churchmen by tamper-

[27] Gash, *Reaction and Reconstruction*, p. 108.
[28] *Ibid.*, p. 107.

ing with the areas of grievance. Disestablishment and religious equality provided that absolute of pure principle which Dissenters needed to put up a good fight; it placed the grievances within a wider cause which could capture the imagination. Moreover, by placing sweeping, ultimate demands in view, the militant Nonconformists, whilst they probably delayed the arrival of some concessions, also changed the climate of what was thinkable politically and thereby paved the way for greater and more thorough concessions in the medium term, and even disestablishment itself, in the case of Ireland.

By adopting the cause of removing Nonconformist grievances and by offering a coherent political worldview to Dissenters which was not effectively countered by any alternative vision from within their own camp, the militant Nonconformists moved the political centre of gravity amongst Nonconformists in a more radical direction. More moderate Dissenting leaders such as J. A. James and Robert Vaughan, while they could slow down the radical march on certain issues and in regard to specific techniques, rhetoric and methods, did not offer an alternative rallying point. To the extent that they were an opposition party within the internal world of Dissenting politics, they were one which could sometimes effectively critique the ruling one, and give people pause about its schemes; but their section of opinion did not offer a rival political theory of its own and therefore was in no danger of actually setting a different political course for the community as a whole.

E. D. Steele, in a recent study, has argued that Palmerston successfully pacified Dissent by certain skilful actions he took in office and thereby weakened the radical nature and overall influence of militant Nonconformist politics, wooing the Dissenting community more toward the middle ground. He even claims: 'Palmerston shaped his policy accordingly, with the result that relations between Churchmen and Dissenters were better at the time of his death than they had ever been, or were to be again for the rest of the century and beyond.'[29] As to politics, he argues, 'The closer integration of political Dissent with the Liberal party and the consequent dilution of middle-class radicalism may be followed through the growing Palmerstonianism of Edward Baines.'[30] Scattered throughout the book are several principal lines of argument regarding how Palmerston is said to have achieved this end, notably by making ecclesiastical appointments which bolstered Evangelicalism or the Low Church party, by making efforts to remove some of the Nonconformist grievances, by giving baronets, administration and cabinet positions and similar honours to influential Nonconformists or radicals, and by the

[29] Steele, *Palmerston*, p. 8.
[30] *Ibid.*, p. 177.

influence of Palmerston's step-son-in-law and religious adviser, Lord Shaftesbury.

While these actions by Palmerston did make a notable impression on the official Wesleyan leadership (which was coming from the direction of Toryism, not radicalism), they did not work as a moderating influence upon Dissenting politics.[31] Quite to the contrary, far from Palmerston achieving a high point of peace, co-operation and mutual understanding between the Church and Dissent, his administration was marked by a rising tide of bitterness, confrontation and militancy. The early 1860s witnessed the rise of the Church Defence movement, the aggressive clashes provoked by the Nonconformist commemorations in 1862 of the Great Ejection, unprecedented bitterness over church rates and the decline of the moderate Dissenting Deputies and the corresponding rise of the Liberation Society as the authentic voice of Dissenting politics.[32] The true picture, as this study has shown, was exactly the reverse: militancy was leavening Dissent as a whole, rather than moderation leavening militant Dissent.

The effect of Palmerston's actions on Dissenters has been over-estimated. Nonconformists were more likely to view Palmerston's approach on the issue of their grievances as, at best, half-hearted and, at worse, obstructionist, than to be delighted with efforts he is claimed to have made. Wesleyans were impressed by some of Palmerston's actions mentioned by Steele, but rank-and-file Congregationalists and Baptists and Nonconformist political activists were so far removed from the Church of England that appointments to bishoprics made little impression upon their political agenda. Moreover, Steele asserts, 'The Dissenters' religious independence was compatible with eager deference to Shaftesbury's exposition of the social and political dimensions of faith.'[33] Once again, it was the reverse which was actually the case: Dissenters were happy to combine a deference for Shaftesbury's genuine piety and common Evangelicalism with maintaining their own independent views of social and political matters. Steele cites the life of Edward Baines the younger as an example of the shift of Dissent from radicalism to Palmerstonianism. Baines, however, started his political journey as a solid Whig, not as a radical and so, if anything, the position he arrived at

---

[31] See, for Palmerston's successfully winning of Wesleyan support, *Wesleyan Methodist Magazine*, April 1857, pp. 362–3.

[32] For the commemoration of the Great Ejection, see Timothy Larsen, 'Victorian Nonconformity and the Memory of the Ejected Ministers: the impact of the bicentennial commemorations of 1862', in R. N. Swanson (ed.), *The Church Retrospective* (Studies in Church History 33), Woodbridge, Suffolk: The Boydell Press for the Ecclesiastical History Society, 1998.

[33] Steele, *Palmerston*, p. 173.

during the Palmerstonian era underlines the contention of this study that
militancy was increasing in Dissenting politics. Baines kept aloof from
the Anti-State Church Association for years after it had been founded,
but even he eventually succumbed to its gravitational pull. By Palmerston's death, the radical element in Dissenting politics was a stronger
influence on the political thinking of the whole Nonconformist community and the relationship of Dissenters with Churchmen was significantly more strained than it had been a decade or two before.

Although absolute principles had the power to galvanise the Dissenting community into action, they also had their limits. Repeatedly, when
major areas of national concern emerged, no such guiding principle was
found and therefore the Dissenting worldview could offer no clear
response. When forced to examine deeply, Nonconformists admitted
that going to war was not invariably wrong and thereby lost a coherent
line on a major aspect of foreign policy, having it increasingly replaced
by a temptation to want to rescue victims, establish justice and generally
do some pressing good by means of military force which other principles
told them was right. Few were willing to admit a principle which claimed
that the vote was every man's right, and so a coherent Dissenting
campaign could not be made on the issue of suffrage, despite a widespread sense that something ought to be done. No 'total and immediate'
demand could be made, and so the matter was handed over to the
practical politicians who would judge what the current situation needed,
rather than what ultimate standards demanded. Every political philosophy, when applied in government, finds itself facing issues which do
not neatly fall under the aegis of any of its guiding doctrines. The leaders
of mid-Victorian Dissenting politics offered a genuine political worldview in the sense that they had a coherent ideology which they were
willing to attempt to apply comprehensively. They were not, however, a
kind of opposition party which offered an official plan of action for every
affair of state. Perhaps we may excuse a religious group for attempting to
offer a prophetic voice which reminds people of absolutes of justice on
issues where such a standard seems clearly applicable, rather than
devaluing its currency by presuming to have an administrative expertise
which could wisely pronounce on everything from the allocation of a
budget among competing departments down to the last penny to the re-
drawing of electoral boundaries so that every village was unquestionably
in the right constituency. The love of principle which the Dissenters
possessed, and the nature of the principles which they held, set a natural
boundary on the areas of public policy which they attempted to influence
as a body.

Manhood suffrage was championed as a necessity of principle by only
a few Nonconformists of note and pacifism did not pass the test of being
an absolute principle under pressure, but the greatest would-be absolute

of them all to crumble in this period was state non-interference. Nonconformists had experienced government interference as an evil throughout much of their history. The civil powers had interfered with their efforts to meet together, to worship, to build chapels, to preach, in short, to be Dissenters. Moreover, their political experience had repeatedly reinforced a pattern in which the solution to problems was the removal of restraints: Dissenting grievances, slavery, Corn Laws and state churches could all be solved by an abolitionist response. Victorian Nonconformists believed in the practical possibility and virtuous effect of individuals practising self-help and willing people acting voluntarily together to tackle problems and accomplish great ends. Their political ideology, championing as it did liberty and religious equality, was happy to welcome their sister, retrenchment, as well. Therefore, their religious history, political history, economic interests, societal ideals and intellectual instincts all lent themselves to their embracing *laissez-faire* as the ideal approach for a government to adopt.

Sir James Graham's proposed Factory Bill in 1843 reinforced to a Dissenting community already suspicious of government interference the dangers of the education of the young being in the hands of the state. Graham was willing to create a school system in which the children of the nation were formed by the leadership, teaching and worship of the Church of England. In effect, state education would be a kind of parallel institution with the State Church. It was not unnatural for Dissenters to apply their alternative theory for the one to the other: not state religion but voluntary religion, not state education but voluntary education. If the people could themselves build their own chapels, train and appoint their own ministers and generally organise themselves religiously without the help of the government, then surely they could build schools, train and appoint teachers and generally take on the whole business of education as well. Any doubts regarding the feasibility of the latter seemed to imply a slur on the sacred truth of the former. Moreover, the concerns of Dissenters regarding the kind of social control which government education might produce were not without foundation. One of their achievements was to ensure that state education, when it eventually did come, handled the convictions of minority groupings within society with greater sensitivity and respect. It is another example of the distorted picture of Dissenters which still persists that historians of education have neglected this contribution which Nonconformists made to the formation of national education and some have even made it appear as if Dissenters themselves were one of the leading groups amongst those who wished to indoctrinate the nation's children.[34] At

---

[34] Adams, *Elementary School Contest*, p. 129; McCann (ed.), *Popular Education*.

the end of this period, Dissenters admitted to themselves that educational Voluntaryism had failed and accepted the idea of government education and with it the abandonment of the pure ideal of state non-interference. They must share the blame with obstinate Churchmen for the delay of this goal, but perhaps they alone deserve credit for ensuring that when it did come, the rights of children and their parents to think differently from the doctrines of the State Church, or even of Christianity itself, were respected.

State non-interference was a double-edged sword. It made Dissenters reluctant to endorse needed reforms such as state education and legislation regulating the hours which children could work in factories. It also, however, made them disinclined to attempt to enforce their religious and moral standards through legislation. The nobility of principle, for all those who cherish it, is that it is allowed to cut both ways impartially. For these Dissenters, this meant, for example, if government money should not go to Roman Catholics, it should not go to their own denominations either. Or again, the state should not force people to become educated, but neither should it force them to become teetotal. In the end, as with pacifism, Dissenters were forced to admit that there was no such absolute principle as government non-interference. They lost the struggle for Voluntaryism in education and by the closing days of this study had to admit defeat, even to themselves. The period which followed was therefore one of new challenges. Religious equality was much easier to implement within the context of a minimalist state. The immediate cause of the decline of the doctrine of state non-interference, the issue of national education, amply proves this. It is not easy for the state to educate without assuming some religious stance or implying a secularist one. The more active and interventionist government became, the more likely it would be that some specific philosophy would need to inform those activities and Evangelical Dissenters naturally would be tempted to propose their own. The increased popularity of prohibition was the product not of a Dissenting political vision *per se*, but of a political vision in which the state was interventionist. Therefore, there was much that was left unresolved by the political worldview of mid-nineteenth-century Dissenters, sheltered as they were from so many decisions by their commitment to state non-interference, not the least being the fundamental question of the very meaning of the notion of a 'Christian' nation.

The politics of Nonconformists in the eras immediately subsequent to the years covered in this study have been covered in detail by David Bebbington.[35] James Munson has placed Dissenting political activity in

---

[35] Bebbington, *Nonconformist Conscience*.

the Gladstonian era and beyond into a wider cultural context.[36] Both Bebbington and Munson end their studies circa 1914. Arguably, the Gladstonian era was a time when Dissenters asserted an increased desire to impose standards of personal morality in the political arena and upon society as a whole along with a continuation of the emphasis on religious equality. Certainly, men like J. Guinness Rogers and R. W. Dale continued to assert the principle of religious equality and to attempt to apply it to specific political issues; albeit it is clear that other currents, sometimes conflicting ones, could also move Dissenters politically in those decades. Perhaps by the years after the Great War there was truly a section of Dissenters who knew not Miall and the political vision he represented. The Baptist historian, W. T. Whitley, might serve to represent them. He published a history of British Baptists in 1923 and a revised edition in 1932. In this work he hints that it would have been better if Victorian Baptists could have received government money to build their chapels, concentrates on the Divorce Bill as one of the most significant measures of the years of this study (Dissenters at the time made little of it and were not afraid to praise it as a step in the right direction), suggests that Catholic Emancipation was an error and admires the Plymouth Brethren denomination for not allowing their best men to pursue political careers.[37] This is a long way from the politics of mid-nineteenth-century Evangelical Baptist ministers such as F. A. Cox, J. P. Mursell and J. H. Hinton, as this study has shown. To return to the broad brush labels offered in the introduction, the phases of Dissenting political attitudes might be sketched as the following: an early nineteenth-century quest for 'toleration', followed by the development of a distinctive political philosophy in the middle of the century which called for 'equalisation'; toward the close of the century some Dissenters felt a temptation to pursue cultural 'domination' and, by the inter-war period, an awareness of the declining public influence of the Nonconformist community had generated a movement for 'separation' from the political sphere.[38]

If the Dissenters of the mid-nineteenth century left many questions unanswered for their heirs to face, they also bequeathed to them a worthy inheritance. True, they did not provide a blueprint for how to

---

[36] James Munson, *The Nonconformists: In Search of a Lost Culture*, London: SPCK, 1991.

[37] W. T. Whitley, *A History of British Baptists*, London: Kingsgate Press, revised edition, 1932, pp. 283–5, 287–8, 293, 303. The *Nonconformist* wanted the Divorce Bill 'as speedily as possible', criticising it only for being sexist: 10 June 1857, p. 441.

[38] For this latter phase of 'separation', see John Wolffe (ed.), *Evangelical Faith and Public Zeal: Evangelicals and Society in Britain, 1780–1980*, London: SPCK, 1995, chs 7, 8 and 9.

square Christian moral standards and convictions with the principle of religious equality in the context of an interventionist state. They did, however, rule out one false option: concurrent endowment. Almost everyone else in the world of mid-nineteenth-century politics flirted with this option: for example, the great party leaders – Peel, Derby, Russell, Gladstone, Palmerston and Disraeli – all supported the Maynooth grant. Without the pressure provided by the Dissenters, which sprang from the clarity of their vision, concurrent endowment almost certainly would have been the course which was increasingly pursued. If the path of religious equality had created new problems for which the Dissenters of this era provided no answers, concurrent endowment would certainly have become progressively more untenable and absurd as society became increasingly pluralistic. The stubborn fidelity to principle which the Dissenters maintained spared Britain from this muddle. The principle of religious equality itself, however, was the greatest gift which these Dissenters left for future generations. It is a fundamental part of the true Nonconformist conscience in politics. Concerns about Sabbatarianism and issues of personal morality were part of an Evangelical conscience which was also attractive to Dissenters and increasingly politicised for them as well as state intervention became more acceptable. Far from this Evangelical conscience being uniquely Nonconformist, it can be traced all the way back to the prominent Evangelical Anglicans at the start of the century who organised their Society for the Suppression of Vice with its desire to see Sabbath breakers prosecuted.[39] It is interesting to note that the figure who is perhaps most associated with the 'Nonconformist conscience', Hugh Price Hughes, was not from one of the denominations of Old Dissent, but rather was a Wesleyan Methodist. The unique contribution of mid-Victorian Dissenters to politics was not concerns regarding personal morality, but their vision of religious equality. It set them apart from the Whigs and the Tories, the Wesleyans and the Roman Catholics; it was their distinctive contribution to the political arena. The term 'Nonconformist conscience' was first used in 1890, during the controversy over Parnell's personal life.[40] This is not the place to investigate whether the impression which this origin gives – that the dominant political concern of Dissenters during the late Victorian period was with issues of personal morality – is accurate. This study, however, has shown that this impression is a false one, if applied to Dissenters in the middle decades of the nineteenth century. Mid-Victorian Dissenters were a group of

[39] Ian Bradley, *The Call to Seriousness: the Evangelical Impact on the Victorians*, London: Jonathan Cape, 1976, chapter 5.
[40] John F. Glaser, 'Parnell's Fall and the Nonconformist Conscience', *Irish Historical Studies*, XII, 46 (October 1960), pp. 119–38.

people who believed passionately in their own religious vision, but who had a political vision, formed from this religious one, which led them away from attempting to use the power of the state to establish their Christian convictions. In the light of the history of the twentieth century which stands between us and the Victorians, a century which saw some totalitarian regimes using the power of government to attempt to suppress religion and various Fundamentalists attempting to use the power of the state to compel people to submit to their religious scruples, we may be inclined to value more highly the legacy of the Evangelical Dissenters of England. In the mid-Victorian period they struggled to develop a coherent view of the duties of government and so bequeath to posterity the notion of religion equality before the law.

BIBLIOGRAPHY

Contents

Manuscripts 271
Official Publications 271
Reference Works 272
Annuals 272
Newspapers and Journals 272
Contemporary Printed Material 272
Biographies and Autobiographies 276
Diaries, Letters and Speeches 279

Secondary Sources:
Books 279
Articles and Essays 285
Unpublished Theses 289

Manuscripts

Baines Papers, West Yorkshire Archive Service, Leeds
John Blackburn Papers (New College London MSS), Dr Williams's Library, London
Bright Papers, British Library, London
Dale Papers, Birmingham Central Library
'Dictionary of Quaker Biography', Friends' House, London
Dissenting Deputies Papers, Guildhall Library, London
Gladstone Papers, British Library, London
'The Personal Narrative of Me, George Hadfield, M.P.', Manchester Central Library
Liberation Society Papers, London Metropolitan Archives
New College Manuscripts Collection, Dr Williams's Library, London
National Public School Association Papers, Manchester Central Library
Letters Relating to the *Patriot*, Congregational Library, London
Sturge Papers, British Library, London

Official Publications

Census of Great Britain, 1851, Religious Worship. England and Wales. London: George E. Eyre and William Spottiswoode, 1853 (reprinted: *British Parliamentary Papers*, Population 10, Shannon, Ireland: Irish University Press, 1970).
Hansard's Parliamentary Debates, 3rd series.

Reference Works

Dictionary of National Biography
Baylen, Joseph O. and Gossman, Norbert J. (eds) *Biographical Dictionary of Modern British Radicals, vol. 2: 1830–1870*, Brighton, Sussex: Harvester Press, 1984.
Cook, Chris and Keith, Brendan *British Historical Facts 1830–1900*, London: Macmillian Press, 1975.
Lewis, Donald M. (ed.) *The Blackwell Dictionary of Evangelical Biography, 1730–1860*, Oxford: Blackwell, 1995.
Peel, Albert *The Congregational Two Hundred, 1530–1948*, London: The Independent Press, 1948.
Vincent, J. and Stenton M. (eds) *McCalmont's Parliamentary Poll Book, 1832–1918*, Brighton, Sussex: Harvester Press, 1971.

Annuals

Annual Report of the Society for Promoting Ecclesiastical Knowledge
Baptist Handbook
Baptist Manual
Congregational Year Book
Minutes of the [Wesleyan] Methodist Conference

Newpapers and Journals

Baptist Magazine
British Banner
British Quarterly Review
Christian Witness
Congregational Magazine
Ecclesiastical Journal
Eclectic Review
English Independent and Free Church Advocate
Friend
Inquirer
Leeds Mercury
Liberator
Methodist New Connexion Magazine
Nonconformist
Patriot
Primitive Methodist Magazine
Wesleyan Methodist Association Magazine
Wesleyan Methodist Magazine
United Methodist Free Churches' Magazine

Contemporary Printed Material

Anon. ['A Lay Churchman'] *Church and Party: Being Some Remarks on the Duty of Churchmen in and out of Parliament; with Particular Reference to the Coming General Election*, London: Rivingtons, 1865.
Anon. *A Full Report of the Proceedings of the Ministerial Conference on the Suppression of the Liquor Traffic, Held at Manchester, in the Town Hall, on June 9th, 10th and 11th, 1857*, Manchester: United Kingdom Alliance, 1857.

Anon. *A Plan for the Establishment of a General System of Secular Education in the County of Lancaster*, London: Simpkin & Marshall, 1847.

Anon. [John Rippon] *The Ultimate Principle of Religious Liberty: The Philosophical Argument*, London: Ward & Co., 1860.

Adams, Francis *History of the Elementary School Contest in England*, London: Chapman and Hall, 1882 (reprinted: Brighton, Sussex: Harvester Press, 1972).

Anti-Corn Law League *Report of the Conference of Ministers of all Denominations on the Corn Laws* [Manchester 1841], Manchester: J. Gadsby, 1841.

Arnold, Matthew *Culture and Anarchy*, London: Smith, Elder, & Co., 1897 [originally 1869].

Baines, Edward *Letters to the Right Hon. Lord John Russell, First Lord of the Treasury, on State Education*, London: Simpkin, Marshall, & Co., 1846.

Bennett, James *The History of Dissenters, from the Revolution to the year 1808*, 2nd ed., London: Frederick Westley and A. H. Davis, 1833.

Blackburn, John *The Three Conferences held by the Opponents of the Maynooth College Endowment Bill . . . Containing a Vindication of the Author from the Aspersions of the Dissenting Press*, London: Jackson & Walford, 1845.

Bogue, David and Bennett, James *History of Dissenters, from the Revolution in 1688, to the year 1808*, 4 vols, London, n.p., 1808–12.

Brown, John *Centenary Celebration of the Bedfordshire Union of Christians*, London: Congregational Union, 1896.

Chambers, George F. *The Church-and-State Handy-Book of Arguments, Facts, and Statistics Suited to the Times*, London: William Macintosh, 1866.

Chambers, George F. *The Church Defence Movement: An Answer to the Question 'What is it?'*, London: Wertheim, Macintosh and Hunt, 1862.

Conder, Josiah *The Law of the Sabbath: Religious and Political*, London: Holdsworth and Hall, 1830.

Conder, Josiah *The Political Position of Protestant Dissenters in 1853: Eight Letters Addressed to Evangelical Nonconformist Members of the House of Commons*, London: Patriot Office (William Tyler), 1853.

Congregational Board of Education (sponsor), *Crosby-Hall Lectures on Education*, London: John Snow, 1848.

Congregational Board of Education, *Report of the Congregational Board of Education*, London: J. Unwin, Gresham Stean Press, 1852.

Congregational Union of England and Wales, *Bicentenary Lectures,* London: Congregational Union of England and Wales, 1889.

Dale, R. W. *History of English Congregationalism*, London: Hodder and Stoughton, 1907.

Drysdale, A. H. *History of the Presbyterians in England: Their Rise, Decline and Revival*, London: Presbyterian Church of England, 1889.

Evangelical Voluntary Church Association, *Evangelical Voluntary Church Association*, n.p., n.d.

273

Gregory, Benjamin *Side Lights on the Conflicts of Methodism*, London: Cassell, 1899.

Hale, W. H. *The Designs and Constitution of the Society for the Liberation of Religion from State Patronage and Control, Stated and Explained*, London: Rivingtons, 1861.

Hall, Newman *Dissent and the Papal Bull, No Intolerance: A Response to the Cry of "No Popery"*, London: John Snow, 1850.

Halley, Robert *Lancashire: Its Puritanism and Nonconformity*, Manchester: Tubbs and Brooks, 1869.

Harris, William *The History of the Radical Party in Parliament*, London: Kegan Paul, Trench, & Co., 1885.

Hinton, John Howard *The Romish Hierarchy in England: A Sermon preached at Devonshire Square Chapel, London, on the 2nd November, 1850*, London: Houlston and Stoneman, 1850.

Hook, W. F. *A Church Dictionary*, rev. ed., London: John Murray, 1852.

James, John Angell 'The Sabbath, Its Religious Observance a National Duty and a National Blessing' (1848), in Thomas James (ed.), *The Works of John Angell James*, vol. XVI, London: Hamilton Adams, 1862.

Kay-Shuttleworth, James *Four Periods of Public Education*, London: Longman, Green, Longman and Roberts, 1862 (reprinted: Brighton, Sussex: Harvester Press, 1973).

Liberation Society *The General Election. Hints to Electors*, London: Reed and Pardon, 1859.

Liberation Society *Standard Essays on State-Churches*, London: Arthur Miall, 1867.

Macaulay, T. B. *Critical and Historical Essays*, London: Longmans, Green, and Co., 1894.

Maitland, S. R. *The Voluntary System*, second edition, London: J. G. Rivington, 1837.

Manchester Peace Conference, *Brief Statement of the Labours of the Manchester Peace Conference*, [1858].

Mann, Horace 'On the Statistical Position of Religious Bodies in England and Wales', *Quarterly Journal of the Statistical Society*, XVIII, Part II (June 1855).

Masheder, Richard *Dissent and Democracy: their Mutual Relations and Common Object: An Historical Review*, London: Saunders, Otley, & Co., 1864.

Miall, Edward *The British Churches in Relation to the British People*, second edition, London: Arthur Hall, Virtue & Co., 1850.

Miall, Edward *The Politics of Christianity*, London: Arthur Miall, 1863.

Miall, Edward *Title-Deeds of the Church of England to Her Endowments*, London: Longman, 1862.

Mill, J. S. *Utilitarianism, On Liberty, and Considerations on Representative Government*, London: J. M. Dent & Sons, 1972 [*On Liberty* was first published in 1861].

Molesworth, I. E. N. *The Necessity and Design of Church Defence Associations*, Manchester: Thos. Sowler and Sons, 1860.

National Education Union, *Opening Address of Edward Baines, Esq., M.P., at the Educational Conference Held at Leeds December 8th, 1869*, London: Longmans, Green, Reader, & Dyer, n.d.

Noel, B. W., et al. *The Christian Sabbath, Considered in its Various Aspects. By Ministers of Different Denominations*, Edinburgh: Religious Tract and Book Society of Scotland, 1856.

Noel, B. W. *Essay on the Union of Church and State*, London: James Nisbet and Co., 1849.

Peirce, William *The Ecclesiastical Principles and Polity of the Wesleyan Methodists*, new edition, London: Hamilton, Adams, and Co., 1868.

Porritt, Arthur *The Best I Remember*, New York: George H. Doran, n.d.

Pulman, John *The Anti-State Church Association and the Anti-Church Rate League, Unmasked*, London: William Macintosh, 1864.

Reid, William *The Temperance Cyclopaedia*, second edition, Glasgow: Scottish Temperance League, n.d. [1856?].

Religious Freedom Society, *Report presented at the First Annual Meeting of the Religious Freedom Society* [London, 7 May 1840], London: W. Tyler, 1840.

Rigg, James H. *Congregational Independency and Wesleyan Connexionalism Contrasted*, London: James Nichols, 1851.

Ritchie, J. E. *The London Pulpit*, London: Simpkin, Marshall, and Co., 1854.

Shipley, Orby (ed.) *The Church and the World: Essays on Questions of the Day*, London: Longmans, Green, Reader and Dyer, 1866.

Skeats, H. S. *History of the Free Churches of England, 1688–1851*, London: Arthur Miall, 1868.

Skeats, H. S., and Miall, C. S. *History of the Free Churches of England, 1688–1891*, London: Alexander & Shepheard, 1891.

Spurgeon, C. H. *Our National Sins: A Sermon*, London: Partridge & Co., 1857.

Stoughton, John *Religion in England, 1800–50*, 2 vols., London: Hodder and Stoughton, 1884.

Street, J. C. et al. (eds) *Proceedings of the International Temperance and Prohibition Convention*, London: Job Caudwell, 1862.

Thomson, Adam *A Comparative View of English and Scottish Dissenters*, Edinburgh: William Oliphant and Son, 1839.

Vaughan, Robert *English Nonconformity*, London: Jackson, Walford, and Hodder, 1862.

Vaughan, Robert *Popular Education in England*, London: Jackson & Walford, 1846.

Vaughan, Robert *Religious Parties in England*, London: Thomas Ward, 1839 [originally 1838].

Waddington, John *Congregational History*, vols. 4 and 5, London: Longmans, Green, and Co., 1878/1880.

Wayland, F. *The Principles and Practices of the Baptist Churches* (edited and introduced by J. H. Hinton), London: J. Heaton & Son, 1861.

Biographies and Autobiographies

ASHWORTH, JOHN
Calman, A. L. *Life and Labours of John Ashworth*, Manchester: Tubbs and Brook, 1877.

BAINES, EDWARD (senior)
Baines, Edward *The Life of Edward Baines*, London: Longman, 1851.

BINNEY, THOMAS
Hood, E. Paxton *Thomas Binney: His Mind, Life and Opinions*, London: James Clarke, 1874.

BRIGHT, JOHN
Ausubel, Herman *John Bright: Victorian Reformer*, New York: John Wiley & Sons, 1966.
O'Brien, R. Barry *John Bright: A Monograph*, Boston: Houghton Mifflin, 1911.
Mills, J. Travis *John Bright and the Quakers*, 2 vols, London: Methuen, 1935.
Robbins, Keith *John Bright*, London: Routledge & Kegan Paul, 1979.
Robertson, William *The Life and Times of the Right Hon. John Bright*, Rochdale: 'Observer' Printing Works, 1877.
Smith, George Barnett *The Life and Speeches of the Right Hon. John Bright, M.P.*, 2 vols, London: Hodder and Stoughton, 1881.
Trevelyan, G. M. *The Life of John Bright*, London: Constable and Company, 1913.
Vince, C. A. *John Bright*, London: Blackie & Son, 1898.

BROCK, WILLIAM
Birrell, Charles M. *The Life of William Brock, D.D.*, London: James Nisbet, 1878.

BURNS, JABEZ
Burns, Jabez *A Retrospect of Forty-five Years' Christian Ministry*, London: Houlston, 1875.

CAMPBELL, JOHN
Ferguson, Robert and Brown, A. Morton *Life and Labours of John Campbell, D.D.*, London: Richard Bentley, 1867.

COBDEN, RICHARD
Edsall, Nicholas C. *Richard Cobden: Independent Radical*, Cambridge, Massachusetts: Harvard University Press, 1986.
Hobson, J. A. *Richard Cobden: The International Man*, London: Ernest Benn, 1968 [originally 1919].
Morley, John *The Life of Richard Cobden*, London: T. Fisher Unwin, 1903.

COLMAN, J. J.
Colman, Helen Caroline *Jeremiah James Colman: A Memoir*, London: privately printed at the Chiswick Press, 1905.

CONDER, JOSIAH
Conder, E. R. *Josiah Conder: A Memoir*, London: John Snow, 1857.

COOK, THOMAS
Ingle, Robert *Thomas Cook of Leicester*, Bangor, Gwynedd: Headstart History, 1991.

COOPER, THOMAS
Cooper, Thomas *The Life of Thomas Cooper*, Leicester: Leicester University Press, 1971.

DALE, R. W.
Dale, A. W. W. *The Life of R. W. Dale of Birmingham*, London: Hodder and Stoughton, 1898.

DAVIDSON, SAMUEL
Davidson, Anne Jane *Autobiography and Diary of Samuel Davidson*, Edinburgh: T. & T. Clark, 1899.

HALL, NEWMAN
Hall, Newman *Newman Hall: An Autobiography*, London: Cassell, 1898.

HAMILTON, RICHARD WINTER
Stowell, W. H. *Memoir of the Life of Richard Winter Hamilton*, London: Jackson and Walford, 1850.

HOOK, W. F.
Stephens, W. R. W. *The Life and Letters of Walter Farquhar Hook*, London: Richard Bentley & Son, 1881.

JAMES, JOHN ANGELL
Dale, R. W. *Life and Letters of John Angell James*, London: James Nisbet, 1861.

MARTINEAU, JAMES
Drummond, James and Upton, C. B. *The Life and Letters of James Martineau*, 2 vols, London: James Nisbet & Co., 1902.

MCKERROW, WILLIAM
McKerrow, J. M. *Memoir of William McKerrow*, London: Hodder and Stoughton, 1881.

MIALL, EDWARD
Miall, Arthur *Life of Edward Miall*, London: Macmillan & Co., 1884.

MURSELL, JAMES PHILLIPPO
Mursell, Arthur *James Phillippo Mursell: His Life and Work*, London: James Clarke, 1886.

NEWDEGATE, CHARLES N.
Arnstein, Walter L. *Protestant versus Catholic in Mid-Victorian England: Mr. Newdegate and the Nuns*, Columbia, Missouri: University of Missouri Press, 1982.

PARKER, JOSEPH
Adamson, William *Life of the Rev. Joseph Parker*, London: Cassell, 1902.
Parker, Joseph *A Preacher's Life: An Autobiography and an Album*, London: Hodder and Stoughton, 1899.

PETO, MORTON
Anon. *Sir Morton Peto: A Memorial Sketch*, London: Elliot Stock (printed for private circulation), 1893.

RICHARD, HENRY
Miall, Charles S. *Henry Richard, M.P.: A Biography*, London: Cassell, 1889.

ROGERS, J. GUINNESS
Rogers, J. Guinness *J. Guinness Rogers: An Autobiography*, London: James Clarke, 1903.

RULE, W. H.
Rule, W. H. *Recollections of My Life*, London: T. Woolmer, 1886.

LORD JOHN RUSSELL
Walpole, Spencer *The Life of Lord John Russell*, 2 vols, London: Longmans, Green and Co., 1889.

SALT, TITUS
Balgarnie, R. *Sir Titus Salt, Baronet: His Life and Its Lessons*, London: Hodder and Stoughton, 1877 (reprinted: Settle, Yorkshire: Brenton Publishing, 1970).
Burnley, James *Sir Titus Salt and George Moore*, London: Cassell, 1885.
Reynolds, Jack *The Great Paternalist: Titus Salt and the Growth of Nineteenth-Century Bradford*, London: Maurice Temple Smith, 1983.

LORD SHAFTESBURY
Hodder, Edwin *The Life and Work of the Seventh Earl of Shaftesbury, K.G.*, 3 vols, London: Cassell, 1887.
Finlayson, G. B. A. M. *The Seventh Earl of Shaftesbury, 1801–1885*, London: Eyre Methuen, 1980.

SMITH, JOHN PYE
Medway, John *Memoirs of the Life and Writings of John Pye Smith*, London: Jackson and Walford, 1853.

SPURGEON, C. H.
Spurgeon, C. H. *C. H. Spurgeon's Autobiography*, 4 vols, London: Passmore and Alabaster, 1897.

STOUGHTON, JOHN
Stoughton, John *Recollections of a Long Life*, London: Hodder and Stoughton, 1894.

STURGE, JOSEPH
Hobhouse, Stephen *Joseph Sturge: His Life and Work*, London: J.M. Dent & Sons, 1919.

Richard, Henry *Memoirs of Joseph Sturge*, London: S. W. Partridge, 1864.

Tyrrell, Alex *Joseph Sturge and the Moral Radical Party in Early Victorian Britain*, London: Christopher Helm, 1987.

VAUGHAN, ROBERT

Anon. *Robert Vaughan, D.D.: A Memorial*, London: James Clarke & Co., 1869.

WARDLAW, RALPH

Alexander, W. L. *Memoirs of the Life and Writings of Ralph Wardlaw, D.D.*, Edinburgh: Adam and Charles Black, 1856.

WILLIAMS, WILLIAM

Evans, Daniel *The Life and Work of William Williams*, Llandyssul, Wales: Gomerian Press, n.d. [1940].

CARDINAL WISEMAN

Ward, Wilfrid *The Life and Times of Cardinal Wiseman*, London: Longmans, 1897.

Diaries, Letters and Speeches

BRIGHT, JOHN

Leech, H. J. (ed.) *The Public Letters of the Right Hon. John Bright*, second edition, London: Sampson Low, 1895 (reprinted: New York: Kraus Reprint, 1969).

Rogers, J. E. T. (ed.) *Speeches of John Bright, M.P.*, 2 vols, second edition, London: Macmillan, 1869 (reprinted: New York: Kraus Reprint, 1970).

Walling, R. A. J. (ed.) *The Dairies of John Bright*, New York: William Morrow, 1931.

BUNTING, JABEZ

Ward, W. R. (ed.) *Early Victorian Methodism: The Correspondence of Jabez Bunting, 1830–1858*, Oxford: Oxford University Press, 1976.

THIRLWALL, CONNOP

Perowne, J. J. Stewart (ed.) *Remains Literary and Theological of Connop Thirlwall: Charges*, 2 vols, London: Daldy, Isbister & Co., 1877.

TRELAWNY, JOHN

Jenkins, T. A. (ed.) *The Parliamentary Diaries of Sir John Trelawny, 1858–65* (Camden Fourth Series 40), London: Royal Historical Society, 1990.

Secondary Sources

Books

Addison, William George *Religious Equality in Modern England, 1714–1914*, London: SPCK, 1944.

Adelman, Paul *Victorian Radicalism: The middle-class experience, 1830–1914*, London: Longman, 1984.

Altholz, Josef L. *The Religious Press in Britain, 1760–1900* (Contributions to the Study of Religion 22), New York: Greenwood, 1989.

Bebbington, D. W. *Evangelicalism in Modern Britain: A History From the 1730s to the 1980s*, London: Unwin Hyman, 1989.

Bebbington, D. W. *The Nonconformist Conscience: Chapel and Politics, 1870–1914*, London: George Allen and Unwin, 1982.

Bebbington, David *Victorian Nonconformity*, Bangor, Gwynedd, Wales: Headstart History, 1992.

Beck, G. A. (ed.) *The English Catholics, 1850–1950*, London: Burns Oates, 1950.

Belchem, John *Class, Party and the Political System in Britain, 1867–1914*, Oxford: Basil Blackwell, 1990.

Bellot, H. Hale *University College London, 1826–1926*, London: University of London Press, 1929.

Best, Geoffrey *Mid-Victorian Britain, 1851–75*, London: Fontana Press, 1979.

Best, G. F. A. *Temporal Pillars*, Cambridge: Cambridge University Press, 1964.

Biagini, Eugenio F. *Liberty, Retrenchment and Reform: Popular Liberalism in the Age of Gladstone, 1860–1880*, Cambridge: Cambridge University Press, 1992.

Biagini, Eugenio F., and Reid, Alastair J. (eds) *Currents of Radicalism: Popular radicalism, organised labour and party politics in Britain, 1850–1914*, Cambridge: Cambridge University Press, 1991.

Binfield, Clyde *So Down to Prayers: Studies in English Nonconformity, 1780–1920*, London: J. M. Dent & Sons, 1977.

Binns, Henry Bryan *A Century of Education*, London: J. M. Dent, 1908.

Bowen, Desmond *The Idea of the Victorian Church: a study of the Church of England, 1833–1889*, Montreal: McGill University Press, 1968.

Bradley, Ian *The Call to Seriousness: the Evangelical Impact on the Victorians*, London: Jonathan Cape, 1976.

Briggs, J. H. Y. *The English Baptists of the Nineteenth Century* (History of the English Baptists 3), Didcot, Oxfordshire: Baptist Historical Society, 1994.

Briggs, John and Sellers, Ian (eds) *Victorian Nonconformity*, London: Edward Arnold, 1973.

Brown, Kenneth D. *A Social History of the Nonconformist Ministry in England and Wales, 1800–1930*, Oxford: Clarendon Press, 1988.

Burgess, Henry James *Enterprise in Education: The story of the work of the*

Established Church in the education of the people prior to 1870, London: SPCK, 1958.

Burn, W. L. *The Age of Equipoise*, London: Unwin University Books, 1968 [originally 1964].

Carlile, John C. *The Story of the English Baptists*, London: James Clarke & Co., 1905.

Chadwick, Owen *The Victorian Church*, 2 parts, London: Adam and Charles Black, 1966/70.

Clark, G. Kitson *The Making of Victorian England*, London: Methuen, 1962.

Cliff, Philip B. *The Rise and Development of the Sunday School Movement in England, 1780–1980*, Nutfields, Redhill, Surrey: NCEC, 1986.

Coleman, B. I. *The Church of England in the Mid-Nineteenth Century: A Social Geography*, London: The Historical Association, 1980.

Conacher, J. B. *The Peelites and the Party System, 1846–52*, Newton Abbot, Devon: David and Charles Ltd., 1972.

Cowherd, Raymond G. *The Politics of English Dissent*, London: Epworth Press, 1959.

Cunningham, Valentine *Everywhere Spoken Against: Dissent in the Victorian Novel*, Oxford: Clarendon Press, 1975.

Currie, Robert et al. *Churches and Churchgoers: Patterns of Church Growth in the British Isles since 1700*, Oxford: Clarendon, 1977.

Davidoff, Leonore and Hall, Catherine *Family Fortunes: Men and Women of the English Middle Class, 1780–1850*, London: Routledge, 1987.

Dingle, A. E. *The Campaign for Prohibition in Victorian England*, London: Croom Helm, 1980.

Donajgrodzki, A. P. (ed.) *Social Control in Nineteenth Century Britain*, London: Croom Helm, 1977.

Ellens, J. P. *Religious Routes to Gladstonian Liberalism: The Church Rate Conflict in England and Wales, 1832–68*, University Park, Pennsylvania: Pennsylvania State University Press, 1994.

Everitt, Alan *The Pattern of Rural Dissent: The Nineteenth Century*, Leicester: Leicester University Press, 1972.

Fraser, Derek *Urban Politics in Victorian England*, London: MacMillan Press Ltd., 1976.

Garrard, John *Leadership and Power in Victorian Towns, 1830–80*, Manchester: Manchester University Press, 1983.

Gash, Norman *Politics in the Age of Peel: A study in the Technique of Parliamentary Representation, 1830–1850*, London: Longmans, Green and Company Ltd., 1953.

Gash, Norman *Reaction and Reconstruction in English Politics, 1832–52*, Oxford: Clarendon Press, 1965.

Gay, John D. *The Geography of Religion in England*, London: Duckworth, 1971.

Gibson, William *Church, State and Society, 1760–1850*, Basingstoke, Hampshire: MacMillan, 1994.

Gilbert, Alan D. *Religion and Society in Industrial England: Church, Chapel and Social Change, 1740–1914*, London: Longman, 1976.

Gowland, D. A. *Methodist Secessions: The Origins of Free Methodism in Three Lancashire Towns*, Manchester: The Chetham Society, 1979.

Halévy, Elie *A History of the English People in the Nineteenth Century*, vol. 4, London: Earnest Benn, 1951.

Hamer, D. A. *The Politics of Electoral Pressure: A study in the History of Victorian Reform Agitations*, Hassocks, Sussex: Harvester Press, 1977.

Hanham, H. J. *Elections and Party Management: Politics in the time of Disraeli and Gladstone*, Hassocks, Sussex: Harvester Press, 1978.

Harrison, Brian *Drink and the Victorians: The Temperance Question in England, 1815–1872*, London: Faber and Faber, 1971.

Hempton, David *Methodism and Politics in British Society, 1750–1850*, London: Hutchinson, 1987 [originally 1984].

Henriques, Ursula *Religious Toleration in England, 1787–1833*, London: Routledge and Kegan Paul, 1961.

Hilton, Boyd *The Age of Atonement: The Influence of Evangelicalism on Social and Economic Thought, 1785–1865*, Oxford: Clarendon Press, 1988.

Holt, Raymond V. *The Unitarian Contribution to Social Progress in England*, London: George Allen & Unwin, 1938.

Horstman, Allen *Victorian Divorce*, New York: St Martin's Press, 1985.

Howe, Anthony *The Cotton Masters, 1830–1860*, Oxford: Clarendon Press, 1984.

Howsam, Leslie *Cheap Bibles: Nineteenth-century publishing and the British and Foreign Bible Society*, Cambridge: Cambridge University Press, 1991.

Howse, Ernest Marshall *Saints in Politics: The 'Clapham Sect' and the Growth of Freedom*, London: George Allen & Unwin, 1971 [originally 1953].

Isichei, Elizabeth *Victorian Quakers*, Oxford: Oxford University Press, 1970.

Johnson, Mark D. *The Dissolution of Dissent, 1850–1918*, New York: Garland Publishing, 1987.

Jones, R. Tudur *Congregationalism in England, 1662–1962*, London: Independent Press, 1962.

Kirk, Neville *The Growth of Working Class Reformism in Mid-Victorian England*, Sydney: Croom Helm, 1985.

Koss, Stephen *Nonconformity in Modern British Politics*, London: B. T. Batsford, 1975.

Lovegrove, Deryck W. *Established Church, Sectarian People: Itinerancy and the Transformation of English Dissent, 1780–1830*, Cambridge: Cambridge University Press, 1988.

Machin, G. I. T. *Politics and the Churches in Great Britain, 1832 to 1868*, Oxford: Clarendon Press, 1977.

Machin, G. I. T. *Politics and the Churches in Great Britain, 1869 to 1921*, Oxford: Clarendon Press, 1987.

Mackintosh, William H. *Disestablishment and Liberation*, London: Epworth Press, 1972.

Manning, Bernard Lord *The Protestant Dissenting Deputies*, Cambridge: Cambridge University Press, 1952.

McCann, Phillip (ed.) *Popular Education and Socialization in the Nineteenth Century*, London: Methuen & Co, 1977.

McLeod, Hugh *Religion and the Working Class in Nineteenth-Century Britain*, Basingstoke, Hampshire: Macmillan, 1984.

Munson, James *The Nonconformists*, London: SPCK, 1991.

Murphy, James *Church, State and Schools in Britain, 1800–1970*, London: Routledge & Kegan Paul, 1971.

Murphy, James *The Religious Problem in English Education: The Crucial Experiment*, Liverpool: Liverpool University Press, 1959.

Norman, E. R. *Anti-Catholicism in Victorian England*, London: George Allen and Unwin, 1968.

Norman, E. R. *The Conscience of the State in North America*, Cambridge: Cambridge University Press, 1969.

Norman, E. R. *Church and Society in England, 1770–1970*, Oxford: Clarendon Press, 1976.

Obelkevich, James *Religion and Rural Society: South Lindsey, 1825–1875*, Oxford: Clarendon Press, 1976.

Parry, J. P. *Democracy and Religion: Gladstone and the Liberal Party, 1867–1875*, Cambridge: Cambridge University Press, 1986.

Parry, Jonathan *The Rise and Fall of Liberal Government in Victorian Britain*, New Haven, Connecticut: Yale University Press, 1996 [originally 1993].

Parsons, Gerald (ed.) *Religion in Victorian Britain*, vols. I, II, and IV, Manchester: Manchester University Press, 1988.

Patterson, A. Temple *Radical Leicester: A History of Leicester, 1780–1850*, Leicester: University College, 1954.

Payne, Ernest A. *The Baptist Union: A Short History*, London: The Carey Kingsgate Press, 1958.

Paz, D. G. *The Politics of Working-Class Education in Britain, 1830–50*, Manchester: Manchester University Press, 1980.

Paz, D. G. *Popular Anti-Catholicism in Mid-Victorian England*, Stanford, California: Stanford University Press, 1992.

Peel, Albert *These Hundred Years: A History of the Congregational Union of England and Wales, 1831–1931*, London: Congregational Union of England and Wales, 1931.

Read, Donald *Press and People, 1790–1850: Opinion in Three English Cities*, Westport, Connecticut: Greenwood Press, 1961.

Robinson, W. Gordon *A History of the Lancashire Congregational Union, 1806–1956*, Manchester: Lancashire Congregational Union, 1955.

Royle, Edward *Victorian Infidels*, Manchester: Manchester University Press, 1974.

Salbstein, M. C. N. *The Emancipation of the Jews in Britain: The Question of the Admission of the Jews to Parliament, 1828–1860*, London and Toronto: Associated University Press, 1982.

Salter, F. R. *Dissenters and Public Affairs in Mid-Victorian England*

(Twenty-First Lecture of the Friends of Dr Williams's Library), London: Dr Williams's Trust, 1967.

Searle, G. R. *Entrepreneurial Politics in Mid-Victorian Britain*, Oxford: Oxford University Press, 1993.

Sellers, Ian *Nineteenth-Century Nonconformity*, London: Edward Arnold, 1977.

Shiman, Lilian Lewis *Crusade Against Drink in Victorian England*, London: MacMillan Press, 1988.

Simon, Brian *Studies in the History of Education, 1780–1870*, London: Lawrence & Wishart, 1960.

Sims, Basil H. *The Dissenting Deputies*, London: Independent Press, 1961.

Snell, K. D. M. *Church and Chapel in North Midlands: Religious Observance in the Nineteenth Century*, Leicester: Leicester University Press, 1991.

Shipley, C. E. (ed.) *The Baptists of Yorkshire*, Bradford: Wm. Byles & Sons, 1912.

Stanley, Brian *The History of the Baptist Missionary Society, 1792–1992*, Edinburgh: T. & T. Clark, 1992.

Steele, E. D. *Palmerston and Liberalism, 1855–1865*, Cambridge: Cambridge Unversity Press, 1991.

Stewart, Robert *The Foundation of the Conservative Party, 1830–1867*, London: Longman, 1978.

Stewart, Robert *Party and Politics, 1830–1852*, London: MacMillan Education, 1989.

Sturt, Mary *The Education of the People: A history of primary education in England and Wales in the Nineteenth Century*, London: Routledge & Kegan Paul, 1967.

Sutherland, Gillian *Elementary Education in the Nineteenth Century*, London: The Historical Association, 1971.

Tholfsen, Trygve R. *Working Class Radicalism in Mid-Victorian England*, London: Croom Helm, 1976.

Thompson, David M. (ed.) *Nonconformity in the Nineteenth Century*, London: Routledge and Kegan Paul, 1972.

Underwood, A. C. *A History of the English Baptists*, London: Baptist Union, 1947.

Vincent, John *The Formation of the British Liberal Party, 1857–68*, Harmondsworth, Middlesex: Penguin, 1972 [originally 1966].

Vincent, J. R. *Pollbooks: How Victorians Voted*, Cambridge: Cambridge University Press, 1967.

Ward, W. R. *Religion and Society in England, 1790–1850*, London: B. T. Batsford, 1972.

Watts, Michael R. *The Dissenters: Volume I: From the Reformation to the French Revolution*, Oxford: Clarendon Press, 1978.

Watts, Michael R. *The Dissenters: Volume II: The Expansion of Evangelical Nonconformity, 1791–1859*, Oxford: Clarendon Press, 1995.

Whitley, W. T. *A History of British Baptists*, second edition, London: Kingsgate, 1932.

Wigley, John *The Rise and Fall of the Victorian Sunday*, Manchester: Manchester University Press, 1980.

Wigmore-Beddoes, Dennis G. *Yesterday's Radicals: a study of the affinity between Unitarianism and Broad Church Anglicanism in the Nineteenth Century*, Cambridge: James Clarke, 1971.

Wolffe, John (ed.) *Evangelical Faith and Public Zeal: Evangelicals and Society in Britain, 1780–1980*, London: SPCK, 1995.

Wolffe, John *God and Greater Britain: Religion and National Life in Britain and Ireland, 1843–1945*, London: Routledge, 1994.

Wolffe, John *The Protestant Crusade in Great Britain ,1829–1860*, Oxford: Claredon Press, 1991.

Articles and Essays

Allen, Janet E. 'Voluntaryism: a "Laissez-faire" Movement in Mid Nineteenth Century Elementary Education', *History of Education*, 10 (1981), 2.

Anderson, Olive 'Gladstone's Abolition of Compulsory Church Rates', *Journal of Ecclesiastical History*, XXV, 2 (April 1974).

Anderson, Olive 'The growth of Christian militarism in mid-Victorian Britain', *English Historical Review*, LXXXVI, CCCXXXVIII (January 1971).

Anderson, Olive 'The Reactions of Church and Dissent towards the Crimean War', *Journal of Ecclesiastical History*, 16 (1965).

Beales, D. E. D. 'Parliamentary Parties and the "Independent" Member, 1810–1860', in Robert Robson (ed.), *Ideas and Institutions of Victorian Britain*, London: G. Bell and Sons, 1967.

Bebbington, D. W. 'The Baptist Conscience in the Nineteenth Century', *Baptist Quarterly*, XXXIV, 1 (January 1991).

Bebbington, D. W. 'Baptist M.P.s in the Nineteenth Century', *Baptist Quarterly*, XXIX, 1 (January 1981).

Bebbington, D. W. 'Gladstone and the Baptists', *Baptist Quarterly*, XXVI, 5 (January 1976).

Bebbington, D. W. 'Gladstone and the Nonconformists: a religious affinity in politics', in Derek Baker (ed.), *Church, Society and Politics* (Studies in Church History 12), Oxford: Basil Blackwell, 1975.

Bebbington, D. W. 'The Life of Baptist Noel: its setting and significance', *Baptist Quarterly*, XXIV, 8 (October 1972).

Bebbington, D. W. 'Nonconformity and Electoral Sociology, 1867–1918', *Historical Journal*, 27 (1984), 3.

Best, G. F. A. 'The Religious Difficulties of National Education in England, 1800–70', *Cambridge Historical Journal*, XII (1956), 2.

Bowers, Brian and Bowers, Faith 'Bloomsbury Chapel and Mercantile Morality: The Case of Sir Morton Peto', *Baptist Quarterly*, 30, 5 (January 1984).

Brent, Richard 'The Whigs and Protestant Dissent in the Decade of Reform: the case of Church Rates, 1833–1841', *English Historical Review*, CII, CCCCV (October 1987).

Clarke, P. F. 'Electoral Sociology of Modern Britain', *History*, 57 (1972).

Close, David 'The formation of a two-party alignment in the House of Commons between 1832 and 1841', *English Historical Review*, LXXXIV, CCCXXXI (April 1969).

Conway, Stephen 'John Bowring and the Nineteenth-Century Peace Movement', *Historical Research*, 64, 155 (October 1991).

Cornford, James 'The Transformation of Conservatism in the Late Nineteenth Century', *Victorian Studies*, VII (1963).

Dekar, Paul A. 'Baptist Peacemakers in Nineteenth-Century Peace Societies', *Baptist Quarterly*, XXXIV, 1 (January 1991).

Dick, Malcolm 'The Myth of the Working-class Sunday School', *History of Education*, 9, 1 (1980).

Ely, Richard 'The Origins of the Debate over "Secular" Instruction', *History of Education*, 9 (1980), 2.

Embree, Ainslie T. 'Christianity and the state in Victorian India: confrontation and collaboration', in R. W. Davis and R. J. Helmstadter (eds), *Religion and Irreligion in Victorian Society*, London: Routledge, 1992.

Feheney, J. Matthew 'Towards Religious Equality for Catholic Pauper Children, 1861–68', *British Journal of Educational Studies*, XXXI, 2 (June 1983).

Field, Clive D. 'The social structure of English Methodism: eighteenth-twentieth centuries', *British Journal of Sociology*, 28, 2 (June 1977).

Fraser, Derek 'Edward Baines', in Patricia Hollis (ed.), *Pressure from Without*, London: Edward Arnold, 1974.

Fraser, Derek 'Voluntaryism and West Riding Politics in the Mid-nineteenth Century', *Northern History*, XIII (1977).

Glaser, John F. 'English Nonconformity and the Decline of Liberalism', *American Historical Review*, LXIII, 2 (January 1958).

Glaser, John F. 'Parnell's fall and the Nonconformist Conscience', *Irish Historical Studies*, XII, 46 (October 1960).

Grant, A. Cameron 'A Note on "Secular" Education in the Nineteenth Century', *British Journal of Educational Studies*, XVI (Feb. – Oct. 1968).

Gurowich, P. M. 'The Continuation of War by other Means: Party and Politics, 1855–1865', *Historical Journal*, 27 (1984), 3.

Harrison, Brian 'The British Prohibitionists 1853–1872: A Biographical Analysis', *International Review of Social History*, XV (1970).

Harrison, Brian 'Drink and Sobriety in England 1815–1872: A Critical Bibliography', *International Review of Social History*, XII (1967).

Harrison, Brian 'Religion and Recreation in Nineteenth-Century England', *Past and Present*, 38 (December 1967).

Harrison, Brian 'The Sunday Trading Riots of 1855', *Historical Journal*, VIII (1965), 2.

Hempton, David 'Wesleyan Methodism and Educational Politics in Early Nineteenth-century England', *History of Education*, 8 (1979), 3.

Henderson, Gavin B. 'The Pacifists of the Fifties', in his *Crimean War Diplomacy and other Historical Essays*, Glasgow: Jackson, Son & Co., 1947.

Hilton, Boyd 'Peel: A Reappraisal', *Historical Journal*, 22 (1979), 3.

Inglis, K. S. 'Patterns of Religious Worship in 1851', *Journal of Ecclesiastical History*, 11 (1960).

Johnson, Richard 'Educational Policy and Social Control in Early Victorian England', *Past and Present*, 49 (November 1970).

Jones, D. K. 'The Educational Legacy of the Anti-Corn Law League', *History of Education*, 3, 1 (January 1974).

Jones, D. K. 'Horace Mann, the American common school and English provincial radicals in the nineteenth century', *History of Education*, 15 (1986), 4.

Jones, D. K. 'Lancashire, the American Common School, and the Religious Problem in British Education in the Nineteenth Century', *British Journal of Educational Studies*, 15 (Feb. – Oct. 1967).

Joyce, Patrick 'The Factory Politics of Lancashire in the Later Nineteenth Century', *Historical Journal*, XVIII (1975), 3.

Larsen, Timothy 'Bishop Colenso and his Critics: the strange emergence of biblical criticism in Victorian Britain', *Scottish Journal of Theology*, 50 (1997), 4.

Larsen, Timothy ' "How Many Sisters Make a Brotherhood?" A case study in gender and ecclesiology in early nineteenth-century English Dissent', *Journal of Ecclesiastical History*, 49, 2 (April 1998).

Larsen, Timothy 'Victorian Nonconformity and the Memory of the Ejected Ministers: the impact of the bicentennial commemorations of 1862', in R. N. Swanson (ed.), *The Church Retrospective* (Studies in Church History 33), Woodbridge, Suffolk: The Boydell Press for the Ecclesiastical History Society, 1998.

Machin, G. I. T. 'Gladstone and Nonconformity in the 1860s: the formation of an alliance', *Historical Journal*, XVII (1974), 2.

Machin, G. I. T. 'Lord John Russell and the Prelude to the Ecclesiastical Titles Bill, 1846–51, *Journal of Ecclesiastical History*, XXV, 3 (July 1974).

Matthew, H. C. G. 'Disraeli, Gladstone, and the Politics of Mid-Victorian Budgets', *Historical Journal*, 22 (1979), 3.

McLeod, Hugh 'Class, Community and Region: The Religious Geography of Nineteenth-Century England', in Michael Hill (ed.), *A Sociological Yearbook of Religion in Britain*, 6, London: SCM, 1973.

Parry, J. P. 'Religion and the Collapse of Gladstone's First Government, 1870–1874', *Historical Journal*, 25 (1982), 1.

Partridge, M. S. 'The Russell Cabinet and National Defence, 1846–1852', *History* 72 (1987).

Pickering, W. S. F. 'The 1851 religious census – a useless experiment?', *British Journal of Sociology*, 18 (1967).

Ralls, Walter 'The Papal Aggression of 1850: A study in Victorian Anti-Catholicism', *Church History*, 43 (1974).

Roberts, M. J. D. 'The Pressure-Group Politics of the Church of England: The Church Defense Institution 1859–1896', *Journal of Ecclesiastical History*, 35, 4 (October 1984).

Roper, Henry 'Toward an Elementary Education Act for England and

Wales, 1865–1868', *British Journal of Educational Studies*, XXVIII, 2 (June 1975).

Salter, F. R. 'Congregationalism and the "Hungry Forties"', *Transactions of the Congregational Historical Society*, 17 (1955).

Short, K. R. M. 'The English Indemnity Acts, 1726–1865', *Church History*, 42 (1973).

Short, K. R. M. 'The English Regium Donum', *English Historical Review*, LXXXIV, CCCXXX (January 1969).

Short, K. R. M. 'London's General Body of Protestant Ministers: its Disruption in 1836', *Journal of Ecclesiastical History*, XXIV, 4 (October 1973).

Simon, Alan 'Church Disestablishment as a Factor in the General Election of 1885', *Historical Journal*, XVIII, 4 (1975).

Smith, Paul 'Disraeli's Politics', *Transactions of the Royal Historical Society*, Fifth Series, 37 (London 1987).

Stanley, Brian 'Christian Responses to the Indian Mutiny of 1857', in W. J. Sheils (ed.), *The Church and War* (Studies in Church History 20), Oxford: Basil Blackwell, 1983.

Stanley, Brian 'Commerce and Christianity: Providence Theory, the Missionary Movement, and the Imperialism of Free Trade, 1842–60', *Historical Journal*, 26 (1983), 1.

Stannard, Kevin 'Ideology, education, and social structure: elementary schooling in mid-Victorian England', *History of Education*, 19 (1990), 2.

Summerton, N. W. 'Dissenting Attitudes to Foreign Relations, Peace and War, 1840–90', *Journal of Ecclesiastical History*, 28, 2 (April 1977).

Thompson, David M. 'The 1851 religious census: problems and possibilities', *Victorian Studies*, 11, 1 (September 1967).

Thompson, David M. 'The churches and society in Nineteenth Century England: a rural perspective', in G. J. Cuming and Derek Baker (eds), *Popular Belief and Practice* (Studies in Church History 8), Cambridge: University Press, 1972.

Thompson, David M. 'The Liberation Society, 1844–1868', in Patricia Hollis (ed.), *Pressure from Without*, London: Edward Arnold, 1974.

Thompson, David M. 'The Religious Census of 1851', in Richard Lawton (ed.), *The Census and Social Structure*, London: Frank Cass, 1978.

Thompson, F. M. L. 'Social Control in Victorian Britain', *Economic History Review*, 2nd series, XXXIV, 2 (May 1981).

Tyrrell, Alexander 'Making the Millennium: the mid-nineteenth century peace movement', *Historical Journal*, 20 (1978), 1.

Tyrrell, Alex 'Personality in Politics: The National Complete Suffrage Union and Pressure Group Politics in Early Victorian Britain', *Journal of Religious History*, 12, 4 (December 1983).

Wadsworth, A. P. 'The First Manchester Sunday Schools', in M. W. Flinn and J. C. Smout (eds), *Essays in Social History*, Oxford: Clarendon Press, 1974.

Ward, J. T. and Treble, J. H. 'Religion and Education in 1843: Reaction to the "Factory Education Bill" ', *Journal of Ecclesiastical History*, XX, 1 (April 1969).

Wilson, Alexander 'The Suffrage Movement', in Patricia Hollis (ed.), *Pressure from Without*, London: Edward Arnold, 1974.

Wolffe, John 'The Evangelical Alliance in the 1840s: an attempt to institutionalise Christian unity', in W. J. Sheils and Diana Wood (eds), *Voluntary Religion* (Studies in Church History 23), Oxford: Basil Blackwell, 1986.

Wolffe, John 'Evangelicalism in mid-nineteenth-century England', in Raphael Samuel (ed.), *Patriotism: The Making and Unmaking of British National Identity*, vol. 1, London: Routledge, 1989.

Unpublished Theses

Brownell, K. G. 'Voluntary Saints: English Congregationalism and the Voluntary Principle, 1825–62', Ph.D. thesis, University of St. Andrews, 1982.

Ellis, George Mark 'The Evangelicals and the Sunday Question, 1830–1860: Organized Sabbatarianism as an Aspect of the Evangelical Movement', Ph.D. thesis, Harvard University, 1951.

Lowerson, J. R. 'The Political Career of Sir Edward Baines (1800–90)', M.A. thesis, University of Leeds, 1965.

Martin, H. R. 'The Politics of the Congregationalists, 1830–1856', Ph.D. thesis, University of Durham, 1971.

Newton, J. S. 'The Political Career of Edward Miall', Ph.D. thesis, University of Durham, 1975.

Rugg, Julie 'The Rise of Cemetery Companies in Britain, 1820–53', Ph.D. thesis, University of Stirling, 1992.

Salbstein, M. C. N. 'The Emancipation of the Jews in Britain, with Particular Reference to the Debate Concerning the Admission of the Jews to Parliament, 1828–1860', Ph.D. thesis, University of London, 1974.

Welch, Allen Howard 'John Carvell Williams, the Nonconformist Watchdog (1821–1907)', Ph.D. thesis, University of Kansas, 1968.

INDEX

Acworth, James 180
Adams, Francis 160
Affirmations Bill 251–2
Africa 219
Aldis, John (sons of) 64
Alexander, G. W. 142–3
Allen, Stafford 143
America/Americans 87, 90–1, 92, 98, 178, 211, 261; see also United States
American Civil War 98, 100, 219–20
American Revolution 24
Anderson, Olive 243, 244, 245
Anglo-Catholics 95; see also High Church; Tractarians
Anti-Catholicism 4, 5, 9, 104, 130, 225–42, 248 (n. 183)
Anti-Compulsory Vaccination League 116
Anti-Corn Law League 2, 117, 121, 217
Antidisestablishmentarianism 97–8; see also Church defenders
Anti-Sabbatarians 189, 191, 198, 199, 201, 203–4
Anti-Semitism 130
Anti-slavery see Slavery
Anti-State Church Association 2, 31, 32, 34, 35, 36, 37, 71, 81, 82–3, 87, 93, 99, 108, 111, 112, 117, 119, 172, 180, 183, 220, 227, 258, 260, 265; see also Liberation Society Executive Committee 36, 81, 94
Anti-transubstantiation declaration 94, 226
Arbitration 28, 210
Armitage, Elkanah 158
Arnold, Matthew 81, 204, 205
Art Treasures Exhibition 180
Artisan culture 185; see also Class
Ashley, Lord see Shaftesbury, 7th Earl
Ashworth, John 186, 187–8, 199, 210
Atheism/atheists 4, 19, 135, 225, 249, 251–2; see also Secularists; Irreligious; Infidels

Baines, Edward (Jr.) 18 (n. 14), 33, 58, 67, 83, 106, 120, 139–40, 142, 143, 144, 148, 150–51 153, 154, 155, 156, 162, 163, 164, 165 (n. 129), 167, 171–2, 196, 214–15, 223, 224, 233, 235 242, 264–5
Baines, Edward (Sn.) 25, 47
Baines, M. T. 58
Baines, William 47, 48, 53, 220
Ball, Edward 38, 51
Band of Hope Union 181, 182 (n. 38)
Baptist Board 193
Baptist Handbook 181
Baptist Magazine 32, 46, 48, 57, 62, 84, 134, 142, 146, 149, 154, 163, 180, 183, 184, 195 196, 197, 199, 204, 211, 212, 219, 228, 236 (n. 136), 237, 241, 245
Baptist Missionary Society 261
Baptist Union 57, 83, 93, 111, 180, 181, 182, 188, 224, 242
Baptist Union of New Zealand 182
Baptists 16, 23, 29, 38, 42, 55, 57, 64, 83, 86, 89, 128, 141, 142, 143, 157, 174, 175, 180–84 185, 195, 200, 213, 219, 233, 241, 253, 255, 256, 261, 262, 264, 268
Barrett, Joseph 143
Batey, John 181
Baxter, W. E. 68, 73
Beaumont, Lord 241
Bebbington, David 4, 38, 267–8
Bedfordshire 23, 174
Bennett, James 86, 87, 106
Berkshire 174
Biagini, Eugenio 6–7, 253
Bible Christians 18, 63, 175
Bible printing monopoly 118–20, 236
Bible societies 120
Binfield, Clyde 4, 164
Binney, Thomas 19, 20, 22, 29, 34, 41, 155, 216, 245
Birmingham 22, 25, 30, 80, 95, 96, 165, 188, 233
Birrell, C. M. 182

Birth registration grievances 43
Bishops 67, 127, 232, 260, 264
  Roman Catholic 230, 232
Blackburn, John 25, 82, 85, 93, 228, 261
Bogue, David 86, 87
Bourne, F. W. 63
Bowly, Samuel 28
Bowring, John 84
Bradford 22, 30
Bradley, James 24
Brewster, Patrick 185
Briggs, William 158
Bright, Jacob 158
Bright, John 27, 29, 30, 46, 51, 53, 111, 117, 118, 165, 179, 188, 191, 193, 204, 214, 216 218, 224, 232, 233, 234, 236, 245, 252
Bristol 83, 90, 172, 231
British and Foreign Anti-Slavery Society 143
British Banner 34, 36, 54, 127, 155, 157, 194, 197, 208, 213, 218, 221, 223, 227, 231, 235 244
British Ensign 34, 223
British Library 114
British Museum 196
British Quarterly Review 21 (n. 26), 33, 37, 41, 53, 59, 61, 66, 68–9, 70, 72, 74, 91, 106, 110 112, 113, 116, 122, 134, 138, 141, 155, 156, 187, 194, 195, 201, 214, 217, 228
British Society 137
British Standard 34
Brock, William 29, 142, 210, 216, 219
Brougham, Lord 57
Brown, A. M. 120
Brownell, K. G. 10
Brussels 210
Buckinghamshire 23, 174
Bungay 119
Bunting, Jabez 26, 27, 152, 190, 253
Bunyan, John 16, 23
Burgess, Henry 166
Burial law grievances 43, 44, 53–7, 68, 70
Burke, Edmund 234
Burnet, John 29, 210, 211, 257
Burns, Dawson 180, 181, 184
Burns, Jabez 172–3, 176, 180, 210
Burritt, Elihu 211
Burt, Thomas 185

Buxton, Charles 64
Byron, 6th Baron 49

Calvinistic Methodists 175
Cambridgeshire 23, 38
Cambridge University 44, 59, 61–2, 64, 66
Campbell, John 34, 35–6, 71, 85, 94, 119, 120 (n. 56), 127, 157, 185, 212, 213, 223, 249 (n. 185)
Canada 102
Canadian Clergy Reserves Bill 102
Canon law 237
Card, Nathaniel 177
Catholic Emancipation Act 238, 268
Catholicism, Roman/Roman Catholics 1, 4, 11, 18, 65, 99, 100, 113, 138, 157 (n. 93) 182, 200, 225–42, 267, 269; *see also* Anti-Catholicism
  Irish Catholics 5, 103–5
Cemeteries 54
Census *see* Religious Census
Chadwick, Owen 5–6, 7, 10, 35, 121, 197, 204
Chambers, George 99
Chartists 98, 185, 220–21, 224
Cheap Bread Herald 117
Cheshire 174
Childs, John 119–20
Chown, J. P. 182
Christian government/nation, idea of 246–50, 267
Christian Witness 34, 36, 45, 48, 58, 60, 89, 94, 193, 198
Christian's Penny Magazine 34
Church Defence Associations 97–9
Church defenders 50, 69, 80, 97–9, 108, 122, 264
Church establishments, idea of 39, 79, 80, 81, 88, 90, 95, 100, 102, 110, 118, 121, 145, 172 217, 235, 236, 247, 254, 256, 261
Church government *see* Ecclesiology
Church of England 5, 15, 17, 18, 19, 21, 22, 23, 24, 40, 41, 42, 43, 45 51, 53, 55, 56, 58, 65, 67, 75, 82, 86, 87, 89, 95–102, 118, 130, 136, 138, 141, 144, 157, 165, 166, 175, 176, 189, 195, 200, 209, 211, 230, 264, 266; *see also* Churchmen
  In Ireland 7, 103–5

Church of England Quarterly Review, The 238
Church of Scotland 117
Church Institution 98–9
Church rate abolition bills 49, 50–1
Church rate martyrs 47, 119, 220
Church rates 25, 26, 27, 41, 44–53, 57, 66, 68, 69, 71, 108, 113, 181, 251, 258, 262, 264
  Lords' Select Committee on 49, 50, 108
Churchmen 6, 21, 32, 41, 50, 51, 60, 62, 65, 70, 85, 90, 92, 97–9, 111, 113, 120, 123, 124, 126–7, 138, 145, 189, 190, 197, 200, 204, 227, 230, 232, 240, 241, 243, 252, 254, 257, 258, 262, 265, 267
Churchwardens 46
Churchyard 43, 53, 55
Class 166, 196–8, 220
  Lower/working 18, 20, 147, 149, 185, 186, 196–8, 201
  Middle 18, 19, 20, 22, 47, 147, 209
Clayton, George 93
Clergymen 53, 54, 55, 56, 57, 58, 67, 95, 117, 175, 211
Close, Francis 162
Cobden, Richard 117, 159, 209, 211, 214, 215, 216, 217
Colenso, J. W. 95
Colman, J. J. 211
Colonies, British 102–3, 105, 207, 225, 236
Committee of the Privy Council for Education 137, 161
Commons, House of 2, 3, 25, 37, 50, 55, 56, 59, 64, 67, 80, 103, 104, 111, 114, 126, 132, 136, 189, 191, 193, 197, 227, 232, 253; *see also* Parliament
Compston, John 181
Compulsory Church Rates Abolition Bill (1868) 51
Concurrent endowment 104–5, 269
Conder, G. W. 29, 210, 226, 233
Conder, Josiah 32, 33, 37, 43, 46, 71, 112, 118, 129, 229, 231, 246, 249
Congregationalists/Congregationalism 15, 16, 17, 19, 20, 22, 23, 24, 29, 42, 63, 81, 82–3, 86–9, 100, 111, 115, 123, 127–8, 138, 140, 141, 142, 145, 147, 153, 154–7, 158–9,

174, 175, 183, 185, 187, 233, 253–6, 259–60, 261–2, 264; *see also* Ecclesiology
Congregational Board of Education 140, 142, 155, 165, 166
Congregational Magazine 82
Congregational Union 19, 30, 58, 82, 93, 94, 106, 107, 111, 124, 140, 154, 158, 159, 160, 183, 193, 216, 224, 243, 246 (n. 176)
Congregational Year Book 70, 82, 110, 128, 161, 243
Conservative Party/Conservatives 2, 27, 37, 38, 111, 136, 189, 264, 269
Constantinople 205
Continental Europe 179, 225
Cook, Thomas 117
Cooper, Thomas 220
Corn laws 25, 117–18, 119, 125, 172, 173, 180, 183, 185, 224, 253, 266
Cornford, P. H. 182
Cornwall 23, 175
Cossham, Handel 90
Cowherd, Raymond 3
Cox, F. A. 29, 80, 81, 86–7, 107, 111, 142, 180, 253, 257–8, 268
Crimean War 212–18, 220, 235, 243
Crossley, Frank 196
Crystal Palace 195, 198, 246
Cutting, Thomas 152

Dale, R. W. 29, 35, 71, 96, 115, 123, 133, 140, 148, 155, 156, 165 (n. 131), 183, 187, 188, 213, 247, 259, 268
Danubian Principalities 213
Darwinism 203–4
Daunt, O'Neill 104, 226
Davidson, Samuel 155, 159, 210
Declaration of Independence 92–3
Dean, D. N. 182 (n. 37)
Denmark 207
Derby, 14th Earl 269
Derbyshire 23
Dillwyn, L. L. 65–6
Disendowment 229
Disestablishment 3, 11, 21, 26, 28, 31, 34, 35, 40, 51, 71, 75, 79–109, 130, 143, 156, 175, 183 (n. 39), 243, 256, 259, 260, 261, 262, 263
  Irish 5, 69, 90, 103–5, 108, 229, 263
Disraeli, Benjamin 1, 111, 130, 189, 269

Dissent, New and Old *see* New Dissent; Old Dissent
Dissenters, 'political' and 'religious' *see* 'Political Dissenters'; 'Religious Dissenters'
Dissenters' Parliamentary Committee 2
Dissenting Deputies 31, 42, 43, 44, 45, 52, 54, 57 (n. 83), 58, 64, 66, 67, 90, 93, 103, 105, 122, 127, 141, 193, 224, 227, 228, 229, 234, 235, 240, 264
Divorce Bill 268
Dobson, J. G. 62, 63, 65
Dr Williams's Library 93, 114
Dorset 23, 174
Dow, Neal 178
Doxsey, Isaac 181
Durham 23
Duty, notion of 146–51

Eardley, Culling 65, 81
Early Closing Movement 197–8
Ecclesiastical Journal 80
Ecclesiastical Knowledge Society 80
Ecclesiastical Titles Bill 230, 234, 235, 236 (n. 138), 237, 240, 241
Ecclesiology 86–9, 99–100, 107, 123, 253–6
    Congregational 16, 86–9, 123, 253–6, 259, 261
    Episcopal 15, 255
    Presbyterian 87, 255
Eckett, Robert 83, 258
Eclectic Review 19, 33–4, 39, 45, 54, 59, 66, 82, 88, 91, 95, 114, 124, 125, 133, 145, 146, 152, 154, 192, 210, 223, 234–5, 245, 247, 252
Ecumenism 90, 98
Edinburgh 189, 210
Education, Minutes of 2, 140–41, 157, 160
Education, secular 154, 155, 157–61, 167, 267
Education, state 2, 10, 28, 33, 105, 116, 137–67, 247, 266–7
Education Act of 1870 137
Elections *see* General Elections
Ellens, J. P. 9, 35, 85, 258–61
Ely, John 106, 121
Embree, A. T. 135 (n. 116)
Endowed schools 44, 65–6

England, Church of *see* Church of England
English Churchman, The 97
English Independent, The 60, 167
English Review, The 120
Equality 91–3, 107, 109, 114, 124, 193, 206, 223, 250, 268; *see also* Religious equality
Erastianism/anti-Erastianism 92, 99, 256
Essays and Reviews 96
Essex 23
Established Church, The *see* Church of England
Evangelical Alliance 257, 258
Evangelical Voluntary Church Association 80, 257
Evangelicals/Evangelicalism 8, 16, 35, 80, 92, 124, 126, 150, 171, 185, 252–3, 255, 257–8, 260, 263, 264, 261, 269
    Churchmen 5, 6, 8, 65, 72, 100–102, 126–7, 251, 253, 263, 264, 269
    Nonconformists 1, 3, 8, 9, 60, 90, 91, 126, 129, 150, 238, 251, 252, 256, 257–8, 259, 267, 270
    Pan-Evangelicalism 8, 10, 253
Everitt, Alan 23
Exeter Hall 210

Factory Bill, Sir James Graham's (1843) 2, 82, 138, 145, 152, 153, 266
Fast Days 243–6, 247
Ferguson, Robert 119
Forbes Mackenzie Act 174
Foreign policy 207–20, 265
Foster, C. J. 62
Fox, W. J. 189
France 218, 225
Franchise reform 28, 98, 164, 220–25, 265
    And women 223
Frankfurt 210
Fraser, John 185
Free Church of Scotland 181
Free trade 28, 117–21, 179
    In Bibles 118–20
French Revolution 24
Friend, The 51, 54, 87, 110, 129, 143, 177, 198, 213, 236 (n. 136), 237, 244
Friends *see* Quakers

Friends' Temperance Association 178,
198
Fry, Elizabeth 55
Fundamentalism 205, 270

Gardner, Richard 131
Gash, Norman 2–3, 8, 121, 262
Gathered church, idea of 88–9, 123
General Body of Ministers of the Three
Denominations 93, 117, 193, 224,
232 (n. 116)
General Elections 2, 29, 30, 35, 164
of 1847 1, 2, 3, 141, 252
of 1852 112, 117–18
of 1857 216, 222
of 1865 113, 226
of 1868 164, 172, 199
of 1874 172
Geographical distribution of
denominations 22–4
Of ministers at prohibition
conference 174–5
Germany 207, 240
Gibson, William 5
Gilpin, Charles 252
Gladstone, W. E. 3, 40, 50, 60, 61, 68,
69, 75, 105, 164, 256, 269
Gladstonian era 1, 7, 268
Glaser, J. F. 171
Glorious Revolution 21
Gloucestershire 145
Golden rule 125
Goring, Charles 127
Government interference/non-
interference 115–21, 137, 138,
151, 156–7, 162, 163, 185, 187–8,
195, 207–9, 266, 267, 269
Graham, James, see Factory Bill
Gray, John 104
Great Ejectment of 1662 15, 79, 111,
264
Bicentennial of 79, 96
Great War, The 268
Green, T. 67
Greville, C. C. F. 232
Grey, George 55
Grievances see Nonconformist
grievances
Guardian, The 29
Gun Powder Plot 239

Hadfield, George 31, 47, 51, 53, 54,
67–9, 73, 74, 80, 117, 188, 196,
208, 211, 216, 233, 248, 252, 253,
261
Hale, W. H. 85, 97, 98, 120
Halévy, Elie 121, 160
Hall, Newman 50, 60, 63, 184, 211,
221, 233, 236
Halley, Robert 25, 159, 216
Hamer, D. A. 2, 90
Hamilton, R. W. 83, 106, 140, 160
Harrison, Brian 176
Havelock, Henry 219
Heathcote, William 55, 57, 64
Helmstadter, Richard 7, 253
Hempton, David 27, 152 (n. 72), 225
Henshaw, Robert 63
Henslowe, W. H. 55
Hertfordshire 23, 31
Heywood, James 61, 63
High Church 29, 56, 58, 60, 65, 97,
99; see also Tractarians; Anglo-
Catholics
Hilton, Boyd 148
Hindus 92, 132–5
Hinton, J. H. 29, 79, 142, 147, 149,
166, 180, 236, 254, 268
Homerton College 82
Holyoake, G. J. 252
Hook, W. F. 99, 154, 159
Hope, A. J. 130
Howard, H. C. 241
Howell, George 185
Hughes, H. P. 269
Hull 233
Hume, Joseph 189
Hunt, G. W. 67
Huntingdonshire 23, 174
Huxley, T. H. 203
Hyde Park riots (1855) 201

Imperialism 219
Indemnity Acts 42–3
Independents, see Congregationalists
India 92, 132–5, 246, 247
Indian Mutiny 132–3, 218–19, 243,
245, 246
Infidels 85, 123, 185, 194, 200; see also
Irreligious; Secularists; Atheism
Inglis, Robert 126, 127, 129, 130, 189
Inquirer, The 60, 72, 153
Inquisition, The 239
Ipswich, mayor of 67

Ireland   90, 103–5, 174, 226, 227–9,
    230; *see also* Disestablishment,
    Irish
Irish in Britain   240
Irish Famine   243, 244
Irreligious, The   22; *see also* Infidels;
    Secularists; Atheism
Isle of Wight   226

James, J. A.   25, 35, 71, 80, 83, 106,
    108, 165, 183, 202, 205, 210, 213,
    216, 222, 233, 239, 240, 260, 263
James, T. S.   106
Jenkins, T. A.   251–2
Jewish Disabilities Bills   126–32
Jews   1, 11, 42, 114, 126–32, 157, 203,
    248, 257
Johnson, Richard   148
Jones, Ernest   185

Kay-Shuttleworth, James   149, 150,
    153, 161, 163, 166
Kensington Gardens   199
Kent   23
Kershaw, James   158–9

Ladies' Association for the Suppression
    of Intemperance   181
Laissez-faire   116, 118, 120, 254, 266
Lancashire   174
Lancashire Independent College   33,
    153, 155, 157
Lancashire Public School Association
    158, 159, 187; *see also* National
    Public School Association
Latitudinarianism   95, 250
Laymen   18, 22, 30–1, 42, 66
League of Universal Brotherhood   211
Leeds   22, 83, 106, 215, 233
Leeds Mercury   33, 67, 116, 139, 142,
    146, 150, 151, 152, 161, 162, 195,
    199, 207, 214, 221, 222, 223, 225,
    226, 235, 242
Lees, F. R.   183
Legge, George   124
Leicester   22, 31, 47, 81, 220
Leicestershire   23
Lewis, George   68
Liberal instincts   204, 238, 239, 248,
    249, 254
Liberal Party/Liberals   27, 29, 37, 38,
    136, 189

Liberation Society, The   22, 26, 27, 28,
    29, 32, 49, 52, 53, 54, 56, 57, 62,
    63, 65, 66, 67, 69, 72, 74, 79, 84,
    85, 88, 91, 92, 95–9, 101, 104, 105,
    107–8, 115, 118, 120, 122, 133–4,
    183, 189, 222, 224, 226, 227, 229,
    243, 250, 260, 262, 264; *see also*
    Anti-State Church Association
    Executive Committee   62, 96, 99,
    227, 235 (n. 135)
Liberationists   49, 98, 102–3, 109, 254
Liberator, The   52, 68, 84, 90, 92, 94,
    101, 103, 194, 226
Lincolnshire   23
Lindsey   23
Liverpool   80, 157 (n. 93)
Livingstone, David   219
Lloyd Street Chapel   158
Local government   188
Locke, John   135
Locke, Joseph   191, 192
London   25, 29, 31, 42, 82, 105, 111,
    115, 129, 174, 181, 190, 191, 193,
    195, 199, 210, 211, 233
London and Birmingham Railway
    191
London University   62, 156
Lord's Day Observance Society   189,
    200–201
Lords, House of   18, 50, 57, 59, 62, 67,
    127, 131, 136, 260; *see also*
    Parliament
Lovett, William   185
Lucas, Samuel   158
Lynch, T. T.   34

Macaulay, T. B.   2, 128
Machin, G. I. T.   4, 70, 121 (n. 62)
McKerrow, William   28, 80, 117, 124,
    158, 159, 160, 163, 172, 173, 180,
    183, 187, 211, 216
Mackintosh, W. H.   257
Magdalene College, Cambridge   98
Mahon, Viscount   130
Maine Law   172, 177, 178, 187
Maitland, S. R.   145
Manchester   22, 31, 54, 80, 117, 151,
    155, 163, 172, 174, 180, 210, 233
Manchester Examiner and Times, The
    163
Manchester Model Secular School   161
Manchester School   214

Marriage Act (1836) 57
Marriage Act (1856) 58
Marriage law grievances 43, 44, 57–9
Martin, Samuel 111, 197, 243
Martineau, James 63, 94, 213
Masheder, Richard 98
Mathew, Father 182
Mathew, John 182
Maynooth grant 44, 104–5, 227–9,
    240, 269
Mechanics' Institutes 162
Methodists 17, 18, 52, 142, 175, 176–
    7; see also individual
    denominations
Methodist New Connexion 18, 63,
    175, 244, 256
Methodist New Connexion Magazine
    58, 87, 90, 129, 141, 144, 194, 209,
    219, 227, 255
Metropolitan Interment Bills 54
Miall, Arthur 205
Miall, C. S. 101 (n. 101), 143, 245
Miall, Edward 2, 4, 29, 31–2, 33, 34,
    36, 37, 40, 41, 45, 46, 49, 51, 53,
    61, 71, 81–2, 87, 88, 92, 95, 96, 97,
    98, 102, 103, 107, 112, 115, 116,
    119, 124, 125, 133, 140, 147, 148,
    164, 167, 184, 205–6, 210, 212,
    216, 220, 222, 225, 229, 232, 233,
    234, 236, 245, 250, 259, 268
Middlesex 174
Militancy/militants 11, 27, 31, 33, 34–
    7, 39, 40, 41, 49, 51, 52, 56–7, 59,
    63, 64, 66, 68, 69–75 79, 80, 81, 85,
    91, 92, 95, 96, 100–101, 102, 103,
    104, 108–9, 110–12, 114, 119–20,
    122, 124, 125, 126, 127, 135, 139,
    177, 180, 187, 188, 227, 257, 258,
    262–5; see also Radicalism/radicals
Militia Bill 208
Militarism 219
Military, the 208–9
Mill, J. S. 203, 204, 223
Millenarianism 89–90, 98, 122, 223
Ministerial Conference on Prohibition
    173–6, 177, 180–83
Ministers 18, 28, 29, 37, 53, 93, 98,
    109, 117, 163, 173–5, 176, 177,
    180–83, 195, 211, 213, 232, 259,
    266
Missions 209, 260–61
Moderates 11, 31, 32, 33, 34–7, 56–7,

71–5, 80, 81, 108, 128, 198, 228,
    263–4
Monopolies 118–20, 199; see also
    Bible printing monopoly
Moral reform 171–206, 251, 254, 268,
    269
Moral suasion 177, 184, 199
Morley, Samuel 2, 30, 83, 108, 140,
    157, 161, 163, 167, 171–2, 210, 221,
    224, 227, 234, 236
Mormons 135
Moslems 135, 203, 205, 239, 247
Municipal gospel 188
Municipal reform 256
Munson, James 267–8
Mursell, J. P. 29, 80, 111, 213, 220,
    231, 242, 260–61, 268

National Complete Suffrage Union
    81, 98, 220–21, 224, 225
National Gallery 196
National identity 206, 207–50
National Public School Association
    158–9, 160, 165
National Society 137
National Sunday League 199, 205
National Temperance Chronicle 182
National Temperance Society 182
Nationalism 129, 241; see also
    Patriotism
Neate, Charles 62
Nevile, Christopher 100–101
Newdegate, C. N. 61, 68, 69, 73, 189,
    237
New Dissent 17, 23
New South Wales 102
Newton, J. S. 104
Nicholas I, Czar 217, 218
Noel, Baptist 90, 100–101, 108
Nonconformist, The 21, 31, 32, 34, 37,
    39, 40, 43, 45, 48, 50, 53, 56, 57,
    61, 64, 66, 68, 69, 70, 81, 82, 85,
    89, 90, 92, 94, 97, 98, 102, 103,
    108, 113, 114, 115, 119, 138, 139,
    153, 156, 173, 179, 184, 185, 184,
    185, 194, 195, 198, 201, 203, 204,
    208, 212, 220, 221, 228, 229, 230,
    232, 233, 234 (n. 126), 236, 237,
    238, 239, 240, 244, 246, 247, 268
    (n. 37)
Nonconformist conscience 5, 6, 171,
    204, 269

Nonconformist Elector 2
Nonconformist grievances 28, 31, 39–75, 105, 108, 113, 120, 143, 172, 262, 263, 266
Norfolk 55
Norfolk, Duke of; *see* Howard, H. C.
Northamptonshire 23
Norwich 211
Nottingham 114
Nottinghamshire 23

Oakham 52
Oaths 44, 66–9, 105, 217, 251–2
O'Connor, Feargus 220, 221
Old Dissent 3, 16, 17, 23, 27, 31, 269
O'Loghlen, Colman 104
Opium trade 207
Orangemen 242
Oriel College 65
Osborn, George 54
Oxford Movement 99; *see also* Tractarians; High Church
Oxford University 44, 59–61, 62–5
Oxfordshire 175

Pacifism 210, 212, 217, 219, 265, 267
Palmerston, 3rd Viscount 1, 11, 55, 62, 71, 164, 199, 263–4, 269
Palmerstonian era 265
Papal Aggression agitation 225, 227, 229–42, 246
Papal Index of Prohibited Books 122
Paper duties 139
Paris 210
Parker, Joseph 29
Parliament 31, 32, 33, 41, 42, 43, 47, 50–1, 54, 65, 67, 69, 93, 99, 102, 104, 105, 110, 114 120, 125, 126–32, 135, 137, 139, 147, 162, 163, 166, 201, 208, 215, 227, 229, 235, 237, 248, 252; *see also* Commons, House of; Lords, House of
Parliamentary elections *see* General Elections
Parliamentary Oaths Bill 105
Parnell, C. S. 269
Patriot, The 31, 32, 37, 40, 60, 112, 113, 116, 118, 128, 139, 148, 152, 153, 154, 159, 167 184, 195, 198, 214, 226, 232, 238, 239, 244, 247, 248
Patriot Fund 213, 216

Patriotism 129, 216–17, 232, 239, 242–6, 244, 250; *see also* Nationalism
Paz, D. G. 235 (n. 134), 240–41
Peace congresses 210
Peace movement 28, 208–20, 225, 235, 265
Peace Society 210, 211, 212, 213, 218
Pease, Joseph 28, 63
Pease family 191
Peel, Albert 214
Peel, Robert 41, 269
Peelites 2, 38
Pellatt, Apsley 196, 197
Permissive Bill 173, 176, 177, 183 (n. 39), 188, 252
Petitions/petitioning 47, 52, 57, 58, 63, 66, 80, 94, 127, 131, 134, 138, 162, 176
Peto, Morton 30, 55–7, 71, 142, 191, 199 (n. 114), 209, 216, 236 (n. 138)
Philanthropists 28, 30, 147–8
Phillimore, Robert 58
Pillans, J. 74
Pitt, William 43
Pius IX, Pope 229, 230, 232
Plymouth Brethren 268
Political Dissenters 25, 27, 29, 36, 52, 257; *see also* Religious Dissenters
Pollbooks 27, 37
Poor Law Board 58
Poor Law Guardians 57, 182
Portsmouth 214
Postal service 116, 123, 192–3, 196, 202
Prayer Book 53, 57, 65
Presbyterians 3, 15, 16, 28, 42, 158, 172, 175, 261; *see also* Ecclesiology
Pressure group politics 2, 29, 30, 35, 37, 80, 141, 250, 254
Price, Thomas 33, 81, 122, 258
Priests (Roman Catholic) 227–9, 236
Primitive Methodists 18, 20, 54–5, 165, 175, 256
Primitive Methodist Magazine 18 (n. 14), 55, 56, 57, 59, 84, 103, 142, 176, 188, 193, 196, 197, 207
Principle, notion of 105–8, 110, 116, 118, 138, 151, 163, 181, 195, 200, 201, 204, 217, 218, 219, 224, 249, 252–3, 257, 261, 262, 263, 265–6, 267

Prohibition 28, 171–89, 198, 206, 222, 267
Protectionists 2, 38
Protestant Alliance 229, 240
Protestant Episcopal Church of Scotland 230
Protestant Succession 249
Protestantism/Protestants 15, 124, 157 (n. 93), 189, 225–42, 250, 255, 259
Prount, Peter 181
Pulman, John 98
Puritans/Puritanism 1, 15, 79, 192, 202, 204, 205

Quakers 16, 27, 51, 55, 63, 110, 142–3, 158, 177–9, 210, 215, 216, 220, 231, 244
Qualification for Offices Bill 67–9, 73, 74, 105
Queen's printer 118
Quietism, political 24, 28

Radicalism/radicals 24, 25, 40, 50, 52, 53, 69, 71–5, 81, 110, 112, 114, 115, 121, 133, 135, 180, 188, 191, 196, 211, 220, 221, 222, 246, 248, 258, 262, 263, 264–5; see also Militants/militancy
Radical Party 37, 189
Raffles, Thomas 80
Ragged schools 197
Railways 118, 191
Rast Gafter 92
Record, The 252
Reform Bill of 1832 242, 256
Reform Act of 1867 1, 164, 224
Reformed Presbyterian Church 175
Registration of Births, Deaths and Marriages Bill 43
Regium Donum 7, 36, 44, 93–4
Irish 94, 105
Reid, William 185
Religious Census of 1851 20, 21, 22, 123, 175
Proposed one in 1861 123
'Religious Dissenters' 25, 101, 257–8; see also 'Political Dissenters'
Religious equality 1, 3, 11, 12, 85, 110–36, 153, 156, 159, 160, 161, 166, 167, 171, 182, 183 (n. 40), 185, 189, 192, 194, 199, 202, 204, 225, 226, 227, 229, 231, 232, 235,

236, 237, 238, 240, 241, 243, 246–50, 255, 256, 257, 260, 261, 262, 263, 266, 267, 268, 269, 270
Religious Freedom Society 80
Religious houses 236, 237
Religious pluralism 105, 136
Religious toleration; see Toleration
Respectability 28, 30, 41, 54, 57, 59
Retrenchment 137, 162, 208–9, 266
Revised Code (1861) 161, 162
Richard, Henry 30, 143, 210, 245
Rigg, J. H. 255
Rippon, John 114–15, 135
Rivulet controversy 34
Roberts, M. J. D. 99
Rochdale 22
Roebuck, J. A. 189
Rogers, Henry 155
Rogers, J. G. 29, 71, 72, 104, 113, 154, 156, 268
Roman Catholic Oaths Bill 226, 227, 240
Roman Catholicism see Catholicism, Roman
Rothschild, Baron Lionel de 3, 128, 129, 132
Rowntree, John 28
Rowntree, Joseph 28
Rowntree, William 63
Royal Botanic Garden 189
Royal proclamations 243–6
Royal Statistical Society 182
Royal supremacy 86, 99, 230–31, 234
Rule, W. H. 200
Rural areas 23, 54, 151, 193
Russell, Lord John 2, 43, 61, 104, 129, 130, 139, 140, 141, 145, 157, 230, 236, 241, 269
Russia 213–18

Sabbatarianism 4, 171, 189–206, 251, 252, 255, 256, 269
St Martin's Hall 203
Salbstein, M. C. N. 132
Salford 155, 180
Salomons, David 114
Salt, Titus 30, 46, 106, 221, 224
Salvation Army 200
Sanitation reform 116
Saturday half-holiday 197–8
Savoy Declaration 86
Scholefield, William 158, 252

Scotland 16, 80, 118, 120, 174, 191
  Scots 16, 174, 189
Searle, G. R. 146
Secularism 250, 258, 259, 261
Secularists 157, 159, 160, 161, 185,
  203–4, 249, 252; see also Atheism;
  Infidels; Irreligious
Self-help 266
Selwyn, C. J. 63, 65, 66
Shaftesbury, 7th Earl 5, 30, 126, 135,
  175, 192, 193, 238, 264
Skeats, Herbert 21, 39, 226
Slavery 28, 125, 143, 185, 219, 217,
  224, 253, 260, 266
Smith, Culling see Eardley
Smith, Edward 143, 178
Smith, G. C. 181
Smith, J. P. 36, 82, 89, 94, 117, 157,
  211, 254, 260
Snell, K. D. M. 23
Social control 148–50, 166, 266
Social stigma 41, 42, 58
Society for the Suppression of Vice
  269
Society of Friends see Quakers
Solemnisation of Marriages Bill 43
Soteriology 253
Spencer, Herbert 187
Spooner, Richard 189, 229, 253
Spring Hill College 155, 156
Spurgeon, C. H. 26, 29, 57, 204, 216,
  218, 246
State, the role of 115, 116, 149, 186–8,
  247, 254, 261, 267, 269, 270; see
  also Government interference
State education see Education, state
Steane, Edward 52
Steele, E. D. 8, 11, 71, 263–5
Stephens, J. R. 26
Stockport 199
Stockton and Darlington Railway 191
Stoughton, John 85, 107, 253
Stovel, Charles 142, 182
Sturge, Charles 219
Sturge, Joseph 2, 28, 30, 35, 114, 125,
  133, 143, 191, 206, 211, 213, 214,
  220, 219, 221, 223, 233, 249
Sturt, Mary 162, 166
Suffolk 23
Suffrage see Franchise reform
Sunday bands 190, 191, 200, 206
Sunday closing 184, 198–9

Sunday opening 195–8
Sunday recreation 195–200, 205–6
Sunday trading 193–5, 197, 200–201
Swaine, Edward 159

Tamworth Manifesto 41
Taunton Commission 164
Taxes on knowledge 118
Taylor, John 179
Teetotalism 175, 176, 182, 183, 184,
  185, 198, 267
Temperance 171, 179, 181, 182, 183,
  184, 188
Territorial church, idea of 88–9, 123
Test and Corporation Acts 42–3, 66,
  256
Thanksgiving Days 243–6
Theology 1, 5, 7, 9, 10, 86–8, 95–7,
  99, 108, 114, 121, 124–5, 128, 130,
  205, 223, 236 (n. 136), 237–8, 246,
  249, 253–7, 258, 259, 261
Thirlwall, Connop 130
Thirty-Nine Articles 101
Thompson, David 22, 257
Thomson, Adam 119–20
Thomson, Dr 189
Thorne, James 63
Thorogood, John 25, 47, 48
Times, The 119, 140, 241
Toleration 15, 43, 111, 230, 252, 268
Tories see Conservative Party
Tractarians 100, 240; see also High
  Church; Anglo-Catholics
Trelawny, John 49, 50, 251–2
Trinitarianism 261
Turkey 213, 217
Tyrrell, Alexander 260

Uniformity, Act of 79
Unitarians/Unitarianism 3, 15, 56, 60,
  62, 63, 72, 84, 85, 94, 130, 145,
  153, 252, 253, 256, 261
United Kingdom Alliance 172–77,
  180–83, 185, 187, 189, 198, 204,
  252
United Methodist Free Churches 18,
  255, 256
United Methodist Free Churches'
  Magazine 52, 122, 176, 197, 207,
  248
United Presbyterian Church 175
United Presbyterian Magazine 195

United States 172, 190, 225, 232; *see also* America
University College London 33
Universities 43, 44, 59–65, 70, 113, 118, 127, 136, 236

Vaccination 116, 182
Vaughan, Robert 19, 26 (n. 41), 33, 37, 63, 71–2, 88, 116, 138, 140, 141, 153, 154, 155–6, 157, 163, 167, 187, 194, 211, 233, 263
Victoria, Queen 214, 230, 232 (n. 116), 233, 231, 232, 242–46
Vince, Charles 95
Vincent, John 9, 27, 252
Voluntaryism/Voluntaries 10, 11, 48, 49, 80, 85, 88–9, 102, 104, 105, 107, 116, 118, 119, 120, 121, 130, 145, 153, 161, 200, 227, 228, 236, 246, 249–50, 254, 258, 262, 266
  educational Voluntaryism 10, 11, 138–67, 187, 256, 266–7
Voluntary Church Associations 10, 80, 145, 172
Voluntary Church Magazine 80
Voluntary School Association 10, 142–3, 145

Waddy, Samuel 73
Wadsworth, A. P. 166
Wales 20, 151, 174
  Welsh 21, 174
Walmsley, Joshua 189, 196, 197
Walpole, S. H. 55
Walter, John 63
War 209–20, 265
Ward, W. R. 11, 198 (n. 104)
Wardlaw, Ralph 202, 258
Ware, Hertfordshire 31
Watchman, The 100
Watts, Michael 4, 5, 8–9, 11, 20, 34, 42, 141, 257
Wesley, John 17, 26
Wesleyan Methodism/Wesleyans 17,

18, 23, 26–7, 34, 40, 52, 53, 66, 73, 100, 104, 138, 141, 145, 152, 153, 157, 162, 175, 176, 189, 190, 191, 198, 200, 222, 225, 229, 232, 237–8, 241, 251, 253, 255, 256, 262, 264, 269
  Leadership 51, 53, 73, 176, 223, 264
  Lord's Day Committee 190
  'no politics' rule 26
Wesleyan Methodist Association 18, 83, 175, 176
Wesleyan Methodist Association Magazine 48 (n. 40), 49, 70, 82, 89, 103, 107, 141, 143, 186, 194, 195, 209, 212, 216–17, 236 (n. 136)
Wesleyan Methodist Magazine 17, 51, 60, 104, 126, 132, 176, 190, 201, 205, 222, 225, 238, 242, 248 (n. 183)
Wesleyan Reformers 175
Westhead, J. P. 126
Whig Party/Whigs 2, 3, 37, 208, 256, 264, 269
Whitehead, George 181
Whitley, W. T. 268
Wigley, John 204
Wilberforce, R. I. 99
Wilberforce, Samuel 62, 131
Williams, Carvell 53, 65, 245
Williams, Charles 182–3
Williams, Daniel 93
Wilson, Joshua 19, 22, 221
Winter, Thomas 83
Wiseman, Nicholas 230, 234, 239
Wood, J. J. 181
Wormegay, Norfolk 55
Wurtemberg 190

Yearly Meeting (Quaker) 27, 178, 179, 244
York 154, 238
Yorkshire 23, 47, 138, 174, 181, 222
Yorkshire Baptist Association 47, 231
Yorkshire Tribune 185